Research Methods
in Africana Studies

BLACK STUDIES & critical thinking

Rochelle Brock and Richard Greggory Johnson III
Executive Editors

Vol. 64

The Black Studies and Critical Thinking series
is part of the Peter Lang Education list.
Every volume is peer reviewed and meets
the highest quality standards for content and production.

PETER LANG
New York • Washington, D.C./Baltimore • Bern
Frankfurt • Berlin • Brussels • Vienna • Oxford

Serie McDougal III

Research Methods in Africana Studies

PETER LANG
New York • Washington, D.C./Baltimore • Bern
Frankfurt • Berlin • Brussels • Vienna • Oxford

Library of Congress Cataloging-in-Publication Data
McDougal, Serie, III.
Research methods in Africana studies / Serie McDougal III.
pages cm. — (Black studies and critical thinking; vol. 64)
Includes bibliographical references and index.
1. African Americans—Study and teaching. 2. African American philosophy.
3. Social sciences—Methodology. 4. African Americans—Research.
5. Critical theory. 6. African Americans—History. I. Title.
E184.7.M3484 2013   973'.0496073—dc23   2013031491
ISBN 978-1-4331-2461-7 (hardcover)
ISBN 978-1-4331-2460-0 (paperback)
ISBN 978-1-4539-1207-2 (e-book)
ISSN 1947-5985

Bibliographic information published by **Die Deutsche Nationalbibliothek.**
Die Deutsche Nationalbibliothek lists this publication in the "Deutsche
Nationalbibliografie"; detailed bibliographic data is available
on the Internet at http://dnb.d-nb.de/.

Cover art: *Tehuti* by Kimberly Monique Coy

Contents

Speak to the Posterity

The discipline of Africana Studies' activist-intellectual tradition goes back as far as classical African civilizations such as ancient Kemet (Egypt). In ancient Kemet, the Sesh, or scribe, was expected to use knowledge and skill to serve the people by ensuring justice, caring for the vulnerable and the environment, respecting persons and bearers of dignity and divinity, and working for future generations. The administration of ancient Egyptian civilization was carried out with the assistance of the Sesh, who experienced decades of rigorous training consisting of:

1. schooling in the village school at a very early age;
2. the study of classical literature, which they undertook in their twelfth year;
3. instruction in reading and writing complex texts. In addition, they received instruction in various medu neter (hieroglyphs) that required the ability to draw with a pen. (Obenga, 2007)

The Sesh's command of writing was essential in making Kemet the most highly organized and prosperous state in the ancient world. In addition to mastering the skill of writing, the Sesh was expected to master the highest standards of beauty and deep thought (Hilliard, 1998). The Sesh was not an individual who was concerned with personal advancement, but instead was concerned with immortality. The discipline of the Sesh was writing in accordance with the precepts of *Maat*—

truth and justice. In addition to truth and justice, Maat is the ancient Kemetic divine principle that represents the proper ordering and construction of the individual, society, and the universe. The ancient Kemetic sage Ptah Hotep, in his book of wise instruction, proclaimed:

> If you listen to my sayings all of your affairs will go forward. Their value resides in their truth. The memory of these sayings goes on in the minds of men and women because of the worth of their precepts. If every word is carried on, they will not perish in this land. If advice is given for the good, the great will speak accordingly. This is a matter of teaching a person to speak to posterity. He or she who hears it becomes a master hearer. It is good to speak to posterity. Posterity will listen. (Hilliard, Williams, & Damali, 1987)

Ptah Hotep's proclamation charges one to produce *enduring knowledge*. Like Ptah Hotep's wise instructions, the sacred duty of the Sesh was to speak to posterity or future generations. This goal was to be accomplished by producing writing and deep thought that was in accord with Maat. These sacred writings would endure for generations because of their truth and high standards.

Tehuti, the "Divine Tongue"

In ancient Kemet, *Tehuti* was the ancient neter (deity) who was the father of the written language and the patron of the Sesh. Tehuti is credited with the invention of the medu neter, the world's oldest writing system. The name Tehu is an ancient Kemetic term meaning *to measure in relation to the moon*. Tehuti, or the divine tongue, was the personification of deep thought emerging from knowledge and wisdom. Most of the ancient Kemetic neter (deities) are represented by one or more animals. Tehuti is often represented by the head of an ibis or stork-like bird. He is also depicted holding a scroll and papyrus, which are symbols of the Sesh. Like the Sesh and Tehuti, the scholar in Africana studies is charged with producing knowledge of the highest standards of deep thought that will be of benefit to future generations of people of African descent, the larger society, and the universe. This goal is achieved by the systematic study of the lived experiences and prospects of people of African descent.

The Problem

What is a problem? In the context of conducting research in the social sciences, a "problem" doesn't always have to indicate a negative situation. A problem exists whenever there is a gap between a *present condition* and a *better condition*. The role of the Sesh was to aid society in closing the distance between the two; such is also the role of the scholar in Africana Studies. The imperfection of the human condition ensures the constant presence of problems that must be addressed, and the scholar-activist in Africana Studies stands at the ready. How does a scholar-activist approach problems? W.E.B. Du Bois once said that "true lovers of humanity can only hold higher the pure ideals of science, and continue to insist that if we would solve a problem we must study it" (Du Bois, 1898, p. 23). This book attempts to help sharpen the necessary skills for the process of studying and solving problems that arise in the lived experiences of people of African descent. Mastering the information in the pages of this book does not require that the reader possess any tremendous amount of prior knowledge on the topic of research methods. All you must have to become a great researcher in general and in the context of the Africana experience is:

1. intrigue and interest in furthering yours and others' knowledge and understanding;
2. the courage to accept the responsibility of service to your community, society, and the world;
3. the discipline necessary to develop the skills needed to carry out the complex work that is essential for understanding and addressing social challenges.

This text is not written for the reader as simply a consumer of information or as a student; it is written for the reader as an active agent in his or her society and as a thinking person in the world.

Acknowledgments

This text is dedicated to my mother, my father, my sister, my people, and the discipline of Africana Studies. Without them nothing I have ever accomplished would have been possible. Thank you mom, for teaching me resilience and that anything is possible. Thank you dad, for teaching me to be disciplined and strategic. Thank you big sister for always being supportive, for being the most multitalented person I have ever known, and for always helping me to think of things from a different perspective. A special thanks to my close friends: Oron Marshall, for being my best example of free thought; Michael Tillotson, for being my best example of relentless work and aggressive scholarship; Paul Easterling, for being my best example of a decolonized imagination; Crystal Guillory, for being my best example of victorious consciousness, and Justin Gammage, for being my best example of what a principled scholar should be. Thank you all for being the warrior scholars that you are and for always helping me sharpen my tools of analysis; steel sharpens steel. A special thanks to my mentors: Rev. John W. Brazil, for being a third parent and educator to me; Marc McConney, for seeing something in me that I didn't see in myself; Daniel Johnson, for teaching me how to organize in the institutional setting; Marcia Sutherland, for teaching me what it means to be a scholar; Sonja Peterson-Lewis, for teaching me what research is all about; Molefi Asante, for teaching me what an academic discipline truly is and how to be a professional; Ama Mazama, for teaching me centeredness; Dorothy Tsuruta, for teaching me how to be a mentor to students; and Rochelle Brock, for taking an interest in my work. A special thanks to Ms. Sureshi Maduka Jayawardene for her unwavering encouragement and for helping me through every step of the editorial process. A special thanks to all of my former and current students for their challenging questions and comments. Last, thanks to my creator and my ancestors for helping me to do my best to honor you through my work.

CHAPTER ONE

Africana Studies and the Science of Knowing

...the limits of knowledge in any field have never been set and no one has ever reached them.
—PTAH HOTEP (CITED IN HILLIARD, WILLIAMS, & DAMALI, 1987)

As long as there is room to improve the society in which we live, research will be necessary. In professional and educational settings, people are advised or required to learn methods of research. Some wonder why research methods are relevant to them, especially if they do not intend to pursue a profession that requires them to conduct research. They often ask what is meant by the word "research" and why they should learn it. This chapter first explains the relationship between research methods and **Africana Studies**. Second, it explains some of the most common ways of knowing and the most common errors that occur during the process of investigation. Third, this chapter identifies the best ways of avoiding common roadblocks to critical thought in scientific research. Once researchers understand the techniques of engaging in systematic research, they must begin to engage in the process of explaining variation in human thought and behavior. This chapter describes the means of explaining variation and causality in scientific research. The following sections explore some of these basic concerns.

What Is Meant by "Research"?

In the 25th century B.C., the African philosopher Ptah Hotep spoke of the limitless nature of knowledge. Training in scientific research is meant to prepare people for the endless pursuit of knowledge. This is of critical importance because knowledge is necessary for advancing society; thus it is relevant to enhancing the lived experiences of people of African descent. **Research** is something that most people are already intimately familiar with. In this book you will be gaining a deeper understanding of things you already understand to some degree, and a more complex knowledge of things that you already know to some extent. This notion of familiarity is not meant to give readers a false sense of prior knowledge; however, people should not be led to think that research methods are something totally foreign to them. They are a part of our nature. We all engage in research to some degree. The difference is that in this book you will be introduced to research in a much more deliberate, formal, and systematic way. **Scientific Research** has to be distinguished from casual, everyday research. Scientific research refers to systematic investigation; it involves the discovery, explanation, and description of a subject or topic. People engage in different forms of casual research on a daily basis. For example, we may need to find out the details of a new mobile phone to see if it has our desired features before making a purchase. We may need to find directions to the hotel at which we have a dinner engagement by calling and questioning some of the people we expect to be there. Before purchasing a new computer we examine those at a computer store to identify the one that works best for us. These are all forms of casual research. What happens if these forms of casual research turn out to be wrong or mistaken in any way? We might

> buy the wrong phone,
> be late to dinner, or
> buy a keyboard that is uncomfortable for the wrist.

Clearly, in casual research there are consequences for mistakes that we must correct or learn to live with. However, for scientific researchers, research must be systematic and methodical as opposed to casual. Being systematic and methodical is necessary because when engaging in study about social problems that affect people's lives in an instrumental way, the stakes are much higher than what is at stake in, for instance, being late to dinner. Social research contends with issues such as unemployment, academic achievement, housing discrimination, and police brutality. The greater the problems and challenges that researchers investigate, the greater the consequences of error. In many cases Africana scholar-activists are conducting research that directly or indirectly leads to saving lives, improving people's overall well-being, or changing the way people think about critical issues. Africana Studies,* by definition, is designed to contribute to the emancipation of people of African descent and humanity by virtue of that contribution. Therefore, mistakes that are affordable in casual everyday research are hardly so in Africana Studies research. For these reasons, researchers of phenomena in the Africana world must be prepared with an adequate knowledge of scientific research.

Why Learn Research Methods?

The world is increasingly centered on information—having access to it and the ability to understand and produce it. Therefore, it is critically important to have a basic knowledge of the science of research. One of the goals of learning **research methods** is to equip people with the skills to carry out their own research. Learning research methods also gives people the ability to interpret, evaluate, and critique research produced by others.

The purpose of textbooks on research methods is to introduce readers to the tools and techniques for studying problems or social conditions. Within the discipline of Africana Studies, studying problems prepares researchers to formulate data-driven, reliable conclusions about the problems and challenges faced by people of African descent. Moreover, such information helps scholars formulate data-driven, evidence-based *solutions* to those problems. After reading a text on research methods, you should be familiar with the processes of scientific research. You should be familiar with every step in the process from formulating a research question, systematically stating the problem, reviewing the literature, collecting and analyzing the data, applying theory, and drawing conclusions. The study of research methods prepares people to produce practical research that will benefit the African world and sustain the utilitarian relevance of Africana Studies in the everyday lives of people of African descent. It is likely that no matter what profession you pursue or are currently in, you will be required to evaluate information and make choices based on the assessment of information. Knowledge of research methods provides people with an awareness of methods of collecting and processing information that will help prepare them to make informed decisions. Accurate and reliable information is the key to making effective decisions. Training in research methods teaches people how to judge the value and quality of data or information necessary

---

* The term "Africana Studies" will be used throughout this book as synonymous with "African American Studies," "Afro American Studies," "Pan-African Studies," "Black Studies," and "Africology."

for making critical choices. Access to information is expanding, and this makes the ability to evaluate the quality of information all the more critical.

Africana Studies Domain Theory

By definition, **Africana Studies** is the critical and systematic study of the thought and practice of people of African descent in their past and present unfolding (Karenga, 2002). Beyond its definition, every discipline has a *domain of inquiry*: for example, political phenomena for political science and psychological phenomena for psychology. The **domain of inquiry** refers to the specific aspects, subsets, or dimensions of reality on which a discipline focuses its thought. The term "Africana" is the label that represents Africana Studies' domain of inquiry. "Africana" is a term that refers to African phenomena. It is an umbrella term that refers to people, geography, and culture (Carr, 2007). Carr (2007) explains that *Africana* refers to people of African descent and African-descended communities wherever they are found globally. Geographically, Africana refers to the study of Africa as well as any physical space occupied by African-descended peoples. Culturally, Africana refers to the study of the concepts, practices, materials, and cultural products that African-descended people have created to live and interact with themselves, others, and their environments inside and outside of the African continent (Carr, 2007). Africana Studies' domain of inquiry is the *African world*. The African world stretches beyond time, space, political boundaries, and continental shores. Africana Studies is relevant everywhere in the universe that African influence can be detected and studied.

> One of the first things I think young people, especially nowadays, should learn is how to see for yourself and listen for yourself and think for yourself. Then you can come to an intelligent decision for yourself…. This generation, especially of our people, has a burden, more so than any other time in history. The most important thing we can learn today is think for ourselves.
>
> —MALCOLM X

Much of what human beings know is based on agreement and belief, and very little of it is based on direct experience or personal discovery (Babbie, 2007). In our fast-paced lives we do not always have the time to discover everything for ourselves or learn everything through personal experience. Fortunately, we don't have to take dangerous drugs to learn how they might affect our bodies, stick our hands into fire to learn that it burns the skin, or drink poisonous liquids to know that doing so can kill us. Various methods of knowing keep each generation from having to "reinvent the wheel." However, because every method of knowing has its flaws and drawbacks, science must assume the burden of finding the most reliable and transparent means of knowing. Let's explore some common ways of knowing and the roadblocks to reasoning embedded within them.

Common Ways of Knowing

Tradition

Tradition is a common way of knowing. Traditional knowledge is based on custom, ritual, and habit. It is transgenerational and passed down from generation to generation. Tradition ties people together. People of a common culture accept certain knowledge about how the world works. This accepted knowledge varies from culture to culture. Traditional knowledge is considered the common knowledge accepted by the group. Traditions contain truths, which makes them continuously relevant. However, society has a tendency to accept traditions simply because they have been practiced or accepted for a long time and not because they make sense. Can you think of any examples? Here is one: Many people traditionally believe that the two-parent nuclear family model consisting of a married male and a female in a sexual relationship is the most stable and effective family model. This traditional belief carries with it certain truths, given that in the United States single-parent households are more likely to be poorer and have fewer resources. This is especially significant because 48% of African American families are headed by single mothers, compared to 16% for Whites and 27% for Hispanics (Fields, 2003).

The drawbacks of traditions stem from their very strengths. Sometimes people follow traditions neither because they understand them nor because they are the most logical, but because they are just the way things have always been done or what people have always believed. Traditions develop over long periods of time as people develop patterns of thinking and behavior. Therefore, they can become resistant to change even when newer understandings emerge or information is discovered that contradicts the traditional beliefs (Imagine yourself questioning something that "everybody knows"). Just accepting traditional assumptions and beliefs in totality without inquiry or question can present a barrier to social progress or the continuous advance of knowledge. It is problematic when we accept things without being critical or without fully understanding them, simply because "that's the way we've always done things." One of the basic requirements of a social scientist is the courage to test assumptions. After all, it was once tradition for African Americans to enter some White-owned establishments through the back door, because Whites treated Black people as if they were inferior. To advance knowledge and society, traditions must always be subject to scrutiny.

Take, for example, the belief that the two-parent nuclear family model is superior to the single-parent family and other family structures. Despite this traditional belief, there is current research that indicates that it is not always the case that two parents are better than one (Trammel, Newhart, Willis, & Johnson, 2008). Recent studies indicate that non-traditional fathers and non-custodial fathers can be *more* effective parents than resident fathers (Dubowitz, Lane, Grief, Jensen, & Lamb, 2006). Moreover, same-sex relationships are changing the demographic makeup of family structures. This research suggests that emphasis should be placed on the quality of relationships within families and not just household composition.

Traditional beliefs can be very effective, but when they are accepted without question they can lead to broad overgeneralizations and misguided advocacy. Reliance on traditional beliefs can lead one to label a family as dysfunctional because of its structure and not the quality of its functioning. What happens if a social worker accepts without question traditional beliefs about two-parent families or the belief that low marriage rates are due to lack of value of marriage? What happens when social programs for low-income parents are designed to promote family values among the poor, when lack of values is not their primary dilemma? This is the danger of tradition as a primary source of knowledge. In fact, recent studies suggest that the belief that low-income fathers place less value on marriage and family values than their peers at other income levels is actually an overgeneralization, and that in fact they place just as much value on marriage, family, and parenthood as their higher-income peers (Edin & Kefalas, 2005; Waller & Plotnick, 2001). Keep in mind that it was once a traditional belief that the earth was the center of the universe—and flat. The researcher must have the courage to question assumptions and beliefs that are widely accepted and taken for granted, especially when they are not entirely accurate. As Franz Fanon stated in his classic book *Black Skin, White Masks*, "My final prayer: O my body, always make me a man who questions!" (Fanon, 1952, p. 232).

I don't know, ask an expert.

Authority

What we believe can be based in large part on the authority of the information provider or information source. Imagine that someone tells you that cobalt, a super alloy found in abundance in the Democratic Republic of the Congo, does not melt until it reaches more than 2,723 degrees Fahrenheit. Are you more likely to believe your physics professor, who has a degree in geology and mining engineering, or a person you just met on the subway on the way home from work? You would probably choose the physics professor because of that person's position of authority or status. The professor most likely had to meet certain criteria before being hired to teach, such as having earned a degree in physics. One of children's first sources of knowledge is their very own authority figure: a parent. Authority becomes a source of knowledge when people rely on the knowledge of persons they recognize as having a grasp on some aspect of reality. When people accept information as true, they generally do so based on the authority of the information provider. If someone occupies a special status, people often consider that person's information legitimate— which is good, because that is the purpose of specialization and expertise. Specialization is one of the primary reasons for increased production in countries. Experts carry out important functions in given fields such as psychology, education, banking, engineering, and construction.

Among many people of African descent, elderly persons are traditionally given a great deal of respect as authority figures based on the wisdom they have accumulated over the course of their lives. Because African Americans have a tendency to describe themselves as religious or spiritual (Barna Group, 2005), it is important to make note of the fact that they often place emphasis on the authority of religious leaders as sources of knowledge. In many African countries, people place lots of credibility on traditional healers as sources of knowledge. But people don't rely on them simply because of tradition. Traditional healers are trained for many years and have to be tested; they have to prove themselves, and they have to be accurate. But what happens when they are not? What are the drawbacks to authority figures as sources of knowledge? Have you ever heard the phrase "Certification doesn't always mean qualification?" This statement means that just because people hold specialized degrees or occupy a certain specialized job or status doesn't mean that they always know what they are talking about. In certain infamous cases, individuals in positions of authority have been able to get away with inaccurate and superficial knowledge simply because their powers of persuasion attracted followers and they thereby gained positions of authority. Take, for example, the case of the religious leader Jim Jones, who led over 900 of his followers to mass suicide in Guyana, South America, in 1978. He told them that by committing suicide they would ensure their transition into paradise, and many people *believed* him. Sometimes persons with specialized knowledge can hide their ignorance by using professional jargon. For example, if you know nothing about cars, you consult a mechanic about why your engine is making noise. You expect the mechanic to give you a reliable explanation for the problems with your engine. However, a mechanic who is baffled by the sounds coming from your engine might hide that fact by speaking in specialized mechanical jargon to convince you to accept what you are being told.

Authority as a source of knowledge is something that has to be critically analyzed. Oppressed people and underrepresented racial groups must be aware of how this challenge relates to them. For example, African Americans have been chronically underrepresented in professional, managerial positions in American business, just as women are underrepresented as chief executive officers (CEOs). In addition, diversity training and culture-specific knowledge are still scarce in the curricula of American universities. For example, a Black person who seeks psychological counseling still cannot be certain that her clinical psychologist is familiar with the best practices of the Association of Black Psychology, because such competence is not presently required by the American Psychological Association. Parents of an African American son cannot be certain that their son's teacher is familiar with African American learning styles or teaching methodologies found to be generally more effective with African American males; such knowledge is not universally required for accreditation in institutions of higher education. Consequently, African Americans cannot be certain that individuals in positions of authority are knowledgeable about the unique needs and interests of the Black community. This deficiency brings attention to issues related to institutionalized racism and lack of cultural competence and sensitivity training in education.

There is also the issue of those persons in positions of authority who speak outside of their fields of knowledge. An example is Andrew Fraser, an associate professor of law from Macquarie University in Australia, who railed against allowing people of African descent to migrate to Australia with his infamous message that "Those of African background had lower levels of intelligence than White people, and were criminally inclined" (Limb, 2005). Fraser exploited his background in law to make racist claims. Unfortunately, some people do accept as true what individuals like Fraser have to say on the basis of their professional credentials. There are clearly positives and negatives to tradition and authority as sources of knowledge. Authority as a source of knowledge is highly valuable, but it must be constantly questioned because, like all sources of knowledge, it has its drawbacks.

Common Sense

What is called common sense or conventional wisdom can also be a major source of knowledge. Common sense represents the conventional wisdom of a people based on their common experiences. One of the problems with conventional wisdom is that it can be inaccurate and contradictory. For example, many people accept as correct the conventional wisdom of the saying "birds of a feather flock together" while also accepting the phrase "opposites attract." The problem with conventional wisdom is that it is applied broadly to many different aspects of human thought and behavior, often not in a very rigorous or systematic way. People have to interrogate the so-called *common sense* beliefs and assumptions that they hold and be cautious when applying them to social issues. One of the hallmarks of a good researcher is the willingness to question the things that people often take for granted. Doing so may not make you the most popular person in the room, but it will get you into the habit of becoming a careful consumer of information. Because so much of the history and experiences of people of African descent has been misunderstood by laypersons and scholars, it is important to be critical of conventional wisdom.

News and Media

They get enveloped by the vision teller/The television tell 'em their vision/So now it's hard for them to make decisions.
—ANDRE 3000 ON THE REMIX OF THE SONG "30 SOMETHING"

Presently, the news media is a major source of knowledge for billions of people worldwide. The Internet makes information instantly available to more people than ever before. News media foster the immediate formation of world opinion about various topics and issues. But what is the quality of such information? Scientific research can be compared to the journalism that goes into the news media. Journalists gather fragments of information, draw conclusions based on those pieces of information, and come up with new ones every day and send them to presses. Reporters weave those bits of information into incomplete stories, or newsbytes, just to keep up with the fast pace of news reporting. People read news sources because they, too, are working at a fast pace and need sound bites of information to keep up with what is going on in the world—the latest oil spill, earthquake, hurricane, playoffs, elections, and more. Because reporting can lack the rigor of a long scientific research investigation, news media can suffer from some information inaccuracies. This can become problematic because people make important decisions based on information provided by the news media. As rapper Andre 3000 creatively expresses it, the media can be a powerful force that can replace critical thought if its information is accepted uncritically.

Scientific researchers take a much more systematic approach. They commit more time and resources to the process of investigation, so they do not have to jump to conclusions like the average news service or the general population. Ideally, scientific research benefits from accuracy, precision, a systematic approach, trained observers, forethought, and planning. African Americans are overrepresented in the media as perpetrators of crime, despite the fact that arrest and crime victimization data indicate that the typical criminal in the United States is White (Walker, Spohn, & Delone, 2012). Media distortions have serious consequences such as perpetuating racial stereotypes about crime, victimization, and public policy. Let's explore some of the major roadblocks to critical thought.

Analytical Misjudgments and Roadblocks to Critical Thought

I realized that evidently the social scientist could not sit apart and study in vacuo, neither on the other hand, could he work fast and furiously simply by intuition and emotion, without seeking in the midst of action, the ordered knowledge which research and tireless observation might give him.
—W.E.B. Du Bois (Du Bois, 1944, pp. 56–57)

It is necessary to discuss some of the common mistakes made by human beings in their attempt to understand the world around them through tireless research and observation. Without an accurate understanding of the roadblocks to critical thought, it is difficult to properly engage in systematic research. However, as a systematic researcher, you will often have to swim upstream against the currents of baseless opinions, assumptions, and conjecture that Du Bois speaks of. These roadblocks to critical thought are the cobwebs of casual thinking. Let's clear some of those cobwebs away so that we can prepare for more scientific inquiry.

Overgeneralization

Don't let your mouth write a check that your tail can't cash.
—Bo Diddley

As a researcher, you must not (to loosely quote Bo Diddley, one of the pioneers of rock and roll) *make a claim* your *evidence* cannot *support*. One of the most common roadblocks to critical thought is overgeneralization. Overgeneralizing involves drawing blanket conclusions about those who were not part of your research population. For example, imagine that you want to know how many of your fellow students want your university to start a College of Ethnic Studies. You decide to conduct a research investigation in which you find that most of the students on your campus are in favor of starting such a college. Moreover, you think this new College of Ethnic Studies should be modeled on the College of Ethnic Studies at San Francisco State University, the only one in the country. You decide to present the results of your study to the U.S. Department of Education. In your report you declare that *the majority of college students in the United States are in favor of starting Colleges of Ethnic Studies*. Oops! You have just made an error in inquiry called an overgeneralization. You have assumed that because the majority of students at *your* campus are in favor of starting a College of Ethnic Studies, students across the country feel the same way. Your mistake is generalizing beyond the population your research involved or speaking beyond your evidence. The solution to this error in inquiry involves three things. First, remember to stick to drawing conclusions about the population involved in your research. Second, increase your population size—the more people you sample, the more people you can draw conclusions about. Third, repeat your research on different populations. Every time you repeat your study and gain similar results, your conclusions become more dependable. If you are interested in making generalizations about college students across the country, then you need to select a sample population that includes students from across the country.

Scientific research must constantly reveal overgeneralizations because they can be harmful in very practical ways. If a researcher were to conduct investigations into the development of breast cancer in women in New York by using a sample population of White women, it would be important for that researcher to avoid generalizing the conclusions about breast cancer to all women in New York regardless of race. Why? Breast cancer does not behave the same in all women regardless of race. In fact, research shows that Black women are more likely than White women to develop breast cancer tumors that are resistant to hormone-based treatments, which means they must be treated differently (Stewart, 2007). In this case, knowledge of the specifics and the avoidance of overgeneralization may save lives. Breast cancer is also a case that demonstrates that sometimes treating people equitably doesn't mean treating them exactly the same.

In the 1960s, one of the problems that Black psychologists identified with the American Psychological Association (APA) was its practice of designing standardized achievement and intelligence tests that had been normed on populations of White students and using them to measure the intelligence and knowledge of Black students. One of the mistakes Black psychologists accused the American Psychological Association of making was overgeneralization. The APA was in the habit of designing tests that successfully measured the intelligence of and predicted academic success of White students and expecting those same tests to accurately do the same for Black students, despite cultural and socioeconomic differences. The advocacy of organizations such as the Association of Black Psychologists led to the removal of culturally loaded items and other biases from many tests. Overgeneralization has been a fundamental feature of **Eurocentrism**, or placing European culture and ideals at the center of all thought and behavior and imposing Western culture and ideology on other non-European-descended peoples. Eurocentrism involves the assumption that what the White world defines as modern is the default definition of modernity for all people. When operating from a Eurocentric perspective, it is difficult to avoid making overgeneralizations. It is the job of a critical researcher to avoid this kind of hegemony and ethnic chauvinism in reasoning.

Selective Observation

> *All seems infected that the infected spy, as all looks yellow to the jaundiced eye.*
>
> —ALEXANDER POPE

In many cases, selective observation occurs when, in the research process, people acknowledge only things that are consistent with their preconceptions. When researchers approach situations and observe facts selectively, they are more likely to engage in poor thinking and subsequently reach false conclusions even without doing so consciously. Imagine, for example, that you are interested in conducting research on school violence by observing classroom behavior. If you are of the preconception that African Americans are more likely to be violent, you could be more apt to notice the Black students who engage in violent behavior and ignore or pay less attention to those who are behaving peacefully. Or, you might be less likely to notice White, Chinese American, Japanese American, and Mexican American students who are also behaving violently. This is how selective observation manifests itself and confounds or confuses the validity or truthfulness of well-intentioned research. To avoid making selective observations, it is important to review the relevant literature (existing research) on your topic before you conduct your own research. By reviewing the literature you will discover previous research on your topic that may disconfirm your preconceptions, give you a broader perspective, and provide you with background and context on your topic. In addition, it is impossible for you to purge yourself of all of your biases. If you can't get rid of them, then turn them into strengths by using them to improve your research. It is important to be conscious of your biases and to consciously look for observations that disconfirm your preconceptions. Researchers' biases can harm them only if they allow them to lead to obstinacy or the inability to admit when their preconceptions have been contradicted or proven wrong. If researchers have a preconception that children of single mothers will have poor academic performance, then they need to make a conscious effort to test their preconceptions by looking for instances in which those same children may perform highly and consciously guard against ignoring them.

Inaccurate Observations

Inaccurate observations in research occur when you simply misrecord the facts or data. Inevitably you will face a situation where you have been on the phone with someone and thought they said something that was merely similar to what they actually said. You thought your teacher said a paper was due on October 15th when he or she actually said it was the due on the 17th. You thought the traffic light was green, or at least that's what you told the officer. What was the person who was standing next to you in the grocery store line wearing on the first day of class? If you truly had to answer that question you might misremember the color of his pants, or the type of top he had on. This is okay in everyday casual observance, but you must guard against this kind of mistake in empirical (systematic) research. To do so, you must be sure to take a more systematic and deliberate approach. For example, if you went to the first day of class deliberately trying to take note of what the person sitting next to you wore, you would probably do a much better job in recounting it later on. What's more, you might even create a chart to make sure that you systematically record the person's shoes, top, pants, hat, and earring(s).

To observe problem behavior in school classrooms, Schrank and Woodcock (2002) developed a classroom observational form for the purpose of observing classroom behavior in a systematic way. Their observational form includes a chart that lists different types of problem behaviors such as inattentive, overactive, impulsive, uncooperative, anxious, withdrawn, and aggressive, and a section for "other" inappropriate behavior. In addition, their chart includes a range of times so that they can take note of just how long each student was engaged in any of those problem behaviors. This is a systematic and deliberate approach that guards against selective observation. If the researchers go into classrooms to observe classroom behavior without some idea about the specific things to look for, then they run the risk of making scattered observations. Guard against inaccurate observations by being systematic and deliberate about what you intend to observe.

Vested Interests: Shaping the evidence around the conclusions instead of shaping the conclusions around the evidence

Researchers have a vested interest when they will benefit personally from a certain outcome. This presents a problem when researchers allow the vested interests they have in certain research conclusions or outcomes to influence the accuracy of their research. When researchers are influenced by a vested interest, they are compelled to violate the ethics of research in order to ultimately come to a conclusion that confirms their preconceptions or preferred outcomes. Vested interest is the problem of *shaping the evidence around the conclusions instead of shaping the conclusions around the evidence*.

Researchers often decide to make their research conclusions consistent with their own prejudices and preconceptions. For example, a researcher may design a financial literacy workshop for members of a poor, inner-city community. To demonstrate that the financial literacy workshop was successful, the researcher may desire to show an increase in the financial literacy of the majority of the community members who participated in the financial literacy workshop. To do so, the researcher may give the participants a financial literacy test at the beginning of the research project and again at the end to identify any increase in the financial literacy levels of the participants. But what if the tests indicate that the majority of the participants' financial literacy scores did not show any significant improvement as a result of the workshop? Those who have conducted this research are now at an ethical crossroads. The ethical course is to report the truth (the workshop was ineffective), even if it does not reflect favorably upon the effectiveness of the financial literacy workshop. However, some would unethically choose to allow vested interests to shape their research by falsely reporting increases in the financial literacy levels of the participants. They may fill out the correct answers of several financial literacy tests and replace the low-scoring tests with high-scoring tests, making the financial literacy workshop appear to have been more successful than it actually was. This is the vested interest problem, and it confounds the validity of research. Avoid the vested interest problem by being true to the ethics of good research.

Illogical Reasoning

Illogical reasoning refers to ways of thinking that are not based on any systematic or critical judgment. During the early 19th century, some White social scientists believed that enslaved African people who either attempted to escape or escaped from slavery were suffering from a mental illness. Samuel Cartwright, who was known as a psychologist of the slave, labeled slaves who escaped as *mentally ill*; specifically, he called their illness *drapetomania*, the "flight from home" disease (Kambon, 1999a). This conclusion wasn't based on any science or logic. It was supported because it justified racism, the status quo, and existing power relations in America. This is a case of illogical reasoning that justified White supremacy. To avoid illogical reasoning it is important to be intentionally logical and to ground current research in previous scientific research. Scientific research avoids many of these roadblocks to critical thought by being deliberately systematic, logical, transparent, and evidence based. However, even scientific research can be wrong. Although scientific research does its best to eliminate as much risk of error in inquiry and roadblocks to rational reasoning as possible, one must not believe that science can eliminate all error.

Mistakes in Racial/Cultural Reasoning

It is indeed no accident that in this society the subjects of social and psychological studies are in some capacity the powerless. It is, in fact, the powerful who study the powerless. Social scientists of all disciplines have traditionally occupied positions of economic, political and psychological superiority over the people they select to study. In a very real sense, the position of the social scientist is similar to that of the colonial master and his subject people.

—WADE NOBLES (2006, P. 123)

Because so much of the history of social science has been the study of the powerless by the powerful, researchers must be cautious of engaging in **scientific colonialism**, which occurs when the center of gravity for the acquisition of knowledge about a people is located outside of that people's lived reality (Galtung, 1967). Nobles (2006) explains that scientific colonialism can leave a researcher conceptually incarcerated or capable only of using non-African concepts, ideas, and perspectives to study people of African descent. There are several common misleading approaches and assumptions that have historically been made and continue to be made in the process of researching people of African descent. Several mistakes in racial/cultural reasoning as they relate to people of African descent are *transubstantive error* (Nobles, 2006), the *hierarchical comparative analysis problem*, the *fallacy of homogeneity*, the problem of the *orientation/solution deprivation* cycle, *ethnologic ahistoricism*, the *disregarding social regularities reaction*, and *self-censorship*.

Transubstantive Error

When researchers do not respect or give adequate weight to the cultural perspective of the people being studied, they are prone to committing what Nobles (2006) calls the transubstantive error. According to Nobles (2006), transubstantive error occurs when a researcher uses the cultural substance of one ethnic group to define, explain, and interpret the cultural substance of another group. Both historically and presently, the thought and behavior of African American people have been examined and judged from a Eurocentric perspective. It is the responsibility of the researcher to ask first how the people being studied define themselves on their own terms and in their own cultural context. For example, in their study of conceptualizations of intelligence among the Luo people of Kenya, Grigorenko and colleagues (2001) studied how the Luo define intelligence on their own terms. Had they simply taken traditionally Western notions of intelligence and applied them to the Luo people to see how they measured up, they would have ignored the cultural definitions of the Luo people and committed the transubstantive error. Instead, they found that Luo understandings of intelligence go beyond the traditionally Western tendency to associate intelligence with cognitive functioning (mental processes, including knowing, perceiving, and remembering). They learned Luo concepts such as *rieko*, *luoro*, *paro*, and *winjo*, which refer to skill, competence, communalism, creativity, strategic capability, knowledge of traditional wisdom, and judgment. Had they committed the transubstantive error, they would never have learned of Luo understandings of intelligence. They would only have learned how the Luo look in the light of Western definitions of intelligence. The transubstantive error is closely related to the hierarchical comparative analysis problem.

Hierarchical Comparative Analysis Problem

Comparative studies date back to the late 18th and 19th centuries when European anthropologists conducted a series of comparative studies that contrasted the physical attributes of Black and White people, looking at characteristics such as skin color, hair texture, skull size, skull shape, facial structure, and posture. In these comparative studies, the differences were always found to favor Whites, and the implication always went far beyond the physiological. For example, physical differences were said to account for intelligence, lack of intelligence, superiority, and inferiority. This tendency is demonstrated clearly in the legacy of scholarship in American psychology. As Belgrave and Allison (2006) state:

> A large percentage of studies done in American psychology have focused on differences between African Americans and Whites. During the 1st part of the 20th century, most of the research conducted on African Americans involved comparative studies that contrasted African Americans and Whites on individual difference traits (Guthrie, 1976/1998). This focus on differences led to African Americans being viewed as having deficits on many psychological characteristics. (p. 10)

When researchers fail to use culturally specific methods of analysis, there is a tendency to use comparative analysis. When researchers use the comparative approach, it is easy to accept the doctrine of cultural monism. Comparative analyses are known for identifying behavioral differences. However, while differences may indicate cultural pluralism or cultural diversity, those differences are often interpreted as evidence of deviance or deficiency. The major weakness of the comparative model is that sometimes researchers end up identifying one cultural set of norms as superior and another as inferior. These analyses have the tendency to give meaning to the thoughts and behaviors of one cultural group based on how similar or different they are from another cultural group. Comparative analysis can be rich in identifying and appreciating cultural difference and diversity. However, the benefits of comparative analysis can be spoiled by the tendency to add a hierarchical element.

The problem with the race-comparative paradigm is not with the comparative method itself, but rather with the user(s) of the method. Many scholars who have used the comparative method have had the tendency to equate the *differences* they discover with *inferiority* or *inadequacy*. In scholarship that has used the comparative paradigm, there has been a tendency to equate the characteristics of those who hold a greater share of power with what it means to be standard, ideal, and normative. Therefore, there has been a tendency to equate the characteristics of those who prove to be different with inferiority and consequently to evaluate them negatively (McLoyd, 1991). According to McLoyd (1991), the comparative paradigm can produce an intellectual foreclosure that positions difference as an end in itself, as opposed to seeking out the cause of difference. When social problems are framed as being caused by difference from the norm, the solution can easily be understood as assimilating to the norm. For example, A is wrong because it is different from B; therefore, A must become more like B. One of the noted shortcomings of the race-comparative paradigm is that, when used exclusively or heavily relied upon, little if anything can be learned about variation and dynamism within the African American population itself, because emphasis is placed on difference between races rather than within them.

Fallacy of Homogeneity

Another error in racial/cultural reasoning is the *fallacy of homogeneity* (Stanfield, 1989), which refers to the assumption that all people of African descent are the same. This assumption, usually latent in some social scientific research, ignores the fact that all people of African descent—African Americans, for example—are extremely diverse. As Belgrave and Allison (2006) assert, African Americans are male, female, young, old, Baptist, Muslim, atheist, Buddhist, rich, middle class, and poor. This fallacy is also evident in the tendency of researchers to overwhelmingly focus their investigations on low-income African Americans and African Americans in urban areas and to generalize their findings to all African Americans (Belgrave & Allison, 2006). This is a fallacious approach to investigation, given that most people of African descent are not poor (National Urban League, 2010). This phenomenon will be explained further in the next section.

Problem Orientation/Solution Deprivation

Prejudice and racism are embedded into the social fabric of America in ways that are individual, institutional, intentional, and unintentional. They may vary in the forms they take, but their most consistent, constant, unswerving feature is their outcome. Scholars and researchers are not immune to their influences. In the research context, the problem orientation manifests itself in the tendency for researchers to focus on underachievement, calamity, depravity, deficiency, and failure when researching people of African descent. This problematic orientation does not emerge in a vacuum; it is a manifestation of the *deficiency paradigm*. The deficiency paradigm is an approach to studying peoples of African descent that we will explore further in the following chapter. The consequence of the focus on underachievement is that Black children in advanced placement or those who are simply performing above average are an under-researched population. The focus on family dysfunction leaves healthy Black family functioning an under-researched phenomenon. Overwhelming focus on uninvolved fathers leaves the nurturing Black father an invisible reality in the research world. Research guided by this orientation tends to leave solutions under-researched. However, the problem is embedded within the orientation itself: the tendency to focus on problems creates a poverty of solutions. Why? Why do solutions escape the researcher guided by the problem orientation? Simple: they were not looking for solutions to begin with. The consequences of under-researched Black success, healthy functioning, high achievement, wealth, and agency is a lack of knowledge about how healthy families function, how community organizations successfully create change, the reasons why high-achieving students are successful, and so on. Researchers avoid this mistake by being self-critical and asking themselves whether or not they are taking a balanced approach to studying the lived experiences of Black people.

Ethnologic Ahistoricism

One of the most common limitations of research about people of African descent is ahistorical analysis. Ethnologic ahistoricism occurs when researchers engage in the study of a racial or ethnic group at a single point in time without placing their findings into historical context. When the contemporary conditions of a people are not placed into historical context, research can be very fragmented. Such research may be descriptive but lacking in explanation. Connecting the past with the present helps researchers to provide an understanding of how present conditions developed and how the past is still unfolding. A lack of historical context can lead to analytical misjudgments such as the problem of orientation/solution deprivation and deficit thinking. For example, an ahistorical analysis of the present conditions of the African American family might lead a researcher to conclude that African American families suffer from multiple dysfunctions as a result of their own internal inadequacies. Such an analysis might never explain the role that slavery, segregation, migration, economic events, changes in welfare policy, and institutional racism played in fostering family dysfunction. This error is avoided by reviewing past literature and historically situating research subjects.

Disregarding Social Regularities Reaction

An additional problem that is the opposite of the fallacy of homogeneity is the problem of *disregarding social regularities*. Black people have often been stereotyped such that certain qualities have been presumed to apply to all members of Black populations based on no scientific evidence. One hasty yet understandable reaction to this is the dogmatic focus on individuality and turning a blind eye to social regularity. This problem is important to recognize because, in the effort to establish and proclaim the diversity among people of African descent, social scientists can fail to see the commonalities—patterns of thinking and acting—that represent cultural cohesion among people of African descent.

One must be careful not to preclude the absence of social regularities between people of African descent without bothering to establish the presence or absence of social regularities. For example, there are many different ethnic groups on the African continent, but their commonalities become apparent after studying them. There are African Americans of different income levels, educational levels, and religions, but their commonalities become apparent after examination. Amid all of the diversity and uniqueness among different people of African descent, there are social regularities, patterns of thinking, and behavior. Social regularities are what culture is based on. Identifying the differences and commonalities between people can be the pretext for collective action. However, assuming the absence of such social regularities would not allow the researcher the benefit of appreciating the commonalities that constitute African American, Afro Cuban, and Afro Brazilian culture. Such precluding represents an abandonment of the scientific method. This is an accepted exception to the rule that researchers must examine the facts before drawing conclusions.

This assumption of the absence of commonality would also disallow the researcher from recognizing and acting on what research tells us about the learning styles that are most commonly found among African American students, the counseling techniques that have proven more effective in treating psychological distress among many African Americans, or the child-rearing techniques that have generally proven more effective with Black children than children of other races and ethnicities (Belgrave & Allison, 2006). These patterns in thinking and behavior allow service providers to better serve Black populations. They never represent absolutes, but social scientists rarely discover any absolutes. They study patterns in thinking and acting, not absolutes in human thinking and acting. Remember that social scientists primarily look for social regularities and seek to explain variation in human thinking and acting. The diversity that exists among African Americans only complements the fact that there are patterns of thought and behavior that are more commonly found among people of African descent.

This is different from overgeneralizing, which declares that all members of a group think or act in the same way. The social scientist has to be able to make the distinction between overgeneralizing and recognizing patterns. Recognizing patterns of thought and behavior should not lead one to assume that all people of African descent are the same. Similarly, recognizing the uniqueness and diversity among people of African descent should not lead one to ignore their commonalities. If it does, you might "miss the forest for the trees," as the age-old proverb goes.

Self-Censorship: The Dirty Laundry Quandary

We scared of almost everything, afraid to even tell the truth
So scared of what you think of me, I'm scared of even telling you
—LUPE FIASCO (JACO) (2011)

The moral agency to be truthful maintains the integrity of the researcher and his or her research. Africana Studies research is meant to be conducted in the service of the people, and this necessitates the ability to deal honestly in the world of information. The researcher must always be willing to report truth whether or not it is interpreted to reflect positively or negatively upon the researcher(s), the research participant(s), society's institutions, or society's power holders. Unwillingness to do so will lead one down the slippery slope of roadblocks to critical thought and reinforcement of the status quo. Such self-censorship does no service to the masses. In addition to the mistakes in racial cultural reasoning, the next chapter discusses an additional two: the *inferiority paradigm* and the *cultural deficit paradigm*.

Now that you are familiar with these errors in different types of human inquiry, you have to apply them. Now that you know the principles of systematic thought, you have to think about one of the major preoccupations of social scientists. This preoccupation is the ever-present need to explain variation in human thought and behavior. Social scientists of all sorts attempt to account for such variation. They believe that if they can gain a greater understanding of human attitudes and actions, they can take steps toward improving people's lived experiences. This variation we speak of can be accounted for by explaining the relationship between different variables. This section explains what variables are and how to explain the relationship between them.

Variables

Why do people's attitudes about race vary? Why do people's test scores vary? Why do people's behaviors vary? There are many possible answers to these questions. How do you go about explaining this variance? Let's begin by explaining exactly what the term "variables" means. Simply put, things are called variables because they vary. Because of the inherent problems in defining a word using the word itself, we cannot stop there. A **variable** is a concept (trait or characteristic) with two or more categories or attributes. Research cases can vary based on the categories they belong to. Skiba, Michael, and Carroll Nardo (2000) conducted an investigation that found that Black public school students were more likely to be expelled from school than their White peers for committing the same infractions. In this case, whether or not students were expelled from school *varied* based on those students' races. One variable in question in this study is "race" (Exhibit 1.1). Race is a variable because it is a characteristic with two or more categories. Rate of suspension is a variable because

Exhibit 1.1

VARIABLE	ATTRIBUTES \ LEVELS
Race	African American \ Black
	European America\ White
	American Indian or Alaska Native
	Latino\ Latina American
	Asian Indian
	Chinese
	Filipino
	Japanese
	Korean
	Vietnamese
	Native Hawaiian
	Guamian or Chamorro
	Samoan
	Other Asian
	Other Pacific Islander

Exhibit 1.2

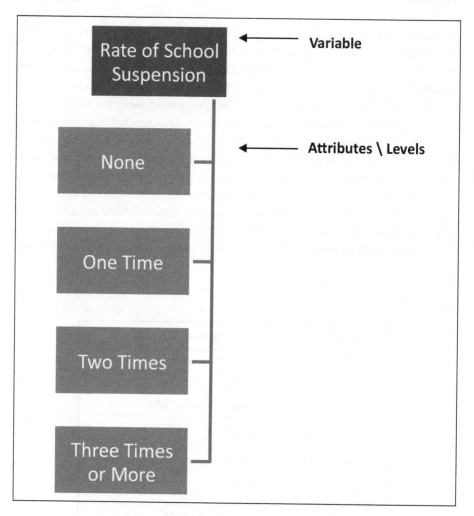

Exhibit 1.3

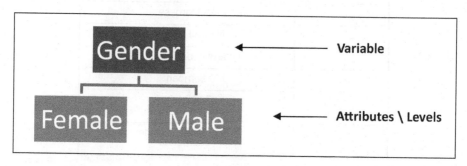

it varies based on race (Exhibit 1.2). In this case, race is a variable with as many cat-egories as there are racial distinctions. What if we wanted to know whether there was any *variation* in the suspension or expulsion of Black students who committed disciplinary infractions based on their gender? For example, were Black males more likely to be suspended or expelled than their Black female peers? Our new variable is gender/sex. If gender is a variable, then what are its attributes? The attributes of gender are typically presented as *male* and *female* (Exhibit 1.3), but should also include transgender and gender queer. With this variable, we can determine whether or not Black students' suspension or expulsion rates vary based on their gender.

For the purposes of research, variables are classified as either independent or de-pendent. The **independent variable** (IV) is known as the predictor variable or the causal variable because it determines changes in the dependent variable (DV). The **dependent variable** is affected by or dependent upon the independent variable. Put another way, changes in the dependent variable(s) are a result of changes in the independent variable(s). If, for example, we are trying to determine why Black stu-dents have higher suspension and expulsion rates than their White peers, our de-pendent variable would be student suspension rates and student expulsion rates. Why? Because these variables are dependent variables (suspension rates and ex-pulsion rates), as they vary based on race. Race is the independent variable because it has an effect on student suspension rates.

Research has shown that African Americans have the highest rate of cigarette smoking in Illinois by race (Simmons, 2009). Right away we know that the rate of cigarette smoking among Illinois residents varies based on race. But what are the independent and dependent variable(s)? The dependent variable is the rate of cig-arette smoking. But the rate of cigarette smoking among Illinois residents varies based on something. Whatever that something is, it is going to be the independ-ent variable because it is having an effect on the dependent variable (rate of ciga-rette smoking). In this case, the independent variable is race. Also remember that there can be more than one independent or dependent variable. It was also found that the rate of smoking varied based on age (Simmons, 2009). Now we have a new variable: age. Among adults, males smoked more than females. Among high school students, females smoked more than males. It was also found that the poor and less educated smoked at higher rates. Care to identify the new variables? What are they? If you are tempted to say "less education," "lack of education," or "poor," you are on the right track, but you are stating these new variables in an unbalanced or biased way. Instead of identifying the variable as "less educated," state it as "level of education"—which could be low, moderate, or high based on an individual's high-est earned degree. Instead of identifying the variable as "poor" or "poverty," state it as "level of income." The two variables, then, are level of education and level of in-come. Note that each of these variables is related to *stress*. However, by examining the relationship between the independent and dependent variables, we have a much better understanding of how that relationship works and the other factors that are involved. Often people relieve stress by smoking. Remember, you state the variable instead of one of its attributes. When you state the variable as "level of income" and "level of education," it is clear that these variables can vary because they can have different levels.

Although independent and dependent variables are two of the most important types of variables, they are not the only ones. An **intervening variable** (iV) helps to further explain the relationship between the independent and the dependent variables. An intervening variable is defined as "the variable, which is determined by the independent variable but influences the dependent variable, and is often difficult to manipulate or measure" (Bless, Higson-Smith, & Kagee, 2006, p. 183). The intervening variable comes from the independent variable and also influences the variation in the dependent variable. For example, as we know, the independent variable, level of income, influences the dependent variable, rate of cigarette smoking. However, *stress level* is an intervening variable that is a function of the independent variable, and it also influences the dependent variable. Poverty may cause stress, which in turn may compel a person to attempt to relieve the stress by smoking cigarettes. Let's take another example. Imagine that you conduct a study in which you divide your city into districts. You discover that the greater the number of full-service grocery stores available in a district, the less likely those district residents are to experience strokes, high blood pressure, and diabetes. Conversely, you discover that the lower the number of full-service grocery stores in a district, the more likely residents are to experience higher rates of stroke, high blood pressure, and diabetes. What is or are your independent variable(s)? Your independent variable is number of grocery stores. What about your dependent variable(s)? Your dependent variables are the incidence of stroke, high blood pressure, and diabetes among city residents.

You understand that the majority of your city's African American residents are living in those communities with the fewest full-service supermarkets, and the greatest number of corner stores lacking fresh foods. Now comes a very critical moment. What are you going to do with this information? You remember that one of the major objectives of Africana Studies is the emancipation of the African community. You are going to organize the residents of your city, inform your district leader, supermarket brands, the National Black Farmers Association, and other city officials. But wait! How are you going to explain this variation in incidence of stroke, high blood pressure, and diabetes? Why do they vary based on the number of full-service supermarkets in city districts? To do this you need to identify the intervening variable(s). Can you think of any? Try *consumption of fresh produce* (fruits and vegetables). A University of North Carolina study found that predominantly Black neighborhoods' consumption of fresh produce increased 32% for every additional supermarket in the neighborhood (Duenwald, 2002). So your intervening variable is *consumption of fresh produce*, which is a function of the availability of full-service grocery stores. Your dependent variables are rates of stroke, high blood pressure, and diabetes. This is important to know because you may run into some detractors who will attempt to argue that we all have access to fresh produce, and the people who don't eat it don't do so because they choose not to. However, you will be in a position to explain the relationship between your independent and dependent variables and try to influence changes in public policy in your neighborhood that may save lives. Kudos to you. You are a model scholavist (scholar-activist); you are to be commended. Additionally, you did it with your knowledge of independent and dependent variables!

Causality

Discussions about the relationship between variables are incomplete when they do not include the role of causation. A cause is an event or a factor that produces a change in another variable. Simply put, a cause is something that produces a change or an effect in the world (Remler & Van Ryzin, 2011). However, it is important to establish the fact that just because there is a relationship between two or more variables does not mean that one is the cause of the other; relationships don't establish cause and effect. Not every time someone declares that they have discovered a cause have they *truly* discovered one. Sometimes two or more phenomena may occur together, but this doesn't mean that one is caused by the other—they may simply be *related*. For example, when the number of part-time faculty working at a university decreases, there may be a simultaneous decrease in the number of racially/ethnically underrepresented students attending that university. Does this mean that a decrease in the number of part-time faculty working at a university causes enrollment to go down for students of underrepresented racial/ethnic groups? It is tempting to answer "yes," isn't it? But the answer is "No." There is no causal relationship here—only a relationship, and a relationship can only *imply* that there may be a cause. Such implications must be subjected to more scrutiny before one can establish causation.

Here are the three major criteria for establishing causation:

TEMPORAL SEQUENCE: In order for there to be a causal relationship between two or more variables, the cause must precede the effect. It is illogical to claim that something that occurs after the effect is actually the cause. For example, one cannot claim to have caused the light to come on by flipping the light switch if the light came on before the switch was flipped, just as one cannot assert that turning a key started the engine unless the key was turned before the engine started. To establish causation, a relationship must meet the temporal order requirement that the cause must precede the effect. So if one is to claim that the firing of part-time faculty at a university causes student enrollment to decrease for underrepresented racial/ethnic groups, one must establish evidence that there was an increase in the firing of part-time faculty before student enrollment decreased for underrepresented racial/ethnic groups. If this cannot be established, there is likely not a causal relationship. You may assert that placing income restrictions on first-time-buyer housing loans (requiring that occupants have a median family income of $70,000 per year to qualify for occupancy) causes an increase in home ownership for underrepresented racial/ethnic groups. However, you first have to establish that income restrictions were put in place before home ownership rates increased for underrepresented racial/ethnic groups.

ASSOCIATION: In order to establish causation, one must also establish that there is an association between the independent and dependent variables. There must be an empirical relationship between the two variables, meaning that a change in one variable must be associated with a change in another variable. If there is to be a causal relationship between height and weight such that increase in weight causes an increase in height, then as height increases there must be an increase in weight. Someone may assert that high income levels cause people to be more supportive of immigration. He or she would have to meet the association requirement by establishing that there is an empirical relationship between income and attitudes toward immigration. (And, in fact, there is: people of higher income levels tend to be more pro-immigration [Blackwell, Kwoh, & Pastor, 2010]). Or, if one wants to establish that education causes people to be less prejudiced, he or she must demonstrate that—according to the rule of association—as people's levels of education change, there is a change in their levels of prejudice. Although association or correlation is necessary to establish causation, it is still not enough. Remember that one still must meet the temporal sequence requirement and one other requirement: no spurious variables.

NO SPURIOUS VARIABLES: Finally, in order to establish a relationship between two or more variables as causal, one must make sure that there are no spurious variables responsible for the occurrence of both independent and dependent variables. A **spurious variable** is a variable that is the cause of both the independent and dependent variables. For example, what if we discover that a third variable is responsible for both the firing of part-time teachers and decreases in enrollment for students of underrepresented racial/ethnic groups? Consider that some universities respond to budget cuts both by firing part-time professors and raising admissions requirements. By raising admissions standards, it is possible that low-income students who are disproportionately students who belong to underrepresented racial/ethnic groups may be denied entry, thus decreasing the number of such students enrolled. Here is another classic example: One might attempt to establish a relationship between ice cream sales and drowning (Babbie, 2001). As ice cream sales increase, there is typically an increase in instances of people drowning. There is a relationship between these two variables (ice cream sales and drowning). However, that relationship is spurious and not causal because of the existence of a third variable (the spurious variable): temperature. Temperature is a variable that is responsible for both ice cream sales and drowning. People drown because, as temperatures get hotter, more people go swimming and are thus more likely to drown. As the temperature increases, people are also more likely to eat ice cream because it is a cold food that offsets the temperature. Thus ice cream sales will increase.

It was noted earlier that level of education is related to the rate of cigarette smoking. It is an **inverse relationship**, meaning that as levels of education increase, the rate of cigarette smoking decreases. But what steps might we have to take to establish that education causes cigarette smoking to decrease? First, we have to establish temporal order, which means that we have to establish that people's rates of cigarette smoking decrease after they have earned higher levels of education. Second, we must establish an empirical association, which means that as people's levels of education increase, their smoking rates decrease. Finally, we must find out whether or not there is a spurious variable that explains both levels of education and smoking rates.

In addition to spurious relationships, researchers must also be aware of *reverse causation* and *simultaneity bias* (Remler & Van Ryzin, 2011) in studying relationships between variables. Reverse causation refers to instances when the perceived independent variable is actually caused by the perceived dependent variable. For example, one may assert that a low level of education may cause one to have a low income level, when it may be possible that it is the reverse—that it is income level that affects level of education. *Simultaneity bias* refers to the fact that sometimes when someone asserts the existence of a causal relationship between variables, it may be the case that there is a causal relationship between the variables in both directions (Remler & Van Ryzin, 2011). For example, it could be the case that increases in levels of education affect income increases, while increases in income also influence the acquisition of higher education.

Various studies show that students who own library cards read more and perform better on standardized language arts tests (e.g., Whitehead, 2004). So it is not surprising to find some educational leaders attempting to boost academic performance by distributing library cards to all students, as the minister of education did in

New Brunswick, Canada (Communications in New Brunswick, 2004). We are tempted to hope that ownership of a library card itself *causes* kids to read more. However, reverse causation is quite likely in this case: the kids who already read a lot are the ones with the library cards. There could be common causes at work, too, such as parents who value and encourage their children to read *and* own a library card.

Being knowledgeable of the intervening and spurious variables—as well as reverse causation, simultaneity bias, and the criteria for causation—complicates the relationship between variables. However, knowledge of these complexities gives you a more accurate and complete understanding of complex social relationships. With better understanding, researchers can make more evidence-based recommendations for solving social problems and making social change. But as researchers go about studying complex problems, they have to be sure to do so with the utmost regard for the integrity of the populations they are studying. This is the subject of the next chapter.

Key Terms

Africana Studies	Problem
Dependent Variable	Research
Domain of Inquiry	Research Methods
Eurocentrism	Scientific Colonialism
Independent Variable	Scientific Research
Intervening Variable	Spurious Variable
Inverse Relationship	Variable

Thinking about Science

Activity 1

- Research is used to guide many efforts to improve people's life conditions. The provision of education, healthcare, and any number of social services is guided by research. Think of an example of how research can be used to improve some aspect of the lived experiences of people of African descent. Explain your answer.

Activity 2

- Identify an organization committed to improving some aspect of the lived experiences of any people of African descent. Contact this organization and ask one of its representatives if they use research to accomplish any of their organization's objectives. If they do, ask them to give you an example.

Activity 3

- This chapter has explained several errors in inquiry. Go to the websites of some of your local news services. Read some of the editorials until you find an example of an error inquiry. Explain what the error is.

Activity 4

- Think about the mistakes in racial cultural reasoning that were explained in this chapter. Think of an example (not already mentioned in the chapter) of one of those errors and explain how it might affect research about people of African descent. Explain your answer.

Activity 5

- This chapter has discussed independent, dependent, and intervening variables. Identify some variables that you think are related. Identify which of them is the independent variable and which is the dependent variable. List the attributes of those variables. Explain the relationship between them. Now think of a possible intervening variable. Explain its relationship to the independent and dependent variable.

CHAPTER TWO

Methodology in Africana Studies Research

In scientific research, several epistemological tools such as concepts, theories, and paradigms moderate the relationship between the knowing subject and its object. For oppressed people and their descendants, it is important that the intellectual tools guiding the relationship between them and who or what they study is culturally relevant and emancipatory. **Methodology** is the aspect of research that contains the paradigms, theories, concepts, and methods that shape approaches to study and social intervention. These items are explored in this chapter. First the chapter explains the components of methodology in the research process. Second, it explains the unique paradigms, theories, and models in Africana Studies and how they are used to guide research and explain social phenomena. Third, it explains different types of theory and how they are used in the research process. Let's begin by discussing methodology.

Methodology

The difference between the words *method* and *methodology* is more than just the three syllables. As mentioned earlier, a research **method** is a tool of data collection. Methodology includes but goes beyond a researcher's choice of a method of data collection. Africana Studies is sometimes referred to as multidisciplinary or interdisciplinary. This author asserts that the discipline is *unidisciplinary* and has multiple *dimensions.* What distinguishes Africana Studies from other disciplines is primarily its approach to study and its purpose. That unique approach is defined by unique concepts, theories, and paradigms. Given that Africana Studies has its own concepts, theories, and paradigms, it is its own discipline and not a derivative of other disciplines. Africana Studies is multidimensional because it applies its concepts, theories, and paradigms to the African experience through multiple subject areas.

Any group of people can be the subject of study or the object of study. Any scholar can study any people he or she pleases: African Americans, Asian Americans, Nigerians, or any other people. However, even if two different researchers study the same group of people, it is not guaranteed that they will reach the same conclusions, and often they may not reach the same conclusions because they didn't follow the same methodology. It is the methodology you are guided by that determines what assumptions you make, your choice of a research method, what questions you ask, what questions you don't ask, what theories you use to make sense out of what you find, or—maybe more importantly—your reasons for engaging in research in the first place. Although the two terms must be recognized for their unique meaning, *methods* can never be divorced from *methodology*. Methods allow the researcher to collect data, but methodology combines methods with the paradigms, assumptions, theories, concepts, and ideas that give life, interpretation, and meaning to data. Let us explain the major components of methodology: paradigms and theories.

Paradigms

In science the conceptual universe takes the form of paradigms which, technically speaking, serve as formalized frameworks that guide descriptions, explanations and evaluations of the empirical world. A paradigm is an instrument for knowing. At the center of the conceptual universe lies a core set of ideas which gives the conceptual universe, which in turn not only determines the people's perception of human capabilities, but also guides the development of new human inventions. How a people define and classify both regular and irregular patterns of social interactions, behavior and development is determined by this conceptual universe. It defines and determines the meaning and purpose of human relationships and experiences.

—NOBLES, 2006, P. 202

All research methods are derived from a particular paradigm or grand theory (Mazama, 2003). Moreover, all academic disciplines have at least one paradigm that guides their development of theories and their conduct of research (Kershaw, 2003).

A **paradigm** is a general way of understanding and approaching knowledge about the world. Paradigms guide a researcher through the experience of acquiring knowledge. A paradigm can also be described, in a practical sense, as a systematic arrangement of explanations and ideas that guide policy and action (Kuhn, 1970). Paradigms are different from theories in the sense that they are larger in scope and cover larger domains of inquiry and areas of human thought and behavior. Dominant paradigms are difficult to displace once they become popular and institutionalized. However, they often serve the interest of a few and must be challenged in order for other explanations to emerge. The existence of multiple paradigms creates a healthy tension in the academic world; however, they ultimately emerge from praxis and can have oppressive or life-affirming, real-world consequences. There are two paradigms in particular that have been applied to people of African descent by scholars in Western science that continue today: the inferiority paradigm and the cultural deprivation paradigm.

Inferiority Paradigm

According to Parham, Ajamu, and White (2011), the inferiority paradigm typifies a framework of analysis that characterizes Black people as inferior based on inadequate genetics and/or heredity. The inferiority paradigm asserts that the substandard social behavior and mental conditions of people of African descent can be explained by their inferior genetic inheritance. A long line of notable European scholars has adopted and continues to adopt this line of reasoning. Linnaeus (1735) asserted that Black people were inferior by nature, possessing qualities such as "capriciousness," "negligence," "slowness," and "cunning." Galton (1869), father of the eugenics movement, argued in *Hereditary Genius* that the average Negro was significantly intellectually inferior to the average White person. G. Stanley Hall (1905), the founding father of the American Psychological Association (APA), provided his professional opinion that Africans in Africa and in the United States were profoundly lazy and prone to theft and hypersexuality. Lewis Terman (1916), a pioneer of intelligence testing, claimed that African Americans were inherently less intelligent than Whites, incapable of abstract thinking, and should be segregated and given special educational instruction. Noted psychologist Carl Gustav Jung (1950) claimed that sexual repression among Americans was due to their living in such close proximity to lower races such as Negroes. American psychologist Arthur Jenson (1969) asserted the genetic intellectual inferiority of Black people. In 2007, the eminent biologist James D. Watson, who won the Nobel Prize for his discovery of the double helix structure of DNA, asserted that people of African descent are not as intelligent as people of European descent (Dean, 2007). These scholars and many more like them represent a tradition, a paradigmatic train of thought that seeks to explain the thinking, behavior, and social conditions of people of African descent by proclaiming their inherent inferiority. These assertions of inferiority locate the nature of social problems within the individual. By doing so, attention is shifted away from the impact of environmental and social conditions on human thought and behavior.

Cultural Deficit Paradigm

The cultural deficit paradigm is known similarly by phrases such as cultural disadvantage, cultural deficit, and cultural deprivation theory, which posit that African Americans experience social dilemmas based primarily on their own internal failures. According to Parham and colleagues (2011), the cultural deficit paradigm is different from the inferiority paradigm in that its proponents cite environmental factors instead of heredity as the source of presumed Black deficiencies. For example, deficit modeling is demonstrated in the idea that African American children experience failure in school because the socialization they receive at home does not provide them with cultural interactions that foster intellectual development. According to the 1964 Conference on Education and Cultural Deprivation held at the University of Chicago, culturally deprived children are described as follows: "We refer to this group as culturally disadvantaged or deprived because we believe the roots of their problem may in large part be traced to their experiences in homes which do not transmit the cultural patterns necessary for the types of learning characteristic of the schools and the larger society" (Banks & McGee-Banks, 2004, p. 18). Some social scientists of the 1960s developed the "culture of poverty" concept, which is part of the cultural deficit paradigm (Banks & McGee-Banks, 2004). The cultural deprivation paradigm became popular in the 1960s and 1970s. It essentially asserts that African American culture is deficient because the values, beliefs, and behaviors it transmits are different from those of Whites (Durodoye & Hildreth, 1995). In the 1960s and 1970s, the cultural deprivation paradigm dominated the discourse to the extent that it was difficult for other explanations to be recognized (Banks & McGee-Banks, 2004). Parham and fellow researchers (2011) explain that the basic assumptions of the cultural deficit paradigm are that White, middle-class values hold that Black people suffer from their underexposure to dominant values, that Black people carry no sophisticated culture from Africa, and that they are in need of cultural enrichment.

Cultural Difference Paradigm

The cultural deprivation paradigm was challenged by the cultural difference paradigm, which gained popularity in the 1980s. Those who advanced the cultural difference paradigm asserted that the culture of Black and other peoples should be considered in understanding their thinking, behavior, and social conditions. According to Parham, Ajamu, and White (2011), this paradigm assumes that thinking and behavior can only be described as appropriate or inappropriate within their own cultural context. Based on this paradigm, each culture has its strengths and limitations, and those who study or work with different populations require cultural awareness and competence. J.A. Banks (1993) argues that cultural difference is being challenged today by the cultural deprivation paradigm, as evidenced by the frequent use of the term "at risk" to describe children who are, in many ways, different. Banks and McGee-Banks (2004) state:

> The at-risk paradigm has become popular, in part, because it was a funding category for state and federal educational agencies. When a term becomes a funding category, it does not need to be defined precisely to attain wide usage and popularity. Another reason the term became popular was because it was used to refer to any population of youths experiencing problems in school. Consequently, every interest group could see itself in the term. Although the phrases are problematic, as Cuban points out in a thoughtful article, it was often used by both researchers and practitioners. (p. 20)

Banks and McGee-Banks (2004) add that the focus on cultural deficits prevents educators from recognizing students' unique strengths and prevents them from looking at the structural changes that need to be made in both schools and society (Banks & McGee-Banks, 2004). Boykin (2000) uses the term "placed at risk" to describe students who are suffering socially and academically because it denotes children whose needs have not received the proper social attention. This stands in contrast to referring to children as "at risk," which connotes that the child has an affliction or less-than-optimal functioning that is the source of underachievement, although that may not be the case. Eggen and Kauchak (2003) refer to students placed at risk as "those in danger of failing to complete their education with the skills necessary to survive in modern society" (p. 44). They state that students placed at risk are in greater need of support, structure, and motivation. The "placed at risk" frame does not make the a priori assumption that the deficiency originates in the person, their family, or culture. This historic and contemporary lens through which the African American experience has been framed informs how African American experiences are framed in the contemporary political arena.

Colonial Paradigm

The colonial paradigm is a lens for understanding the exploitation and underdevelopment of Black communities (Staples, 1976). Based on the colonial model, there are two distinct groups: the dominant group and the subordinate group. In the colonial context, the dominant group maintains dominance and control over those with less power. Those with power use the full institutional apparatus of the state to maintain power (King, 2010). The colonial model focuses primarily on the colonial condition as the interaction among race, ethnicity, and class-based oppression in addition to other forms of oppression. One of the basic assumptions of the colonial paradigm is that the colonized are pressured to abandon their own cultural values and adopt the values of dominant groups. This occurs because the colonized are exposed to the asymmetric power balance in the colonial condition. In using the colonial model, social problems that are educational, economic, political, crime related, and health related are understood as being part of the colonial project. The basic characteristics of colonialism (Staples, 1976, p. 13) are that:

1. The colonized subjects are not in the social system voluntarily, but have it imposed on them.
2. The colonial subjects' native culture is modified or destroyed.
3. Control is in the hands of people outside the native population.
4. Racism is prevalent.

As noted above, institutional racism is part and parcel of colonialism. According to Carmichael and Hamilton (1967), Black people are systematically deprived of power in the racialized colonial contexts; thus, "institutional racism is another name for colonialism" (p. 5). Looking through the colonial model, the Black condition can be explained in some part as the consequence of systematic subjugation. The colonial paradigm positions the revolutionary seizure of power by the colonized as the ultimate solution to colonialism.

Pan-African Paradigm

Theory comes from the lived experiences of communities of human beings. Particularly, Pan-Africanism developed out of the African diasporic community. Pan-Africanism must be understood as distinct from the African diaspora. Pan-Africanism is more of an approach to understanding and advancing the lived experiences of Africa and its diaspora. Pan-Africanism in many ways represents an ideology and a method for liberation as such. Historically and contemporarily, Pan-Africanism has been the driving force behind anti-colonial independence and post-colonial movements in Africa and in the diaspora (Zeleza, 2011). However, it is also a paradigm that can be used to interpret and understand the lived experiences of African communities. Politically and intellectually, Pan-Africanism's ultimate objectives are the liberation (racially, politically, culturally, and economically) and solidarity among African peoples (on political, cultural, and economic matters) (Zeleza, 2011). Lao-Montes (2007) defines Pan-Africanism as "a world historical movement and ideological framework led by activists and intellectuals seeking to articulate a transnational racial politics of Black self-affirmation and liberation" (p. 311). The application and conceptualization of the Pan-African paradigm has been diverse. Some prefer to focus on certain dimensions of Pan-Africanism, while others focus on multiple dimensions. The different dimensions of Pan-Africanism can be understood as political, cultural, and/or economic. Moreover, Pan-Africanism can be applied in continental and/or diasporic ways. Pan-Africanism can be used to analyze the cultural, political, or economic relationships among continental Africans, African countries, and Africa's diaspora. Walters (1993) defines Pan-Africanism by its relationships: among African people and among African states; among African states and African diasporic states (including those in the Caribbean); among African states and African-descended peoples (communities) in the diaspora; among African-origin states in the diaspora and African-origin peoples in the diaspora; and among African-origin communities in the diaspora. One of the basic assumptions of Pan-Africanism is that the proper understanding of and liberation of peoples of African descent requires their political, economic, and/or cultural unity. From a Pan-Africanist perspective, peo-

Exhibit 2.1

Disruptive Conceptualization in Africana Studies: Epistemological Rupture

Christensen (1997) articulated the theory of disruption based on his analysis of how large corporations get toppled by small start-up companies. He found that when small start-up businesses adopted the same models as their larger competitors, they tended to fail. However, when these start-ups designed a model based on the needs of an ignored or less attractive market combined with improvements to existing models, they were more likely to be successful. He called this approach a disruptive strategy. However, there is a corollary to this model in the conceptual world. The theories and paradigms in Africana Studies represent **disruptive conceptualization**. They share similarities with some theories in so-called "traditional disciplines"; however, they reject and debunk some of the fundamental premises of those disciplines and their presumptions. They offer new perspectives based on the unique histories, cultures, and lived experiences of people of African descent. This disruptive innovation in Africana Studies seeks to destabilize dominant approaches to thought. It seeks to relocate the humanity of people of African descent to the epicenter of approaches to studying the African world.

ple of African descent all over the world share a common heritage, and their social, political, economic, and cultural advancement requires them to work for their common well-being and interests (Khapoya, 1998).

Afrocentric Paradigm

Asante (2003a) defines Afrocentricity as a theoretical framework to be used to examine and self-consciously advance African people in every sector of society. According to Mazama (2003), Afrocentricity should function as the meta-paradigm for the discipline of Africana Studies. Afrocentricity means placing African culture, experiences, and ideals at the center of any analysis of African phenomena (Asante, 2003a). The way the Afrocentric scholar thinks about the world is shaped by what Modupe (2003) refers to as Three Pyramidal Elements of Afrocentricity: Grounding, Orientation and Perspective. Grounding refers to knowledge of the history and experience of the African world. Orientation refers to a particular interest in the needs and concerns of people of African descent. Perspective refers to looking at the world in a way that seeks to identify ways to emancipate and empower people of African descent. The basic assumptions of the Afrocentric paradigm are that

- The experiences of people of African descent are worthy of study (Kershaw, 1992).
- African people have unique and distinctive cultural and historical experiences (Kershaw, 1992).
- The best way to understand African people is first and foremost from their own perspective.
- A people's worldview determines what constitutes a problem for them, and how they approach solving problems (Mazama, 2003).
- The fundamental substance of all reality is spirit, and not everything that is important is measurable (Mazama, 2003; Nobles, 2006).
- The ultimate aim of all research in Africana Studies must be to empower and liberate people of African descent (Mazama, 2003; Kershaw, 2003).
- African peoples' experiences can be used to help gain a greater understanding of the human experience (Kershaw, 1992).

There are many key concepts and theoretical frameworks that compose the Afrocentric paradigm, three of which are victorious consciousness, centeredness, and agency. *Victorious consciousness* refers to knowledge and awareness that African people have been victorious in the past and will be victorious in the future (Modupe, 2003). The assumption behind victorious consciousness is that is it difficult to engage in self-determining, liberatory behavior if one does not believe that victory is achievable. *Centeredness* refers to being grounded in the knowledge of the history and culture of African people, and engaging the world from that foundation. *Agency* refers to playing a self-conscious and active role in shaping one's own destiny. These key concepts guide the way the researcher explores, explains, and describes the lived experiences of people of African descent.

When looking through the lens of the Afrocentric paradigm given the principles outlined above, one approaches the study of African phenomena in a particular way. Researchers approaching the study of African phenomena using the Afrocentric paradigm must ask themselves several questions. Where does the phenomenon fit within the larger narrative of African history? How is the phenomenon understood within the context of African peoples' culture(s)? How is it manifested in the unique lived experiences of peoples of African descent? Does the phenomenon enhance or hinder African agency and historical and cultural grounding? How can the phenomenon be approached in a way that promotes African people's development on their own terms? For example, when looking at the problem of mental health

Exhibit 2.2

What does it mean to be a problem? (Du Bois, 1997)

The first assumption in the Afrocentric paradigm is that the Black experience is worthy of study. The initial reaction to such an assumption might be surprise. Why would it not be worthy of study? Why would studying the Black experience be a problem? A strange question indeed, but when it is rife in a society, racism has a way of making otherwise obscene prejudgments seem normal. As W.E.B. Du Bois stated many years ago, "being a problem is a strange experience." Many researchers or scholars of the Black experience have faced the charge that their work is too narrow. Prejudice in the new age has become far more subtle than it was in the past. Sometimes "too narrow" can be the more refined modern corollary to its more candid precursor, "too Black." The unspoken and often spoken assumption is that the Black experience is only worthy of intellectual pursuit when it is studied alongside the legitimizing presence of White people and/or other racial or ethnic groups seen as more legitimate. The aversive racism laden within this charge may not be apparent to the untrained eye. But as Ladson-Billings (2009) explains, scholars are trained to be specific, precise, and to focus their work, and why should that scientific training be temporarily suspended when it comes to studying the Black experience? In various disciplines, scholars focus on specific populations and subject areas without the charge of being too narrow. The Black experience must be understood first and foremost as worthy of study to avoid this conceptual problem. Otherwise researchers may prevent themselves from conducting important research before they even begin.

among a people of African descent—for example, Haitian people—through the Afrocentric paradigm, one must ask questions like these:

- What have African civilizations offered to discussions of mental health and well-being?
- How have African peoples dealt with questions of mental health and well-being in the past?
- What concepts have Haitian people developed to make reference to mental health?
- How have Haitian people approached maintaining well-being or mental health in the past and present?
- How do Haitians' historical relationships with mental health relate to how Haitian people currently approach maintaining well-being or mental health in their own cultural context?
- What mental health conditions currently confront Haitian people?
- What factors are responsible for the current mental health conditions of Haitian people?
- How can Haitians achieve mental health as they define it on their own terms?

It is evident that the Afrocentric paradigm always refers to the culture(s) of people of African descent when approaching the study of any African phenomenon, whether it be psychological, political, education, or any other dimension of reality.

African-Centered Behavioral Change Paradigm

The Institute for the Advanced Study of Black Family Life and Culture (IAS-BFLC) defines the African-centered behavioral change model (ACBCM) as an intervention paradigm (Nobles, Goddard, & Cavil, 2012). The ACBCM is based on the assumptions that behavioral change comes from individual efforts to balance the forces that influence and shape behavior and that culture is central to behavior and behavioral transformation. Several African-based key concepts are central to the ACBCM: maafa, ma'at, person veneration, and human authenticity (Nobles, Goddard, & Cavil, 2012). The maafa is a symbolic representation of disintegration, dehumanization, and negation. It characterizes the cumulative effect of the systematic physical and spiritual domination and oppression that African people have experienced. The ACBCM looks at health and disease within the context of the recent and historical short- and long-term effects of maafan forces.

Ma'at is an ancient Egyptian concept representing the highest ideal or standard for good character and correct human conduct. Ma'at is composed of three critical elements. First, it is distinguished by the idea that the person and life itself are a part of the supreme creative process. Second, ma'at recognizes life as an interconnected process of human causality. Third, it recognizes the spiritual dimension of the human experience. The ACBCM grounds its notion of health and the ability to change and evolve for the better in the seven cardinal virtues of ma'at (or exemplars of good character): order, balance, harmony, compassion, reciprocity, justice, and truth (Nobles, Goddard, & Cavil, 2012). The African concept of veneration of the person ensures that African people are looked upon as cultural phenomena, with human agency, and as human beings who are repositories of divine energy. The African conception of human authenticity asserts that African people must have a sense of their connection to their own ancestry and that which brought them into being (the divine). Once African people have this authentic core, they will have a sense of essence and the drive to make the proper response to the demands of life (Nobles, Goddard, & Cavil, 2012). According to the ACBCM, behavioral change "occurs through the process of culturization" (Nobles, Goddard, & Gilbert, 2009, p. 231). Culturization minimizes negative social conditions and maximizes prosocial and life-affirming social conditions. This is accomplished by way of three particular techniques: cultural realignment, cognitive restructuring, and character refinement. Cultural realignment is a process in which African people are realigned with traditional African and African American cultural values. The purpose of doing so is to draw upon this essence in order to enhance their well-being (Nobles, Goddard, & Gilbert, 2009). Cognitive restructuring is a process by which people restructure how they think of themselves and the world in which they are located so that they can assume their rightful place. Character refinement is a process by which people adjust their mental and ethical character traits so that they are aligned with their cultural essence. Based on the ACBCM, human service providers must be knowledgeable of the cultural meaning and definitions of persons they intend to help if they are to be successful.

Kawaida Paradigm

The Kawaida Paradigm is a "cultural and social change philosophy which is defined as an ongoing synthesis of the best of African thought and practice in constant exchange with the world" (Karenga, 2010, p.260). The central concept in Kawaida is culture, "the totality of thought and practice by which a people creates itself, celebrates, sustains and develops itself and introduces itself to history and humanity" (Karenga, 2010, p. 261). Kawaida maintains that the key challenge of Black people is the crisis of culture, specifically, being displaced from their own historical and cultural foundations and being relegated to the margins of European history and culture. The solution to this crisis must begin with a cultural revolution, defined as "the ideological and practical struggle to rescue and reconstruct African culture, break the cultural hegemony of the oppressor over the people, transform persons so that they become self-conscious agents of their own liberation, and aid in the preparation and support of the larger struggle for liberation and a higher level of human life" (Karenga, 2010, pp. 261-262). This revolution requires African people to identify models of excellence in every area of human life, particularly in the seven fundamental areas of culture: history, ethics and spirituality or religion; social change organization, economic organization, political organization, creative production, and ethos. To guide the African liberation struggle, the Kawaida paradigm puts for the Nguzo Saba (seven core values of the Kawaida paradigm): Umoja (unity); Kujichagulia (self-determination); Ujima (collective work and responsibility); Ujimaa (cooperative economics); Nia (purpose); Kuumba (creativity), and ; Imani (faith).

Literary Pan-Africanism

Literary Pan-Africanism is a paradigm designed to guide the "proper explanation of the content, form, and function of African literary creations" (Temple, 2005, p. 4). Literary Pan-Africanism is a particularly appropriate tool for the analysis of texts in which an author representing one region of Africa and the diaspora writes about a literary character from another region of Africa and the diaspora (Temple, 2006a). Literary Pan-Africanism is meant to ensure that Pan-African literary works are placed in proper historical context and evaluated based on their practical relevance and problem-solving capacity (Temple, 2006b). Works that reflect the paradigm of literary Pan-Africanism possess the following characteristics or qualities (Temple, 2005, p. 4): (1) the text seeks to regenerate relationships between Africans and descendants of the Africans dispersed through the European slave trade; (2) the writer recognizes and nurtures relationships between Africans and African Americans; (3) the philosophy and ideals of the narrative reflect Pan-African ideology; (4) the text uses language reflective of "return"; (5) the author's approach is Pan-African, Afrocentric, and/or African-centered; and (6) the author usually has spent some time among African American communities in the United States. The primary objective of literary Pan-Africanism is to demonstrate how such works can generate unity among people of African descent through discourse (Temple, 2005).

Sacred Worldview Paradigm

Floyd-Thomas and fellow researchers (2007) position the sacred worldview paradigm as a framework for analyzing and placing the theological tradition of Black churches into historical, cultural, and social perspectives. This sacred worldview paradigm is a point of departure from which Black theologies may be properly understood. Theology is the reflective practice of understanding divine reality and its relationship to creation, the proper order of the universe, and human relationships according to different theological approaches. Floyd-Thomas and collaborators (2007) define a theological tradition as "a sustained, communal reflection on practice, teaching, experience and a 'handing on' of both the wisdom and genius of that communal reflection from generation to generation" (p. 75). The Black theological tradition emerges from the Black sacred worldview, which consists of three sources: sacred inheritance, experience, and scripture (Floyd-Thomas, Floyd-Thomas, Duncan, Ray, & Westfield, 2007). *Sacred inheritance* refers to the West African carry-overs or religious wisdom, cultural norms, and practices that continue to manifest in African diasporic cultures throughout the western hemisphere. *Experience* refers to the discrete experience of racial oppression that Black people in the new world have experienced from slavery to segregation, cultural and economic racism, and so on. These unique experiences have influenced the positioning of questions of mercy and justice at the center of African American theological interpretations (Floyd-Thomas et al., 2007). *Scripture* is the third and last source of the Black sacred worldview, and it refers to the unique ways in which Black people have engaged and interpreted biblical scripture—ways that "validated both their humanity and their quest for freedom" (p. 79). The intersection of these three elements produces the sacred worldview that gives shape to the diversity and commonality in African American religion and culture.

Worldview Paradigms Analysis

Kambon (1999b) designed the worldview paradigm as a conceptual approach to understanding and contextualizing the thoughts, beliefs, values, and action of people of African descent. Kambon (1999b) asserts that whether they're conscious of it or not, all people operate from some group concept of reality or understanding of what is real, correct, and appropriate. According to Kambon (1999a), each racial/cultural group has its own unique survival thrust or worldview orientation. Survival thrust refers to the collective environmental adaptations people have made in defining their distinct histories and cultural philosophies. Usually people share beliefs, values, and other cultural patterns with their own indigenous cultural reference group. However, when people identify with a cultural group that is not their own indigenous reference group, then they risk operating from a conception of reality that is unnatural. Kambon (1999a) defines appropriate behavior as culturally relative. According to Kambon (1999b), when people think and behave in ways that are consistent with their own indigenous cultural experience, they are behaving appropriately and normally. But when they think and behave in ways that are not, they are behaving inappropriately. Worldview represents the distinct unifying cosmological, ontological, epistemological, and axiological principles representing a racial-cultural group's natural cultural or conceptual orientation, outlook, or perspective on and construction of reality. The worldviews paradigm makes the following assumptions about the origin, development, and function of worldview systems:

- Every culture generates its own distinct approach to and experience of reality (i.e., indigenous definitional system, philosophy of life, or fundamental/basic assumptions about life, nature, the universe), which we might call its cosmology or worldview. It grows out of their distinct (collective) bio-genetic and geo-historical condition in the world.
- The worldview system naturally evolves through and reinforces the survival maintenance of the culture; that is, its cumulative-collective approach to survival.
- Culture varies such that different racial/ethnic groups generate a different culture that is peculiar to their distinct indigenous shared/collective bio-genetic, geo-historical, and experiential-social realities. Thus, culture and worldviews are race-specific phenomena. They are defined and identified by common racial experience (i.e., biogenetic, geo-historical, and environmental condition). This shared culture then defines similarities within a race family and distinguishes between race families.
- There are fundamental differences between the African and European worldviews, just as there are fundamental bio-physical differences between the Africans and Europeans. Thus, the African worldview projects the African survival thrust, and the European worldview projects the European survival thrust.
- Under normal/natural conditions, Africans (Blacks) operate or function in terms of the African worldview, and Europeans (Whites) operate in terms of the European worldview. Hence, it is normal and natural for Africans and Europeans to represent their own distinct worldview orientations.
- Any substantive deviations from these normal/natural relationships or fundamental ontological patterns, therefore, represent unnaturalness, abnormality, or basic cultural disorder as defined by the natural order itself (Kambon, 1999b).

The worldview systems fundamentally represent the different cultural realities, which reflect the distinct approaches that Africans utilize in conceptualizing, organizing, and experiencing reality. These basic assumptions further emphasize that worldview orientation is the index of normality in the psychological functioning and behavior of race-cultural families. According to Kambon (1999a), the adoption of any basic deviations from the indigenous worldview orientation within a race-culture that results from forced intervention/cultural oppression by an external culture is abnormal and a form of basic cultural disorder.

Four of the most critical components of worldview are identified as cosmology, epistemology, ontology, and axiology. These four components make up the philosophical structure of the worldview construct and the manner in which it defines cultural reality indigenous to the racial/cultural group, which it identifies. Cosmology refers to the structure of reality from a particular racial/cultural perspective or experience. African cosmology is characterized as an interconnected and interdependent edifice; all things in the universe are interconnected and independent, all originating from the Supreme Being, and therefore all in possession of the Supreme Being. The ontological aspect refers to the essence or essential nature of reality based on a particular racial/cultural experience. According to African ontology, spirit is the basis for nature, existence in the universe, and it is this spirit or force provided by the Supreme Being that endows all things. Axiology is the study of values. African axiology is based on harmony with nature, cooperation, and communalism. The epistemological aspect of worldview refers to the method of knowing and understanding reality based on a particular racial/cultural experience. A race or cultural group's epistemology explains how that group approaches knowledge acquisition. African epistemology emphasizes affective cognitive synthesis as the way of knowing reality, as well as through symbolic imagery. Affect refers to the feeling self, the emotive self engaged in experiencing phenomena holistically (physically, spiritually, and mentally), or putting one's self into the experience and not separating one's self from the totality of the phenomena (Moore, 1996). African epistemology is a sociocentric (collective, interactive) way of learning. With all of its components, worldview determines the meaning we attach to the events in our day-to-day existence; it informs our definitions, concepts, values, and beliefs. Worldview determines how people perceive and respond to various phenomena that characterize the ongoing process of everyday existence within a culture.

Positivist Paradigm

Quantitative science has been associated with Eurocentricity and racism due in part to its close association with positivism. Positivism is a term that was coined by August Comte to refer to "the empirical study of phenomena" (Vogt, 1999, p. 217). Positivism applies the principles of research in the natural sciences to the study of social phenomena. Positivism grew out of a rejection of much of the knowledge that accrued from religion and metaphysics. This paradigm identifies society as a phenomenon that can be studied scientifically. Positivism asserted that science should involve the use of the five senses instead of belief alone. It is a reductionist philosophy in that its intention is to reduce ideas and social phenomena into small categories and variables that can be measured. Numeric measures are central to positivist social scientific research. The paradigm asserts that ideas, emotions, morality, and other human qualities can be studied quantitatively (Vogt, 1999). But, alas, positivism is not a method; it is a paradigm. It is a way of viewing the world that favors quantification.

Paradigms are not research methods; they are a part of research methodologies. The Afrocentric paradigm is in conflict with certain aspects of the positivist paradigm. Afrocentricity rejects the idea that all valid knowledge is external (Akbar, 1994) and that human beings are fundamentally material. From an Afrocentric perspective, reality is, in fact, fundamentally spirit. However, this does not take away from the Afrocentric social scientist's responsibility to learn how to scientifically measure material reality, which is fundamentally perceived as the manifestation of spirit. Afrocentricity also rejects the idea that research is or should be value neutral.

Conflict Paradigm

Conflict paradigm is a conceptual framework that sees society as an arena of inequality that creates conflict (Macionis, 1999). It looks at how access to social resources such as education, power, and privilege are distributed inequitably based on variables such as social class, race, ethnicity, gender, and age. Its assumption is that the social structure always benefits some people while depriving others. From this perspective, those who have access to greater power and privilege tend to shape society in a way that maintains their power and deprives others. Through this paradigm society is viewed as an arena in which there is a constant attempt to dominate others and avoid being dominated themselves (Babbie, 2001). Karl Marx focused on the struggle between classes and the distribution of economic resources among different classes of society (Macionis, 1999). For example, a conflict analysis might point out the fact that school perpetuates inequality because it reproduces structural inequality in each new generation through the practice of ability grouping in the form of college preparatory classes and lower tracks for students with lower test scores. This is because ability groups tend to have very little transition from lower to higher tracks, meaning people usually remain in their tracks. There is a relationship between students' family incomes, and their academic achievement levels such that the higher a student's family income, the more likely he or she is to have higher academic achievement, and the lower the family income, the more likely he or she is to have lower academic achievement. Therefore, school actually reinforces and reproduces the social inequality that those students entered school with. Once they graduate with different levels of knowledge and different qualities of education, they will have different levels of access to higher education and employment. According to the conflict paradigm, when those students become parents, their income levels will affect the quality of education they can afford for their children, thus reproducing the cycle of social inequality.

Structural Functionalism

Structural functionalism is a paradigm that sees society as a system whose parts work together to promote overall social stability and solidarity. It sees society as an organism in which every part contributes to the functioning of the whole. The paradigm was designed to create stability during a time of social change, and it assumes that all elements of society are interdependent. It looks at patterns in human thought and behavior to see how they contribute to the overall functioning of society. For example, there is a distinction between two kinds of social functions: manifest and latent functions. Manifest functions are the recognized and intended consequences of a social pattern (Macionis, 1999). Latent functions are the unrecognized and unintended consequences that promote social solidarity and structure (Macionis, 1999). The manifest function of higher education is to provide citizens with skills and knowledge to do jobs and to perform meaningful functions for society. Its latent or unintended function is that it brings people of similar social backgrounds, similar interests, and ambitions into contact with one another. While at universities, people develop bonds in the form of friendships and relationships that may last a lifetime. Higher education also keeps millions of people out of the labor force, where it's unlikely they would all find jobs, and keeps them paying until they finish.

Symbolic Interactionism

Symbolic interactionism is a paradigm that sees society as the product of the meaning created through everyday interactions between individuals. From this perspective society is basically the shared meaning and shared reality that people create as they interact with one another. For example, beauty is something that is negotiated as people interact with one another in different cultures and environments all over the globe. As people interact with one another, they discover what is attractive and unattractive about themselves to others and to themselves. As a result, there are many similarities and differences in what is perceived as attractive body types, complexions, facial structures, and so forth. According to Charles Horton Cooly, as human beings we construct a self-concept as we observe the reactions of people around us (Babbie, 2001). If people around us treat us like thugs, then we conclude we are thuggish; if people around us treat us as intelligent, we conclude we are intelligent. We do this by imagining how others think and feel about us, and in the process we create meaning.

Theory

*An oppressed group's experiences may put its members in a position to
see things differently, but their lack of control over the ideological appara-
tuses of society makes expressing a self-defined standpoint more difficult.*
—PATRICIA HILL COLLINS (2009, P. 44)

Theory is a part of what distinguishes one discipline from another, what gives it its
unique lens of analysis. But what is theory? No doubt you have heard someone say
the words, "I've got a theory," followed by their explanation of how they suspect
that some aspect of the world works. After all, theories are interrelated sets of
propositions that seek to explain some aspect of reality. Theories begin to develop
when people make observations about the society or world around them (Bless,
Higson-Smith, & Kagee, 2006). Sometimes out of curiosity and other times out of
obligation, people attempt to scientifically verify their observations, and when they
do they discover **facts** or valid information. Facts are the cornerstone of knowledge
(Bless et al., 2006). Theory seeks to explain how some facts relate to others by providing elaborate explanations. A **theory** seeks to explain the relationships between
a set of **concepts**. Concepts are abstract ideas that enable one to categorize data
(Vogt, 1999). Concepts are the components of theories, and, taken together, they
explain some aspect of reality. In scientific research, researchers must make systematic observations and test those observations to ultimately develop a theory.
This is important because, in science, theories gain strength and validity the more
they have been tested and verified. One can have confidence in a theory the more
it has been validated by research. Theories seek to clarify some aspect of reality by
explaining the relationship between concepts. Theories explain observed patterns
and regularities and why those regularities occur. Can you think of any social regularities or patterns of thinking and acting that theory could help us to explain?

Let us take, for example, some patterns of behavior among African Americans.
African Americans are in part characterized by their tendency to have an extended
conceptualization of "family." African Americans have a greater-than-average likelihood of living in households with both biologically and non-biologically related individuals considered to be family members or "fictive kin." African American
households have a greater tendency to be composed of multiple generations of family members and extended family members. They also have a tendency to engage in
more religious activity compared to White Americans. African Americans typically
attend church more often, spend more time at church, report praying more often, and
self-report reading the Bible more often than the average American (Barna Group,
2005). These are some interesting patterns in human behavior. But beyond knowing
this information to be true, how do we explain the existence of these behaviors?

Applying Theory to Social Phenomena

Triple Quandary Theory

Boykin (2000) has developed a theory that helps to explain patterns of behavior among African Americans. According to the triple quandary theory, there are three key concepts that represent the three distinct realms of African American culture: mainstream, "minority," and Afro-cultural (Boykin, 2000). *Mainstream* experience refers to beliefs, values, and behavioral styles that are consistent with those of most people who live in the United States. *Minority* experience refers to coping strategies and defense mechanisms used by "minorities" to live in an oppressive social environment. *Afro-cultural* experience refers to the link between contemporary people of African descent and traditional African cultural patterns of thinking and behavior. Allen and Boykin (2000) state that there are nine interrelated dimensions of African American culture: (1) spirituality—a vitalistic rather than mechanistic approach to life; (2) harmony—the belief that humans and nature are harmoniously conjoined; (3) movement expressiveness—an emphasis on the interweaving of movement, rhythm, percussiveness, music, and dance; (4) verve—the special receptiveness to relatively high levels of sensate stimulation; (5) affect—an emphasis on emotion and feelings; (6) communalism—a commitment to social connectedness where social bonds transcend individual privileges; (7) expressive individualism—the cultivation of a distinctive personality or proclivity toward spontaneity of behavior; (8) orality—a preference for oral/aural modalities of communication; and (9) social time perspective—an orientation in which time is treated as passing through a social space rather than a material one (Boykin, 2000).

How might one explain the tendency for African Americans to have an extended conceptualization of family, or to live in multigenerational households? The triple quandary theory is designed to explain African American culture. How might it explain the African American extended family concept? As a minority member in the American context, one has to contend with the fact that the *mainstream* cultural conceptualization of the family is the traditionally European-derived "nuclear family" model, consisting of a man and woman in a sexual relationship and their child(ren). The oppressive conditions that are a part of the *minority experience* also impact the family. For example, the declining economic viability of Black males contributes to the "non-nuclear" African American family structure. For some African American families, living in multi-generational households is influenced by the lack of affordable housing. What Boykin and Cunningham (2002) refer to as the *Afro-cultural dimension* highlights the influence of West African culture on African American behavior. In this case, West African conceptualizations of the family unit were much larger than the nuclear family model of the Western world. The African family unit consisted of aunts and uncles living in the same compound, with almost as much parental authority as biological parents. West African family units often consisted of families with a common lineage—lineages of a common clan and clans of a common ethnic group. All of these factors coming from Boykin's (2000) triple quandary theory attempt to explain why African Americans have a conceptualization of family that is different from the typical American perception of family structure.

How can the triple quandary theory be used to explain the religiosity of African Americans? One of the major components of West African culture was spirituality (Boykin, 2000). The dominant religion in mainstream American culture is Christianity (Barna Group, 2005). As a part of their minority experience, African American people have endured a unique form of oppression in the American context. African people were frequently forced to abandon their spiritual beliefs and forbidden to practice their traditional spiritual systems in the North American system of chattel slavery. In addition, their enslavers' primary religion was Christianity, which in many cases was the only religion African Americans were allowed to practice without punishment (Belgrave & Allison, 2006). The above-mentioned factors demonstrate how the minority, mainstream, and Afro-cultural experiences influence African American religious behavior. Let's look at three non-race/ethnic specific theories (*motivation theory, multiple intelligence theory*, and *teacher expectations theory*) to see what they might offer in the way of explaining African American patterns of behavior along with the triple quandary theory.

Motivation Theory

African American children have been found to perform better academically when they are in cooperative learning (structured group work) contexts (Boykin & Cunningham, 2002). There are several theories that help to explain this behavior, one of which is motivation theory. Most classrooms operate on the teacher-student model in which all the students have to compete with one another to interact with the teacher. Furthermore, they have to concern themselves with the teacher's discretion and approval of their answers or comments as right, wrong, appropriate, or inappropriate. Because of this competition and stress, some students decide not to participate. However, according to motivation theory, students working in groups of other students in a well-structured way can reduce competition to speak and provide students more opportunities to be directly involved in the learning process (Slavin, 1995). Based on motivation theory, this approach to learning can motivate more students to learn. Using motivation theory, one might say that some African American students' likelihood of learning in cooperative settings could be explained by the increased learning opportunities made available to them by way of group learning. Theories don't always do a complete job of explaining social phenomena. For example, motivation theory does not quite explain why so many studies show that African American students have a tendency to respond more positively to cooperative learning than their White classmates (Boykin & Cunningham, 2002). Perhaps triple quandary theory can help to explain this.

Cooperative learning also incorporates three of the nine interrelated dimensions of African culture articulated by Boykin and Cunningham (2002). Communalism, a dimension of African cultural style (Boykin & Cunningham, 2002), represents a commitment to social connectedness in which social bonds transcend individual privileges. Orality is a necessary condition for cooperative learning because it facilitates the social interaction and communication necessary to make cooperative learning successful. Affect, an aspect of African cultural style (Boykin & Cunningham, 2002), represents an emphasis on emotion and feelings. Relatedness refers to students' need to feel connected to others in a social environment and to feel worthy and capable of love and respect (Eggen & Kauchak, 2003). Relatedness can be enhanced through cooperative learning because social interaction is likely to be less competitive. These unique cultural characteristics that many African Americans possess must also be considered in accounting for stylistic preferences of Black students compared to their White counterparts. As you can see, it is sometimes necessary to combine race-specific and ethnic-specific theory with non-race-specific and non-ethnic-specific theory in order to create holistic explanations of social thought and behavior.

Multiple Intelligence Theory

According to Gardner's multiple intelligence theory (Gardner, 1983), a non-race-specific and non-ethnic-specific theory, the traditional approach to conceptualizing intelligence is misguided because there is more than just one kind of intelligence. According to Gardner (1983), there are eight different areas, including linguistic intelligence, logical-mathematical intelligence, musical intelligence, spatial intelligence, bodily kinesthetic intelligence, interpersonal intelligence, intrapersonal intelligence, and naturalistic intelligence. Gardner (1983) explains that educators should acknowledge the multiple areas of intelligence by creating classrooms that tap into the intellectual strengths of more students. Using Gardner's multiple intelligence theory, one might be able to explain more about African American students' increased academic achievement in cooperative learning environments. Multiple intelligence theory could explain why African American students may be more likely to rely upon interpersonal or social and interactive intelligence than some of their counterparts. Moreover, the fact that they perform better academically in cooperative learning settings may be because the cooperative learning simply allows them to use their culturally influenced intellectual strengths to master new information.

Teacher Expectations Theory

Tracking is the practice of placing students into course streams that differentiate the kind and amount of content to which they will have access. Tracking continues today even in the face of serious questions as to whether or not it serves its intended purpose. According to Oakes (1995), Black and Latino students who have similar grades as their White and Asian counterparts are less likely to be assigned to advanced placement (AP) courses. Are there any theories that can help to explain this damaging social regularity? Teacher expectations theory can be used to explain part of the academic underachievement of youth who belong to racially/ethnically underrepresented groups. Eggen and Kauchak (2003) define teacher expectations as "the attitudes and beliefs that teachers hold about students' abilities to learn which influence student achievement" (p. 35). The theory holds that these expectations may have a powerfully positive effect on students' learning—and, unfortunately, an equally powerful negative effect. Lowered teacher expectations have a negative effect on the achievement of African American students in particular (Oakes, 1995). Eggen and Kauchak (2003) state that teachers tend to treat students they perceive as high achievers better than those they perceive as having lower ability by under-serving them in the following four key areas: (1) emotional support, (2) teacher effort and demands, (3) questioning, and (4) feedback and evaluation. The cumulative effect of such differential treatment can be devastating to students perceived by the teacher as having lower ability. Here we have another example of a theory helping to explain a social regularity. Teacher expectations theory explains how teacher expectations affect student performance and teachers' student perceptions, both of which are likely to affect decisions to recommend students for advanced placement courses.

Two Cradle Theory

International studies of human values find many people from African countries to be very collectivist in their social attitudes compared to Western European countries (Hofstede & Hofstede, 2005). Moreover, the country in Africa with the highest scores on measures of individualism is South Africa, which happens to be the country in Africa with the largest population of White people (Hofstede & Hofstede, 2005). Is there a social theory that attempts to explain this social pattern? Diop's two cradle theory (Diop, 1989; Wobogo, 1976) explains the unique patterns of thought and behaviors that developed in the early civilizations of European and African antiquity. During human evolution, different ecologies developed in different geographical locations, and as people adjusted and interacted with their material environment, they developed unique forms of social relationships with one another and their environments. According to Diop (1989), unique patterns of behavior, thought, and systems of belief developed. Diop (1989) asserts that the Southern or African Cradle in the Nile Valley of Northeast Africa was the first cradle of civilization to develop. This Southern or African cradle was characterized by its warm climate, seasonal flooding, and material environment, which was generally supportive of human habitation. According to Diop (1989), the ecology of the Southern Cradle developed in human beings' cultural characteristics such as: matrilineal family structure, communal-collective value orientations, congenial non-racial social relations, and sedentary behavior (Kambon, 1999a). The Northern Cradle—Europe—is characterized by its colder climate, semi-glacial environment, shorter growing season, and competition for resources (Kambon, 1999a). The two cradle theory might explain the general differences in social orientation between African and European people's social attitudes. According to the theory, the origin of African collectivism and European individualism is in part explained by the unique physical environments out of which their cultures developed during the early evolution of human civilizations.

When researching people of African descent it is important to make use of theories that purposefully speak to their own unique experience. It is the due diligence of the researcher to identify theories, concepts, paradigms, and ideas that speak to the unique aspects of the lived experience of the people being studied. Doing so helps guard against many of the roadblocks to critical thought and racial cultural reasoning that we have already discussed. There are many theories dedicated to helping to explain the different dimensions of the lived experiences of people of African descent. Below are descriptions of a few of them. The descriptions are necessarily brief. If you are interested in using any of the following theories for your own research, you should seek fuller explanations of them, since providing such depth is beyond the scope of this text.

African American Family Functioning Model

Mandara and Murray (2002) developed the African American family functioning model based on empirical research. This research was aimed at identifying different family functioning types among African Americans. The African American family functioning model meets the need for an approach to the study of African American family functioning that respects the common and unique sociopolitical, racial, and cultural experiences of African American families. Designed to study the quality of family functioning, Mandara and Murray's (2002) model is a typology of family functioning that facilitates the examination of different interactive variables within and between different family types. The typology examines the relationship between variables such as religiosity, disciplinary strategies, educational expectations, child behavior, self-esteem, African self-consciousness, racial identity, personality, and demographic characteristics within and across different family types. The typology consists of three family types: *Cohesive-Authoritative, Conflict-Authoritarian*, and *Defensive-Neglectful*. The Cohesive-Authoritative type is characterized by high levels of family cohesion, expressiveness, and authoritative disciplinary practices (Mandara & Murray, 2002). The Cohesive-Authoritative family type is also characterized by parents placing a moderate level of emphasis on moral and religious socialization, engaging in high levels of proactive racial socialization and low levels of defensive racial socialization, and less authoritarian and neglectful disciplinary practices than the other two groups. Parents in these families have relatively higher levels of education compared to the other two types. The Conflict-Authoritarian type is characterized by high levels of internal conflict, overbearing authoritarian disciplining, and lack of concern and commitment toward family members (Mandara & Murray, 2002). The Conflict-Authoritarian family type places emphasis on academic achievement but not intellectual stimulation. This family type engages in religious-oriented socialization and a moderate level of racial socialization. Parents in the conflict-authoritarian family type have moderate levels of education, and their children obey less than those in the Cohesive-Authoritarian type. The *Defensive-Neglectful* family type is characterized by high levels of defensive racial socialization (teaching children to dislike other racial groups), low levels of empowering socialization (teaching children to be proud of their heritage), high levels of neglectful parenting, high levels of authoritarian disciplining, low levels of religious and moral socialization compared to the other two family types, and a low incidence of emotional expressions of nurturing and support (Mandara & Murray, 2002). These families have lower levels of education and income than the other two family types. Children who have less intellectual independence and disobey more than children in the other family types also characterize the defensive-neglectful family type. Overall, the model is an empirically grounded tool for understanding African American family functioning and predicting social-psychological outcomes.

African Self-Consciousness Theory

According to Kambon (1999a), Western models for assessing personality are rooted in the history and cultures of people of European descent and are thus inappropriate for assessing the personalities of people of African descent. In fact, when personality models that are products of Western science are applied to people of African descent, they can be misleading. At worst they may result in mischaracterizations and distortions of African reality. Kambon (1999a) proposes African self-consciousness theory as a framework for analyzing the personalities of people of African descent. There are two basic assumptions in African self-consciousness theory. The first assumption is that the Black personality structure is definitively African at its core. However, Kambon (1999a) notes that not every Black person will exhibit African cultural characteristics to the same degree and in the same way based on his or her unique social environment, experience, and exposure. The second assumption is that exposure to European culture and racial oppression has only affected the conscious-level expression of the Black personality. According to Kambon (1999a), African self-extension orientation is the core of the Black personality. African self-extension orientation is the unconscious expression of the African worldview, defined as spirituality by Kambon (1999a). African self-consciousness is the conscious-level expression of the African worldview. Unlike African self-extension orientation, African self-consciousness is subject to change and influence because of exposure to foreign culture and racial/cultural oppression. There are four basic components of African self-consciousness:

1. being aware of one's African history and culture and recognizing one's self as a person of African descent;
2. recognizing the importance of creating institutions that support the values and beliefs of people of African descent;
3. actively participating in the survival and liberation of people of African descent;
4. recognizing and identifying threats to African survival and development, such as racial oppression.

When these elements are present and strong, the Black personality is healthy. For example, research (Pierre & Mahalik, 2005) has indicated that African self-consciousness is related to Black male self-esteem such that as African self-consciousness scores increase, so do Black males' self-esteem scores. According to Kambon (1999a), African self-consciousness can be nurtured and supported or blocked and suffocated based on the presence or absence of institutions, networks, practices, and organizations that promote a culturally supportive environment.

Africana Critical Theory

Africana critical theory is "theory critical of domination and discrimination in classical and contemporary, continental and Diasporan African life worlds and lived experiences" (Rabaka, 2006, p. 133). In addition to critiquing domination, Africana critical theory also critiques anti-imperialistic theory and practice (Rabaka, 2002). The theory draws upon the intellectual and political legacy of historic and contemporary African radicals and revolutionaries as they relate to key questions posed by multiple forms of domination such as racism, sexism, capitalism, and colonialism that have and continue to influence society (Rabaka, 2006). Rabaka (2002) explains that Africana critical theory is interested in how the thought processes and lived experiences of African people (1) have been affected and influenced, corrupted and conditioned by imperialism and the invasion and interruption of African history, culture and society, politics, economics, language, religion, familial structures, aesthetics, and axiology; and (2) may be used to critique domination and discrimination and provide a basis for theory and praxis in the interest of liberation. Moreover, Africana critical theory is a *critical theory*, given that its primary purpose is to identify solutions to the most pressing sociopolitical problems faced by African people. Although it is often overlooked, Africana critical theory emphasizes African continental and diasporan contributions to critical theory (Rabaka, 2006). Africana critical theory is a thought tradition that promotes social activism and political practice geared toward advancing society by identifying (1) what needs to be changed, (2) what strategies and tactics might be most useful in transformative efforts, and (3) which agents and agencies could potentially carry out the transformation (Rabaka, 2006).

Africana Womanism

Africana womanism is a theoretical construct designed for the study of Africana women and the liberation of *all* people of African descent. Hudson-Weems (1994) explains that "Africana" refers to the ethnic identity of the women under consideration, and "Womanism" identifies their unique sex and humanity. The key priorities of Africana womanism are womanhood, family, and community. The theory is grounded in the prerequisite that any study or attempt to advance Africana women must begin with African cultural assumptions. A study of Africana women must also identify the unique experiences, struggles, needs, and desires of Africana women (Hudson-Weems, 1994). Africana womanism accepts that any approach to the study and liberation of Africana women must be grounded in the unique historical truths and sociopolitical circumstances of Africana women, and must prioritize Black women's own criteria for assessing their thoughts and actions (Hudson-Weems, 1994). Hudson-Weems (1994) explains that Africana womanism takes an approach to addressing problems related to Africana men within the context of African culture. Africana womanism also distinguishes itself by its assertion that racism is primary and more central to the marginalization that Black women experience than sexism or gender issues. In fact, for African womanists, racism and classism intersect with but transcend sex discrimination in the lives of Africana women. For Africana womanism, confusion on this point can lead to misguided attempts at liberation. Approaches to study using Africana womanism must consider the fact that Africana womanism is less about the ultimate goal of liberating a single gender and more about the liberation of an entire people. Moreover, Africana womanism's defining characteristics are self-identification, self-definition, family centeredness, collaboration and compatibility with men, flexibility, sisterhood, strength, respect, authenticity, spirituality, respect for elders, adaptability, ambition, mothering, and nurturing.

Africanity Model

The Africanity model is a theoretical approach designed to guide both the study of African American families and research applications and projects for the advancement of Black family life. The Africanity model places the principles that determine the basic nature of African American families at the center of its analysis of Black family life. One of the basic assumptions of the Africanity model is that the Black family cannot be understood unless it is studied in a way that respects the special dignity and value of being Black (Nobles, Goddard, Cavil, & George, 1987). According to Nobles and fellow researchers (1987), the African American family can only be understood if it is "conceptualized, studied and evaluated in terms of its own intrinsic definition" (p. 4). Based on the Africanity model, the African American family must be understood as a system embedded in a Euro-American cultural context, but which derives its primary identity, characteristics, and definition from its African nature. The African American family is not homogeneous or monolithic. African American families are diverse, but amid that diversity are cultural themes that constitute their identity or what Nobles and colleagues (1987) refer to as their Africanity. According to the Africanity model, the African American family is African in its nature; therefore the model itself is based on the African worldview as manifested in contemporary African American life. Nobles, Goddard, Cavil and George (1987) define the African American family as "a particular set of biological, spiritual, physical and behavioral patterns and/or dynamics as a distinguishable entity, as defined by the traditional and contemporary African worldview" (p. 5). The ultimate function of the Africanity model is that it explains how the African worldview manifests itself in contemporary African American families and how it is affected by contemporary social factors such as racism and economic conditions. The model also explains how such knowledge can be used to make African American families and communities viable institutions for growth and development (Nobles, Goddard, Cavil, & George, 1987).

African Feminism

African feminism is a manifestation of the need to ensure the survival and resistance to oppression for African people (Steady, 1992). African feminism pays particular attention to the unique experiences of African women shaped by race, class, gender, and their own unique culture(s), as well as other differences and commonalities. Mekgwe (2003) explains that African feminism "Takes care to delineate those concerns that are particular to the African situation. It also questions features of traditional African cultures without denigrating them, understanding that these might be viewed differently by the different classes of women" (p. 7). African feminism takes a Pan-African perspective of Africana women, examining both the linkages and unique expressions and experiences of African/Black women on the African continent and in the African diaspora. African feminism also distinguishes itself by its emphasis on the agency and power of motherhood, the sacred mother-child relationship, and its culturally relative, culturally defined perspectives on non-antagonistic male/female relationships and collective struggle with Black men (Steady, 1992). African feminists both critique dominant narratives that ignore the nuances of African women's lives and underline the power and agency of Black women's capacity to theorize their own lived experiences from their own socially, culturally situated perspectives (Chilisa & Ntseane, 2010; Mekgwe, 2003).

Afrolatinidad

Conceptually, the term Afrolatinidad refers to the unique lived experience of being both Black and Latina/o. Theoretically, Afrolatinidad is based on a set of interrelated presuppositions that seek to explain this lived experience. These basic assumptions are necessary to guide the understanding and explanation of the Afrolatina/o experience. First, Afrolatina/o identity develops as a unique part of the African diaspora in the Latina/o American context (Lao-Montes, 2007). Second, the lived experiences of Afrolatina/os share both commonalities and distinctions from non-Black Latina/os and other African/Black diasporic peoples (Roman & Flores, 2010). Third, to be properly understood, the history, cultures, and experiences of Afrolatina/os must be centered in the intersecting frameworks of the African, Latina/o, and American histories, cultures, and sociopolitical contexts (Lao-Montes, 2007).

Agency Reduction Formation Theory

Agency reduction formation theory is a framework of analysis designed to expose, situate, and explain ideological trends that are intended to compel African Americans to distance themselves from their collective identity. Michael Tillotson (2011) defines an agency reduction formation as "any system of thought that distracts, neutralizes, or reduces the need and desire for assertive collective agency by African Americans" (p. 60). He identifies the struggle against oppression as an organizing principle for African Americans. The threat to this organizing principle is nowhere more clearly found than in a corpus of ideas called the post racial project. According to Tillotson (2011), the uncritical acceptance of ideas such as postmodernism, colorblindness, essentialism, the social construction of race, and assumptions found in victim blaming and race-neutral discourses not only undermines assertive collective struggle but also shapes within African Americans a psychological infrastructure that is *resistant to resistance* (Tillotson, 2011). Because these ideas are anti-foundational and ignore empirical evidence of the existence of inequality, they must be highlighted, exposed, and translated for what they are so that African Americans can place themselves in a position to advance their collective interests (Tillotson, 2011).

Anti-Life Forces Model

Akbar (1981) developed the Anti-Life Forces model to classify mental disorders in the African American community. Akbar (1981) conceptualized mental health as being reflected in those behaviors that foster mental growth and awareness. He defined mental health as forces or ideas that threaten awareness and mental growth. There are four classifications of disorders in the model: (1) the alien-self disorder, (2) the anti-self disorder, (3) the self-destructive disorder, and (4) the organic disorder. Alien-self disorders are mental conditions manifested in behaviors that represent a rejection of people's natural selves and threaten their own well-being. As a consequence of their condition, they have become alien to themselves. Anti-self disorders include the characteristics of alien-self disorders with the addition of overt and covert hostility toward an individual's group of origin. Self-destructive disorders represent self-defeating attempts to function in a society rife with systemic oppression and inhuman conditions. This condition manifests itself in pimps, drug selling, drug abuse, alcoholism, Black-on-Black homicide, and crime. Organic disorders are manifested as severe mental defectiveness, forms of schizophrenia, and other organic brain disorders. According to Akbar (1981), these disorders are not purely physiological and biochemical, but may also be influenced by social disorder in the form of poverty and other oppressive symptoms.

Black Consciousness Continuum

Milliones (1980) developed a model for explaining the developmental stages of Black consciousness. Milliones's model was developed based on his review of biographical materials from leaders of the Black consciousness movement during the 1960s and 1970s, including Malcolm X, Amiri Baraka, Kwame Ture', and H. Rap Brown. Milliones's (1980) model consists of four stages: (1) the preconscious stage,

(2) the confrontation stage, (3) the internalization stage, and (4) the integration stage. The preconscious stage is characterized by an acceptance of mainstream ideology, a rejection of Black Nationalism, the internalization of racist stereotypes about African Americans, and a general denigration of Black people. A rejection of mainstream ideology and an acceptance of Black Nationalism and the internalization of a binary associating Black with good and White with evil characterize the confrontation stage. The internalization stage is characterized by comfort and pride in one's ethnic identity, deliberate efforts to learn more about one's culture of origin, and a reduction in anti-White sentiment. Finally, the integration stage is characterized by an openness to working with coalitions of Whites or with philosophically different Blacks around issues of relevance to the Black community. Black consciousness has been found to be related to different aspects of self-concept with therapeutic implications.

Black Existentialism

Black existentialism is a system of thought that deals with problems of existence that emerge from the historical and contemporary lived reality of Black peoples. It includes how Black peoples have dealt with concerns of freedom, anguish, responsibility, embodied agency, sociality, and liberation (Gordon, 2000). For example, Gordon (2005) focuses on Black existentialism that emerges in the Americas. According to Gordon and Gordon (2006), the problems of existence for Blacks in the diaspora stem primarily—but not exclusively—from racialized slavery and anti-Black racism, out of which have emerged a sustained Black concern with liberation, freedom, and the meaning of humanity. Black existentialism is expressed in the Black struggle for freedom but also in Black literature, intellectual thought, and music. Black existentialism is concerned with the difficulties and suffering associated with Black existence and Black peoples' struggles to overcome those difficulties and assert their humanity. According to Gordon and Gordon (2006), Black existentialism is an important framework in the articulation of the humanity of dominated people, especially in theories of (1) racism and oppression, (2) the power of the life-affirming aspects of Black music, (3) the rigorous and systematic ways of studying Black people, (4) the interdependent relationships between identity and liberation, and (5) the impact of crises of knowledge on the formation of people in each epoch.

Black Feminist Theory

To understand the thought and behavior of Black women, Black feminist theory asserts that one must place the experiences and ideas of Black women at the center of analysis (Hill Collins, 2009). Black feminist theory is a *critical* social theory meant to be used to theorize about the lived experiences of Black women for their ultimate liberation. Black feminist theory focuses its inquiry on the unique and diverse lived experiences and ideas of Black women for the purpose of social change. Black women have unique experiences and expressions of womanhood as a consequence of being both Black and women. The intersection or convergence of race, class, gender, and sexuality shape the unique and diverse experiences Black women have with womanhood and patriarchy. Hill-Collins (2009) and Gentry, Elifson, and Sterk (2005) identify five key themes that Black feminist theory offers for interpreting the lives of Black women: (1) self-definition and self-validation; (2) the interconnectedness of race, class, gender and sexuality; (3) viewing the experience of Black women as unique—both common and diverse; (4) controlling images constructed for African American women; and (5) structure and agency as a platform for social change.

Black Queer Theory

Black queer theory is an approach to the study of the thought and behavior of lesbian, gay, bisexual, transgender, and queer (LGBTQ; also known as LGBTQIA, meaning lesbian, gay, bisexual, transgender, questioning, intersex, and asexual) Black people and communities. Black queer theory locates the unique racial, historical, cultural backgrounds, and experiences of the Black LGBTQ community at the center of its approach to understanding the thought and behavior of bisexual and same-gender loving people of African descent (Johnson & Henderson, 2005). Black queer theory asserts that these unique racial, historic, and cultural experiences shape how Black people experience and express queerness (Johnson & Henderson, 2005). Black queer theory is based on the assumption that without placing the Black LGBTQ community into its own unique context, intellectual projects will fail to fully understand that community. Moreover, without properly locating Black queer experiences, well-intentioned social movements will be limited. Like other theoretical frameworks in Africana Studies, Black queer theory goes beyond theorizing and is grounded in the idea of producing scholarship to transform systems of privilege, power, and normative status (Cohen, 2005). Black queer theory is grounded in a perspective that privileges the resistance of interlocking and simultaneous oppressions, including but not limited to heteronormativity and heterosexism as they intersect with race, class, and gender (Cohen, 2005). In addition, Black queer theory resists generic homonormative assertions that fail to recognize the unique cultural, historic, and racial specificity of "Black queerness." Black queer theorists also reject approaches that ignore the multiple and intersecting forms of oppression outside of heterosexism such as race, class, and gender-based privilege and discrimination *within* queer communities (Ferguson, 2005). According to

Black queer theory, the Black LGBTQ experience cannot be adequately understood or advanced without recognizing how race, class, and gender interact and intersect with sexuality to create unique experiences for Black people and the Black community as a whole.

Critical Race Theory

Critical Race Theory was conceived by a group of legal scholar activists (faculty, students, and activists) (Crenshaw, Gotanda, Peller, & Thomas, 1995). Its purpose is to guide the production of knowledge about race and racism and to guide action geared toward racial equity. There are several basic assumptions of the critical race theory framework: (1) racism is an enduring and integral part of American life; (2) Whites accept and support equality in the form of laws and policies as long they do not diminish the power and privilege to which they are accustomed (this is known as the interest convergence theory); and (3) the historical context of racism influences present social conditions and outcomes. Derrick Bell is considered to be the father of critical race theory, which was inspired by his seminal work *Faces at the Bottom of the Well* (1992). Critical race theory grows out of the African American intellectual tradition (W.E.B. Du Bois), and the primary unit of analysis of the theory itself has been the African American experience. The theory has since expanded to include the experiences and ideas of other racial/ethnic groups in the form of Latino Critical Race Theory (LatCrit), Asian Critical Race Theory (AsianCrit), and Tribal Critical Race Theory (TribalCrit) (Brayboy, 2006).

Eco-Bio-Communitarianism

Eco-bio-communitarianism is a theoretical framework that examines the relationships among earth, plants, animals, and humans through the lens of an African metaphysical worldview (Tangwa, 2006). Eco-bio-communitarianism is based on the premises that human beings and the natural environment are interdependent, and that human beings and nature are of the same fundamental spirit. Therefore, there is no hard distinction between human beings and the natural environment. According to Godfrey Tangwa (2006), much of the pollution and environmental degradation of the global environment is a consequence of the misguided use of technology. Tangwa (2006) also argues that African people have contributed to environmental degradation on the African continent and must return to the traditional eco-bio-communitarian approach to the relationships among human society, science, technology, and the environment. He does not romanticize traditional or contemporary Africa, nor does he reject science and technology. Instead, Tangwa (2006) rejects the individualistic, domination-oriented philosophical outlook that drives the use of science and technology. He proposes that traditional Africa's outlook offers a more cosmically humble, cautious, respectful, and peaceful relationship with nature. Ultimately, Africa's traditional *live and let live* eco-spiritual approach to nature offers a more sustainable ethic to guide the use of science and industry for the sake of the African continent and the world (Tangwa, 2006).

Education and Schooling Model

Shujaa (2003) conceptualizes schooling as a means by which society maintains existing power relations and institutional structures. Education, however, is a means for transmitting culture, knowledge, and awareness of the needs and interests of the collective from one generation to the next. The education and schooling model is a theoretical framework for understanding how decision making about education and schooling are influenced by three key factors: a society's structural conditions, its members' achievement expectations, and their perceptions about the quality of their lives (Shujaa, 2003). Shujaa (2003) illustrates this process as a series of intersecting circles and bifurcations.

The model consists of four primary bifurcations or key points. Bifurcation one represents any situation in individuals' lives when they evaluate the quality of their lives as either consistent or inconsistent with their achievement expectations. If individuals' quality of life—be it prosperous or impoverished—is consistent with their achievement expectations, they are likely to accept the status quo and allow existing power relations to go unchanged. However, individuals' quality of life or outcomes may also be inconsistent with their achievement expectations. Bifurcation two represents that which individuals attribute their unmet achievement expectations: self or group characteristics or social institutions. Shujaa (2003) explains that maintenance of the existing social order depends upon people attributing their quality of life or life outcomes to their individual characteristics, because it removes stress or culpability from social institutions. However, when life outcomes are attributed to social conditions, people are more likely to challenge society's structures and institutions. Bifurcation three represents the idea that "differing interpretations of one's relationship to the social order are evident in choosing between public school reform and the rejection of public schooling" (Shujaa, 2003, p. 252). The choice of school *reform* and not *fundamental change* may involve changes in schooling's packaging and delivery, but it may reinforce individualistic and materialistic value orientations, which perpetuate existing power relations. In contrast, the rejection of public schooling represents the desire for fundamental change in the schooling process to improve quality of life by home schooling or sending children to independent schools, for example. Finally, bifurcation four represents parents' decisions to send their children to independent schools for reasons that reinforce the existing social order or for reasons that reflect a desire for fundamental change and the collective advancement of Africana people. According to Shujaa's (2003) model, some choose to send their children to African-centered independent schools as an alternative means of achieving personal success and individual wealth in spite of social constraints. Others who differentiate between education and schooling send their children to African-centered schools out of a desire to see fundamental change and collective advance for people of African descent. Each component of the model explains factors that influence decisions that people make about schooling and education.

Extended Self Model

Nobles's (1991) extended self model approaches the African/Black self-concept from the perspective of the African worldview principles of survival of the people and harmony with nature. From this perspective, the African/Black self is an extended self, prioritizing a collective conception of the self instead of an individual conception of the self. This means that individuals can only become conscious of themselves, their responsibility, and identity through others. Using this extended model of self, the individual is perceived as integrally connected to the natural order of the entire universe (interdependence) and tied to the collective well-being of the people (oneness of being). This represents the nature of African people's self-concept. In addition, deviations from it emerge from living under oppressive conditions. The core components of the extended self model are awareness of self in terms of one's (1) historical past, (2) historical future (future as reiteration of the past), and (3) individual and group self-concept (Kambon & Bowen-Reid, 2009).

Holistic/Solutions Framework for Studying African American Families

Hill (1998) presents a theoretical framework for enhancing "knowledge of the status, structure and functioning of African American families" (p. 15). The framework consists of the following dimensions: (1) historical, (2) ecological, (3) cultural, (4) problem identification, and (5) solutions identification. Hill explains that many studies of the Black family are insufficient as a result of their ahistorical character. A holistic perspective on Black families must look at how their characteristics developed over time. A holistic perspective must also take in an ecological perspective that examines how societal, community, family, and individual-level factors affect the structure and functioning of Black families. Not taking into consideration the impact of multi-level factors leads to a deficit outlook on African American families. According to the framework, it is essential that researchers examine the influences of African-based cultural assets and African American cultural identity on the functioning of African American families. The researcher cannot understand African American family structure and functioning without placing them in cultural context. Culture also provides the researcher with an understanding of the culture-based strengths of African American families. Hill identifies five characteristics that have contributed to the survival, stability, and advancement of Black families: (1) strong achievement orientation, (2) strong work orientation, (3) flexible family roles, (4) strong kinship bonds, and (5) strong religious orientation. Hill (1998) also emphasizes the importance of identifying problems that threaten the advancement of African American family functioning, while identifying multi-level solutions to address those problems that build on and enhance African American cultural strengths.

Invisibility Syndrome

Invisibility syndrome is a conceptual model for understanding the intrapsychic processes, behavioral adaptations, and outcomes of African Americans as they manage experiences of racism (Franklin & Boyd-Franklin, 2000). This model is designed for application to African Americans in general, but to African American males in particular because of the real and perceived relationship between their experiences with racism and the subjective experience of invisibility among them (Franklin & Boyd-Franklin, 2000). Franklin (2004) defines invisibility as "an inner struggle with feelings that one's talents, abilities, personality, and worth are not valued or recognized because of prejudice and racism. Conversely, we feel visible when our true talents, abilities, and worth are respected" (p. 4). Franklin (2004) defines invisibility syndrome as a "cluster of debilitating symptoms originating from profound reactions to perceived racial slights that limits the effective utilization of personal resources, the achievement of individual goals, the establishment of positive relationships, the satisfaction of family interactions, and the potential for life satisfaction" (p. 11). According to invisibility theory, the ongoing experience of micro-aggressions (or subtle acts and attitudes that fit a historical pattern of racial disregard) and efforts to manage them have an additive effect that can have harmful psychological and behavioral consequences. The symptoms that may occur as a consequence of invisibility syndrome are (1) frustration; (2) chronic indignation; (3) pervasive discontent and disgruntlement; (4) anger, immobilization, or increasing inability to get things done; (5) questioning one's worth; (6) disillusionment and confusion; (7) feeling trapped; (8) conflicted racial identity; (9) internalized rage; (10) depression; (11) substance abuse; and (12) loss of hope. According to Franklin (2004), the keys to surviving invisibility and nurturing a sense of personal power are (1) recognition—the power of feeling you are being acknowledged by others; (2) satisfaction—the satisfaction of feeling rewarded for what you do; (3) legitimacy—the feeling that you belong; (4) validation—the power of feeling that others share your views and values; (5) respect—the power of feeling that you are being treated as a person of value and worth; (6) dignity—the power of feeling that you are a person of value and worth; and (7) identity—the power of feeling comfortable with the way you are and with who you are.

Laissez-Faire Model of Racism

Laissez-faire racism is a theory that explains the evolution of racial attitudes toward African Americans and the persistence of racial inequality. In the post-Civil War period, Jim Crow racism was at its height. African Americans lived mostly in rural Southern areas doing agricultural work. During this period, racial discrimination was formally accepted. Most White Americans were comfortable with the notion of Black inferiority, and scientific explanations of Black people's inherent biogenetic inferiority were common. However, in the post-World War II era, because of political agency and changes in the position and power of Black people, Jim Crow social structures diminished. The Black population became more socioeconomically heterogeneous and urbanized. Moreover, overt racism became more socially unacceptable and the country adopted more officially race neutral policies. Bobo (1999) asserts that this change did not result in an anti-racist society that embraces a popular ideology of egalitarianism and equal worth and treatment of Black people. Instead, racial inequality is now popularly accepted under the ideology of laissez-faire racism, which is based on the following assumptions: (1) the persistent negative stereotyping of African Americans, (2) the tendency to blame African American people for their position in the current condition of socioeconomic racial inequality, and (3) resistance to meaningful policy efforts aimed at ameliorating racist social conditions because such efforts pose a threat to collective White privilege. According to Bobo, laissez-faire racism has emerged as the popular racial belief system during a time when cultural trends reject notions of biological racism and state policy is formally race neutral and committed to anti-discrimination. In spite of this ideology, race-based inequity persists and has worsened in some respects (Bobo, 1999). As the sociocultural climate has changed, and overt Jim Crow racism is no longer essential to maintaining White privilege, laissez-faire racism defends racial inequality in a socially acceptable manner, thus protecting White privilege.

Lens Theory

The Lens model is an African-centered conceptual framework for analyzing Black male-female relationships (Aldridge, 2007). The Lens model offers a holistic approach to studying Black male-female relationships by looking at the effects of the interplay between *institutional values* and *interpersonal factors* on the nature and substance of gender relations between Black women and men (Aldridge, 2007). The institutional values component of the model consists of a four-pronged set of dominant American value systems that have a counterproductive effect on Black male-female relationships. The four dominant value systems Aldridge (2007) identifies are capitalism, racism, sexism, and the Judeo-Christian ethic. According to the model, capitalism, with its emphasis on private ownership and pursuit of profit, tends to promote human relationships that are based on ownership and objectification. Racism, too, enforces feelings of superiority and inferiority that influence the intra-personal system and the world system of human organization. Sexism in and of itself implies and imposes unequal and exploitative gender relationships. According to Aldridge (2007), the Judeo-Christian ethic is rooted in a tradition that encourages identification with White male dominance and socioeconomic realities.

The Lens model is composed of four basic factors that influence interpersonal interactions between Black males and females: the scarcity of Black men, differential socialization of Black males and females, sexism and women's liberation, and modes of interacting. Black male-female relationships are strained by the shortage of Black males as a consequence of many factors, including but not limited to: shorter life expectancy, rates of homicide, drug addiction, and incarceration rates, as well as factors such as low levels of education and income. Aldridge (2007) also points out that Black males are often groomed to assume socially defined male roles that make it difficult to achieve insight into and empathize with Black females. Sexism and the advent of the women's liberation movement have had the effect of promoting changes in sex-role socialization and political and economic relationships. Finally, according to Aldridge (2007), healthy Black male-female relationships must grow out of a conscious struggle to change values and larger society.

Location Theory

How does one critique scholarly discourse of African American and non-African American writers and critics from an Afrocentric perspective? For this very purpose Asante (1992) developed location theory. According to Asante (1992), through the expression of their writing, authors leave their insignia on their written products. Through the signposts and signals writers leave in their work, researchers are able to locate a text. Asante (1992) identifies several elements involved in locating a text: language, attitude and direction. He uses the concept of *place* to identify the cultural centrality or marginality of the author. Texts produced by authors who have been removed or have removed themselves from cultural Blackness or Africanity are considered either decapitated texts or lynched texts. Decapitated texts refer to texts written by authors who write with no discernible Black/African cultural presence in an attempt to distance themselves from their Black/African cultural identity (1992). The authors of decapitated texts commit to a style of writing that places them outside of their own historical experience. The authors of lynched texts are skilled in literary technique but lack Black/ African historical and cultural knowledge. As a result, such authors' writings have a tendency to reflect Eurocentric perspectives. The author of a lynched text might write a line such as "the warlike natives." In using such language, it is likely that these authors may be rewarded by Eurocentric institutions when they lack cultural centeredness. A text can be located by the language the author uses, specifically the words and nuances that serve as signposts in their writing. For example, an author may use words to describe African people such as "macaca," "Hottentots," "bushmen," "Pigmies," or Native Americans as "wild Indians," or east Asians as "Orientals," and so on. Such language and signposts identify an author who lacks cultural consciousness. Attitude, or the author's predisposition toward a matter, can also be informative in locating a text. One can read a text and get an impression of the writer's motivational attitudes. Direction can also help in the effort to locate a text. Asante (1992) refers to direction as "the line along which the author's sentiments, themes and interests lie with reference to the point at which they are aimed" (p. 240). Direction refers to the authors' ultimate objective or purpose for their writing as indicated through the insignia of their discourse. These concepts help the researcher critique the relationship between the author of literature, the literary work, and people of African descent.

The Multisystems Model

The multisystems model is a theoretical framework designed to guide effective therapy for African American families. However, it is important to recognize that the model has broad-based applicability to all ethnic groups. Boyd-Franklin and Bry (2000) define the multisystems model as "a problem solving approach that helps families with multiple problems to focus and prioritize their issues and that allows clinicians to maximize the effectiveness of their interventions" (p. 226). Based on the assumption that for African Americans to be treated effectively in therapy the clinician must be capable of intervening at multiple levels in multiple systems, the model consists of three main aspects: (1) the treatment process, (2) the multisystem levels; and (3) home-based therapy. The treatment process consists of joining, engaging, assessing, problem solving, and deploying interventions aimed at restructuring and changing family systems (Boyd-Franklin, 2003). The multisystem levels aspect involves the individual, family subsystems, the family household, the extended family, non-blood kin, friends, church and community resources, social service agencies, and other outside systems. Therapist are not required to intervene at each of these levels; however, the model provides them with a framework that would help them to provide treatment successfully at whichever level or levels are relevant to the situation at hand. Finally, home-based therapy is important because office-based treatment often takes place with the least powerful members in African American families (e.g., young mothers and children), while powerful family and extended family members who will not come to the office remain at home. Engaging these family members may have a positive impact on treatment outcomes, while ignoring them might disrupt and weaken the treatment process (Boyd-Franklin, 2003).

Nigrescence Theory

The Cross model of nigrescence (Cross, 1971, 1978) is a theoretical framework for understanding the development and transformation of Black racial identity. The nigrescence model is necessary because racial identity affects the social-psychological well-being of African Americans. Consequently, theories of racial identity are imperative. The word nigrescence itself is a French term that means "to become Black." The nigrescence theory charts the stages that one experiences in the process of becoming racially conscious or aware. These stages have been measured empirically by instruments such as the self-report Racial Identity Attitude Scale (RIAS). The five stages of the nigrescence model are the pre-encounter stage, the encounter stage, the immersion/emersion stage, the internalization stage, and the internalization/commitment stage. The *pre-encounter stage* is characterized by an affinity toward Whiteness and shame of Blackness, acceptance of Eurocentric views, anxiety, defensiveness, poor self-esteem, and feelings of inferiority. The *encounter stage* is characterized by the experience of a racist incident that causes a person to question his or her preconceptions, become conscious of the consequences of Blackness in a racist society, and seek out Black culture. The *immersion/emersion stage* is characterized by the tendency to glorify Blackness and associate Black with good, while denigrating Whiteness and associating White with bad. This euphoria dies down at the latter end of this stage, which is called emersion. The *internalization stage* is characterized by the person settling into a new identity without anxiety, defensiveness, and poor self-esteem. At this stage, the individual has a positive sense of Blackness without denigrating Whiteness. In the *internalization/commitment stage*, the person possesses the same characteristics of the internalization stage with the addition of engaging in social-political advocacy and a commitment to the liberation of Black and other oppressed people.

Nosology of African/Black Personality Disorder

Azibo (1989) developed the nosology of African/Black personality disorder as a diagnostic system for classifying ordered and disordered African/Black personality functioning. Azibo (1989) defines mental health as manifested by behavior that is aligned with the natural order or the African worldview. Based on the model, people of African descent have mental health when they possess African self-consciousness, meaning they (1) recognize themselves as persons of African descent; (2) prioritizes the needs, interests, and developmental goals of people of African descent; (3) respect and perpetuate all things African; and (4) support standards of conduct that neutralize anti-African forces. When a person is in accord with the African worldview and possesses African self-consciousness, he or she is said to have *correct orientation* or *genetic Blackness plus psychological Blackness*. The Azibo (1989) model consists of four categories of disorder: peripheral personality disorder, psychological misorientation, mentacide, and other Black personality disorders. The first category, *peripheral personality disorder*, represents DSM-type disorders such as neurosis that might affect people of African descent. According to the model, such diagnoses are valid to the extent that they do not contradict the basic assumptions of the African-centered perspective. The second category is the most fundamental psychological disorder for people of African descent according to the nosology: *psychological misorientation*, or genetic Blackness minus psychological Blackness. Psychological misorientation is a condition in which a person of African descent operates without an Africa-centered belief system. This disorder predisposes people of African descent to other disorders. The third category of the model represents individuals who are suffering from *mentacide*, which is the deliberate and systematic destruction of an individual or group's mind. People suffering from mentacide have been stripped of any pro-Black or African orientation. They are often positive about the dominant group and attempt to distance themselves from all things African. The experience of mentacide may also engender peripheral personality disorders. The fourth and last category is *other Black personality disorders*, which consist of a host of personality dysfunctions that emerge from psychological misorientation and mentacide. Some of these are materialistic depression, personal identity conflict (individualism, WEUSI anxiety), reactionary disorders (psychological burnout, oppression-violence reaction), self-destructive disorders, organic disorders, and theological misorientation.

Nzuri Theory

Nzuri is an Afrocentric theoretical framework that is Pan-African in scope, and its purpose is contextualizing and guiding the understanding of Africana aesthetic traditions in literary, philosophical, or artistic criticism (Welsh-Asante, 2003). Nzuri theory accepts that beauty and good are synonymous. The theory also perceives the opposite of beauty as ugly, but ugly is not synonymous with bad. Nzuri also builds on the assumption that perceptions and values are complementary entities reflective of culture (Welsh-Asante, 2003). The theory itself consists of seven *aspects* (method, form, meaning, ethos, function, mode, and motif) that draw upon three ontologically ordered *sources*. The aspects are the entities that are used in the production of artistic manifestations or projects. Welsh-Asante defines the aspects as follows:

- **Meaning**: significance of expression in relationship to individual and community;
- **Ethos**: quality of expression that exudes spirit, emotion, and energy;
- **Motif**: incorporation and use of symbolism in the artistic product that reflects a specific culture and heritage mode;
- **Mode**: the manner in which an artistic product is expressed;
- **Function**: the operative relationship of the artistic product to individual and community;
- **Method/Technique**: the practical, physical, and material means of realizing an artistic product;
- **Form**: the status of an artistic product in terms of structure, shape, and composition. (Welsh-Asante, 2003, p. 224)

The sources represent the inner core of the nzuri model based on the premise that everything in the universe is imbued with animating energy (ntu, or vital force). *Spirit* is the invisible metaphysical aspect of the human experience that connects people to divine creativity, ideas, thoughts, and emotions (Welsh-Asante, 2003). *Rhythm* is essential and speaks to the relationship between elements of the universe as well as human reality. Nzuri theory focuses on how well artists negotiate the rhythm of life in artistic expressions. In its analysis, nzuri theory focuses not just on the process of creating. Creativity is placed in a larger context by examining not simply what has been created, but who evaluates the creation, who does the creating, and in what context it is created. The aspects of the nzuri model are supported by three principles: the oral principle, the *ashe* principle, and the *ehe* principle. The oral principle refers to the transmission of art forms through media such as storytelling, song, dance, and literature. The *ashe* principle refers to the use of the artistic product to affirm one's culture through reinforcement, enhancement, and retrieval through creative production. The *ehe* principle recognizes the role of discovery and renewal in the process of artistic production (by individuals who are new and creative participants). Ultimately, nzuri is a framework that can be used to understand and evaluate African aesthetics.

Phenomenological Variant of the Ecological Systems Theory (PVEST)

PVEST is a conceptual framework for examining the process of normative youth development through the interaction of identity and environmental context (Spencer, 1995). Adding to the ecological perspective, Spencer (1995) emphasizes the self-appraisal and meaning-making processes that youth engage in the context of race, class, and gender-laden environmental contexts or developmental spaces. PVEST consists of five interrelated components that describe the identity development process. The first component is the *net vulnerability level*, which consists of the balance between risk-contributing factors and risk-protective factors. Risk protective factors consist of characteristics and contexts that serve as supports that positively affect an individual's development. Risk contributing factors consist of characteristics and contexts that serve as liabilities and could adversely affect an individual's development. Risk-contributing factors consist of phenomena such as poverty, racial discrimination, or gender discrimination. Such risk-contributing factors could be offset or counterbalanced by risk-protective factors or resources such as cultural capital (Swanson, Spencer, Dell'Angelo, Harpalani, & Spencer, 2002). Situations in which risk-contributing factors outweigh risk-protective factors contribute to an individual's net vulnerability. The second component is *net stress engagement level*, which consists of the experiences that challenge or support individuals as they engage risks that threaten their well-being. Youth likely to experience stress in the form of racism, sexism, weight discrimination, class discrimination, puberty, and peer relationships experience care in the form of social supports, racial socialization, and cultural enrichment. An absence or limited amount of such supportive experiences can be dangerous. The third component is the *reactive coping methods*, which are adaptive or maladaptive coping responses to stress. Harmful reactive coping methods are destructive (changing physical features in response to racism, acting out in school), while adaptive coping (resilience, successful problem-solving skills, self-control) are positive and beneficial. Too much challenge and not enough support at an earlier stage can lead to maladaptive coping. The fourth component is *emergent identities*, which refers to "how individuals view themselves within and between their various contexts of development (family, school, and neighborhood)" (Swanson et al., 2002, p. 78). Culture and racial identity, gender identity, individual and peer relationships, and all prior stages shape the identity development of youth. The fifth component, *life-stage, specific coping outcomes*, refers to the adverse or productive behavioral and attitudinal outcomes as a consequence of stresses, vulnerabilities, supports, and identities. Productive outcomes may be good health, positive racial identity, high self-esteem, and positive relationships. Conversely, adverse outcomes may be drug abuse, alcohol abuse, and poor relationships. According to PVEST, these stages help contextualize and explain youth identity development in a holistic way.

Post-Traumatic Slave Syndrome

Post-Traumatic Slave Syndrome (PTSS) is a theoretical framework designed to explain the pattern of psychological and behavioral adaptations to the legacy of oppression among African Americans. Leary (2005) defines PTSS as "a condition that exists when a population has experienced multigenerational trauma resulting from centuries of slavery and continues to experience oppression and institutionalized racism today. Added to this condition is a belief (real or imagined) that the benefits of the society in which they live are not accessible to them" (Leary, 2005, p. 121). Leary (2005) places the resulting patterns of behavior into three categories: *vacant esteem, ever-present anger,* and *racist socialization. Vacant esteem* is the belief that one's self has little or no worth as a consequence of the pronouncements of one's inferiority from three key spheres of influence: society, community, and family. *Ever-present anger* is the emotional response to a persistent legacy of blocked and frustrated access to goals—in addition to violence, degradation, misrepresentation, societal marginalization, and lack of equal opportunity. *Racist socialization* is the adoption of racist standards and the slave master's value system, which holds that all things associated with Whiteness are superior and all things associated with Blackness are inferior. Leary (2005) suggests that PTSS is remediated when Black people know themselves or restore their historical memory, identifying and building on their strengths. Leary (2005) argues that Black people must heal from PTSS by building self-esteem, identifying effective means of redressing mistreatment, and engaging in effective racial socialization.

Sudarkasa's Seven R's Model: Seven Cardinal Values of African Family Life

Sudarkasa's (1996) use of historiographic analysis resulted in the identification of the basic values and precepts that have maintained self-help and cooperation among West African and African American extended families. Sudarkasa found that key values promoted among African American families were very similar to those that were promoted among West African societies. According to Sudarkasa's (1996) analysis, these basic African family precepts had been culturally maintained among people of African descent in the American context. The seven values Sudarkasa (1996) identifies are respect, responsibility, restraint, reciprocity, reverence, reason, and reconciliation. According to Sudarkasa (1996), the first two have clearly remained a key feature of African American family values, while the last two (reason and reconciliation) have diminished in importance due to the influence of the U.S. legal system, in many cases replacing traditional African methods of settling disputes among family. The purpose of understanding the seven cardinal values of African family life is twofold: explanation/description and prescription. First, they are essential to explaining how and why African forms of family organization were maintained and exemplified among Africans in the diaspora. Second, they are prescriptive, meaning they can be helpful for African families facing contemporary threats to family structures and communities.

Along with politics, economics, and other social forces, the cardinal values are a force for social change that can guide African peoples' behavior by returning to traditional African family values. The first value is respect, which African and African American families commanded as a code of conduct that demanded showing deference and honor to all elder persons or persons senior to oneself. Reemphasizing this core precept would help the families of African-descended peoples today. The second value is responsibility. African and African American families traditionally instilled in youth a sense of obligation for supporting one's kinship network. The third value is reciprocity, or the belief that people's own well-being is closely related to their giving back to their family and community. The fourth value is restraint, or the understanding that a person must always consider how the decisions he or she makes will impact the well-being of the collective (immediate and extended) family. The fifth value is African people's characteristic tendency to be spiritual and to honor and find collective empowerment from a higher spiritual power in the universe. The sixth value is reason, or the practice of using rationality, traditional knowledge, and wisdom to settle disputes. The seventh value is reconciliation, or the importance of forgiveness and compassion in defusing hostility. According to Sudarkasa (1996), these values not only represent the principles that have supported African kinship structures for thousands of years. Their revival is also essential to strengthening African American kinship structures in the present.

Social Systems Approach to the Study of Black Family Life (SSASBFL)

According to Billingsley (1968), for Black families to be properly understood they must be viewed as systems that are part of and influenced by other social institutions. The social systems approach to the study of black family life (SSASBFL) is a theoretical framework for critically analyzing Black families that emphasizes the commonality and diversity of Black families and their interdependence with other levels of society (Billingsley, 1968). The SSASBFL consists of four major concepts: (1) social systems, (2) ethnic subsociety, (3) family structure, and (4) family function. Billingsley (1968) defines a system as an "organization of units or elements, united in some form of regular interaction and interdependence" (p. 4). Based on SSAS-BFL, the Black family as a social system is embedded within a network of social systems and is constantly influenced by society's subsystems such as healthcare, education, politics, economics, values, and other subsystems. The Black family can be and has been negatively influenced by and excluded from such institutions, but could be positively influenced by such institutions if the Black family experience were more adequately reflected in their intentions and operations. The SSASBFL also views the Black community as an ethnic subsociety of larger society. According to Billingsley (1968), the Black community possesses ethnic commonality (culture, behaviors, values, etc.) and great in-group diversity (class, geographic differences, etc.). SSASBFL asserts that for Black families to be understood in a holistic way they have to be appreciated for all of their diverse family structures. Billingsley (1968) asserts that Black families can consist of heads of households, children, other relatives, and non-relatives. Moreover, these families can exist in three basic conditions: (1) Nuclear families, which are composed of three basic types: the incipient nuclear family, the simple nuclear family, and the attenuated nuclear family; (2) the Extended Family, which consists of three basic types: the incipient extended family, the simple extended family, and the attenuated extended family; and (3) the Augmented Family, which consists of six basic types: the incipient augmented family, the incipient extended augmented family, the nuclear augmented family, the nuclear extended augmented family, the attenuated augmented family, and the attenuated extended augmented family. SSASBFL also explains that Black family life cannot be adequately understood if too much focus is placed on dysfunction or limited functions of the Black family. According to Billingsley (1968), Black family functions consist of instrumental functions, expressive functions, and functions that are simultaneously instrumental and expressive. Instrumental functions of families refer to the basic economic sustenance of family members in terms of such items as food, clothing, shelter, and healthcare. These instrumental functions are also affected by social structures such as employment, education, and healthcare. Expressive family functions provide for the socioemotional health and psychological integrity of family members. This refers to the idea that families provide the atmosphere that "generates a sense of belonging, self-worth, self-awareness, and dignity" (Billingsley, 1968, p. 26). Still other family functions are both instrumental and expressive—for example, sex, reproduction, and child rearing. The interdependence of all of the different aspects of SSASBFL makes it a theoretical approach designed to guide the holistic study of Black family life.

Site of Resiliency Theory

Yassir Arafat Payne defines site of resiliency theory as a framework of analysis that recognizes "street life" as a context that offers "particular psychological and physical spaces that operate in tandem to produce a site of strength, community, and, ultimately, resilience for street life-oriented Black men (Payne & Gibson, 2009, p. 128). Such men view street life as a personal and economic survival-oriented ideology. Site of resiliency theory also locates the personal construction of resiliency within the complex interaction among race, racism, and concentrated poverty (Payne & Gibson, 2009). Site of resiliency also theorizes that street life offers networking behaviors that come about through illegal and bonding activities such as joking, playing cards or dice, hanging out, rapping, or playing basketball (Payne & Hamdi, 2008).

Situated-Mediated Identity Theory (SMIT)

SMIT is a framework designed to explain the role that identity processes and sociocultural context play in shaping the academic performance of African American youth (Murrell, 2009). Murrell (2009) asserts that "Black achievement is mediated by specific forms of social identification experienced by Black youth in the complex intersections of racial, economic, gender, and class privilege in American society" (p. 98). There are several key concepts in SMIT: situated identity, positionality, and agency. Situated identity refers to the fluid and situational construction of Black youth's sense of identity as influenced by history, culture, and geography or location. This process has to be taken into consideration as identity is constructed, particularly in the school setting. Positionality represents situated identities that youth create to make sense of themselves in the "complex intersections of race, class, gender, and privilege in a variety of contexts" (Murrell, 2009, p. 98). These positionalities mediate youth's school performance and their socioemotional development. Agency refers to how youth use and improvise cultural forms and modes of self-expression to assert their integrity and identity despite others' attempts to negatively position them. These factors and others must be taken into consideration in explaining and understanding African American youth and their academic success (Murrell, 2009).

TRIOS Model

The TRIOS model (time, rhythm, improvisation, orality, and spirituality) is a perspective designed to understand the basic ways that African Americans orient themselves toward living, or how they experience the world and make meaning of their experiences (Jones, 1991). The TRIOS model is based on the premise that Black/African American culture has an African cultural foundation that has adapted and evolved in the American context to produce unique patterns of thinking and behaving. More specifically, the TRIOS model was designed to explain how African Americans have learned to survive, thrive, and maintain psychological well-being in an oppressive environment. TRIOS is a model that stands for five dimensions of the human experience that African people combine in unique ways: (1) a unique disposition toward time; (2) rhythm or a unique way of interacting with the external environment; (3) placing a great deal of value on improvisation; (4) orality, or the use of the spoken word to pass along information and meaning; and (5) spirituality, or the belief in a force or power greater than oneself to make meaning of one's life and to cope with life's challenges. The TRIOS model takes these factors into consideration in explaining how African Americans make meaning of their experiences and maintain resilience in spite of adversity.

Tripartite Model of Racism

Jones (1972) developed a model that explains racism as a phenomenon consisting of three different characteristics: individual, institutional, and cultural. Jones (1972) differentiates prejudice, discrimination, and racism. According to the model, prejudice represents negative pre-judgments about a member or members of a particular race or religion in spite of facts that contradict them. Discrimination is the differential treatment and behavioral manifestation of negative prejudgments about members of a racial or ethnic group or religion. Jones (1991) defines racism as the "exercise of power against a racial group defined as inferior, by individuals and institutions with the intentional or unintentional support of the entire culture" (Jones, 1991, p. 172) The first of the three basic types of racism is *individual racism*. Individual racism occurs when individuals engage in practices that subjugate or "injure, denigrate, or deny services/goods to individuals from racial groups defined as inferior" (Neville & Pieterse, 2009, p. 163). Institutional racism refers to racism that is inherent in the operation of society's institutions and policies. It occurs as a consequence of the conscious or unconscious manipulation of institutions in ways that perpetuate inequality (Jones, 1972). Cultural racism is the assumption of the racially based superiority of one or more groups' cultural beliefs and practices. Jones (1991) asserts that how racism is conceptualized has implications for how it is addressed. For example, if racism is confused with prejudice, then remedies will typically focus primarily on changing attitudes and beliefs. However, understanding that racism is also institutional suggests that racism does not have to be intentional, and its solution must also require the creation of policies and legislation. In addition, understanding that racism is also cultural highlights the role that cultural assumptions and practices play in racial oppression.

Womanism

Womanism is a theoretical framework of analysis that is rooted in the experiences of Black women, with broad application to the human experience. Womanism comes from the language of the African American woman's experiences at the intersection of race and gender. Walker (1983) explains that young Black girls were often called "womanish" (a term derived from the Black American vernacular) (Tsuruta, 2012) for acting willful, courageous, and assertive. Many trace womanism to the famous words of Sojourner Truth in her speech "And Aint I a Woman," in which she critiques the notion of womanhood as it relates to the lived experience of the Black woman. But what is womanism and what is its purpose? Tsuruta (2012) explains that womanism is "a culturally-affirming and transformative ideal of the self-agency and social struggle of Black women to resist all forms of oppression and assert themselves in freedom, confidence and creativity" (Tsuruta, 2012, p. 3). Ogunyemi (1985) asserts that the ultimate goal of womanism is the unification of Black people everywhere. Womanism is concerned with Black women, Black people, and all of humanity (Marsh-Lockett, 1997). According to Phillips (2006), womanism has five overarching characteristics: (1) anti-oppressionist: against all forms of oppression and for all forms of liberation; (2) vernacular: everyday and identified with the grassroots of humanity to the elite; (3) non-ideological: decentralized and avoids rigidity; (4) communitarian: viewing collective well-being as the goal of social change; and (5) spiritualized: recognizes a spiritual essence.

Womanist Identity Development Model

The womanist identity model is a conceptual framework for understanding the gender-related identity development of women across racial and ethnic groups (Ossana, Helms, & Leonard, 1992). Based on the model, healthy development is indicated by positive views of womanhood. The model is built on the ideal of racial identity development and the writings of Black feminist scholars (Moradi, Yoder, & Berendsen, 2004). The model is a framework that outlines the progress toward the "abandonment of external definitions and adaptation of internal standards of womanhood" (Ossana et al., 1992, p. 70). The first stage is the *pre-encounter stage*, which consists of attitudes that conform to rigid societal values that disadvantage women and privilege males. Women in this stage also deny prejudiced thoughts and practices that subjugate women. The second stage is the *encounter stage*, in which women's pre-encounter attitudes are challenged and they begin to become more aware of sexism. As a consequence of the encounter stage, women begin to explore alternative ways of conceptualizing manhood and womanhood. The third stage, *immersion-emersion*, consists of two phases. In the first phase women begin to idealize women while rejecting patriarchy. In the second phase they develop positive conceptualizations of womanhood and seek affiliation with other women (Moradi et al., 2004). The fourth and last phase, *internalization*, is characterized by women integrating their own self-defined positive conceptualization of womanhood into their own identity without reliance on sexist societal norms or the adversary views of men in general. This model of measuring self-definition among women has been found to be related to psychological indicators such as self-esteem, self-efficacy, racial identity, and locus of control.

Sustainable Conceptual Development

As researchers, we must ground ourselves in theories and paradigms related to the topics we are interested in. However, we must not be trapped within the confines of any particular theory. It is important to be able to identify what theories and paradigms explain and fail to explain. Recognizing the limits of different theories' and paradigms' reach is critical. It lets us know what must still be theorized. Sustainable conceptual development is the idea that it is up to theorists to recognize the limitations and inadequacies in existing theories and paradigms. However, to not be trapped in the circular position of being a critic of existing information, the researcher must ultimately move to the next level and become a producer and advancer of knowledge. In addition, it is the scholar's responsibility to add missing components to existing theories and to theorize the dimensions of Africana people's lived experiences that have yet to be theorized from a culturally relevant perspective.

Types of Theory: Inductive and Deductive

Now that you are aware of many different theories, you must also be familiarized with two different approaches to theory development and theory testing. There are inductive and deductive approaches. **Induction** moves from the particular to the general, that is, you move from a specific set of observations to the discovery of patterns in those observations, hypotheses, and theories. **Deduction** moves from an expected pattern of behavior to observations that test whether that pattern actually exists. It moves from established theories to testing the validity of those theories. It can be said that deduction moves from the general to the particular.

One of the functions of research is to test theories. The deductive approach begins with an assumed truth, such as the theory that African American youth perform better academically when they are in cooperative learning settings. A deductive approach would be to test that theory by measuring African American students' academic performance on a test after they have learned in a cooperative learning context, and compare it to the scores of African American students after they have learned in an individual learning context.

What would an inductive approach look like? The inductive approach involves making observations, drawing conclusions, and developing theories or explanations that clarify the observations. For example, an inductive approach may involve observing students as they learn in a variety of learning contexts without making any assumptions about how they might learn. After that, the researcher would look for patterns in the students' test scores, their ethnicity, and the learning contexts they were involved in. Let's assume that the findings indicate that African American students are found to show greater rates of achievement when they have learned in cooperative learning contexts as opposed to individual learning contexts. After testing this theory among different populations and finding the same pattern, a researcher may formulate a theory that explains why African American students learn better in cooperative learning contexts. This is the inductive approach to scientific reasoning. Inductive research often takes place without the benefit of previous research, and it is often used in exploratory research, where there is not much known about the research topic at hand.

Key Terms

Deduction

Disruptive Conceptualiza-
    tion

Induction

Method

Methodology

Paradigm

Theory

Thinking about Science

Activity 1

A high score on a collectivism survey would indicate that a person places the needs of the large group over the individual. A low score would indicate that an individual places his or her own needs before that of the collective. You may want to ascertain the relationship between income level and collectivism among Jamaicans.

- How might you take a deductive approach to studying the relationship between these two things? Explain.
- How might you go about studying the relationship between the two variables inductively? Explain.

Activity 2

Look at the paradigms and theories in the chapter. Pick three of them that you think would offer unique and valuable perspectives on the relationship between collectivism and income level. Explain how a theorist guided by each of the theories you identified might approach studying the relationship between collectivism and income level.

CHAPTER THREE

Ethics in Research

This chapter explains the relationship between values and research by seeking to explain the values that have guided African people's relationship to science. The chapter will also explore how African people's history and experience with science have given rise to guidelines meant to protect those who participate in the research process. How should the values of the people who are being studied influence the topics, processes, and outcomes of research?

Values and Research

Some advance the theory that social research should be value free and objective. However, from an Afrocentric perspective, this kind of objectivity is impossible because culture is essential for understanding any human thought or behavior. Values are a component of a people's culture. It is said that "nothing human happens outside of the realm of culture" (Nobles, 2006, p. 187). This includes research because culture bears upon research, which is a human process. For that reason, research must inevitably negotiate with human values and ethics. **Ethics** refers to the philosophy of morality—what counts as good or bad, right or wrong. In order to guide "proper" behavior, societies and organizations create ethical codes. One of the earliest codes of ethics in human history was developed in the Nile Valley Civilization of Africa. In Ancient Kemet (Egypt), **Maat** represented the ethical principles governing the laws of the universe, the standards by which human society should be shaped, and the principles by which human beings might best live (Obenga, 2004). The concept of Maat dates back to approximately the 28th century B.C. According to Karenga (2002), Maat means "many things, including truth, justice, propriety, harmony, balance, reciprocity and order" (p. 95). There are three levels of Maat: (1) the universal level, expressing the harmony and balance between all of the elements of the universe; (2) the political level, representing the establishment and advancement of justice and order in human society; and (3) the individual level, representing humans living and interacting with one another in accordance with the code of Maat (Obenga, 2004). Maat was the spiritual/ethical ideal of Kemetic society and the moral code for an entire civilization. We all may operate according to some code of ethics. However, because we are all vulnerable to error and capable of violating even our own ethical standards, people have found it necessary to compile agreed-upon ethics to serve as a constant reminder of proper conduct. Today there are codes of conduct for doctors, teachers, lawyers, politicians, and priests. At most people's places of work, there are codes of conduct to which they are held accountable. Nations themselves have codes of conduct embedded within their constitutions. The need to agree upon and uphold a set of human rights is one of the challenges multiple nations around the globe are confronted with. What about those who would engage in the process of scientific research? So, too, must researchers have codes of conduct that guide their practice of research.

The Ethics That Emerged from a Legacy of Abuse

In scientific research, "ethical standards attempt to strike a balance between supporting freedom of scientific inquiry on the one hand and protecting the welfare of participants on the other" (Bless, Higson-Smith, & Kagee, 2006, p. 140). Ethics in research are especially important for people of African descent because they have so often been the victims of unethical research. Often African Americans' mistrust of scientific research is unwisely dismissed as baseless, groundless, and unjustified antiscientific paranoia. However, such a dismissal is ahistorical, hasty, and deficient of critical analysis and careful reflection. Contemporary African American skepticism (both founded and unfounded) of scientific research is the logical consequence of a long, protracted, and largely unacknowledged legacy of inhumane treatment imposed upon them by a racist American scientific community. This legitimate skepticism must first be respected so that the scientific community can go about the process of earning the trust of African-descended people's participation through ethical conduct.

During American slavery, it was common for medical practitioners to experiment on enslaved African people until they devised medicines and procedures suitable to treat Whites (Washington, 2006). In fact, it was not uncommon for doctors to pur-chase enslaved Africans for the purpose of experimentation (Washington, 2006). For example, Thomas Jefferson began experimenting with cowpox injections to inoculate people against smallpox. Jefferson tried to perfect this questionable technique by in-jecting 200 enslaved Africans owned by him and his family. Only after the enslaved Africans were found to have overcome their illness as a result of the injections did Jefferson decide to use the procedure on his own White family (Washington, 2006).

James Marion Simms is widely regarded as a medical pioneer and the father of gynecology. Most of his medical expertise was honed by his "nightmarishly painful and degrading experiments, without anesthesia, or consent, on a group of slave women" (Washington, 2006, p. 61). Simms refused to administer anesthesia to Black women who underwent the pain and humiliation of his experimentation on their genitalia. However, he routinely used anesthesia when he treated the vaginal disorders of White women. Today Simms's legacy is highly honored, and a monu-ment in his honor in stands in New York City's Central Park.

In 1932 the United States Public Health Service began an investigation into how untreated syphilis, a sexually transmitted disease, affects the human body. That study is known as the Tuskegee Study of Untreated Syphilis in the Negro Male. Six hundred low-income Black males from Macon County, Alabama, were recruited to participate in the research study. Three hundred and ninety-nine of them had syphilis and 201 did not. To study the long-term effects of the disease on the men, the researchers intentionally withheld treatment for the disease from them. The re-searchers' objective was to track the effects of the disease on the men's bodies. The participating men were not informed of the purpose of the research, how the dis-ease worked, or the fact that treatment was available. By 1940 the researchers' evi-dence indicated that the mortality rate for the men with untreated syphilis was clearly worse than that of those who were uninfected. Nevertheless, the study con-tinued for a total of 40 years. In 1972, the study ended when a news reporter did an exposé calling public attention to the study. By the time the study ended, 28 par-ticipants had died from the disease, 100 others had died due to conditions related to the disease, 41 of the participants' wives had contracted the disease, and 19 of their children had contracted the disease at birth.

During World War II, the Nazis conducted experiments on Jewish people and others in concentration camps (Beauchamp et al., 1982). Jews were deliberately in-fected with poisons and diseases in order to study the maturation of diseases in the human body. Many of them were also subjected to gas chambers and decompres-sion chambers so Nazi scientists could study the effects of gas exposure and high altitudes on the body. There were also those who had parts of their bodies frozen for the purpose of testing new treatments. When these abuses were made public during the Nuremberg Trials of 1945–1946, the world took notice of how far people might go in the name of research. This also aroused great concern about the need for codified standards for the practice of ethical research. The first effort was the Nuremberg Code of 1946, a direct response to the atrocities carried out by the Nazis. The Nuremberg Code consisted of the principles that a researcher must:

- ensure that participants have voluntarily consented to be in the study;
- avoid unnecessary physical and mental suffering;
- avoid research where death or disabling injury to participants is likely;
- end a research study immediately if its continuation is likely to cause injury, discomfort, or death;
- ensure that highly qualified people using the highest level of skill and care should conduct research studies; and
- ensure that study results are for the good of society and unattainable by any other method.

The Nuremberg Code was limited to medical research. However, in 1966 the Public Health Service (PHS) of the United States declared that all medical research must abide by the following regulations:

- full disclosure of relevant information should be made to the participants;
- the decision to participate must be completely voluntary; and
- researchers must obtain documented, informed consent from participants.

In 1974 the Department of Health, Education, and Welfare (HEW, now the Department of Health and Human Services, HHS) declared that the principles adopted by the PHS would apply not only to medical research but to social research as well. HEW also made it mandatory that research institutions funded by the institution (including universities) establish institutional review boards to review research proposals and make certain that they adhere to the principles of ethical research. The HHS regulations for ethical research became final in 1981 and are located in Title 45, Part 46 of the Code of Federal Regulations. In 1991 the code was revised to include the Federal Policy for the Protection of Human Subjects, which is articulated in the Belmont Report. Those principles are respect, non-malfeasance, and justice. There are several common principles of ethical research that we will cover next, beginning with the principle of informed consent.

Informed Consent

Participation in a research investigation is often a disruption of the lives of participants. Research often requires that individuals take time away from their normal daily activities. Usually participants won't see direct benefits from their participation in research, and they are often asked to reveal personal information as a condition of their participation. For these reasons, it is important that researchers gain the voluntary consent of research participants. But permission is not enough; researchers must have the informed consent of research participants. **Informed consent** refers to research participants' right to know the purpose of a research project, how it may affect them, how it may benefit them, any possible risks of participation, and their right to decline to participate whenever they choose to. Researchers should always take the time to explain the research project to participants in detail. Research institutions require that researchers acquire written consent from all participants in the form of consent forms for participants who are 18 years of age and older. Individuals who are younger than 18 must sign an assent form, which must be accompanied by a consent form signed by their parent or legal guardian. According to Neuman (2009), a consent form should contain the following basic elements:

- a brief description of the purpose and research procedure, including how long the study will last;
- a statement of any risks or discomfort associated with participation;
- a guarantee of the anonymity or confidentiality of data records;
- identification of who the researcher is and contact information that can be used to find out more information about the study;
- a statement that participation is voluntary and that participants may withdraw at any time without penalty;
- a statement of any alternative procedures that may be used;
- a statement of any benefits or compensation that research participants may receive; and
- an offer to provide a summary of the findings when the study is completed.

Non-Malfeasance and Beneficence

Researchers must first commit to do no harm to research participants in the research process. Research should never result in any serious or lasting harm to research participants in the form of either physical or mental distress, including the experience of anxiety or loss of self-esteem. Research participants should not be exposed to conditions that will likely cause them to experience harm. As we now know, enslaved African Americans, participants in the Tuskegee experiments and Jews in Nazi concentration camps were deliberately exposed to physically and mentally harmful conditions. However, research that causes participants to reveal things about themselves or to articulate attitudes they have never had to articulate may result in some level of distress. If a researcher were to show research participants pictures of lynchings to gauge their responses, the pictures might elicit a strong emotional response. In the event that a researcher is working with a vulnerable population such as prisoners, the researcher may trigger emotional reactions. A researcher might interview prisoners convicted of violent crimes about events in their childhood that could be related to their own violent behavior later in their lives. Any particular question might cause them to respond emotionally and engage in behavior that might incriminate them. If researchers design a study that is likely to elicit any unpleasant feelings in participants, they must be sure it is scientifically justifiable and that its potential benefits outweigh the unpleasantness that might be caused by the research process.

Often researchers deal with distress caused in the process of research with a process called "debriefing." Once a study is complete, participants are debriefed to assess their emotional reactions to the study and to reassure them of the purpose of what they experienced. Not only does the researcher have to make sure his or her research does no harm to subjects; it must also go a step further.

It is important that scientific research "not only does no harm but also potentially contributes to the well-being of others" (Bless et al., 2006, p. 141). Researchers have the responsibility to see to it that the population they sample and conduct research on could benefit from research. Conducting research that only serves the intellectual curiosity of the researcher is not enough to justify research with human subjects, especially in Africana Studies. The researcher must be explicit about how the Black community and society at large might benefit from the research.

Right to Privacy

It is also imperative that researchers protect the identity of research participants. This protection is typically provided using two techniques: anonymity and confidentiality. When a researcher guarantees anonymity, it means that neither the people who read about the study nor the researchers themselves are able to link a given response to a given research participant. If researchers conduct face-to-face interviews with someone, they cannot guarantee anonymity because the researcher is able to identify responses with the individual who gave them. Even if the researchers don't tell anyone who gave the responses, or disguise the identity of the research participant, they cannot promise anonymity because they are still aware of the identity of the person who gave the responses. One way to ensure anonymity is to make certain that there are no names or numbers in the data you collect that link the information with the individual it comes from. For example, you can distribute a questionnaire with directions that instruct individuals not to put their name or any identifying numbers on it before mailing it to the researcher.

When researchers guarantee confidentiality, they must make sure that no persons other than the researchers themselves are able to identify any individual participant's responses. A researcher who guarantees participants' confidentiality must make sure not to make public any identifying information about participants. Usually research data is released in aggregate form, meaning that only summary information on how the whole group responded is provided, instead of information about how individual participants responded.

It should now be clear that the difference between anonymity and confidentiality is that with confidentiality, only the researcher can link responses to the individuals who gave them. However, with anonymity, not even the researcher can link responses with individuals who gave them. Anonymity and confidentiality not only protect the privacy of participants, but they also encourage research participants to feel more comfortable about giving responses. This is especially important in research about sensitive topics. It is unethical to breach participants' right to privacy, but it is also unethical to promise participants confidentiality or anonymity when they will not have it. There are many ways to protect individuals' identities during research, including the use of pseudonyms or fictitious names. For example, if a researcher collected data from a school called Martin Luther King High School in Chicago, instead of publishing the school's real name with the research results, a researcher can let it be known that he or she has chosen not to reveal the true name of the high school to protect the privacy of the participants. Instead, the researcher may use a pseudonym such as "James Baldwin High, a predominantly Black high school located in the Midwest of the United States." The pseudonym above also mentions the region in which the school is located instead of revealing the actual city it is located in, making it harder to identify the school.

Several additional concerns in the ethics of social research are deception, quality, and reporting.

Deception

Deception occurs when researchers misrepresent their research to research participants. This practice can harm other researchers' chances of gaining the confidence of potential research participants in the future. However, there are cases in which researchers hide the true intentions of their research from participants to prevent them from changing their natural behavior and responses because of their knowledge of what is being observed. For example, consider the following study on trigger response.

In 2003, a team led by J. Correll flashed random photos of White and Black faces, some superimposed with guns, others with harmless items such as cell phones and wallets. The researchers asked college students to press one key indicating "shoot" the suspect, and another indicating "don't shoot." The students were more likely to mistakenly fire at Black faces that were unarmed compared to unarmed White faces (Munger, 2009). In such a study, it would behoove the researchers to simply inform participants of the trigger response element of the test without informing the participants that the researchers would be looking at the race of the suspects they shot. In this case, deception would assist the researchers in getting more honest responses. Letting the participants know that their racial responses were being observed might influence them to be over-sensitive to their responses to different races, armed and unarmed.

However, researchers who use deception must be certain that their use of deception is warranted. They must demonstrate that the research participants will not be harmed, and that there is no other way to answer their research question without deception. It is also important to debrief participants afterward to make them aware of researchers' intentions, methods, and the results of their analysis.

Quality

Researchers also have the ethical obligation to be sure that they have conducted a properly designed research investigation. Poor research in and of itself is unethical. Poorly designed research is of little or no value to the scientific community because it does not contribute to society. Moreover, if a study is done haphazardly, it effectively squanders the time that research participants have invested in it while offering them nothing in return. More important, if you conduct poor-quality research, you are contributing inadequate information about an important social issue. Scientific researchers must be sure to have proper sampling procedures, choose appropriate methods, and conduct accurate analysis to ensure that they have produced quality research. We will delve into these topics in later chapters.

Reporting

Researchers must always remember that research participants have the right to be informed of the results of the study they participated in. Those results should be presented in an honest and open way. Researchers must be sure to reveal all shortcomings, unexpected results, and contradictory findings. It is unethical to falsify or fabricate research findings. Researchers must also be sure that the results of their study get into the hands of institutions or individuals in positions to benefit society with knowledge of the results of their investigation. Research is of little value if it remains the private personal property of the researchers. Research findings on teaching methods found to be successful in teaching Black girls mathematics in a culturally relevant way is information that should be in the hands of principals of schools with large populations of Black female students, Black parent organizations, and departments of education. Let's consider a couple of investigations that bring to light some ongoing questions of research ethics.

Laud Humphreys (1973) was interested in studying homosexual behavior. He carried out an investigation that raises ethical issues that continue to be debated even now. Humphreys studied casual same-sex acts carried out between men in public restrooms. Typically, these sexual liaisons involved two men engaging in a sexual act in public restrooms (referred to as tearooms by homosexuals who engaged in the acts). There were also "watchqueens" responsible for alerting the men of approaching police or straight men who might interrupt them. Humphreys carried out his observations by playing the role of the "watchqueen" for the men. Whenever possible, he took note of the men's license plates and located their homes by using public motor vehicle records. Humphreys then went to the men's homes and interviewed them without informing them of the true purpose of their interviews. This study has brought about ethical questions concerning Humphreys's decision to observe the men engaged in sexual acts, his decision to record the men's license plate numbers, and then use them to locate and visit the men's homes. When Humphreys visited the men's homes, he disguised himself so that he wouldn't be recognized. He told them he was conducting a survey designed to gather personal information about the men. He found that the men were from stable homes, were married, and had stable jobs. Unlike the perceptions that many held about homosexuals, they were not isolated loners who were out of work and without stable homes. However, none of the men volunteered to be in the study.

Did Humphreys put the men at risk of personal harm by risking their exposure and possible harm to their self-perceptions, careers, and marriages? Did he engage in the violation of his research subjects' privacy? Many criticize Humphreys for his failure to get informed consent from the men and his intentional use of deception. Was it really a violation of privacy if, after all, this activity took place in a public setting? Some say Humphreys was cautious because he didn't disclose the men's tearoom activities. Others say that the study could not be conducted in any other way. What do you think? What might you have done differently, if at all?

Have you ever been on the telephone talking to someone in customer service and gotten the reply "I'm just doing my job"? This is a casual, relatively harmless manifestation of a tendency that has been the subject of much scientific study in its extreme manifestations. Stanley Milgram (1963, 1965, 1974) set out to study how ordinary people came to carry out abuses like those that took place during the Jewish Holocaust. Milgram wanted to study the effect of social pressure on people following orders. He assigned some research participants to play the role of the "teacher" and others to play the role of "pupil." The pupils in the study were located in an adjacent room from the teachers, where they could be heard but not seen by the teacher. The pupil's wrists were hooked up to electric wires. Forty participants were selected to play the role of "teacher." Each teacher sat in front of an electrical panel with dials and switches. Each switch was labeled with a number of volts ranging from 15 to 315. One by one, participants playing the role of the teachers were instructed by the "experimenter" to read a list of word pairs to the pupil in the adjacent room. The teacher tested the ability of the pupil to match the words.

Here is how the experiment worked. Although the teacher could not see the pupil, he saw light flashes at his panel, indicating whether the pupil matched the words correctly or incorrectly. When the pupil matched the words incorrectly, the teacher was instructed by the experimenter to flip one of the weaker switches, administering a low-level shock to the pupil. The teacher was able to hear the pupil's response to the shock each time. As the pupil got more answers wrong, the teacher administered progressively more intense shocks. Eventually, the pupil began to scream, then to kick the walls. Finally, the teacher heard no response from the pupil. Nevertheless, the experimenter instructed the teacher to administer a more intense shock anyway. It was not until the teachers began to hear the pupils kicking the wall that some of them decided not to administer any more shocks. However, out of 40 teachers, 26 continued to administer shocks even after that point. Interestingly, the shocks were not real—pupils were "acting" on behalf of the experiment. The only ones who were not aware of this were the individuals who volunteered to be teachers.

The purpose was to see just how far the "teachers" would go. This study explored the question of how far people were willing to go to hurt others as long as they were *following orders*. After all, this is the excuse many Nazis used at the Nuremberg trials to explain their behavior during World War II. It is also the response used by some of the American soldiers who committed prisoner abuses at the Abu Ghraib prison in Iraq (Levi, 2009). It is a response echoed during the truth and reconciliation hearings by White South African police who committed atrocious abuses against Black people during apartheid.

Ask yourself now: Were any of the principles of research methods ethics violated in Milgram's study? If so, which ones? Was harm brought to participants? Later, some of them would become extremely upset; some even had uncontrollable seizures. Could the researcher have examined obedience in a different or safer way? Let's now deal with the question of how research is designed and why it is conducted.

African Americans and Research Ethics

African Americans remain underrepresented in professional research. The consequences of this underrepresentation are limited generalizeability, limited validity of research studies, and limited knowledge of African American experiences, ideas, challenges and aspirations. This underrepresentation also leads to the underrepresentation of African Americans in the formulation of public policy (Hsin-hsin & Coker, 2010). Let's now explore some of the concerns that Black people identify as causes for their hesitance to participate in scientific research. Hsin-hsin and Coker (2010) identify many understandable reasons that African Americans provide about why they are hesitant to participate (Hsin-hsin & Coker, 2010):

- **Distrust**: There is a long history of documented abuses and institutional racism by the research community. This history includes the Tuskegee Experiment and studies claiming that African Americans are unintelligent. African Americans also express concern about the use of such research to make political arguments to defund social programs. This history has obviously resulted in a widespread sense of mistrust on the part of many African Americans.
- **Lack of understanding of informed consent and the research process**: Many people may not understand what informed consent means or how the research will benefit them.
- **Insufficient recruitment**: Because recruitment of racially/ethnically underrepresented populations may be more difficult, researchers can easily underrecruit and have underrepresentative samples. The fact that some researchers do not actively recruit Black people leads to underrepresentative research samples.
- **Stigma**: There can also be the threat of stigma attached to participating and sharing information with strangers that can be looked upon negatively by family, community, or peers.
- **Financial challenges**: Interrupting daily activities to participate in research may be more costly for many African Americans (in terms of transportation and childcare, for example) and other underrepresented groups than for others.

The reasons that some African Americans are hesitant to participate in research are legitimate when placed in historical and present sociopolitical context. The rate of African American and other underrepresented groups' participation would increase if the research community were to adopt better practices. Many scholars have identified practices that would improve the research process and increase African American participation and the participation of other underrepresented groups (Hsin-hsin & Coker, 2010; Nápoles-Springer et al., 2000; Parrill & Kennedy, 2011; Strauss et al., 2001).

- **Self-examination:** Researchers should question their own motivations for conducting research. Some African Americans are critical of researchers who conduct research for selfish reasons and with no intention of helping. Researchers should (1) be prepared to explain how their research might benefit participants; (2) examine whether or not they are conducting research for money, status, or privilege; (3) be aware of the roles that race, class, and gender oppression play in their research; and (4) be aware of the history of research with African Americans and their legitimate concerns.
- **Financial incentives:** When appropriate, researchers should offer financial incentives such as money for transportation or compensation for participants' time. Researchers may also explore the possibility of offering free services because finance can be a barrier to attracting low-income research participants.
- **Culturally relevant research:** Researchers should also be sure to use concepts and theories that best represent and explain the experiences of people of African descent. Researchers should also balance quantitative approaches with more qualitative approaches that allow participants to define terms from their own perspectives. This is especially important for communities whose voices are underrepresented in mainstream scholarship.
- **Intervention-based research:** Hsin-hsin and Coker (2010) explain that researchers should engage in research designs that are geared toward improving people's conditions. A more aggressive effort should be made to address participants' stated goals and challenges because they are investing their time and energy by participating. This means engaging in more intervention-based research and participatory research that involves community members in the research process. We will further explore participatory research and action research in the following chapters.
- **Build trust:** Researchers should also make an effort to build trust with research participants by volunteering their services for community-related activities unrelated to their own research agenda. Researchers should also seek the research population's input by asking for ideas and topics that people would like explored through research.
- **Build relationships:** It can also be helpful to build relationships with community organizations (neighborhood organizations and task forces)

as well as with church leaders and community organization leaders. As researchers, community leaders are often trusted individuals whose input regarding your research might be valued by community members.

- **Awareness of in-group diversity**: Researchers must also gain an awareness of and respect for the in-group diversity of Black people and avoid the habit of focusing too heavily on low socioeconomic members of Black populations. This encourages researchers to attempt to draw heterogeneous samples of Black people across age, gender, income, and level of education.

These and other practices would not only improve the relationship between the research community and the Black community; they would also improve the overall research process. Incorporating such research practices could make the research process a better instrument of service for Black populations and lead to more research that incorporates a greater diversity of thoughts, concerns, challenges, and solutions.

Key Terms

Beneficence

Deception

Ethics

Informed Consent

Maat

Non Malfeasance

Right to Privacy

Thinking about Science

Association for the Study of Classical African Civilizations
http://www.ascacwesternregion.org/Our-Purose.html

Association for the Study of African American Life and History
http://www.ascacwesternregion.org/Our-Purose.html

Association of Black Anthropologists
http://www.indiana.edu/~wanthro/candice1.htm

Association of Black Psychologists
http://www.abpsi.org/about_mission.html

Association of Black Sociologists
http://associationofblacksociologists.org/about-us/

Activity 1

- Go to the website of one of the scholarly organizations listed above. Locate the organizational description. Explain how the organization's mission or purpose reflects some of the ethical principles explained in this chapter.

Activity 2

- Find out whether or not your school has an Institutional Review Board (IRB). If it does, complete its research certification training process and obtain certification to conduct research.

CHAPTER FOUR

Research Design

Research design refers to critical components in the planning and strategy that guides the execution of research. Research design includes decisions about which methods to use, how to analyze the results, which units of analysis you are using, limits of generalizing conclusions, and how to interpret the relationships between variables (Bryman, 2008). This chapter covers key elements of your research that have implications on what you can say when your research is finished. We will discuss units of analysis, the purpose of research, quantitative and qualitative approaches, and temporal design in research. Research methods—different from research design—are *means* of collecting data. Research design answers the *what*, *why*, and *how* of research, that is, *what* you are going to study, *why* you are studying it, and *how* you choose to go about studying it. Let us first deal with *what* is being studied.

Units of Analysis: The Who and What of Research

The phrase **unit of analysis** refers to the elements on which you measure variables and collect data. They are simply the people or things being studied (Vogt, 1999; Neuman, 2009). Although researchers don't always overtly state them, units of analysis are critical for helping those conducting research. They also assist consumers of research or those who are reading research to clearly think through a study, interpret it properly, and avoid common errors. Units of analysis can be "individuals, groups (family, team), organizations (company, university), social categories (social class, gender, race), social institutions (religion, education, criminal justice, military), and societies (nation)" (Neuman, 2009). Surveys measure attitudes and behaviors; thus the most typical units of analysis in survey research are *individuals*. When the researcher defines the population of inquiry for an investigation according to its personal status, the researcher is usually operating at the individual level of analysis. For example, the groupings single mothers, special education students, valedictorians, and sickle cell patients all identify *individuals* based on an individual status they hold (Monette, Sullivan, & DeJong, 2005). When the unit of analysis in a research study is the individual, the entire analysis must remain at the level of the individual. For example, you could collect a large amount of data from individual African American single-parent fathers and find that their average age was 23. Aggregating the data in this way does not change the unit of analysis, which is still *individuals*.

As we have already established, *groups* are also a unit of analysis. If you went to Chicago to investigate how gangs such as the Black Stones, Gangster Disciples, and Vice Lords interact with one another, then you would be studying group characteristics, not individual ones. Thus, your unit of analysis would be *gangs*; after all, it takes a group to *interact*, not an individual. You are looking for greetings specific to certain gangs, and a greeting requires two or more members. In this case your unit of analysis would be Chicago gangs. Darling-Hammond (1998) notes that "in contrast to European and Asian nations that fund schools centrally and equally, the wealthiest 10 percent of U.S. school districts spend nearly 10 times more than the poorest 10 percent, and spending ratios of 3 to 1 are common within states" (p. 28). If you wanted to compare the educational spending of the districts in your city based on the average income of district residents as indicated by census data, what would your unit of analysis be? Your unit of analysis would be *districts*. If you studied the success rate of rites of passage programs geared toward reducing drug use and violence, what would your unit of analysis be? Your unit of analysis would be the *rites of passage programs*. Why? You are analyzing program success, and therefore your unit of analysis would be *rites of passage programs*.

The National Association of African Americans for Positive Imagery sued the Swisher International Company for targeting Black youth in their advertising campaigns (Gardiner, 2004). There were several methods of study that went into their collection of data to support their case. One of the methods consisted of analyzing the magazines in which Swisher International advertised in the United States. The investigation uncovered the fact that three African American publications—*Ebony*, *Jet*, and *Essence* received a disproportionately higher number of cigarette advertisements than any other magazine. In this study, what is the unit of analysis? The unit of analysis in this case is not an individual or an institution; it is an artifact of sorts.

What is it? That's right: the unit of analysis is *magazines*. That means that you must remember that you cannot draw conclusions about *the media*. The researchers did not study advertisements in the media in general. They studied advertisements in magazines, and therefore their conclusions must be about magazines.

One of the things that knowing units of analysis helps you do is to stay away from faulty reasoning. One type of faulty reasoning is the **ecological fallacy,** which occurs when you investigate an entire ecological unit but come to conclusions about the individuals that make up that group. In short, the fallacy involves drawing conclusions about individuals based on data about groups (Vogt, 1999). If crime rates were high in an area with a large number of children living in single-parent homes, you would be committing an ecological fallacy if you concluded that individuals living in single-parent homes are more likely to commit crime. You could not draw that conclusion based on the information you have, because you have group-level data and not individual-level data. You cannot draw conclusions about individuals with group-level data. Suppose you established monitoring sites in cities all across the United States to measure their air quality by sampling their ozone and small-particle pollution levels. You might find that cities with the largest populations of African Americans are among those with the worst air quality. You would be committing the ecological fallacy if you were to conclude that, based on that data, pollution is more likely to come from the activities of African Americans or that African Americans are disproportionate polluters. This is because you are drawing conclusions about specific racial groups based on *city-level data*. This is a mistake because your unit of analysis is *cities* and not *racial groups*. In fact, African Americans and other people of color are among the least responsible for pollution, although they are among the most vulnerable to the consequences of it (Morello-Frosch, Pastor, Sadd, & Shonkoff, 2009). They are less likely to own vehicles and more likely to use public transportation, which saves energy. It is important to choose the appropriate unit of analysis as you design your study because, as you can see, your choice will influence the remainder of your research. If you wanted to draw conclusions about who pollutes more among different racial groups, you would simply need to collect data on individuals of different racial groups.

The Purpose of Research

There are many reasons for conducting research. Methods are the *means* by which data is collected. However, your means of collecting data cannot be considered in isolation of your *purpose* for collecting data. Try using your GPS system without typing in an end point, and you will know the function of a purpose. Have you ever gone shopping without a purpose? Your purpose is what keeps you from buying everything in the store. (That and your bank account.) It is what helps you make decisions about what store to go to, which isles to browse, and which brands to buy. In the world of research, your purpose is what keeps you from going on an endless pursuit of fragmented information with no apparent end in sight. Your purpose in research as in life is your light at the end of the tunnel. Let's examine several of the general purposes for research.

Exploratory Research

Exploratory research refers to research that looks for patterns, ideas, or hypotheses. Exploratory research is different from research that tries to test or confirm hypotheses and previously formulated theories (Babbie, 2001). Exploratory research is usually done on topics that are new or relatively new—topics on which there is not much research. In many cases exploratory research takes place when a researcher is breaking new ground on a particular topic.

The importance of exploratory research is that it provides insights into topics that have not been studied or have not been sufficiently studied. For instance, there are certain Zulu traditional healers called about whom there is minimal research. They are unique in that, in the process of healing, they communicate with the ancestors of the person who is sick by whistling into the wind and hearing the whistling of the ancestors. The whistling is believed to carry messages from the ancestors. The Sangoma Sabalozi are unique, even among other traditional healers, so if one were to do research on them, he or she would not begin the research with an established theory or hypothesis, or clear expectations, because there is not enough existing research on them. You might ask how they became traditional healers: did they undergo training, what did it consist of, and who are their patients? The exploratory researcher who breaks ground on a new area of study makes it possible for further research to take place. The exploratory research still must do background research on the general area of study. For instance, if researchers conduct exploratory research on the Sangoma Sabalozi, they have to do preliminary research on traditional healers—more specifically, traditional healers in the Southern African community of nations. However, for the most part a researcher conducting exploratory research should be prepared to collect information and identify variables, concepts, and ideas during the research process.

One of the major shortcomings of exploratory research is that it is rarely representative of large populations. Why is this so? The best way to get a detailed understanding of a new issue or idea is to immerse oneself into the community being studied. This is often done by way of comprehensive and detailed interviews, personal observations, and intensive fieldwork. It would be hard to do that with a large sample or population; therefore, it is usually done with a small number of people. So when exploratory research is done, although it is comprehensive, it may not be representative of larger populations because it is done on small groups of people. Another possible exploratory research study would be on a topic such as the indigenous people of the Andaman Islands. These people are of African origin, and local people say they are of *Negrito* origin. Nevertheless, the scientific community was astounded to discover that these indigenous peoples knew before anyone else that the 2004 Indian Ocean Tsunami was approaching, and they began to pack up and leave before anyone else did. An exploratory research study would be to research how the Andaman people study the natural world and predict natural occurrences.

Descriptive Research

Descriptive research is research that describes phenomena as they exist, as opposed to experimental research in which environments are controlled and manipulated. The best example of descriptive research is the country-level population census. In a census, there is a preset combination of variables about which that information is collected. Descriptive research involves collecting information on certain characteristics of an issue. It is usually quantitative because descriptive researchers use statistics to summarize the information they collect. For example, the United States collects information on things like age, sex, household composition, income, wealth, and language. Consider that someone might be interested in how to make Black businesses more suitable to their consumers. You might do a descriptive study of customers who patronize Black-owned businesses. You would have to identify a sample of Black businesses to determine who the consumers or patrons of those Black businesses are by creating a demographic profile of them. You might collect data on their ethnicity, age, marital status, household income, level of education, what they buy, what they wish to buy but cannot, what they read, what they eat, what they wear, when they shop at Black businesses, and how many times per week. This would be a descriptive study. But what if we were interested in why they shopped at Black-owned businesses? We would have to turn to explanatory research for answers.

Explanatory Research

Explanatory research seeks to understand phenomena by explaining the relationship between variables. Explanatory research is a continuation of descriptive research in that once you have descriptive information about a particular issue, you can go on to explain why or how it occurs or works the way it does. Take, for instance, the study of Black businesses. Not only do you want a demographic profile of the people who shop at Black businesses, what they buy, and what their needs are. You also may also want to know why they shop at Black businesses. Explanatory research seeks not to describe or explore but to understand phenomena by discovering relationships between variables. To report the frequency of church attendance would be descriptive research, but determining why certain people and not others attend church is explanatory (Babbie, 2001). Similarly, to report the crime rates of a particular city is descriptive, while discovering or investigating why people in that city commit the crimes they do is explanatory.

It is important to mention that there is a natural relationship among the latter three approaches and that they all depend on one another. Exploratory research brings new issues to the forefront of the research community. On the other hand, descriptive studies designate the characteristics of an issue, while explanatory research helps us understand that issue.

Evaluative Research

Evaluative research is often used to assess or monitor the implementation or effectiveness of a social intervention. A social intervention can be any attempt to change the conditions in which people live (Bless, Higson-Smith, & Kagee, 2006). Social interventions can include initiatives such as drug rehabilitation programs, financial literacy programs, and life skills programs, all of which could benefit from evaluative research. Evaluative research can be used to assess whether or not social interventions are achieving their stated goals. Evaluation research is useful for social interventions that hope to improve themselves. Evaluative research can be used to provide evidence of successes and failures, identify areas of neglect, and pathways to solutions.

Predictive Research

Predictive research focuses on collecting and evaluating information for the purpose of envisaging or forecasting what may happen in the future. Insurance companies create sophisticated formulae to predict the risks associated with insuring certain people or property (Monette, Sullivan, & DeJong, 2005). This predictive research allowed some insurance companies to anticipate and prepare for the 2007 housing market crash in the United States. Predictive research can be used to assess, for example, the developmental impact of providing greater funding to programs such as Head Start and other forms of early childhood education on the educational success of children who participate in them. How might increasing the level of federal funding for community colleges impact the number of people who suffer from cardiovascular disease? How might that funding affect the rate of incarceration? These are questions that could be answered through predictive research. If you are interested supporting a particular political or socioeconomic change, predictive research will help you establish the possible impact of the change you are interested in.

Quantitative and Qualitative Approaches to Data Collection

In scientific research, observations refer to data collection. As a researcher, you make observations or collect data that will help you answer your research question. Research methods are the tools and approaches to data collection. One of the most common ways to differentiate the various approaches to data collection is by classifying them as either quantitative or qualitative. However, qualitative and quantitative approaches overlap with one another.

Quantitative research often—but not always—involves the use of methods such as experimentation and survey/questionnaire design. Researchers often use these methods to study phenomena by using numbers and counts. Quantitative research is generally used to examine cause-and-effect relationships and to test theories. These methods involve taking a numerical approach to research because they involve reducing variables such as attitudes, beliefs, and knowledge to numbers so that they can be easily measured. However, it must be noted that the researcher has to conceptualize and define these beliefs and attitudes. Moreover, the research respondent participating in quantitative research has to make subjective decisions about what those beliefs and attitudes mean to him or her. Therefore, there are some very qualitative dimensions to quantitative research, especially research involving human beings. Quantitative instruments (often surveys or questionnaires) frequently employ close-ended questions with predetermined answers to produce statistical scores. The advantage of data that is quantitative is that it is easily categorized, compared, measured, and summarized. It is also well suited to test cause and effect such as in experimental designs. The drawbacks to quantitative approaches are that they often don't yield the intimate information, detailed context, and deeper understandings that a researcher may get from other more *qualitative* approaches.

Some subjects such as African artistic production and spirituality are difficult to quantify, and therefore different methods are more appropriate, particularly qualitative methods. Using **qualitative research**, the researcher makes use of non-numeric observations of phenomena. Qualitative approaches to research are often carried out using research methods such as ethnography, interviews, questionnaires (with open-ended items), field observations, and analysis of cultural documents. These methods often produce data in the form of words, descriptions, and images to explain phenomena and develop theories.

Qualitative data is often considered rich in meaning because it allows research participants to explain phenomena on their own terms or in their own words. Qualitative research usually yields open-ended data that is analyzed to produce themes and patterns that help to explain phenomena. These qualitative approaches to research are in many cases used to conduct exploratory studies on topics that are new or relatively new. However, there are drawbacks to qualitative research. Qualitative research often yields hours of interview data and pages of notes that can be time consuming to analyze and don't easily lend themselves to quantification. Qualitative research, however, contains elements of quantitative research. Do not be fooled. There is no sharp dichotomy between quantitative and qualitative approaches to research. For example, the data produced by qualitative research must be analyzed categorized, coded, and assigned numerical representation. Therefore, qualitative research can also contain some degree of quantification. Qualitative research, however, is often much more difficult to organize than quantitative data. Each method of research has its own strengths and shortcomings. It is important for a researcher to be familiar with a diversity of research methods because the nature of the problem that is being researched should influence what method(s) the researcher employs. No one method of research is appropriate for all research problems. As Kershaw (2003) states, "In terms of research methods, both quantitative and qualitative methods are appropriate" (p. 29). In fact, **mixed-methods research** is becoming more and more popular. Mixed-methods studies incorporate multiple methods in the research process to employ a more holistic analysis of social phenomena.

Temporal Order and Research Design

The time dimension of research can vary based on the nature of your research. Research can be conducted over a long or short period of time. There are both advantages and drawbacks to each approach, so researchers must be careful to choose the most appropriate temporal research design that fits the purpose of their research. Let's examine cross-sectional and longitudinal designs.

Cross-Sectional Studies

A **cross-sectional study** is a study that is conducted at a relatively single point in time by taking a cross section or snapshot of a sample of a population. Cross-sectional studies collect data on more than one case at a single point in time. Cross-sectional data are collected more or less simultaneously. The U.S. Census, done every 10 years, is an example of a cross-sectional study. You might be interested in conducting a large-scale national survey on racial attitudes by having people answer a few set questions. This would involve taking a measure of prejudice at one point in time, a snapshot. That makes it a cross-sectional study, but such a study has to be examined within its cross-sectional context. For example, consider the results of a cross-sectional study on racial attitudes. Imagine that you find that people who are 65 or older tend to be more prejudiced than people who are 25 or under. This does not mean that as the younger group gets older it is going to become just as prejudiced as the older group. It doesn't mean that it is going to become more prejudiced at all. It also doesn't mean that when the older group was younger it was less prejudiced. This is because cross-sectional studies are snapshots that assess attitudes or circumstances at one single moment in time; they can't tell you much about how a phenomenon develops or what causes it.

These studies are time sensitive: they can take place at a time when racial tensions are heightened by some event that occurs during the time that the study is conducted and influences the results. For example, on January 1, 2010, the San Francisco Bay Area Rapid Transit (BART) police responded to reports about a fight taking place on the train. The police arrived and detained several people. Among them was a young Black man, Oscar Grant. Mr. Grant was handcuffed and laid prostrate on the train platform at the Fruitvale train station in East Oakland. A police officer (Johannes Mehserle) drew his gun and shot Mr. Grant while he lay handcuffed on the platform. The next day there were urban rebellions in downtown Oakland. Remember that cross-sectional research takes place at a single point in time, not over a period of time. The results of a survey on racial attitudes in Oakland on January 2 (the day after Mr. Grant was murdered by the police) would likely be significantly different than a survey on racial attitudes in Oakland on December 31 (the day before Mr. Grant was murdered). However, *longitudinal* designs remedy this limitation by taking place over an extended period of time. However, like all designs, longitudinal designs come with their own limitations. Let's examine a few longitudinal designs such as cohort studies, panel studies, and trend studies.

Cohort Studies

A cohort study involves the study of a specific subpopulation of people over time, but not necessarily the same individual members of that subpopulation each time. Szanton, Thorpe, and Whitfield (2010) investigated the effects of life-course financial stress on the health of African Americans using cohort study data. Their information was based on 699 interviews. Szanton and colleagues' (2010) population came from the Carolina African American Twin Study of Aging (CAATSA), which was designed to study the physical and psychological health of African American twins. The population that CAATSA studied was established by taking a sample of African Americans using birth records and voter registries between 1913 and 1975 in North Carolina. By way of their cohort study, Szanton and fellow researchers (2010) were able to determine that individuals who reported financial strain during their childhood were more likely to report depressive symptoms, be physically disabled, and have lower cognitive functioning than those who reported no childhood financial strain. They also found that financial strain in adulthood was more strongly associated with poor health than financial strain during childhood. This highlights the importance of targeting financial strain among adult African Americans.

Can you think of any cohort studies you might be interested in conducting? What if you decided to conduct a cohort study on the attitudes toward South African national education policies according to South African people who were between the ages of 10 and 15 during the 1976 Soweto uprising, when students protested the racist Bantu Education Act of the South African apartheid government? In a cohort study, such individuals' attitudes toward the South African government's educational policies might be assessed every 5 years. People who were 41–45 years old could be studied in 2009, and people 46–50 years old in 2014. How old would they be in 2019? That's right, 51–55 years old! Totally different people would be studied each time, but they would still be members of the target cohort, which is South African persons who were between the ages 10 and 15 during the 1979 Soweto Uprising in which several hundred men, women, and children were killed by the South African police force. Such a study could tell you much about any lasting effects that being a youth in school in South Africa during that uprising may have on South African people's perspectives on educational policies.

Longitudinal studies are well suited for investigating phenomena that develop, change, and take shape over time. For example, a cohort study might be used to investigate the long-term social, emotional, and educational effects on the children of families who have experienced home foreclosure. A researcher might interview and observe a sample of families from several of the zip codes in Detroit that were hardest hit by home foreclosure in 2007. Using a cohort study design, researchers would need to collect information from the *same* cohort over a period of time. Using another design—panel study—researchers would have to collect data from the same people each time.

Panel Studies

Unlike cohort studies, panel studies examine the same set of people each time. A **panel study** is a long-term study in which data is collected from the same exact people each time. While a cohort study samples from the same population at different times, a panel study examines the same people at different times. Shafer (2010) investigated the effects of marriage on weight gain and obesity in the African American community using panel study data. Shafer (2010) discovered that marriage is associated with the likelihood of becoming obese for African American women. Emily Shafer (2010) used data from the National Longitudinal

Study of Youth, which began collecting data from a panel of 14–21-year-old youth who were interviewed first in 1979 and re-interviewed annually until 1994 and then biannually until 2004. An interesting panel study might follow the recovery and progression of several families from the Lower Ninth Ward of New Orleans, examining their homeownership, household composition, job acquisition, and income levels every 5 years for 25 years. But remember, for this to qualify as a panel study, the same individuals or research participants must be investigated each time. Can you think of an example of another panel study?

Research design answers key questions about a research study. These questions should be answered early on in the research process because they influence the remainder of a study. What or who is studied influences your approach to study. How you go about a study is influenced by your purpose for engaging in that study. Different approaches to study are more or less appropriate depending upon your objective. These questions are all interconnected and critical to the research process.

Key Terms

Cohort Study	Mixed-Methods Research
Cross-Sectional Study	Panel Study
Descriptive Research	Predictive Research
Ecological Fallacy	Qualitative Research
Evaluative Research	Quantitative Research
Explanatory Research	Research Design
Exploratory Research	Unit of Analysis

Thinking about Science

Activity 1

- Use your library's peer-reviewed journal search engines to locate either a panel study or a cohort study. Describe the population that was studied, how often it was studied, and what the findings of the study were.

Activity 2

The following is a list of real research studies. Read the brief descriptions of each of them and identify the units of analysis in each study.

- Simmelink, Lightfoot, Dube, Blevins, and Lum (2013) studied ideas and beliefs about healthcare among East African refugees in the United States. They discovered that East African refugees retained strong cultural beliefs about health that affect their interactions with Western healthcare systems.
- Gagern & van den Bergh (2013) conducted a critical review of fishing licenses made by African, Caribbean, and Pacific countries to distant water fleets. They examined the licenses to determine how beneficial they were to local economies and environments.
- Bryan, Rudd, and Wertenberger (2013) investigated the reasons for attempting suicide among a sample of active-duty soldiers. They found that the soldiers primarily attempted suicide to alleviate emotional distress.

CHAPTER FIVE

Choosing a Topic, Writing a Question, Reviewing the Literature

You may have heard someone ask the question, "What is your research question?" The answer is critical. Novice researchers may struggle against the temptation to begin by saying something to the effect of "I want to prove that...." It is enticing, I know—the chance to achieve some desired outcome and *prove* that you were right all along. This is the wrong way to begin a research project! You should never, ever, ever begin a research project with the intention of trying to prove something. This self-centered way of thinking will lead you into a swamp of roadblocks to critical thought, taking away the validity and reliability of your work. What is the benefit of reading about how some researcher went about attempting to prove a preconception? Even a hypothesis or educated guess is not certain. A researcher who begins with a hypothesis wants to find out whether or not it is true, not to prove that he or she was right all along. A professional researcher never begins with a conclusion. Instead, your objective is to answer a question and let the chips fall where they may. Not just any question—a question with an answer that could conceivably bring clarity to a challenge, illuminate a new way of thinking, or provide a solution to a problem.

Africana Studies' mission centralizes three things: academic excellence, social responsibility, and cultural grounding (Karenga, 2002). How that mission shapes the research process conceptually and technically is the focus of this chapter. Africana Studies is distinguished not by *what* or *who* is studied, but by *how* and *why* it is studied. Africana Studies grounds itself in the cultural location of peoples

Figure 5.1

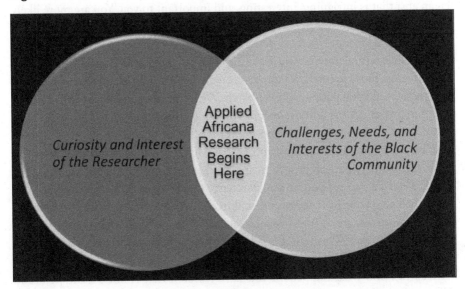

of African descent. The researcher engages in study for the purpose of improving the lived experiences of people of African descent. This chapter outlines how you go about selecting a topic in a way that is consistent with the triple mission of the discipline. This chapter also covers the purpose and process of writing and organizing a literature review.

The Intersecting Interests Theory for Research in Africana Studies

This author asserts the **Intersecting Interests Theory (IIT)** for research in Africana Studies. The realm in which an Africana Studies researcher operates is at the intersection of his or her interests and developing expertise and the needs and concerns of the people (people of African descent). The IIT approach is designed to guide researchers in the process of producing research that is interesting and important to them and relevant to the community. Such an approach is meant to encourage and facilitate the production of scholarship that demonstrates creativity, quality, and relevance. Another purpose of IIT is to help researchers avoid two problems: *researcher-centered research* and *ritualistic research*. It is important that scholars research issues that are important to them and interesting to them. Why? The reason you should identify an area that is of interest to you is because ultimately *you* will need to spend hours reading about it, writing about it, thinking about it, and analyzing it.

It is far more likely that you will do those things and do them well if you have chosen an area that is intriguing, interesting, and important to you. You are more likely to do those important things if you are researching something you are genuinely interested in. You are more likely to develop unique, imaginative, and creative research if you are committed to what you are researching. If you don't have that genuine interest, it is less likely that you will produce quality research. In fact, you are more susceptible to producing poor-quality research. We know from our discussion of ethics in research that poor-quality research is unethical because it means you are contributing poor scholarship to an important issue.

Why does your research have to overlap with the needs and concerns of the larger community? Research in Africana Studies is not meant to be a self-serving act. It is not just about you as a researcher; you are writing for others, too. You should be using your knowledge and skill to conduct research that will provide the information necessary to improve a social condition or bring greater understanding to a critical issue. We are not just trying to produce research that is terribly interesting. We want to make sure that it is relevant as well.

Keep in mind what happens if you have research that is not socially relevant. What if you are conducting research that is simply intriguing to the researcher? This is the definition of speculative scholarship or researcher-centered research. Purely speculative scholarship is outside of the mission of Africana Studies. The same is true for the opposite. What if you conduct research that you are not interested in or committed to? This is the *ritualistic approach* to research, and you are more prone to produce low-quality scholarship if you are engaged in ritualistic research. Research can turn into a dull, boring, and mundane process when you as the researcher have not chosen a topic that is interesting, curious, or intriguing to you. When you choose a topic that is not interesting to you, you may ultimately be hurting the people you are conducting research about by producing low-quality work with unreliable conclusions and unreliable suggestions for improving society.

Developing Topics and Questions

Finding Topics

Where do ideas about topics come from? In short, topics may emerge from anywhere and everywhere. New topics can come from previous research you have done. Previous research tends to leave you with lots of new questions. One of those questions may be the start of a new topic for research. Your own personal experiences, conversations, and observations can be sources for new research topics, as can existing theories and ideas. You may explore one of your interests or someone else's idea, test a preexisting theory, or test an assumption. Look at the topics and titles of articles written in scholarly journals such as the *Journal of Black Studies*, the *Journal of Black Psychology*, the *Journal of African American Studies*, or the *Western Journal of Black Studies*. Look at some topics others have pursued and think about trying to improve on their research.

It is customary to start off with a general interest such as the education of African American youth. This is an okay place to start, but it is too general. What aspect of your general interest might you be tempted to pursue further? Try to think of the different aspects and dimensions or subcategories of your topic. Let's brainstorm some dimensions of African-centered education:

- African American learning styles
- African-centered school designs
- Educational motivation among African American youth
- Use of digital technology in educating Black youth
- African Americans in gifted education programs
- Hip Hop as a pedagogical tool for African American youth
- School discipline strategies for African American youth

The list goes on and on. Make your own list, and think of which one(s) you are most interested in pursuing. Perhaps you are interested in the relationship between culture and education. You may investigate the role of "African-Centered Curriculum at African-Centered Charter Schools." However, this is a rather broad topic. It is okay to start with a broad topic just as long as you begin to carve it down into a more manageable and researchable topic. Once you have developed a topic, think of how its different parts might relate to or affect one another. For example, you might be interested in how the use of digital technology affects the educational motivation of African American youth. You may also consider how your topic has changed over time. For example, you might be interested in how approaches to African-centered curricula have changed in the past 50 years. You might compare your topic to a similar topic. For example, you might study how an African-centered curriculum relates to culturally grounded Native American approaches to teaching and learning. Developing a question forces you to be more specific.

Developing Research Questions

Lace your boots and put on your hardhat. The bottom line is this: in order to get some answers about your topic, you have to learn to develop questions. Not just questions, but *research* questions. A **research question** is a question representing the problem you intend to investigate in your study. What question do you want to ask about your topic? If your topic is interesting to you, it should compel you to ask some questions about it. What would you like to know—but do not know—about the topic you are interested in? As Booth, Colomb and Williams (1995, p. 39) suggest, the starting point of good research is always *"what do you not know or understand but feel that you must?"* Is anything coming to mind? The questions are there. Find them.

You might decide that your question is *"Culturally relevant approaches to teaching Black youth."* But, alas, there are criteria that your research question must meet. First, it must be in the form of a question. *"Culturally relevant approaches to teaching Black youth"* is not a question; it is a statement. A question would be *"What are the culturally relevant approaches to teaching Black youth?"* The second criterion—that your research question should also suggest a relationship—is not always necessary, but it can be helpful. After all, science is about studying relationships. Relationships between what? Relationships between variables. *"What are the culturally relevant approaches to teaching Black youth?"* does not suggest a relationship between variables. There are no independent or dependent variables in this question. Here is a new question: *"What are the effects of culturally relevant teaching on the education of Black youth?"* This question is phrased in the form of a question, and it suggests a relationship. The independent variable is clearly *culturally relevant pedagogy* and the dependent variable is *education.* However, a third criterion that a question must meet is that it must be testable—in other words, measureable. You must be able to find a plausible empirical answer to this question. You must make your variables specific. In the question *"What are the effects of culturally relevant teaching on the education of Black youth?"* the variables are not worded specifically enough to be empirically tested. "Education" is too vague, and "culturally relevant pedagogy" is acceptable, but it could be further refined to a more specific type of culturally relevant pedagogy if the researcher were interested in one. Here is an example of a more testable research question: "What are the effects of African-centered pedagogy on the achievement levels of Black youth?" This question is phrased in the form of a question, it suggests a relationship between variables, and it is answerable. This research question meets the basic criteria, but from here you must also decide upon a research method and a population. Exhibit 5.1 explains a more comprehensive approach to writing a research question.

Writing a Literature Review

Literature, in scientific research, is a term that refers to past research on a particular topic. A **literature review** is a survey of scholarly articles, books, chapters of books, and dissertations relevant to a particular issue. The literature review provides a description and critical evaluation of each work. The general purpose of writing

Exhibit 5.1

A More Comprehensive Approach to Writing Your Primary Research Question

The following is a different approach to writing your primary research question. For example, do culturally centered approaches to teaching African American students actually increase the knowledge and achievement of African American students? You can develop such a question about your interest. However, you will need to develop a research question. Below is one approach to developing research questions. Using this approach the research question must contain several different elements: an independent variable (IV), a dependent variable (DV), a population (POP), and a method (METH). Each of these elements should be present in this kind of research question. Observe the following example:

Are dietary habits, as assessed by the Dietary Habits and Nutritional Orientations Scale influenced by the neighborhood household income levels among African American adults in four different zip codes in San Francisco (94224, 93123, 94122 and 94132)?

Can you see the independent variable(s)? Do you see the dependent variable(s)? Do you see the population or the method(s)? Let's take another look?

Are **dietary habits**, as assessed by the **Dietary Habits and Nutritional Orientations Scale** influenced by **the neighborhood household income** levels among **African American adults** in four different zip codes in San Francisco (94224, 93123, 94122 and 94132)?

The dependent variable is **dietary habits score**. In this situation, the variable that is dependent or effected by or dependent upon the independent variable is the dietary habits score that members of the population earn after having taken the Dietary and Nutritional Orientations Scale. The dependent variable is "dietary habits *score*" and not simple "dietary habits" because the variable should be stated in terms that indicate that it will be measured. The independent variable is **Neighborhood household income levels** because this is the variable that determines changes in the dependent variable, dietary habits score. Remember the researcher who asked this question to find out how Neighborhood Household Income Levels influence dietary habits. Since Neighborhood household income levels is the variable that is doing the influencing, it is the independent variable. The population in this question is clearly **African American adults**. They are the population because they will be the research participants in this study. Data will be collected from them, therefore they are the population. Now, on to the matter of the method of this research question. The method is the means by which data will be collected from a sample population. Methods consist of experiments, surveys, questionnaires, observations, interviews, discourse analysis, content analysis, etc. Methods are tools of data collection. In this case the method is the **Dietary Habits and Nutritional Orientations Scale** because it is the means by which the researcher(s) will collect data on African American adults' dietary habits. Here is another example:

Cont. on p. 112

Exhibit 5.1 cont.

According to the Parental Involvement Questionnaire (PIQ), what are the effects of parental involvement score on the level of academic achievement of 10th-grade students at De LaSalle, Dunbar, and Martin Luther King Jr. High schools in Chicago?

Can you see the independent variable(s)? Do you see the dependent variable(s)? Do you see the population or the method(s)? Let's take another look?

According to the **Parental Involvement Questionnaire (PIQ)**, what are the effects of **parental involvement score** on the **level of academic achievement** of **10th-grade students** at De LaSalle, Dunbar, and Martin Luther King Jr. High schools in Chicago?

The dependent variable here is level of academic achievement because this is the variable that is being effected in the questions above. Therefore, it is the variable that is being impacted or influenced by another variable. What is that other variable that is having an effect on level of academic achievement? The independent variable is parental involvement score because the researcher is looking for the effect it has on levels of academic achievement. The population here is 10th-grade students because they are the sample population from which information will be collected.

Based on ethnographic interviews with 12–14 year-old African American students at Bayard Rustin Middle School, what is the relationship between type(s) of hip hop music they listen to and their social attitudes?

Can you see the independent variable(s)? Do you see the dependent variable(s)? Do you see the population or the method(s)? Let's take another look?

Based on **ethnographic interviews** with **12–14 year-old African American students** at Bayard Rustin Middle School, what is the relationship between **type(s) of hip hop music** they listen to and their **social attitudes**?

This question presents a slight exception to the rule that every question must have an independent variable and a dependent variable. Sometimes when a research question is looking at the relationship between two or more variables there may not be a clear dependent or independent variable because the researcher(s) may not be looking for a causal effect that one variable has on another. So when researchers are simply looking at a relationship between two or more variables it is necessary to simply identify those variable. In this case what are those variables? One variable is the **type(s) of hip hop music** listened to. The other variable is **social attitudes**. The population is…you guessed it, **African American youth ages 12–14 years old.** The method is **ethnographic interviews.** Now that you know how to construct research questions, be sure to interrogate your research question thoroughly. You should be coming up with a question whose answer helps to provide necessary understanding about something that is not sufficiently understood.

the literature review is to create an overview of significant research on a topic. Having this overview of research is meant to familiarize the writer/researcher and the reader with the current state of the problem that is being studied. Having this familiarity helps the researcher choose the best way forward. This section will cover the functions of a literature review, the kinds of literature a review should consist of, how to find literature, how to maximize reading the literature, how to write and organize the literature review, and how to summarize and close a literature review.

Functions of the Literature Review

Think of the benefits of knowing history in general and you will have begun to understand why it is important for a researcher to write a literature review. Those who attempt to make history without bothering to study it are bound to repeat it. The following are the general functions that a literature review serves for both the writer of the literature review and whoever reads it.

- It informs the researcher and the reader about what is known about the topic.
- It can expose the researcher and the reader to knowledge gaps and weaknesses in existing research on the topic.
- It helps the researcher narrow a general topic down to a more specific general topic.
- It provides the researcher with examples of the styles that other researchers have used to present literature on their topics.
- It provides researchers with examples of designs, methods, and techniques that they might use in their own research.
- It exposes the researcher and the reader to different theories used to understand their topics.
- It provides the researcher and the reader with different definitions of key terms used in previous studies.
- It helps the researcher and the reader identify connections and contradictions between the findings of previous research studies.

What's Known about Your Topic?

When you review the literature you get a sense of what has already been covered thoroughly and exhaustively and what has been underresearched or incompletely researched. Many unintentional research mistakes have been made that were completely avoidable. Nonetheless, they occur because of failure to review literature on a topic before conducting research. Many of the major blunders in the world have been the consequence of individuals so anxious to *make history* that they never bother to *study it.* Your literature review is like history in the sense that it is a critical review of the past research studies on your topic.

Of all our studies, history is best qualified to reward our research. And when you see that you've got problems, all you have to do is examine the historic method used all over the world by others who have problems similar to yours. Once you see how they got theirs straight, then you know how you can get yours straight.

—MALCOM X (CITED IN BREITMAN, 1965, P. 8)

Knowing what has already been done is important because you want to know that what your study offers is something that has yet to be done or something new to your topic. Knowing the previous literature helps you avoid reinventing the wheel.

Weaknesses and Gaps in the Literature

Knowing the literature does more than help a researcher avoid reinventing the wheel. One of the most important reasons for reviewing previous literature is that it allows researchers to identify gaps in knowledge about their research topics and weaknesses in previous studies about their topics (Bless, Higson-Smith, & Kagee, 2006). Reviewing the literature lets a researcher know what has been studied and *what has yet to be studied.*

Helps Narrow Your Scope

Knowing what has already been done is important because you want to know that what your study offers is something that has yet to be done or that your study is offering something new to an old topic. Once you find out what has already been done, you gain a more expansive knowledge of the details and particular dimensions of your topic. Because you gain a more thorough understanding of your topic, you can be more specific about exactly what you want to research relative to what others have researched, thereby narrowing your topic.

Provides Stylistic Models

Reviewing the literature also provides you with examples of different styles and methods that you could use in your own research. Before you put your pen to paper to write a literature review, you need to read several good literature reviews. The literature you review presents you with examples of different styles, structures, and formats. When you start reading the literature you will find that there is a particular pattern or scheme in the way the studies are being presented. The pattern in which the information is being presented is important because it gives the study flow, direction, and a trajectory. Most important, it gives you ideas for how you might want to organize and structure your own literature review. In addition, reviewing existing research also shows you what kinds of styles to avoid. You will observe flaws in the way other studies are presented that you don't want to repeat when you start writing your own research. Not only does reviewing existing literature give you models for how others have structured and organized their literature reviews; it also gives you examples of how other researchers have organized and completed their entire studies. This kind of exposure gives researchers models for how they can organize their completed studies.

Provides Examples of Methods

A review of the past literature on a topic provides the researcher with examples of the methods that previous researchers have used to collect data on topics similar to yours. By observing the methods of other researchers, you can develop ideas for what methods you want to use to collect data to answer your own research questions. You have to choose whether you want to use questionnaires, interviews, observations, experiments, or a combination of methods. Reviewing past studies will help show you which methods will be most appropriate for collecting data to answer *your* research question.

Exposure to Different Theoretical Approaches

By reviewing studies done on your topic you will observe relevant theories, paradigms, and concepts. Being exposed to a variety of theories and concepts used by other researchers will give you more options to choose from in selecting the most appropriate theoretical frameworks for your own investigations. This allows you to become familiar with the technical language and specialized terminology associated with your topic. The familiarity you gain with this language will help you to explain your own study. A review of existing scholarship may reveal to you that culturally appropriate concepts and theories have yet to be applied to the topic that you are interested in researching.

Greater Knowledge of Definitions

Variables and key terms must be defined and operationalized. However, key terms and variables are not always defined in the same way by different researchers, even if they are investigating the same topic. By reviewing the literature on your topic you will observe many different and similar definitions of key terms. Not only does reviewing the literature allow the researcher to see many different definitions; it also reveals the strengths and weaknesses of different definitions. It is important to see many different definitions of key terms so that you can define key terms clearly and concisely in your own research.

Exposure to Connections and Contradictions

Reviewing previous studies helps researchers identify the connections and contradictions between the results, claims, and conclusions of different studies on their topics. This is important because addressing, explaining, and reconciling connections and contradictions between previous research results can form the beginning of a new investigation. Any researcher investigating topics gains more legitimacy if he or she is able to acknowledge and explain the relationship between previous research findings on the topic in question. Your research may seek to explain why those contradictions exist or how to avoid them in the future.

Caution! A Word of Warning to Reviewers of Literature

As exciting as reviewing the literature may be, it carries with it a seductive danger. As researchers review literature, they encounter the risk of accepting without criticism the outcomes, explanations, and conclusions of previous researchers. A researcher must be careful to review past literature while thinking critically and being open to new possibilities and ways of thinking about their topics. In a phrase, *think critically and creatively*. Researchers must be aware of this risk so that they can avoid becoming trapped within existing frameworks of viewing phenomena when there may be better ones.

What Kind of Literature Do I Review?

A researcher writing a literature review should be reviewing articles in scholarly journals, books, reports, and relevant chapters of books and dissertations. Additional sources will be found by looking through the bibliographies or reference sections of sources to gain access to other articles and books that may be relevant to the research topic. If you are doing an empirical research study, most of the literature that is reviewed should be studies that are organized in like fashion to the study you are organizing. If you intend to conduct your own empirical study, it is important that you review empirical studies. You should review studies with literature reviews, methods sections, data collection, and analysis sections. This does not mean staying away from conceptual articles that mostly discuss the topic you are interested in theoretically. Those articles are important, but your literature review should certainly include empirical studies because you are doing one. You should review theoretical articles as well, since sometimes you will find that the problem with some of the studies you will review is that they have taken a flawed theoretical approach to studying the problem. Sometimes you will discover that they have taken an approach that does not include culturally relevant theories and concepts that are more appropriate for your topic or population. However, if you are designing an empirical study, you need to be sure that you are reviewing empirical studies, because you are planning to do more than conceptualize about your topic. You are planning to take it to a different level by collecting information, analyzing it, coming to conclusions, and making recommendations.

How to Find the Literature

Start with a library database. If you are a student, use your school library's online database. Search your library database by subject, author, or key words related to your topic. Look for books and chapters of books on your topic. Use the library database to search professional journals for articles on your topic. It is also helpful to seek the advice of social scientists with experience and expertise in the area of the topic you are interested in. Such experts may be able to direct you to important resources and provide you with advice. Try to find approximately 50 sources on your topic. You may not ultimately use every source that you find, but it is best to start with a lot of sources so that you may settle on a few. Some of the studies you find will be more relevant than others.

Maximize Your Reading: How to Carefully Read the Literature

As researchers read through studies on their topics, they must be sure to get the most out of their reading. As you read previous research, read critically. Pay attention to a study's research question, the problem it is addressing, its methods of data collection, findings, and conclusions. Remember, when you are reading a study, it is not enough to pay attention to the author's conclusion; you must also evaluate the arguments that support those conclusions (Booth et al., 1995). As you read one study, think about how that study relates to other studies you have read. Pay attention to inconsistencies between the findings of one or more studies you have reviewed. If you do find that authors have similar findings, go a step further and find out whether or not they explain their findings in different or similar ways (Booth et al., 1995). Consider what, if any, new questions a study's conclusions give rise to.

Ask yourself as you read different studies on your topic, "What is the significance of this study?" and "What are the strengths and weaknesses of this study?" As you read a study, be sure to take note of the theoretical approaches the authors have used to guide their study and interpret their findings. Think about what those theories offer to the research question. How well do the theories authors use help to explain and contextualize their research findings? As you read literature on your topic, you should also be thinking about how to organize your own literature review.

Organizing a Literature Review

Begin your literature review with a paragraph that clearly states its purpose. There is likely to be a diversity of sources of literature on your topic, and you will therefore need to explain the criteria you will use to determine what literature you will use in your own literature review. Explain the kind of literature that you were looking for. Explain whether or not you were looking for peer-reviewed sources. Discuss the sources you got your literature from and why you chose those sources. You may even explain any key words you used in searching for your literature. Your objective in the first paragraph of your literature review should be to describe your strategy for finding sources in such a way that another researcher could replicate it. You should also provide an outline of your literature review for the reader. A good way to do this is to explain the subsections that your literature is organized by. Provide a brief description of the literature that will be covered in each subheading and how it relates to the entire body of literature on your topic.

Your reviews of past research on your topic should follow the first paragraph of your literature review. Reviews of previous studies should include (1) the purpose of the study, (2) any theories that are used, (3) any hypotheses that are made, (4) a description of the study's population and sample size, (5) methods of data collection, and (6) findings. However, you are not to simply summarize previous studies on your topic. Explain whether or not the study you are reviewing confirmed its hypotheses. If the authors of the study you are reviewing point out the implications or consequences of their findings, you should include them in your review as well. Sometimes the authors will point out their own limitations, but if they do not, you should do so.

As you know, you are not just summarizing previous studies, but also critiquing them. However, you should not just be thinking critically, but also creatively about the studies you review. This means that you should think not only of their limitations, but how the studies you review can be improved upon. It is important to think of how previous studies can be improved upon because this will help you tailor your own study toward addressing one or more of the weaknesses of previous studies on your topic.

Alas, researchers! You must beware of writing a literature review that reads like a list of summaries of articles one after the other (Neuman, 2009). Your literature review must be organized into a coherent whole and should be presented in an organized fashion. A researcher should try to organize the literature into subcategories based on common themes between articles. You might choose to divide and organize your literature based on subject matter. If you want to do this, you can identify four or five different dimensions linking studies you have read. Then separate your articles into those that fit into the different dimensions. You might review three or four scholarly articles in each section. Shockley and Frederick's (2010) literature review on African-centered education is divided into subsections based on subject matter. The subheadings the authors used were identity and Pan-Africanism; African culture and values; reattachment; Black nationalism; community control and institution building; education, not schooling; and implications for policy and practice. Each of these subsections of Shockley and Frederick's review consisted of critical analysis of different dimensions of African-centered education. What will the subsections of your own literature review be?

You might also divide your literature review into different sections based on methods of data collection. To do this, you could separate your reviews by placing those studies that were conducted using experimental designs into one subsection, those conducted using interviews into a second subsection, those conducted using observations into a third subsection, and those conducted using questionnaire data into a fourth subsection.

You could also divide your literature into different subcategories based on sample population characteristics such as age, race, or sex. Finally, you could organize your literature based on theoretical approaches.

What is the best way to organize your literature review into a coherent whole? The choice is yours. Nevertheless, your research must be organized in a logical and systematic way. However, your literature review should not just be a string of reviews one after the other in no logical sequence. To find out the best way to organize your literature review, you must comb through all of your sources to find out how they relate to one another, how they are distinct from one another, and what themes you can find connecting your sources. Group your studies together based on the common themes you are able to identify. Once you have finished with the body of your literature review, you must organize the last section of your literature review into a final summary.

Final Summary

In the final paragraph(s) of your literature review you should summarize all of the studies you reviewed with a focus on the patterns you noticed in the existing literature. You must explain to the reader how the reviewed studies relate to your own study. Make sure that your final section summarizes the most important studies, captures the major themes of your review, and suggests why there needs to be more research on the topic. The final section should not be too long, so you should not mention every study covered in your literature review. It should focus on those studies that are most directly related to your topic. In addition to summarizing the major findings of the studies you reviewed, summarize the major contradictions, gaps, and limitations of those studies. Explain what future research needs to do to address those gaps. Explain the things that future research must address to advance the topic. In this final section it is time for you to explain how the research that you are proposing addresses one or more of the gaps in previous research that you have pointed out. Explain existing needs for new research, and how your proposed study seeks to address one or more of those needs.

Referencing and Citing Sources

Citing sources or referencing past research on your topic as you write is very important. Referencing other scholars lets the reader know that you are knowledgeable of the historical development and existing information on your topic. It also lets people know that you understand how your research fits into or builds upon the research of other scholars who have studied your topic or related topics (Bryman, 2008). Referencing is also a way for writers to demonstrate their understanding of their subject areas. You indicate or reference your sources in the text of your writing and in a references or works cited list at the end of your paper. In the text of your document you use in-text citation. Your literature review should be the most heavily cited section of your research proposal. Remember that if you make a claim, you are responsible for providing a citation to back it up. Your reader should not have to take your word for it. For directions on how to style in-text citations and works cited/bibliography sections, see the APA website (http://www.apastyle.org) or the MLA website (http://www.mla.org/).

The Structure of a Research Proposal

A **research proposal** is a detailed description of the research project that you intend to pursue. If you intend to carry out a research project, you may have to write a research proposal first. Your research proposal should include several basic components: an introduction, a literature review, a methodology, a works cited section, and several appendices. Each of these basic components consists of the subsections explained below.

Introduction

The purpose of your introduction is to establish what you are researching, why it's important, and what you intend to accomplish by researching it. The introduction is composed of two things: a statement of the problem or condition and a statement of the purpose. Your **statement of the problem** should be an explanation of the importance of your topic. You can establish this by explaining who and how many people are affected by it and how. Use evidence to state your case. However, be sure to be realistic and not to exaggerate the problem. Your statement of the problem should explain why your research topic is important to society, the Africana (Black) community, or some segment of the Africana (Black) community. According to Booth and fellow researchers (1995), you can think of the statement of the problem as having two objectives. The first is to establish that there is some condition of incomplete knowledge or understanding about your topic. The second objective is to explain the consequences that continuing with this flawed or incomplete knowledge and understanding will have for the African/Black community and society at large. Your **statement of the purpose** should be an explanation of why you are conducting your research project. This statement should explain how your research will help society to better understand or address the problem you have stated in a more fruitful way.

Literature Review

Your literature review should follow your introduction. The literature review allows you to go into more depth than you did in your introduction. After reading your literature review, your readers should know what other aspects of your topic other researchers have investigated, what approaches they have taken, what methods they have used, what results they have found, and the implications of those results. The reader should be aware of any gaps in the existing research. Regarding your own research, the reader should be aware of your own research question(s) and how your research will attempt to fill one or more of those gaps.

Methodology

Your methodology section should include a description of any paradigms, theories, or models you will use in your research. It should also explain why those concepts are the best suited to guide and explain your research. Your methodology should also include a description of any methods, procedures, and analytical tools you will use. After you explain the frameworks you will use, your methodology should include a methods section that explains what tools of data collection you intend to use: interviews, questionnaires, ethnography, and so forth. You must also include a section describing your participants, instruments, and procedure.

PARTICIPANTS/ELEMENTS: You must describe your participants by explaining their characteristics in terms of race, gender, age, grade, socioeconomic status, or any other important features. Explain how many participants you intend to have (It should not be an arbitrary number). Then explain why you need the population size that you state. If you are not using human subjects, explain whatever unit of analysis you intend to study. If you are not researching human beings but are instead studying some objects, they are called *elements* and not *participants*. Are you researching a population that has any mental or physical handicaps? Will the participants have any health problems? You must also explain how you will gain access to this population. How will you recruit them? If you are going to get access to a population by going through an institution, then explain how you will go about acquiring permission. Place any letters in your appendices.

INSTRUMENTS: You must provide a detailed explanation of any data collection tools that you will use. Describe the purpose, dimensions, and items of your instrument. Provide an operationalization of your variables. If applicable, state how you will calculate scores, what the scores will mean, and how you will interpret them. If you are conducting an experiment, describe in detail what stimulus you will use, and why. What will different responses mean or indicate? If you will be using observation, describe in detail what variables you will be observing, how you will observe them, and why. Also include an observation code sheet that charts specifically what you will be looking for. Include a copy of your instrument in an appendix.

PROCEDURE: You must also explain your research procedure. It should include a description of what your research participants will experience from start to finish. Also include all of the steps you will take in your research process from start to finish using times, dates, lengths, and durations.

DISSEMINATION PLAN: Your dissemination plan should include at least three specific institutions with which the results of your study will be shared. In this section, you should name those institutions and provide a justification for why you have chosen to share the results of your studies with them. You must explain why the institutions you have chosen are in the best positions to improve people's lives with the results of your study.

Works Cited

The works cited section of your paper should include an alphabetized list of your sources in a proper and consistent style (APA, MLA, etc.).

Appendices

Finally, your appendices should be located after your works cited section. You should provide copies of several documents in your appendixes. There should be one item in each appendix, and each appendix should be labeled properly (i.e., Appendix A, Appendix B, etc.). In your appendices, you should provide a copy of your questionnaire, survey, interview questions, observation code sheets, and so on. Each should be in a separate appendix. You should provide a copy of your consent form. If necessary, include your assent form and parental consent forms for your participants and their legal guardians to complete. You should also provide a copy of your letter(s) of permission written to any institutions that allow you access to people or other units of analysis. Also include copies of any advertisements for posting or distribution at institutions or agencies for the purpose of recruiting people to participate in your study. Create an appendix that includes your research certification (certificate), any letter confirming that you have gained approval to conduct your research, or any letter granting you access to an institution.

Key Terms

Intersecting Interests

Theory

Literature Review

Research Proposal

Research Question

Statement of the Problem

Statement of the Purpose

Thinking about Science

Activity 1

Using a library search database such as Academic Search Complete, JSTOR, or Proquest, locate the full text of the following study:

Cunningham, G., & Regan, M. (2012). Political activism, racial identity and the commercial endorsement of athletes. *International Review for the Sociology of Sport*, 47(6), 657–669.

- Read the article and identify the following information:
- What is the authors' research question?
- What theoretical framework(s) do the authors refer to?
- What are the key variables in the study?
- What method(s) of data collection are used in the study?

- What unit of analysis is examined in the study?
- What are the key findings of the study?
- What is the significance of the study? How can the data be used to benefit the population being studied?
- What were the strengths and limitations of the study?
- If there were limitations, how could future studies improve upon this study's findings?

Activity 2

Design your own study. Identify the following components of the study you would like to propose.

- Topic: _____
- Research question: _____
- Variables (independent and dependent): _____
- The unit of analysis: _____

CHAPTER SIX

Measuring Social Reality

Through exacting long-term observation, our ancestors determined that seasonal cycles, vegetation growth cycles, and even animal migration and mating cycles correlated with the cyclic changing position of the moon and sun. That information provided them with a reliable and perpetual time frame—a calendar—to schedule their social festivals and rituals and to know the optimum planting and harvest times. Their culture, along with their economy, was wedded to the sky. In striving for greater calendrical accuracy, the astronomer priests of many African families, such as the Dogon of Mali in Africa, incorporated the rising and setting of certain stars or groups of stars into their various calendars. Such accuracy was necessary to make certain that the sacred holy days coincided precisely with the end or beginning of one of nature's basic cycles, thus maintaining their community's harmonious relationship with nature. Politics was also involved: priests derived their power and influence by keeping an accurate calendar.

—HUNTER HAVELIN ADAMS III (2001)

Ancient Africans and other traditional societies around the globe used scientific observations of the world around them to organize and improve their societies. Presently, social scientists who are interested in using research to improve their communities and the world around them make similar use of scientific observation.

The health consequences of pollution make it necessary to measure the levels of carbon dioxide in the air. Presidential campaigns make it necessary to measure public opinion about political issues. Racial gaps in learning outcomes make it necessary to measure the achievement levels of students by race.

Imagine that you are interested in the growth of a particular Black-owned business. You might simply count the number of customers who enter that business. You would be conducting measurement. You might decide to organize a systematic schedule with predetermined days and times for you to observe. Which days of the week? What times of the day? In time you would be able to draw conclusions about the levels of consumer traffic at the business over a period of time. You might be able to state at what times of the day traffic is lower or higher. This is measurement. Before analysis can be done, researchers conceptualize and define variables so that they can be measured. How variables are defined determines how you can measure them and at what level you can measure them. Once you determine how to measure variables, the measurements must be assessed to determine how reliable and valid they are. These issues are explained in this chapter.

Measuring

Suppose you are leading a new and innovative program aimed at increasing adult literacy in your community. How will you know your program is working? How will you identify what aspects of your program are working and those that need to be cancelled or improved? You would need to measure any changes in adult literacy scores as a result of your program. How will you decide what school you want to attend or what school you want your child to attend? Would you look at different school graduation rates? Would you be interested in the rate at which a school's graduates are accepted to 4-year colleges? These questions require measurement. The president might be interested in setting aside money for job growth for cities in the country with the highest levels of unemployment. Targeting this kind of community development would require the careful measuring of unemployment rates. These are measurements that help people make decisions and improve human services. Make no mistake; measurement is a critical component of advancing a society.

Measurement refers to "the process of describing abstract concepts in terms of specific indicators by assigning numbers or other symbols to these indicants in accordance with rules." (Monette, Sullivan, & DeJong, 2005, p. 100). Measurement is an essential part of the process of moving research from the abstract to the concrete or from conceptualization to application. It is the process of transforming abstract ideas into concrete data. Measurement is not something that is totally foreign to you. In fact, it is something that you do in your daily life. You may have started a new exercise regimen to reduce your body fat. To *measure* the effectiveness of your new regimen, you may get onto a digital body-fat scale to monitor changes in your body fat over time. If you want your rice to turn out just right, you may need to be sure to add exactly two cups of water. A *measuring* cup may be your tool of choice. When you were a child you may have been interested in how much taller you were from year to year. Do you remember how you found out how much taller you grew? Did you make marks on your wall? Did you find out at the hospital after a doctor had you stand next to a long ruler? Each of these is a form of measurement. In the social world, you might also want to *measure* the effectiveness of an afterschool math tutoring program. You might measure the effectiveness of that program by evaluating the math scores of the students participating in the program.

Measurement begins at the conceptual level. A researcher must have a conceptual understanding of what is to be measured. This meaning is developed through the process of conceptualization. Conceptualization occurs when a researcher begins to put his or her thoughts about an idea into words. This process leads to the development of concepts. A *concept* is an abstract representation of an idea. In scientific research, concepts are represented as the variables in a research question. Concepts are generally used to organize ideas about the social world. Researchers often begin with concepts that they intend to refine into variables and ultimately measure (O'Sullivan, Rassel, & Berner, 2010). A variable is a refined concept, and its meaning is initially expressed through a conceptual definition (O'Sullivan et al., 2010). *Racism* is a concept, and the process of conceptualization leads to a conceptual definition of it. A **conceptual definition** is an abstract description of a variable that a researcher intends to measure. Conceptual definitions are like the definitions you are likely to find in a dictionary in that they are stated in the abstract rather than measureable or quantifiable terms.

Imagine that a researcher begins to conceptualize racial identity. Janet Helms and Thomas Parham (1996) conceptually define *racial identity* as a sense of collective identification based on one's membership in a particular racial group. However, that definition is a conceptual definition; it doesn't tell you how racial identity can be measured. The next step in the process of conceptualization is to move from a conceptual definition to an operational definition. An **operational definition** is a definition stated in terms of the specific procedures and operations necessary to measure a variable. An operational definition explains how a variable will be measured. First, consider all dimensions of the variable to be measured. Concepts such as racial identity often consist of several dimensions. To measure the racial identity of African American youth, Belgrave et al. (1994) define several dimensions of racial identity, including an *affective* dimension, a *cognitive* dimension, a *behavioral* dimension, and *physical attributes*. Once the dimensions are defined, it is necessary

Figure 6.1

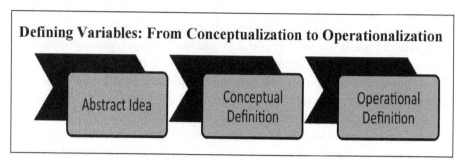

to have *indicators* of a variable if the variable is to be measured. An **indicator** is an observation of evidence of the attributes or properties of a phenomenon. An indicator can come in several forms. A question or a series of questions can be indicators of a phenomenon. For example, if completed by a person, a self-esteem questionnaire may be filled with questions or statements that indicate something about a person's self-esteem. If researchers wanted to interview individuals to measure the relationship between their levels of education and overall life satisfaction, they might ask the person a question as an indicator of how much education they have received, such as "What is the highest level of education that you have completed?" Structured observation is another means by which indicators of vari-

Exhibit 6.1

Operationalization of Racial Identity

Racial identity was assessed using the Children's Black Identity Scale. Although methodology exists for a more comprehensive assessment of racial identity among children, a short paper\pencil measure was desired because of time constraints. This nine-item scale developed by Belgrave (NTU project, 1994) assesses the extent to which the student endorses affective ("I feel good about being an African American"), cognitive ("African Americans have many good qualities"), and behavioral aspects of racial identity ("African Americans should learn to live and act more like White Americans"), and physical attributes of Black people ("Black people who have light skin and straight hair are more attractive than Black people with darker skin and hair that is not straight"). A 3-point scale was used. Students circled 1 if they agreed with the statement, 2 if they disagreed with the statement, and 3 if they were unsure. Students' scores were summed and then averaged to obtain a composite score that could range from 1 to 3. Cronbach's alpha coefficient for internal consistency using the current sample was .68.

ables can be observed. For example, if a researcher were interested in observing *disruptive behavior* in a classroom, s/he may pay attention to students arguing with the teacher, refusing to follow instruction, fighting, and inappropriately running around the classroom as some indicators of disruptive behavior.

In addition to Belgrave, Cherry, Cunningham, Walwyn, Letlaka-Rennert, & Phillips's (1994) definition of racial identity and the dimensions into which it has been divided, it is necessary to have some operational means of measuring the dimensions of racial identity by assessing their indicators. For example, as an indicator of the extent to which a research participant endorses affective racial identity, Belgrave et al.'s (1994) instrument includes the item "I feel good about being African American." Respondents may reply to this statement by indicating whether or not they agree, disagree, or are unsure about the statement. Additionally, Belgrave et al. (1994) have designed a questionnaire including several indicators of each dimension of racial identity, ultimately producing scores representing each participant's racial identity attitudes. Look at Belgrave's operational definition of racial identity attitudes (Exhibit 6.1).

Defining Variables

Reliability

Reliability refers to the consistency of a measure. A measurement is considered reliable when it yields consistent results. Researchers should not expect to design a measure that is completely reliable or valid; however, they should strive to create measures that are both as reliable and as valid as possible. The more reliable and valid a measure is, the more believable, dependable, and truthful it is considered to be.

Three aspects of reliability are **stability**, **internal reliability**, and **inter-observer reliability**. You may have a scale that measures body fat. Suppose that you get on the scale and it indicates that you have 27% body fat; then you get off the scale and step back onto the scale, repeating this process three more times. If the body fat scale is reliable, it should give you a measure of 27% each time. An unreliable scale would give you different percentages each time, even when your true body fat percentages have gone unchanged. This is the aspect of reliability called *stability*. **Stability** is the aspect that refers to how consistent a measure's results are over time. If a measure is stable, a researcher can be confident that the measure will have little variation over time. The best way of checking the stability of a method is the *test-retest method*. To implement the test-retest method, the researcher must administer the test on one occasion (T^1) and again on another occasion (T^2). A correlation is a measurement of the strength of the relationship between two or more variables. After administering the test-retest method, a researcher should expect to have a high correlation (strong relationship) between the outcomes observed during the first test and those observed during the second test.

$$T^1 \quad T^2$$
$$Obs^1 \quad Obs^2$$

There is evidence that high rates of religious activity are associated with lower blood pressure and hypertension. African Americans as a racial group engage in higher-than-average rates of religiosity (Barna Group, 2005). Loustalot, Wyatt, Sims, Ellison, Taylor, and Underwood (2011) investigated the relationship between the daily spiritual experiences of African Americans and their systolic blood pressure and hypertension levels. The instrument they used is called the Daily Spiritual Experiences Scale (DSES). The DSES is a 16-item measure that is designed to assess feelings of closeness to God and the everyday experiences that grow out of those feelings. To test the stability of the DSES, it has been subjected to the test-retest method. It has yielded high correlations, indicating that the measure appears to be stable and that its respondents' answers can be relied upon.

Internal reliability refers to the degree to which the indicators that make up an instrument are consistent and relate to one another. This is important because sometimes a researcher may have an instrument with multiple indicators that are supposed to be measuring the same thing. However, it may be the case that the indicators are not all measuring the same thing and are unrelated to one another. Suppose you created a 20-item self-esteem measure. When respondents complete your questionnaire, their answer to each question contributes to an overall self-esteem score. It is important to know that each of those items is related to the others, giving you a coherent instrument that measures self-esteem. But how do you know? Internal reliability is often gauged by implementing the *split-half approach* to assessing reliability. Using the split-half method of reliability, the indicators of an instrument are randomly divided in two, with each half being treated as a separate scale. A correlation is then calculated between people's responses to questions in the two halves. A correlation of r=.80 or higher is necessary to have a strong degree of reliability. To test the reliability of your self-esteem instrument, you would administer your instrument to a group of respondents. Then the 20 indicators would be divided into two halves at random. Next, your respondents' answers to each of the groups of ten questions will be calculated. If the instrument is reliable, the respondents' answers to each set of ten questions should be relatively the same. You can use statistical software such as the Statistical Package for the Social Sciences (SPSS) to calculate the correlation between the two sets of answers.

Baro, Onyenania, and Osaheni (2010) assessed the information-seeking behavior of Nigerian undergraduate students to improve the library information and library management services at universities within Nigeria. The authors created a 30-item information-seeking questionnaire called Information Seeking Behaviour of Undergraduate Students in the Humanities Questionnaire (ISBUSHQ). To establish the reliability of their instrument, they employed the split-half approach. This means that they divided their 30 items into two halves and performed a statistical correlation to determine the strength of the relationship between each half. Their calculations produced a correlation coefficient of .78, indicating a moderate level of reliability that comes close to the conventionally accepted level of .80.

The split-half method has some limitations. The correlation coefficients that come from the split-half method can underestimate the reliability of a measure. Longer scales are generally more reliable, however, because the split-half method involves dividing a scale into two independent halves so they can be compared; each scale is analyzed at half of the size it would be in a single scale. The problem is sometimes corrected by using the Spearman-Brown formula:

Exhibit 6.2

Illustrating the Spearman-Brown Formula

To illustrate the effect of the Spearman- Brown formula, suppose we have a 20-item scale with a correlation between the two halves of $r_i = .70$, which is smaller than the minimum needed to demonstrate reliability. The Spearman – Brown formula corrects as follows:

$$r = \frac{(2)(.70)}{1+.70} = \frac{1.40}{1.70} = .82$$

It can be seen that the Spearman – Brown formula has a substantial effect, increasing the uncorrected coefficient from well below .80 to just over it. If we had obtained the results with an actual scale, we would conclude that its reliability was now adequate. (Monette, Sullivan and DeJong, 2005, p 117).

In the above equation, .70 represents the uncorrected correlation coefficient, and r represents the corrected correlation coefficient. **Inter-observer reliability** refers to an assessment of how similar or how consistent observers or interviewers are when measuring the same research subject or object. If multiple researchers are observing classroom disruption in the same 20 math classes, we would want to be confident that their assessments should be the same or very similar. This is because we do not want our measurements to be too reliant on the personal biases and opinions of the observers.

Validity

A measure can be reliable and consistent but lack validity, such as a scale that consistently gives you the wrong weight (off by two pounds every time!). If you are assessing the validity of a measure, you are asking the question, "Does this measure accurately measure the variable or concept that it is intended to measure?" **Validity** refers to the truthfulness, correctness, and accuracy of a measurement. When people ask whether or not an instrument that is intended to measure emotional health actually measures emotional health, they are questioning the validity of that instrument. When people question whether or not the Body Mass Index (BMI) accurately reflects whether a person is over or underweight, they are questioning the validity of the BMI. Similarly, when students in a class question whether or not their score on the last quiz was an accurate reflection of their knowledge, they, too, are questioning the validity of the last quiz. To ensure validity, it is important to be sure that there is a clear relationship between the way a variable is conceptually defined and how it is operationally defined. There are several different types of validity that reflect the different ways of gauging the validity of a measure.

FACE VALIDITY is concerned with whether or not there is a reasonable relationship between a variable and a measure. Face validity is the minimum requirement that a measure must meet. It is an intuitive judgment by people who are knowledgeable about the variable in question. Imagine that someone constructs a measure of healthy dietary habits that consists of asking participants how many apples they eat per week. The measure clearly lacks face validity because healthy dietary habits are far more dynamic that how many apples an individual eats per week. If a measure apparently reflects the content of the variable it is intended to measure, then it can be said to have face validity. It is the easiest and also the weakest measure of validity, but any measure must at the very least have face validity.

CONTENT VALIDITY refers to the extent to which a measure's items or indicators accurately represent the phenomena being assessed. For example, if a test on African American history had only questions about slavery, it would not be content valid because it would not be representative of the entire subject area (Vogt, 1999). Content validity represents how well a measure captures the range of meanings in a concept. The Gender Inequality Index is a measure that assesses the country-level disadvantage of women in three key dimensions: reproductive health, empowerment, and labor market. Reproductive health is indicated by the maternal mortality rate and the adolescent fertility rate. Empowerment is indicated by the percentage of seats in Parliament that each sex holds, and the education attainment levels of each sex. The labor market dimension is measured by women's participation in the workforce. Obviously, Gender Inequality is a multidimensional construct. If the Gender Inequality Index attempted to measure gender inequality only by observing women's levels of participation in a country's workforce, it would lack content validity because it would not accurately represent the multidimensionality of gender inequality.

CRITERION VALIDITY indicates a concept by way of a standard or criterion. To establish the criterion validity of a measure, it is compared to another measure of the same concept or variable. One type of criterion-related validity is *concurrent validity*, in which a measure or instrument under evaluation is compared to another existing measure, or data collected simultaneously in another study. If a researcher were interested in determining the validity of a questionnaire measuring the college readiness of high school students, he or she might calculate the correlation between the scores they obtain by way of the college readiness instrument and scores from some other measure. Can you think of a criterion? For example, a researcher might correlate the scores obtained by way of the College Readiness Questionnaire with teacher ratings on how college ready each student participant is. If there is a strong correlation between the teachers' rating of college readiness and the scores students earn on the College Readiness Questionnaire, this can be taken as evidence of the validity of the College Readiness Questionnaire. It is conventionally accepted that having a correlation of $r = .50$ is the minimum required to establish the criterion-related validity of a measure. Often concurrent validity is assessed when a researcher selects a concurrent criterion on which people are known to differ and that is also relevant to the variable in question. For example, an instrument might be put together to assess high school students' school satisfaction by way of a School Satisfaction Scale. To measure the validity of the School Satisfaction Scale, it would be helpful to identify a criterion on which students are known to differ and that is related to the variable in question, school satisfaction. An example is student absenteeism. (Some students are more likely to miss school than others.) The researcher might calculate a correlation to determine if students who are more satisfied with their schooling are more likely to attend school regularly, and vice versa. If it is determined that there is no relationship between school satisfaction scores and absenteeism, the validity of the School Satisfaction Scale will be questionable, and there will be doubt about whether or not it truly measures school satisfaction.

The drawback to assessing criterion-related validity often lies in the validity of the existing measure that is used for comparison. If that measure lacks validity, then all a researcher can conclude is that his or her measure is as valid as an invalid comparison. For example, if the College Readiness Questionnaire results are compared to racially biased teacher ratings of students' college readiness, then the teacher ratings are not a good comparison and do not validate the College Readiness Questionnaire. For this reason, if criterion-related validity is to be used to assess the validity of an instrument, researchers must be careful to be sure that the measures they use for comparison have already been established to be valid.

PREDICTIVE VALIDITY is a kind of criterion validity in which a measure or instrument's validity is assessed based on its prediction of some future state of affairs (Monette et al., 2005). The difference between predictive validity and concurrent validity lies in the fact that predictive validity uses future criteria instead of already-existing or contemporary criteria as a measure of validity. A researcher using predictive validity would take future school attendance rates as a criterion against which the validity of the School Satisfaction Scale would be assessed. Again, the difference between predictive and concurrent validity is that in predictive validity, future criteria are used instead of simultaneous or already-existing criteria.

CONSTRUCT VALIDITY is a type of validity that is derived from a theory that is relevant to the concept in question. Using construct validity, an instrument is validated by analyzing how it is correlated with the concepts and assumptions of a theoretical framework designed to explain the relevant variable. If it is discovered that there are significant correlations between an instrument and the concepts and assumptions of a theoretical framework associated with the variable at hand, the instrument can be said to have construct validity. New cases of sexually transmitted diseases (STDs) and sexually transmitted infections (STIs) disproportionately affect adolescents (DiClemente et al., 2010). Some social scientists have studied the social/environmental factors that contribute to adolescent risk-taking behaviors; however, there is a growing body of knowledge looking into personality constructs that may be associated with sexual risk-taking behavior (DiClemente et al., 2010). Sexual sensation seeking refers to the seeking of different levels and kinds of sexual sensations and the willingness to incur different kinds and levels of risks for those experiences. Knowing the sexual sensation-seeking attitudes and behaviors of youth can aid interventions that seek to prevent the acquisition of STIs and STDs. DiClemente and fellow researchers (2010) validated the Sexual Sensation Seeking Scale for African American Adolescent Women (SSSA) using many measures including construct validity. Theoretical constructs suggest that there is a relationship between sexual sensation seeking and negative coping strategies such as sexual compulsiveness, sexual risk taking, alcohol abuse, drug abuse, and possessing an external locus of control. DiClemente and colleagues (2010) found the SSSA to be significantly correlated with negative coping strategies, number of lifetime vaginal, oral, and anal sex partners, having sex while high on alcohol or drugs, and the amount of time one could go without sex. These significant correlations with concepts that come from theoretical frameworks that seek to explain sexual risk-taking behavior establish the construct validity of the SSSA as an instrument. Simply stated, the theory says these relationships exist, and the evidence shows that they indeed do exist; therefore there is construct validity. However, in assessing construct validity, one must be careful to make sure that the theory or theories being used are not misguided. Use of a misguided theory can lead a researcher to draw a false conclusion about an instrument's construct validity. Remember that theories explain relationships between variables. When the data collected show evidence that those relationships exist, the measure can be said to have construct validity.

Reliability, Validity, and Preventing Error

Reliability and validity are two distinct concepts, but they are related. If you have collected data in a reliable way, you have collected them consistently and not sloppily, erratically, or inconsistently. This only makes your data dependable. Reliability is a necessary requirement for having validity. You cannot have validity without having reliability; however, you can have reliability without having validity. You may have a clock that is 5 minutes too fast. You can rely on that clock to wake you when it reaches 5:00 a.m. every morning. However, in reality it is waking you up at 4:55 a.m. The clock is reliable, but it is definitely not giving you a valid (accurate) measure of the time. On the other hand, a clock that tells you it is 5:00 a.m. when it really is 5:00 a.m. is both reliable and valid. Therefore, in social science, you can have a reliable measure that is also an invalid measure.

To avoid the risk of conducting unreliable and invalid research, there are several things that a researcher must be sure to do. Many researchers run into reliability and validity issues because they are not completely clear on what they are measuring. For this reason it is important that researchers operationalize their variables before conducting research so that they are clear on the indicators of their variables. It is also important to actively pretest and pilot measurements before actually conducting research. This is important because researchers get helpful feedback by actively seeking it from subjects about the clarity of their questions and instructions. When constructing measurement instruments, it is important to use multiple indicators. As discussed above, measurements are more reliable when there are more indicators. Moreover, where feasible, it is important to seek the highest level of measurement possible to improve the quality of data collected.

Levels of Measurement

Researchers have the responsibility of conceptualizing and defining the variables they attempt to measure. However, variables differ in how they can be measured

Table 6.1

LEVELS OF MEAS-UREMENT	MUTUALLY EXCLU-SIVE CATEGORIES	RANKED/ FIXED ORDER	EQUAL DISTANCE BETWEEN CATEGORIES MEASURED	TRUE ZERO
Nominal	Yes			
Ordinal	Yes	Yes		
Interval	Yes	Yes	Yes	
Ratio	Yes	Yes	Yes	Yes

and what conclusions can be drawn about them. Because of this diversity, there is a set of rules that explains what mathematical procedures can be performed on data at different levels. Those rules are explained by levels of measurement. **Levels of measurement** are determined by the characteristics of the concept or variable that you as the researcher are trying to measure. The characteristics of the concept you are attempting to measure limit the levels of measurement you can use and the mathematical operations you can perform. There are continuous variables and discrete variables. **Continuous variables** have an infinite number of values such as temperature, age, and income (Neuman, 2009). By contrast, **discrete variables** have a fixed, limited, and distinct set of values or categories such as gender (e.g. male, female, transgender, and gender queer), race (African American, Asian, Caucasian, etc.), religion (Christian, Muslim, Jewish, etc.). There are four levels of measurement: nominal, ordinal, interval, and ratio (Table 6.1). Discrete variables are nominal- and ordinal-level variables, while continuous variables are interval- and ratio-level variables. Whether or not a variable is continuous or discrete affects its level of measurement.

NOMINAL MEASURES classify observations into mutually exclusive categories. Nominal data are capable only of indicating differences between categories. They merely offer names and labels for characteristics. Numbers have no order or value in nominal data; they are only used to categorize data. Nominal-level measures classify data into mutually exclusive categories that represent data in name at the theoretical level. Some nominal-level variables are race, sex/gender, ethnicity, religion, state of residence, and political party. For example, in the 2010 Census (U.S. Census Bureau, 2010), the variable *sex* is defined as a dichotomous variable consisting of two categories: male and female. For the purpose of data analysis, we might assign a number to represent each category. For example, we could represent females as 1 and males as 2. However, remember that with nominal-level data the numbers are purely arbitrary, meaning that they are not to be ranked. They possess no mathematical significance, magnitude, or order. None of the mathematical operations such as adding, multiplying, or dividing can be done legitimately on nominal data, because they are merely symbols representing different categories. For example, a male could just as easily be represented as a 1 and a female as a 2. The fact that females are represented as 2 and males are represented as 1 doesn't mean that females have twice as much of the variable "sex" as males. The following questions collect nominal-level data on the variable political party.

> With what political party are you a member? (circle your answer)
> - Democrat
> - Republican
> - Independent
> - Other:_____

Remember that political party is a nominal variable whose categories cannot be rank ordered. If we coded Democrats as 1, Republicans as 2, Independents as 3, and Other as 4, this does not mean that Republicans are more political than Democrats, or that Independents are three times more political than Democrats. A relationship survey might pose the question:

> What is your marital status? (circle your answer)
> 1. married
> 2. single
> 3. separated
> 4. divorced
> 5. widowed
> 6. engaged
> 7. annulled
> 8. cohabitating

This is yet another nominal variable: it will indicate how many participants in a study are married, single, and so forth. However, because it is a nominal variable you cannot conclude that someone who is engaged has more "marital status" than someone who is separated. For example, a city concerned with its citizens' preparation for extremely cold weather might produce a housing survey asking individuals what type of heating they have in their housing unit. The options might be 1 = electric, 2 = gas, 3 = oil, 4 = none, 5 = other. Like other nominal measures, it would be meaningless to calculate a numerical mean for this measure. What would an average of 2.5 mean? It would mean nothing because this measure is only useful for categorizing the types of heating residents have.

Sometimes variables are conceptualized and operationalized in such a way that they have an inherent order. **ORDINAL MEASURES** indicate order and rank among the categories of a variable. Ordinal measures represent a higher level of measurement than nominal measures because, in addition to being made up of mutually exclusive categories, categories can be rank ordered in ordinal-level measures. A typical example is the agreement scale with these response options: strongly disagree, disagree, undecided, agree, and strongly agree. It is clear that "strongly agree" represents a greater level of agreement than "agree," and so on. If you were studying the quality of dietary habits in inner-city neighborhoods, you might ask residents the following question:

How often do you eat from fast food restaurants? (circle your answer)
- Every day
- 3–5 times a week
- Once a week
- Once a month
- Never

What makes the question above an ordinal measure is the fact that when measuring ordinal variables, the categories of those variables can be rank ordered, indicating that one response represents more or less of the variable in question than another. For example, an individual who responds by filling in the circle next to "Every day" eats from fast food restaurants more often than an individual who fills in the circle next to "3–5 times a week." The categories of ordinal measures are not, however, equally spaced. This means that even though the difference between the first and second responses in the fast food question are one rank apart, the distance between them is not necessarily the same. If person #1 selects response one (Every day) and person #2 selects response two (3–5 times a week), you can say that person #1 eats at fast food restaurants more often than person #2. However, you cannot tell how much more often. The lack of equal spacing between ranks in ordinal measurements limits the mathematical operations that can be performed on the data. As with nominal measurements, one cannot add, subtract, multiply, or divide ordinal scales. The only characteristic that separates nominal measurements from ordinal measurements is the fixed order among categories in ordinal measurements.

When measuring interval variables, the distances between categories are identical. **INTERVAL MEASURES** possess the same characteristics as both nominal and ordinal variables, with the addition of the fact that there is a fixed distance between points in interval measures. This makes interval measurements a higher level of measurement than both nominal and ordinal measures. However, interval data does not have a true zero point. Two examples of interval measurements are Fahrenheit and Celsius measurements of temperature. Unlike nominal and ordinal measures, the different temperatures have a fixed distance between categories. For example, the difference between five degrees and six degrees is the same difference between six degrees and seven degrees. The difference is one degree. However, neither Celsius nor Fahrenheit possesses a true zero point, in which a score of zero represents an absence of the variable in question. Instead, they both possess an arbitrary zero point. For example, a temperature of zero does not indicate that there is no temperature outside.

Another example of an interval measurement is the Intelligence Quotient (IQ) score. It has a fixed distance between categories, meaning that the difference between a score of 95 and 96 is the same as the difference between 96 and 97. However, like temperature, it does not have a true zero, but an arbitrary zero point, meaning that a score of zero does not indicate that an individual has zero intelligence, even though he or she has a score of zero. All measures like addition, subtraction, multiplication, and division can be performed on ratio-level data. However, because there is no true zero, one cannot claim that an individual with an IQ score of 180 is twice as intelligent as an individual with an IQ score of 90. There is considerable debate over the level of measurement of attitude scales like frequency scales (never, rarely, sometimes, most of the time, and always) or agreement scales (strongly disagree, disagree, undecided, agree, and strongly agree). The argument that attitude scales can be treated as interval scales is based on the belief that the difference between categories like *most of the time* and *always* is the same as the difference between *rarely* and *never*. Nevertheless, the debate over the level of measurement status of attitude scales goes on.

RATIO MEASURES possess all the characteristics of nominal, ordinal, and interval measures with one exception. The ratio level of measurement is a higher level of measurement because its measures also possess a true zero point, in which a score of zero is meaningful and represents an absence of the variable in question. Consider the following question:

Fill in the blank.
The last time you went to the gym, how many minutes did you spend on the treadmill?_____

The above question is a ratio question. Like an interval measure, there is a fixed distance between points, such that the difference between an individual who ran the treadmill for 15 minutes and one who ran for 16 minutes is one minute, the same as the difference between a person who ran 17 minutes and one who ran 18 minutes. However, unlike interval measures such as IQ and Fahrenheit, there is a true zero in the above (treadmill) measure, such that an individual who writes zero into the blank truly did not run for any number of minutes, whereas a temperature of zero doesn't mean there is no amount of temperature outside. Can you imagine there being no temperature outside? No, you can't, and that is because temperature is a variable without a true zero. One measure is absolute and the other is arbitrary. Remember that all measures such as addition, subtraction, multiplication, and division can be performed on ratio-level data. In addition, one can make comparisons such as the statement that an individual who ran for 20 minutes ran for twice as long as an individual who ran for 10 minutes. The following are ratio measurements.

> Fill in the blanks.
> - How old are you? _____ years
> - How much do you weigh? _____ pounds

It is important to appreciate that the level of measurement depends on how a variable is defined. For example, the questions above could be redefined at the ordinal level. For example, one could ask:

> - How many years of education have you completed? _____ years
>   (fill in the blank)

The above question is a ratio-level item. But it could just as well be asked as an ordinal-level item, as here:

> How many years of education have you completed? (circle your answer)
> - 0–6 years
> - 7–10 years
> - 11–12 years
> - 13–15 years
> - 16–18 years
> - 18 or more

It could also be asked in the following ordinal manner:

> What is the highest level of education you have attained? (circle your answer)
> - No School
> - Nursery school to 4th grade
> - 5th grade or 6th grade

- 7th grade or 8th grade
- 9th grade
- 10th grade
- 11th grade
- 12th grade, no diploma
- High school graduate— high school diploma or the equivalent (for example, GED)
- Some college credit, but less than 1 year
- 1 or more years of college, no degree
- Associate's degree (for example, AA, AS)
- Bachelor's degree (for example, BA, AB, BS)
- Master's degree (for example, MA, MS, MEng, Med, MSW, MBA)
- Professional Degree (for example, MD, DDS, DVM, LLB, JD)
- Doctoral degree (for example, PhD, EdD)

Key Terms

Conceptual Definition	Levels of Measurement
Construct Validity	Measurement
Content Validity	Nominal Measures
Continuous Variables	Operational Definition
Criterion Validity	Ordinal Measures
Discrete Variables	Predictive Validity
Face Validity	Ratio Measures
Indicator	Reliability
Inter-Observer Reliability	Stability
Internal Reliability	Validity
Interval Measures	

Thinking about Science

Activity 1

Let's create eight questions that attempt to measure the extent to which someone is currently receiving a *quality education*. We have to operationalize quality education. What is a quality education? First, use the Internet to search for definitions. Second, write your own conceptual definition of quality education. Third, think of four aspects/dimensions of a quality education. Then develop two questions (indicators) for each dimension, giving you a total of four indicators of a quality education.

Activity 2

What are the levels of measurement for the following variables?

- Race (African American/Black, White, Asian, etc.)
- Marital Status (single, married, divorced, separated, widowed)
- Number of people living in household
- Score on Scholastic Aptitude Test (SAT)

CHAPTER SEVEN

Sampling Procedures

According to a *New York Times*/CBS News poll taken in April 2009, for the first time in CBS poll-taking history a majority of African Americans reported U.S. race relations to be "good." Fifty-nine percent of African Americans polled indicated that race relations were good, compared to only 29% who answered similarly less than one year before. The poll indicated a 30% rise (CBS News/*New York Times*, 2009). (Consider the fact that the poll was taken shortly after the election of Barack Obama, the first Black president of the United States). White Americans have consistently seen race relations as generally good, however—even White Americans' perceptions of race relations as such rose nearly 10% (from 55% to 65%) (CBS News/*New York Times*, 2009). The poll was conducted by way of a national random sample of 973 Americans, interviewed by telephone April 22–29, 2009. Of the 973 respondents, 701 were White and 212 were Black. Researchers sampled phone numbers using random digit dialing (RDD) of landline telephones and cell phones. CBS and *The New York Times* were both involved in the sampling process. In this chapter we will discuss how CBS and *The New York Times*'s sample of over 900 people can actually represent the attitudes of millions of people. In addition, we will discuss the strategic limitations of the study conducted by CBS News and *The New York Times* and how to avoid them.

When you are running water to take a bath or a shower, how do you know when the water is hot enough or warm enough? You may put your hand into the water stream to *sample* its temperature and adjust the nozzle until the water reaches the temperature you desire. What if your sister invites you to eat a new kind of chicken soup she has come up with during Thanksgiving dinner? What if she is known for putting too much salt in her food? Yuck! How will you make sure the soup is not too salty for you to eat? You may *sample* the soup by sipping half a teaspoon of the soup to be sure that it is not too salty. A mother may warm up a bottle of milk for her newborn to drink, but she may wonder whether or not the milk is too hot. How will she make sure the milk will not be too hot on her baby's tongue? She may *sample* the milk by letting a drop fall on her finger to test the temperature. These are all instances in which people do casual *sampling* in their day-to-day lives. It is not a foreign idea; it is typical and commonplace. Most important, it is a familiar and natural procedure.

The same process of *sampling* is necessary when studying human populations and other units of analysis, such as the study of attitudes about race in the United States just after the election of the United States' first Black president. Once the researchers develop research questions and design a process for answering them, the work is not done. The next step in the process is sampling, which involves selecting the research subjects or participants who will allow you to answer your research question. This chapter describes when different sampling techniques are appropriate or inappropriate. In addition, their strengths and limitations are explained so that you can make important decisions about how to go about selecting a smart sample for your research.

Consider the study of Black and White attitudes about racial progress. What is most significant is not the group of 973 research participants in the above-referenced study. Rather, it is what those participants reveal about the larger population and about the attitudes and thinking of the communities, nations, and the larger world we live in. This is why samples are important. In a casual and everyday sense, you stick your hand in the bathtub hoping it reveals something about the temperature of the whole body of water in the bathtub, and you sample the soup in the hope that it tells you how spicy the whole bowl is. However, what if you stick your hand in the end of the pool that is warm, while the other end is cold? What if you sample a spoonful of soup only to discover that the second spoonful has pepper in it and is too hot? These concerns raise the issue of *sampling error* and *generalizability*. **Generalizing** occurs when you apply the results of the study of a sample to a larger population or a larger reality. This is important, especially in quantitative research, because you sample a population when it is unrealistic to study the entire population. This is one of the strengths of sampling. Sometimes it is unrealistic, too time consuming, cumbersome, or expensive to study an entire population. When this is the case, sampling allows you to study a feasible number of cases from the larger group to draw conclusions that will be relevant to the larger group. This is why CBS News and *The New York Times* didn't study the more than 281 million people in the Unites States: they selected a sample of 973. Second, it is sometimes better to get information from a carefully selected sample than from an entire population. Hard to believe? For example, the census is conducted every 10 years. A census is the name given to a study that attempts to collect data from an entire population. However, the problem with the census comes in the difficulties of studying any large population—*undercounts*. Whenever the census is conducted, some constituencies file lawsuits claiming that they were undercounted and thus are underrepresented. Samples, however, allow a researcher to study a much smaller, manageable population. Studying a sample makes it easier to ensure that a subpopulation is equally *represented*. But wait! Can knowledge gained from a few cases be true for the whole population? This is the question of representativeness. Examining the external validity or generalizability of conclusions drawn about a sample depends on how representative that sample is of the target population it was drawn from. If the sample that is studied is a representative sample, then the conclusions drawn from it can be accurately applied to the larger population.

In qualitative research, the objective of sampling is often different from that in more quantitative research. In qualitative investigation, researchers are often less interested in finding representative samples of a large population than they are in studying some key aspect of social life in a smaller population. For this reason, sampling in qualitative research is sometimes referred to as *theoretical sampling*. Qualitative researchers are less concerned with large populations than they are with finding informative sources that will help deepen their understanding of some aspect of social life. Qualitative studies are usually done on smaller populations and, as a result, they produce data that are not generalizable in the statistical sense (Remler & Van Ryzin, 2011). However, it is said that they produce generalizable theories (Remler & Van Ryzin, 2011). Through more in-depth and detailed observations on small samples, qualitative researchers can identify general features and patterns in data.

The Language of Sampling

A **population** of interest (represented as N) refers to the broad collection of elements (people or things) from which you select your sample. The population need not consist of people; instead, a researcher could be studying nations, cities, regions, photographs, teams, businesses, or houses. For example, you might be interested in Chicago-area public high school students. A target population refers to all of the possible cases of whatever or whoever is being studied in your research—for example, the registered 14–18-year-old high school students at Martin Luther King High School, Paul Robeson High School, and Whitney Young High School. Researchers then use these samples to make *inferences* or generalizations about the population of interest. A **sample** (represented as n) is the specific segment of cases or elements that is selected from a population of interest for the purpose of investigation. Once you have a target population, you can move forward by making or acquiring a sampling frame. A *sampling frame* is a listing or inventory of all of the sampling elements of your target population. If you are studying Chicago-area high school students, your sampling frame may come from the administrative office's lists of all of its currently registered students. Allen, Davey, and Davey (2010) investigated the role that African American church leaders and lay psychologists play in the delivery of mental health services to parishioners. They used a sampling frame that included approximately 25 associate pastors/ministers, 50 deacons/deaconesses, and 200 congregational caregivers/deacon aides (Allen, Davey, & Davey, 2010). From this sampling frame, a sample of 112 participants was randomly selected.

Bias in Sampling

Coverage Bias

Under ideal circumstances, the sampling frame covers the entire target population. However, sampling frames are often limited in some ways. When this occurs, a study can suffer from coverage bias. **Coverage bias** occurs when members of the sampling frame are significantly different from the target population (Remler & Van Ryzin, 2011). This is a problem that is increasingly challenging for telephone-based surveys. Telephone surveys based on listed numbers are limited because many households are unlisted, and those who are listed are often older, male, and of a higher income level. In addition, younger, unmarried, and more mobile segments of the population are more likely to use cell phones. In fact, African Americans use cell phones more often than White Americans. All of these factors make telephone-based surveys vulnerable to coverage bias. One solution to this problem is random digit dialing (RDD), which will be discussed later. What is most important to take away from the discussion of coverage bias is the need for researchers to constantly ask themselves how well the sampling frame represents their target population.

Non-Response Bias

The response rate in a study can also be a source of bias. Most research involves some degree of **non-response,** meaning that some members of a sample population are likely to decline participation in a research study. The **response rate** refers to the percentage of a population that agrees to participate in a study. The calculation of a response rate is a bit more complicated. Some people will refuse to participate in a study; some will leave a large number of items unanswered or blank; and others may quit part way through the study, making their input unusable. Thus, the response rate in a study contains two main components: (1) the *contact rate*, and (2) the *cooperation rate*. Contact rates indicate how well researchers do at contacting people or units to be a part of their research. Cooperation rates indicate how willing people or units who are contacted are to participate in research. Calculating the response rate of a study involves multiplying its contact rate by its cooperation rate (response rate = contact rate × cooperation rate) (Remler & Van Ryzin, 2011). Renauer and Covelli (2011) studied African American and Latino/a perceptions about whether or not police use race and ethnicity unfairly in making traffic stops. They conducted a telephone survey of 1,431 Oregon residents—741 from a stratified statewide random sample by county, with 164 African Americans and 161 Hispanics over samples. For the sake of demonstrating response rate, let's imagine that 60% of the households on their list answer the phone (contact rate), and 70% agree to be interviewed (cooperation rate). The response rate would then be .60 × .70 = .42, or 42%.

Non-response is not only a problem for telephone surveys; it is also a problem for mail surveys. Surveys administered through the mail often suffer from changes of address, but also because many people ignore questionnaires they receive through the mail (non-response). Online surveys also suffer because they are sometimes filtered into spam folders, and people often don't trust them and decide not to complete them (non-response). Sampling is often done so that researchers can come to unbiased conclusions. Non-response is expected in most research; however, it can be problematic when non-response leads to biased conclusions. The key question here is "What is the cause of non-response?"

Consider the CBS News/*New York Times* telephone survey. Eric, for example, is an African American male who voted for Barack Obama for president and feels that Obama's election represents the racial progress of the United States and the marginality of racism in contemporary U.S. society. Regina, an African American female who also voted for Barack Obama for president, believes that his election in no way represents the declining significance of race or racism in the United States, because there has been no evidence of a decrease in police racial profiling, housing discrimination, banks' lending discrimination, racism in medical care, and poorer teacher expectations for Black children since Obama's election. Regina argues that there has, in fact, been an increase in hate crimes since the president's election. Eric may be excited about participating in a telephone interview about race in the United States and racial progress, given his enthusiasm over the election of the country's first Black president. Regina, however, may fear that her feelings about racism and the election may not be received well or that she may be perceived as cantankerous or complaining. Because of this, Regina may be less likely than Eric to participate in the study. If certain people's propensity to respond is directly related to what a study is trying to measure, the study runs the risk of producing biased results. For example, if people like Eric—who are optimistic about the state of race in the United States—cooperate more than people like Regina—who have less positive attitudes about race in the United States—then the study's results will be biased.

Non-response produces bias in cases where the cause for non-response is directly linked to what the study is trying to measure. However, it is not always the case that non-response causes the outcome of a study to be biased, because sometimes the factors that influence non-response may be different from the factors that affect the outcomes of a study. For example, one might conduct a case study at a school to examine the relationship between school satisfaction (how students rate their overall satisfaction with their school) and their levels of academic achievement. But what happens if this study is conducted on a day that a stomach illness is going around the school? The stomach illness may affect students' willingness to participate in the study, but it is not necessarily related to students' school satisfaction levels. Therefore, the non-response in such a study does not bias the results.

Probability Sampling

Probability in research refers to likelihood or possibility. **Probability sampling** refers to sampling techniques in which people or elements of a population have a *known chance* of being selected. Developing a sample using a **random sampling** selection process means that each element or person in a population has an equal chance of being selected. Random selection is most likely to produce a sample that is representative of the population it was selected from. In order to select a random sample, one must have an accurate sampling frame listing the elements of the target population. A random number table or a computer program designed to draw random numbers, such as the website www.random.org, should be used. Random number tables and randomization computer programs are designed to limit human subjectivity in the selection process.

Random sampling is the foundation upon which a lot of important data have been collected: medical, educational, criminal justice–related, economic, and other social statistics. Governments around the world use data based on random sampling to make important decisions and formulate social policy. Some examples of data sets based on random samples are:

- Labor department statistics on employment levels
- Crime victimization statistics from the National Crime Victimization Survey (NCVS)

- Data on Islamophobia, racism, and sexism in the General Social Survey (GSS)
- Data on national math achievement and literacy levels from the National Assessment of Educational Progress (NAEP)

SIMPLE RANDOM SAMPLING is the most basic kind of probability sample. Simple random samples ensure that every element in a target population has an equal chance of being selected for inclusion in a sample. Usually simple random samples are used in small-scale projects that deal with moderate-sized populations from which it is easier to gather an accurate sampling frame. Studies show that there are regional development factors that contribute to residents' likelihood to engage in physical exercise, such as availability of recreational facilities and gyms, access to parks and playground structures, neighborhood crime, and safety (Flournoy & Treuhaft, 2002). If we wanted to estimate the percentage of African Americans in Stockton, California, who engage in regular physical exercise, we might do so by issuing questionnaires to the 3,086 African American residents in that city. Let's say we select a simple random sample of n = 400 African Americans. We can use p to represent the sample proportion who indicate that they engage in some level of physical exercise on a regular basis. The following are our results (p represents the sample proportion, μ represents the sample mean or average, and N represents the total population):

N = 3,086
p = 200 engage in regular exercise
n = 400 total in the sample
μ = .5 or 50%

The above sample estimate of the percentage of African Americans who engage in some level of physical exercise (p) on a regular basis is = 50% based on a simple random sample of 400 African Americans. This study would be unbiased because theoretically every member of the population had an equal chance of participating. Because this sample was drawn at random, a researcher can be confident that it is representative and close to the total population mean, μ. In fact, according to Flournoy and Treuhaft's (2002) analysis of African American samples, 50% of Black adults do not participate in regular light, moderate, or vigorous physical activity compared to 35% of White adults. However, if we were to conduct the above study again using another simple random sample, we would probably not get exactly 50%. Each sample can vary from another separate sample. This is called sampling error or sampling variability.

Now imagine that we want to apply for federal funds to organize Healthy Living Campaigns in low-income, underserved Black communities. To make a strong argument, we will want to be sure of the validity of our findings regarding regular exercise among *all* African Americans. To ensure the validity of the findings we may draw over 1,000 samples for the African American population, each consisting of a sample population of n = 400 people. It is likely that each time we will get slightly different estimates of exercise rates. A **sampling distribution** represents the distribution of scores or percentages on a variable. However, because the samples are randomly selected, a pattern should emerge, and the estimates will center on the true percentage of African Americans who engage in regular exercise, P (where P represents the proportion of the total population that engages in regular exercise). Half of the sampling means should be below the population mean, and half should be above the sampling mean. With 1,000 samples, the sampling distribution begins to form a pattern called a **normal distribution**, referring to a clustering of the sample means around the unknown population mean. The average of the sampling means, represented by $\bar{x}$, converges around the true population mean, μ. The population mean μ is truly unknown, which is the reason that we study samples p, to attempt to estimate it with sample means. If a distribution is a normal distribution, then there are certain claims we as researchers can make about the population the samples were drawn from. To make these claims, we need to know a statistic called the **standard error of the mean**, which tells us how much a sample mean is likely to differ from a population mean, μ. This statistic can be calculated using statistical software such as SPSS.

According to sampling theory, if we know that a curve is normal:

- 68% of all of the sampling means in the distribution will fall within ± (plus or minus) 1 standard errors of the population mean, μ.
- 95% of all of the sampling means in the distribution will fall within ± (plus or minus) 2 standard errors (exactly 1.96) of the population mean, μ.
- 99.7% of nearly all of all of the sampling means in the distribution will fall within ± (plus or minus) 3 standard errors of the population mean, μ.

Using this sampling theory, a researcher can calculate a **confidence interval** or an estimate of the margin of error in his or her sample mean. The confidence interval indicates how precise a sample is. If the mean percentage of African Americans who exercise regularly in our sample of 400 people is .5, or 50%, and we determine that our standard error of the mean is .011, then we can be 95% certain that the population mean will be between

$$.5 + (1.96 \times .011)$$

and

$$.5 - (1.96 \times .011)$$

This means that we can be 95% certain that the population mean will be .5 ±.022 or 50% plus or minus 2.2 percentage points. We now know with 95% certainty that the percentage of African Americans who regularly exercise, μ, will lie somewhere between 47.8% and 52.2%.

SYSTEMATIC RANDOM SAMPLING involves selecting every kth element in a sampling frame. When researchers use systematic sampling, they often use a table of random numbers to select a random starting point in their sampling frame. The symbol k represents the **sampling interval**, determined by dividing the population size (count of the sampling frame) by the desired sample size. We might be concerned that some children who need chelation treatments for lead poisoning may be going undiagnosed, as so many racially/ethnically underrepresented children do. Because of our concern, we might study the prevalence of lead poisoning (elevated blood lead levels) among children living in a multi-building housing project in Brooklyn, New York. We might use a listing of youth under the age of 18 living in the buildings as our sampling frame. Let's say that the total population of children living in the housing project is 500, and we want to select a sample of 50. Then our sampling interval would be 10. To select our sample, we would begin at a random starting point and select every tenth child until we have the 50 children we need for our sample. If it turns out that the random starting point is in the middle, you simply jump back to the beginning and continue until you have the desired sample size.

Researchers usually use systematic sampling when they draw samples by hand instead of by computer. It is especially useful when population data or records are recorded or listed on paper. At present, election exit polls are conducted using systematic sampling. They ensure that the samples are random and use a sampling interval, k. Researchers calculate exit polls by waiting outside polling places and surveying every kth voter, asking them about their vote. The challenge of systematic sampling is the periodicity or recurring pattern in the sampling frame. In some cases the sampling frame may be organized in a particular fashion that may bias the sample that is drawn. Returning to our study of the blood lead levels of the children in a Brooklyn project, it could be that the sampling frame is organized by building and floor number, or it could be that certain floors in each building have larger units that families with children are more likely to rent. The random starting point might cause a substantial number of children living in those units to be skipped. To avoid problems such as periodicity, researchers often randomize or rearrange the list to eliminate the problem. It is important for a researcher using systematic sampling to be sure that there is no inherent order to the sampling frame, and if there is, the solution is to randomize it.

When using simple random sampling, or systematic random sampling, the target population is treated as a single impartial whole. **Stratified random sampling** divides the population into strategic strata or subgroups. After the population is divided, a sample is drawn separately and randomly from each stratum. When this is done, the strata must encompass or include the entire target population. Every element in the target population has to fit into a stratum. This sampling technique is used when researchers want to be sure that their sample reflects certain diversity in a target population. The landmark study *Toxic Wastes and Race in the United States* illustrated that race was the strongest demographic predictor of the location of waste facilities in the United States—beyond poverty, land values, and home ownership (United Church of Christ Commission for Racial Justice, 1987). You may decide to take a present-day sample of the U.S. population to examine how close individuals live to waste facilities. However, if you want to make sure that each geographic region of the United States is represented and receives even coverage, you might have to divide the population into strata based on region.

The United States can be divided into the following strata: Northeast, South, Midwest, and West (Table 7.1). You want to draw a stratified random sample of 1,000 people from the U.S. population, making sure each region is adequately represented. To do so you must consider that the Northeast represents 18% of the U.S. population (55,574,197), The Midwest represents 22% of the U.S. population (67,924,018), the South represents 37% of the US population (114,235,849), and the West represents 23 % of the U.S. population (71,011,474) (U.S. Census Bureau, 2010). Here the regions represent the strata of this stratified sample. If you drew a random sample of 1,000 Americans, you could not be sure that 18% of your sample would be from the Northeast, or that 22% would be from the Midwest. Instead it is likely that each region will not be adequately represented just based on simple chance. However, stratification takes care of this problem because—at least theoretically—you can be sure that 30% of your sample is drawn from the North-

Table 7.1

REGION	POPULATION	PERCENTAGE OF TOTAL POPULATION	STRATIFIED SAMPLE OF 1,000 PEOPLE
United States	308,745,538	100%	—
Northeast	55,574,197	18%	180
Midwest	67,924,018	22%	220
South	114,235,849	37%	370
West	71,011,474	23%	230

east. Thirty percent of 1,000 is 180, so you randomly select 180 people from the Northeast; 22% of 1,000 is 220, so you randomly select 220 people from the Midwest; 37% of 1,000 is 370, so you randomly select 370 people from the South; and 23% of 1,000 is 230, so you randomly select 230 people from the West. When you are finished, you have selected a stratified random sample with each region of the United States adequately represented.

Stratified sampling is often used along with **disproportionate sampling** or **oversampling**. This is a technique used in stratified sampling in which the researchers select a disproportionately large number of elements from a particular stratum or group that might otherwise yield too few subjects. Sometimes proportionate sampling results in too few minorities or members of a small or uncommon population in a sample. For example, consider a research project comparing attitudes toward the death penalty among African Americans (13% of the U.S. population), Latino/as (16%), and White Americans (72%). When proportionate sampling might result in too few voices from small populations, researchers often oversample small populations so that each race is evenly represented. This can only be done by oversampling the smaller or uncommon groups so that each is equally represented. For example, imagine that you are interested in studying the parenting styles of African American single mothers and African American single fathers, when 48% of Black children are raised by a single mother and only 5% are raised by a single father (Fields, 2003). If a proportionate sample of 500 parents were collected for such a study, then there would be 475 single African American female parents and only 25 single African American male parents. Proportionate sampling would result in too few single fathers in such a study, and the researcher would not be able to make any meaningful comparisons based on such a small sample. Disproportionate sampling would allow the researcher to draw enough single African American male parents to make meaningful comparisons. In other probability samples, each element in a population has an equal chance of appearing in the sample. In proportionate sampling, each element in each stratum has an equal chance of appearing in the sample.

Sampling Underrepresented Populations

Drawing representative samples helps researchers make valid generalizations. However, this can be a challenge when dealing with racially/ethnically underrepresented populations. Latino/as represent 16% of the U.S. population, African Americans represent 12%, Asians represent 4%, and American Indians represent 0.9% (U.S. Census Bureau, 2010). Consequently, a racially proportionate sample of 1,000 Americans would include 120 African Americans, 40 Asians, 160 Latino/as, and 9 American Indians. As noted earlier, small numbers result in a higher error rate, especially for minority groups, who often constitute small percentages of samples (Monette, Sullivan, & DeJong, 2005). This increases the risk of making incorrect inferences about minority populations. Small percentages also make it difficult to assess the within-group differences in minority groups based on socioeconomic status, gender, sexuality, and so on. Some researchers address the problem by oversampling minority populations in studies.

Cluster sampling, also called *area sampling* or *multi-stage sampling*, is a procedure in which the final grouping of elements in a sample are drawn from larger units of elements called clusters. It is sometimes called multi-stage sampling because it involves working down in scale from larger clusters to smaller clusters. Cluster sampling is often useful in situations where there is no sampling frame listing the elements in a population. For example, you might be interested in interviewing teachers at Afrocentric schools in the United States about their teaching philosophies. To use a simple random sample, you would need a sampling frame. But what if there is no such listing? Instead you could use multi-stage cluster sampling. A cluster represents a grouping of elements in the sample you are interested in. While you cannot get a list of all such teachers, you can develop a list of Afrocentric schools. You begin by sampling the clusters. Each Afrocentric school represents a cluster, and, instead of a listing of individuals, a listing of Afrocentric schools in the United States is your sampling frame. Just for the purpose of this example, you might randomly select 25 of 100 Afrocentric Schools. Each one of these schools has a listing of teachers. Next, you draw a random sample of five teachers from each cluster—or school, in this case. Now you have a sample of $5 \times 25 = 125$ teachers. This is a big help for you because, in a situation where you could not get a sampling frame of the elements in your population (Afrocentric school teachers), you were able to get a sampling frame of clusters. Once you create a sampling frame of clusters, it is easier to get a sampling frame of the elements within those clusters.

Cluster sampling is easier to manage and less expensive than simple random sampling, but it has its limitations. Cluster sampling does suffer from some loss of precision because clusters often have characteristics that set them apart from the larger target population. King, Mallett, Kozlowski, and Bendel (2003) studied African American attitudes toward increasing cigarette taxes. To draw their sample they used multi-stage cluster sampling. They sampled clusters from the four strata (the U.S. census regions mentioned earlier—Northeast, Midwest, West, and South). Ten congressional districts (clusters) were selected from within the four geographic regions (strata). One hundred households were randomly selected from each congressional district to be a part of the final sample. A sampling frame of African Americans was unrealistic, and a random sample might result in some geographic regions being underrepresented. In this case, cluster sampling increased the representativeness of the study. Sometimes probability samples are unrealistic, depending on the timing or subject of research.

Non-Probability Sampling

While probability sampling refers to sampling techniques in which each population element has a known probability of being included in a sample, **non-probability sampling** refers to sampling techniques in which each population does not have a known probability of being included in a sample. Random samples usually produce the most accurate and generalizable results. However, it is sometimes impossible or difficult to draw a random sample. Moreover, random sampling is often costly and impractical. In these cases, researchers sometimes make use of non-probability sampling. Non-probability samples are often useful and functional in three particular circumstances: (1) when the research goals are to explore the relationship between variables and not to generalize results beyond the sample to a larger population; (2) in qualitative research, when the research goals are only to develop a greater understanding of a particular population, element, or social condition; and (3) when it is not possible or realistic to develop a sampling frame or list of all elements in a population (Monette et al., 2005). The term *non-probability sampling* refers to several different types of sampling techniques such as voluntary sampling, convenience sampling, snowball sampling, and quota sampling. The major limitation of non-probability samples is that their conclusions cannot be generalized beyond the sample cases studied.

VOLUNTARY SAMPLING refers to instances when population elements are selected by putting out an explicit call for volunteers, such as an Internet post or paper-posted advertisement for participants. Consider the following recruitment for research participants posted on Facebook:

> Are you or someone you know a mother of a 3rd grader? Are you African American or White? Researchers at UNC-Chapel Hill and NCSU are looking to recruit mothers and children to participate in a study of children's understanding of emotions in dyadic interactions.
>
> What's involved: Each mother and child pair will be asked to visit the DIISP (Duke Interdisciplinary Initiative in Social Psychology) lab at Duke University to complete a series of questionnaires and 2 emotion related conversations. Each visit will last approximately 2–2.5 hours.
>
> Compensation: Each family will receive $55 for participating in this one-time lab visit.
>
> If you're interested in participating, or if you have any questions, please contact ########### at ######@email.unc.edu or by phone (919) 843-####.

People who end up participating in a study like this based on this kind of post are considered a voluntary sample. There is a concern that accompanies this kind of sampling that is called **volunteer bias**. Volunteer bias refers to the possibility that volunteers may differ from a more representative sample in ways that affect the outcomes of a study. Mothers who volunteer for a study such as the one mentioned above may have more strong feelings about the importance of emotion in dyadic interactions than the general population. Imagine that there was a similar post on a popular website in South Africa recruiting South African participants to volunteer for a study of South African attitudes about Zimbabwean immigrants. It could be that the South Africans who volunteer for such a study may be more open to and accepting of immigration than the general South African population. In either case, volunteer bias is a problem when people's propensity to respond is related to the outcome of the study in question.

A **CONVENIENCE SAMPLE** is a sample based on population elements that are available to the researcher. You see convenience samples all the time if you watch television. If you are watching the news, you might see a news reporter interviewing people on a street corner about political or casual issues as they walk by. The United States Postal Service workforce is 21% African American (African Americans make up only 13% of the national population) (Balani, 2011). Imagine that a post office supervisor in Chicago decided to distribute questionnaires assessing how a recently proposed cut of 220,000 postal jobs in the United States might affect the Black community. It is likely that the supervisor would get a good response rate, but the sample would likely be biased. This is because convenience samples, by their very nature, suffer from **coverage bias**. Coverage bias represents the problem presented by convenience samples in which the subjects that are conveniently accessible to the researcher are not representative of the target population. The problem with the postal supervisor's sample is that we do not know what population they represent. They are simply the postal workers that the supervisor has immediate access to. They are not representative of African American postal workers as a whole.

This does not mean that convenience samples should never be taken. If the researcher (the supervisor) is interested in doing a more representative study of postal workers in Chicago or in the nation as a whole, it would be a good idea to conduct a pilot study (a preliminary study)—a study using the workers he personally supervises. Piloting a study on a population that will not be part of the main study is a good way for researchers to find out whether or not their questions are clear. It is also a good way to find out if people are answering certain questions in common ways. Keep in mind that convenience samples do not always suffer from this bias; they are biased when people's likelihood of being involved in the study is related to the outcomes of the study.

ONLINE SAMPLING has emerged in recent years with the increased popularity of the Internet as a tool for research. Many organizations and individuals post and distribute web polls. Such polls, however, risk a high degree of volunteer bias because respondents are often those who are most intrigued and excited by the topics. For example, imagine that you posted a series of questions on a popular website asking people about their opinions on the legalization of marijuana. It is likely that those who are advocates of legalization of marijuana will be more likely to respond, while those who are not strong advocates may be less likely to respond. This kind of response biases the results of such a poll in favor of those who are strong advocates of marijuana legalization. However, the problem of volunteer bias in online research is remedied through the creation of *Internet access panels*. These are email lists of individuals who make a prior agreement to participate in a series of online studies. The Internet access panels differ from other online research studies in that the respondents are not completing studies based on their passion for specific issues. However, debates about the bias in online research continue despite efforts to remedy the problem.

In addition, researchers must keep in mind the **racial digital divide** when conducting online research. This is the problem presented by different levels of accessibility to information and communication technologies. These considerations should not prevent scholars from using the Internet for research. However, it is important that they take measures to prevent the following disparities from biasing research, especially that which includes minorities and poor people.

- In the United States, 51% of African Americans have access to a home computer compared to 74.6% of White Americans (Fairlie, 2005).
- In the United States, 40.5% of African Americans have access to the Internet at home, compared to 67.3% of White Americans (Fairlie, 2005).
- There is also a global digital divide resulting in an imbalanced access to the Internet between wealthy and poor countries.

PURPOSIVE SAMPLING is used in qualitative sampling of people or non-human elements. When researchers engage in purposive sampling, they often select individuals or elements they believe possess unique characteristics or perspectives that will provide insight into a particular topic. In purposive sampling, the researchers are less interested in generalizing their findings to a large population and consequently use their informed judgment to select cases that will best serve the purpose of their research. Friedman, Corwin, Rose, and Dominick (2009) used purposive sampling to select 25 African American men for a study of their information-seeking behaviors, awareness, and recommendations regarding prostate cancer and treatment. The researchers were interested in studying the unique behaviors and ideas of African American men because—unlike the general U.S. male population—African American men 45 years of age and older have the highest rates of prostate cancer both in the United States and the entire world (Friedman et al., 2009). The study revealed unique barriers to treatment. However, if the study included a random sample, it would have gotten more variation based on age and race and a host of other variables that were not of direct interest to the researchers.

SNOWBALL SAMPLING is a type of convenience sampling in which researchers make initial contact with a small number of research participants, and then use them to gain access to additional research participants. Initial participants are asked to refer others to the researcher for participation in the study, gradually building the sample size. The name refers to the analogy of a snowball rolling down a snowy hill, picking up snow as it continues to roll. Like the literal snowball, snowball sampling is based on the assumption that certain research participants may have knowledge of other possible research participants with similar characteristics. This technique is often used when there is no sampling frame or no available/accessible sampling frame for a population of interest. It is especially useful in cases where researchers are studying sensitive topics, vulnerable populations, or subcultures in which members are in routine contact with one another. Snowball sampling is often used in qualitative research in which the researchers are not as interested in generalizability. Hasnain, Levy, Mensah and Sinacore (2007) studied the relationship between educational attainment and HIV/AIDS risk among active African American intravenous drug users (IDU), collecting data from them while offering counseling and treatment. They used snowball sampling to gather their research participants, since there is no sampling frame of active African American IV drug users, and members of such a population are not likely to identify themselves because they are engaged in an illegal activity that is also looked down upon as social deviance. Such a technique could also be helpful in sampling populations such as rape victims, illegal immigrants, and other subgroups and vulnerable populations.

In using snowball sampling it is especially important to protect the confidentiality and privacy of participants. Qualitative researchers, like quantitative researchers, also need to be concerned about the issue of non-response, because in a respondent-driven sampling technique like snowball sampling, there may still be some bias in the characteristics of those individuals who choose to participate and those who do not. The researchers have to ask themselves what kinds of participants might be unaccounted for in their research.

QUOTA SAMPLING is a technique that involves dividing a population into categories and selecting a quota or certain number of them from each category. It is not as representative as random sampling; however, it takes measures to add more representativeness than other non-probability sampling techniques. Quota sampling is used more in political polling and medical research than in academic social research. It is used to produce samples that reflect population characteristics such as race, gender, age group, and socioeconomic status. It is similar to stratified sampling, with the difference that random selection is not used.

There are several steps involved in carrying out quota sampling (Neuman, 2009). The first step is to identify the categories of people (or elements) that are important to the research. These categories could be males and/or females, certain racial groups, specific age groups, or some other categories. The next step is to decide upon the number of units to select for each category (for example, 10 African Americans, 10 Latino/as, 10 males, 10 females—that is, 5 males and 5 females for each ethnic group). Once you have selected the categories and number of units needed for each, you can begin to select the specific units. For example, you may go about interviewing visitors to a health clinic in Oakland by interviewing African Americans and Latino/as who enter the clinic until you have reached each quota. When you have interviewed 5 African American males, you have to skip all the other African American males who enter the clinic because you have met that quota. You continue with this process until each quota is met. This approach is an improvement upon convenience sampling because the categories within the population that the researcher is interested in are represented, whereas in convenience sampling everyone interviewed may be of only one particular category. Quota sampling is still limited in that it involves selecting only a few predetermined population categories when the target population may differ in many other respects.

Random Digit Dialing

Sometimes researchers are interested in sampling a large segment of the population by telephone. However, the drawback of taking this approach is the limitation of the telephone directory as a sampling frame. According to Neuman (2009), published telephone directories miss four kinds of people:

- people without telephones
- people who have recently moved
- people with unlisted numbers
- people who only use a cell phone

The study in the epigraph at the beginning of this chapter conducted by CBS and *The New York Times* on the topic of perceptions of race relations made use of **Random Digit Dialing** (RDD). This technique has been useful as a means of accessing samples because telephones were once considered standard equipment in households. RDD gives both listed and unlisted telephone numbers an equal chance of being selected. RDD works by replacing the last digits of listed telephone numbers with randomly selected digits. Once the random digits are selected, the numbers are called. Some of them turn out to be non-working numbers, fax numbers, or business numbers. However, others will turn out to be what the researcher is looking for: listed and unlisted household numbers. Each of these numbers has an equal chance of being selected because the numbers are generated randomly. RDD avoids the bias that comes with using listed numbers. RDD organizations keep accurate lists of up-to-date working area codes and generate random samples that are then used by survey researchers. When RDD is done properly, researchers are persistent and call numbers in their random samples 7–10 times before they move on, call on different days of the week and different times of the day, and make call-backs for those who request it (Remler & Van Ryzin, 2011). The researcher's choice of sampling procedure varies depending on the objective of the research project at hand. If the researchers are aware of the strengths and weaknesses of each sampling technique, they can choose the technique best suited to produce high-quality data.

Key Terms

Cluster Sampling	Racial Digital Divide
Confidence Interval	Random Digit Dialing
Convenience Sample	Random Sampling
Coverage Bias	Response Rate
Disproportionate Sampling	Sample
Generalizing	Sampling Distribution
Non-Probability Sampling	Sampling Interval
Non-Response	Simple Random Sampling
Normal Distribution	Snowball Sampling
Online Sampling	Standard Error of the Mean
Oversampling	Stratified Random Sampling
Population	Systematic Random Sampling
Probability Sampling	Voluntary Sampling
Purposive Sampling	Volunteer Bias
Quota Sampling	

Thinking about Science

Activity 1

Imagine that a research consortium is interested in studying the educational persistence of Black/African American PhD students who are currently enrolled at a major university. The research group is particularly interested in getting a representative number of African American males because they are underrepresented among PhD students.

- Given the research group's objectives, what sampling technique should it use? Explain why it should use the technique you suggest.

Activity 2

Now let's assume that the research group plans to recruit its sample by setting up tables around the campus during midday (11:00 a.m. to 2:00 p.m.) and explaining the purpose of its study to African American/Black passersby.

- What potential coverage bias issues might the research group confront?
- What adjustments to its recruiting strategy might it make to resolve these potential biases?

CHAPTER EIGHT

Non-Reactive Methods

Unobtrusive or non-reactive research refers to measures that are not obtrusive. In obtrusive research, participants modify their reactions or responses when they know that they are involved in a study. In unobtrusive research, people are not aware that they are being studied and so are not reactive to the research practice. An unobtrusive approach can make it easier to collect data. Analysis of physical evidence, secondary analysis, and content analysis will be addressed in this chapter.

Physical Evidence

> *Broken glass everywhere, people pissing on the stairs, you know they just don't care*
>
> —GRANDMASTER FLASH

A researcher can learn about social life through analysis of **physical evidence**. Analysis of physical evidence refers to the analysis of physical objects that are indicators of the variable(s) researchers are studying. Analysis of physical evidence is plausible when a researcher can establish that there is some physical evidence that indicates the presence of a variable of interest. Neuman (2009) points out several examples of the study of physical evidence as a non-reactive measure of variables:

- looking at family portraits in different historical eras to study how seating patterns reflected gender relations within families;
- studying public interest in exhibits by noting worn floor tiles in different parts of a museum;
- comparing graffiti in male and female high school restrooms to examine gendered themes;
- Examining high school yearbooks to compare the high school activities of people who later had psychological problems with those who did not.

Analysis of physical evidence can be used to confirm or contradict evidence gathered from reactive measures. A researcher might be interested in studying the genres of Hip Hop music that fans listen to most. Kitwana (1994) categorized of Hip Hop music by several genres: (1) recreational rap (themes of partying and fun); (2) conscious rap (dealing with cultural, political consciousness); and (3) sex-violence rap (dealing with sexual conquest and violent themes). If a sample of participants were interviewed about the Hip Hop genres they listen to most often, they might be inclined to answer that they listened to conscious Hip Hop music most often if they want to sound more intelligent and socially aware. Likewise, if they were completing a questionnaire assessing the genres of Hip Hop they listen to most often, they still might indicate that they listen to socially conscious songs, as opposed to music in the category of sex-violence. Non-responsive research avoids much of this kind of bias. A researcher employing analysis of physical evidence might examine the iPod playlists of research participants to see how many songs from each genre participants had, and which songs from different genres they listed to most often. This method might confirm that data derive from reactive measures such as questionnaires. Questionnaires might reveal that an individual listens to sex-violence rap far more than recreational rap or conscious rap. Sometimes non-reactive methods can be more accurate than reactive measures. Neuman (2009) identifies the five things that a researcher needs to do to conduct a study with physical evidence:

1. Identify a physical evidence measure of a behavior or viewpoint of interest.
2. Systematically count and record the physical evidence.
3. Identify and measure the variable(s) of your hypothesis.
4. Consider alternative explanations for the physical data and rule them out.
5. Compare the variables of your hypothesis using quantitative data analysis.

Limitations of Analyzing Physical Evidence

Because analysis of physical evidence is an indirect measure, the researcher often has to make inferences or educated guesses about what physical data reveal about people's attitudes or behaviors. For example, you may infer that because the person's iPod playlist shows more sex-violence rap than any other genre that this is the music they like most, or that they listen to most. It could be that the person has more than one iPod, shares his or her iPod with someone else or let someone else borrow it, or accidentally downloaded some music. For these reasons it is important to use non-reactive measures alongside reactive measures to confirm research findings and to use larger samples to minimize error. It is important to confirm the meaning of physical evidence by ruling out alternative explanations. In analyzing physical evidence it is also important to protect individuals' privacy. To do so, a researcher must make an effort to protect people's anonymity or confidentiality. For example, if an individual is examining trash or waste products, it is important that they record relevant information and not individuals' names, addresses, or other data that could allow them to be personally identified.

Content Analysis

Content analysis is a research technique that allows one to systematically analyze the hidden and visible content in messages. The word *content* here can refer to words, meanings, pictures, symbols, ideas, themes, and messages that a given *text* communicates. Text can be found in many different forms of communication media, including speeches, books, magazine articles, newspaper articles, DVDs, lyrics, official documents, pictures, clothes, and art. *Visible content* refers to the obvious and apparent meaning or messages in communication. *Hidden content* refers to the latent, subtextual, or beneath-the-surface meaning in texts. Content analysis is often a technique used along with reactive research methods because interviews often result in extensive transcripts, just as surveys with open-ended questions result in pages of answers that need to be coded.

Content analysis has mostly been used to analyze communicated messages in print materials and mass media items. It is a non-reactive method because the producer of the words and images in the texts is not aware that his or her products will one day be the subject of study. Content analysis allows the researcher to identify aspects of texts and communications that are difficult to see or may go unnoticed through ordinary reading, viewing, or hearing. It allows you to analyze content across multiple texts using quantitative techniques.

Content analysis is a technique that has been used to study:

- the variation in the frequency and quality of newspaper coverage of criminal athletes by race (Mastro, 2011);

- different expressions of positive social relationships between men in Hip Hop lyrics (Oware, 2011);
- analysis of body-type depictions of Black women through analysis of front-cover photos of select magazines (Thompson-Brenner, Boisseau, & St. Paul, 2011);
- comparison of how the behaviors of hurricane victims of different races were depicted in news broadcasts during the first week following Hurricane Katrina in New Orleans, Louisiana, in 2005 (Johnson, Dolan, & Sonnett, 2011).

This method could also be used to study:

- themes in different genres of music;
- trends in newspaper coverage;
- the ideological tone of newspaper articles on a particular topic;
- how people of different races are depicted in television commercials; and
- messages about physical appearance in men's and women's magazines.

Advantages of Using Content Analysis

Content analysis is a transparent research method. Its coding schemes, coding manuals, and sampling procedures make it easy for a researcher to replicate findings and conduct follow-up studies. It is an inexpensive method that allows researchers to collect data over an extended period of time. The fact that it is an unobtrusive, non-reactive approach means that its data are less likely to be affected by the reaction bias that occurs when people know they are being studied. It is also a flexible method that can be applied to many different forms of data, given its broad diversity as a tool of inquiry.

Sampling and Criteria for Inclusion in Content Analysis

Sampling procedures are as much a part of content analysis as most other analytical techniques. As mentioned earlier, one might measure the variation in the frequency and quality of newspaper coverage of criminal athletes by race. However, he or she would have to specify which newspapers to select articles from. Would they be national or local newspapers? What would those newspapers have to be about to be included? Within what time frame would articles be collected? Usually researchers focus on just a few sources of text. To study the different expressions of positive social relationships between men in Hip Hop lyrics, Oware

(2011) analyzed lyrics selected from 25 top-selling albums by male Hip Hop artists from 2003 to 2008. The study yielded a sample of 478 songs.

Every study using content analysis must explain not only its sampling procedure, but also its criteria for including or excluding sources. For example, to study variation in the frequency and quality of newspaper coverage of criminal athletes by race, Mastro (2011) sampled all articles addressing athletes associated with criminal activity appearing in *The New York Times*, the *Los Angeles Times*, and *USA Today* over a period of three years (January 1, 2005–December 31, 2007). This information, though necessary, is still insufficient. Researchers must also explain their criteria for including and excluding articles from the sources they have selected. In Mastro's (2011) study, the following reasons are given for including or excluding articles:

- Articles were included if they discussed at least one collegiate, professional, or Olympic athlete by name.
- Articles were included if they directly identified the individual to be associated with illegal activity.
- Articles exclusively addressing steroids were excluded because (a) they focused on illicit activity within the context of sportsmanship and within the sporting domain, whereas Mastro's (2011) focus was on illicit activity outside the sporting domain; and (b) because the Mitchell Report was released during the time of the research, possibly biasing the coverage of the topic of steroids.
- Articles solely addressing high-profile National Football League quarterback Michael Vick's dog-fighting case and/or the Duke University men's lacrosse team rape case were also excluded because of their inordinate coverage compared to other cases.

Mastro (2011) located articles through newspaper library databases—LexisNexis, NewsBank, and ProQuest—using specified search terms. This search yielded 475 articles for analysis. But data collected for content analysis must be systematically analyzed or coded.

Coding in Content Analysis

Coding is the part of content analysis that involves synthesizing text into systematic categories of data (sometimes quantitative data). Operationalization, as in all other research, is necessary in content analysis. To operationalize variables in content analysis, a researcher must create a **coding system.** Using a coding system allows the researcher to make observations in an organized and systematic way. Researchers create this system to provide themselves and readers with written rules

Table 8.1

CONTENT ANALYSIS CODING SCHEDULE			
Press Coverage of the Environmental, Crime/Courts and Political Issues			
A. NEWSPAPER	☐	1. The Standard 2. The Sunday Mail	
B. DATE (dd/mm/yyyy)	☐		
C. HEADLINE (copy verbatim)	☐		
D. NEWS CATEGORY (beat)	☐	1. Crime/Courts 2. Environment 3. Politics	
E. TYPE OF ITEM	☐	1. News Item 2. Feature 3. Editorial 4. Other	
F. INTRODUCTORY PARAGRAPH (copy verbatim)			
G. DOMINANT THEME IN INTRO	☐	Crime/Courts C1–Fraud C2–Robbery C3–Murder/Culpable Homicide C4–Sexual Assault C5–Property Disputes C6–Drug Trafficking C7–Illegal Currency Exchange C8–Other	Environment E1–Water/ Sanitation E2–Climate E3–Energy E4–CBNRM E5–Bio-Conservation E6–Livestock Disease E7–Habitat E8–Other	Politics P1–Elections P2–Demonstrations P3–Inter-Party Violence P4–Intra-Party Conflict P5–General Party Coverage P6–International Relations P7–Land Reform P8–Other
H. PLACEMENT	☐	1. Top Banner (Lead) 2. Mid (Ordinary) 3. Bottom (Anchor)	
I. PAGE LOCATION	☐		
J. PICTURE	☐	1. Yes 2. No 3. Head and Shoulders 4. Stand Alone	
IF 4 ABOVE, PROCEED.			
K. CAPTION (verbatim)			
L. THEME (from G above)	☐		

that explain how observations are classified or categorized. The coding system should be designed to match the topic or subject under study. Coding schemes usually change as they are being used. A researcher can approach coding deductively by creating codes based on his or her understanding and prior studies found in the literature on their topic. Coding can also be done inductively simply by analyzing and interpreting qualitative data. However, during the research process, codes are often renamed, split apart, or collapsed. The coding system includes both a coding schedule and a coding manual.

Coding Schedule

Researchers using content analysis must also specify a schedule of observations or a coding schedule. The **coding schedule** is a form on which all data related to a particular item are recorded. It should provide a space for the researcher to observe each relevant dimension of what is being studied. Table 8.1 is a coding schedule designed to analyze newspaper press coverage of environmental, crime/courts, and political issues (Envirocom, 2007). The coding dimensions were the newspapers, dates, headlines, news categories, types of items, introductory paragraphs, dominant themes, placements, item locations, pictures, and captions. The coding schedule allows the researcher to systemically observe each relevant dimension of every unit of analysis.

Coding Manual

The **coding manual** is a statement of instructions for coding. It includes all possible categories for each dimension being coded. Each dimension and corresponding category should be operationalized. The coding manual is important because it provides the researcher with guidelines on how to interpret the dimensions of the coding schedule. Friedman, Laditka, Laditka, and Price (2011) conducted a content analysis of the cognitive health content of 20 high-circulation magazines in the United States between 2006 and 2007. To guide their observations, they created a coding manual describing the dimensions and categories of the variables they studied in each magazine (Table 8.2).

Types of Coding: Manifest and Latent

MANIFEST CODING refers to the coding of the apparent and surface content of a document. **Surface coding** refers to analyzing what different documents are clearly about. In manifest coding, the researcher counts the number of times specific words, images, or characters appear in a document. Manifest coding is considered

Table 8.2

INTEREST AREA AND PUBLICATION*	MAGAZINE FOCUS AREAS
General Interest	
AARP Magazine (1)	World's largest circulation; for ages 50+; diet, fitness, health conditions, lifestyle, finance, travel
Reader's Digest (2)	Shared stories of readers; inspiration, community, learning, family-friendly, humor
Time (7)	Weekly national & world news; business, law, health, science, technology, environment, arts, culture
Newsweek (15)	Weekly national & world news; business, science, technology, society, arts, entertainment
U.S. News & World Report (31)	Weekly national & world news; health topics, money, business, education
Health	
Prevention (12)	Health focus; fitness, cooking, beauty, health
Health (61)	Health & lifestyles; food, fashion, beauty, fitness, relationships, well-being
Weight Watchers (71)	Weight loss & well-being; healthy recipes, weight loss, fitness, personal success stories
Women	
Good Housekeeping (5)	For busy women; food, nutrition, home, garden, health, fashion, culture, beauty
Ladies Home Journal (6)	Women's lifestyles; health, wellness, family, empowerment, community
Women's Day (8)	Style, health, eating well; solutions for relationships, family, self-esteem
Family Circle (9)	Parenting solutions; family activities, healthy recipes, diet, fitness, fashion
Men	
Men's Health (40)	For active, professional men; fashion, grooming, health, nutrition, fear, entertainment news
GQ (89)	Style & culture; news, fashion, gear, gadgets, health, entertainment, travel, trends
Men's Journal (133)	Active lifestyles; outdoor adventure, health, fitness, style, fashion, gear
Esquire (134)	Fashion, food, relationships, travel, lifestyle
African American	
Ebony (59)	One of oldest for African Americans; politics, culture, arts, education, technology, health, lifestyle
Essence (83)	Culturally relevant articles & editorials; career, finance, health, lifestyle, fashion, beauty
Jet (106)	Politics, culture, arts, education, technology, health, lifestyle
Vibe (108)	Urban, popular culture; celebrities, fashion, lifestyle, new media, business

* Advertising Age® Circulation Ranking, 2006

highly reliable because a word, image, or characteristic is either present or is not. The weakness of manifest coding is, ironically, related to its strength. Manifest coding often does not get to the deeper meanings, contexts, connotations, and multiple meanings of the words, images, and characters that it codes so well. Lack of depth weakens the validity of manifest coding.

LATENT CODING refers to coding for the deeper meanings that lie beneath the surface of a text. Latent coding requires more inference and interpretation on behalf of the researcher. In latent coding, the researcher often has to read entire documents to determine whether or not certain themes are present. Latent coding is sometimes considered less reliable than manifest coding because it relies more on the researcher's ability to pick up on subtleties and identify the hidden social meanings behind text. However, latent coding is believed to have more validity than manifest coding. This is because human beings communicate in indirect ways that carry *contextual meaning*. They also communicate in ways that carry *multiple meanings* that the mere presence of words and images may not reveal.

Units of Analysis: What to Look for in Analysis of Content

Remember that units of analysis are the *what* of research. They are the units on which you measure variables and collect data. Clearly, they are the people or things being studied (Vogt, 1999; Neuman, 2009). What are the units of analysis in content analysis? Common units of analysis in content analysis are actors, frequency, images, subjects, themes, dispositions, spaces, and prominence. They are indicators of what researchers are trying to measure. Below we list several common units of analysis.

Significant Actors

When you are studying a source of information using content analysis, it is important to identify the characteristics of the producers of that information. Who was the source of the information? What is the expertise of the author, organization, or institution? Is the author a specialist, news reporter, author, or scholar? Is the answer to these questions vital in interpreting the data that comes from these sources? Who are or is the main focus of the article, book, or other document? Is it a politician, an athlete, or an organization? Who are the alternative voices on the subject at hand? What was the context of the data in a content analysis? Was the data in the form of an interview, a movie, a book, or a commercial? Information about the significant actors in content analysis data is important for contextualizing the data you are analyzing.

Frequency

Frequency refers to how often something occurs within a text, for example, how often African Americans appear in college advertisements on a television channel in the time span of one week. How often do they have speaking roles in those commercials? What percentage of criminals in reality television shows about police arrests are of a particular race during a specified time span? These questions all deal with frequency. One element related to frequency is the use of words. Sometimes researchers using content analysis calculate the frequency with which certain key words are used. Sometimes the use of certain words can be an indicator of perspectives, attitudes, or feelings. According to Asante (1992), the use of words to describe African people such as "macaca," "Hottentots," "bushmen," and "Pigmies" is an indication of an author's Eurocentric perspective in approaching the study of African people. Dunning, Murphy, and Williams (1988) studied the sensationalizing of disturbances at football games by calculating British press use of emotive words such as "hooligan," "lout," and "war" when less dramatic words could have been used instead.

Subjects and Themes

On other occasions researchers analyze texts by categorizing them in terms of certain subjects and themes. In this kind of thematic coding, the researcher has to take a much more interpretative approach. In this case the researcher is looking at latent—or hidden, less obvious—aspects of phenomena. The researcher using this technique has to look deeply into the text being studied. Oware's (2011) analysis of expressions of positive social relationships between men in Hip Hop lyrics was a thematic analysis. Oware (2011) was looking for expressions of positive male relationships in the rap lyrics. The most common expressions of positive male relationships will represent his themes.

Dispositions

Sometimes a researcher looks for apparent dispositions in the text(s) being analyzed. One may be interested in whether or not reporters, when reporting on an issue in a newspaper, are doing so favorably or unfavorably. In this case, authors' dispositions might be coded in terms of being favorable, unfavorable, or neutral/descriptive only.

Space and Prominence

Researchers using content analysis often make use of measures of size, volume, time, or physical space. For measures of visual or audio material, a researcher might measure length of time. In measuring the appearance of Black people on televisions shows, a researcher would take note of the length of time that Black people are present in the commercials being studied. Prominence is also a characteristic related to space. In studies of television shows, a researcher would want to take note of the time of day certain shows appeared (for example, in prime time as opposed to 3 a.m.) because it is an indicator of prominence. Similarly, a newspaper article appearing on the front page has more prominence than one appearing in the middle of the newspaper.

Semiotics

Researchers using content analysis often analyze semiotics. **Semiotics** involves the analysis of signs and symbols and the meanings they carry. Semiotics often accompanies what we have previously described as content analysis. A researcher using semiotics looks for the intentional or unintentional meaning of signs and symbols. The critical study of signs requires an understanding of two critical elements: the signifier and the signified. The signifier is the thing that points to meaning, and the signified is the meaning (Bryman, 2008). Signs also carry denotative and connotative meaning. *Denotative meaning* is the obvious meaning that the signifier carries. *Connotative meaning* is the meaning the signifier carries in association with a certain context in addition to the denotative meaning. Klassen (2004) examined the semiotics of the communicative power of African American Methodist women's style of dress. Klassen (2004) found that dress was used by the women to communicate respectability and legitimacy. Semiotics helps the researcher see beyond the apparent, or beneath the surface. However, as an analytic tool, it is criticized for its reliance on arbitrary interpretation.

Categorizing Themes

Categories developed by way of content analysis must be *exhaustive* and *mutually exclusive*. A category is considered to be exhaustive when every element in an analysis can be categorized in one place or another. However, in some cases it is nearly impossible to have an exclusive category for every element. In these cases it is important to categorize the most common elements into categories, creating a miscellaneous category for others. For example, a researcher may analyze all of the speeches a president makes in which he directly mentions African Americans. The researcher may be interested in taking note of what issues the president mentions African Americans in relation to (voting, crime, education, housing, neighborhood conditions, healthcare, etc.). There may be up to 20 different categories of issues African Americans are mentioned in relation to. However, 20 may not be exhaustive, in which case a researcher might use the most common issues as categories and make an additional category for "other" issues. Mutual exclusivity means that each coded item must fall into one and only one category. There should not be any conceptual or empirical overlap between the categories created by the researcher. This means that categories have to be defined precisely. Low levels of mutual exclusivity have a negative effect on the reliability of a coding system.

Reporting Themes

Researchers employing content analysis must descriptively report the patterns they discover. They must also report them and illustrate them quantitatively. In Oware's (2011) thematic analysis of expressions of positive social relationships between men in Hip Hop lyrics, three major themes were discovered (Table 8.3). Rappers tended to express positive relationships with other males in three common ways: (1) friends and family, (2) success by association, and (3) loss of friends. Oware (2011) descriptively explains his findings:

> These topics included rappers defining their male friends as family members (friends are family), rappers utilizing their personal achievements for the benefit of their male friends (success by association), and finally lamenting or mourning the incarceration or death of a companion (loss of friends). Specifically, coding was based on the presence of these themes in individual songs. Instances of "friends are family" were based on references wherein rappers equated friendship with familial ties, for example, "we are more than friends we are family," or a similar sentiment. "Success by Association" entailed cases where rappers mentioned sharing their material wealth or other resources with their friends, an example being "my money is your money" or something to that effect. Finally, "loss of friends" referred to rappers lamenting the loss of their buddies to incarceration or death; for example, "I am sad he died" or a similar emotion. (Oware, 2011)

Oware (2011) illustrates his findings in Table 8.3.

Basic Steps in Content Analysis

Neuman (2009) identifies the basic steps in carrying out content analysis as follows:

STEP 1: Formulate a research question. Keep in mind as you formulate your question that content analysis is best suited for questions dealing with the study of symbols of manifest or latent messages in text.

Table 8.3

ARTIST	ALBUM TITLE	SONG	THEMES		
			FRIENDS ARE FAMILY	SUCCESS BY ASSOCIATION	LOSS OF FRIEND
2003 Compact Discs					
DMX	Grand Champ (N=20)	Where the Hood	X	0	0
		Dogs Out	X	0	0
		Untouchable	0	X	X
		We Bout to Blow	X	0	0
		A 'Yo Kato	X	0	X
Chingy	Jackpot (N=13)	Chingy Jackpot	0	X	0
		We Getting It	0	X	0
		Represent	0	X	0
		Bust	0	X	0
Outkast	Speakerboxx/-Love Below (N=16)	Tomb of Boom	X	X	0
		Flip Flop Rocks	X	0	0
		Reset	0	0	X
50 Cent	Get Rich or Die Tryin' (N=18)	Many Men	0	0	X
		High All the Time	0	X	0
		Don't Push Me	0	0	X
		Gotta Make it to Heaven	0	0	X
G-Unit		Betta Ask Somebody	X	X	X
		G'd Up	0	0	X
2004 Compact Discs					
D12	D12 World (N=18	Loyalty	X	0	X
		How Come	X	X	0.
		40oz.	0	X	0
		American Psycho	X	0	X
Twista	Kamikaze (N=16)	Hope	X	0	X
		Sunshine	0	X	0

Table 8.3 continued

ARTIST	ALBUM TITLE	SONG	THEMES		
			FRIENDS ARE FAMILY	SUCCESS BY ASSOCIATION	LOSS OF FRIEND
Lil' Flip	U Gotta Feel Me (N=20)	All I Know	O	X	O
		Bounce	X	O	O
		Check (Let's Ride)	O	X	O
		Dem Boyz	O	X	O
		Dem Boyz (remix)	O	X	O
		Drugs (screwed)	O	X	O
		Rags to Riches	O	X	O
		Sun Don't Shine	O	O	X
		Throw up Yo' Hood	O	X	O
		Y'all Don't Want It	O	X	O
Kanye West	College Dropout (N=16)	Get 'em High	O	X	O
		Family Business	X	O	O
Nelly	Sweat/Suit (N=24)	American Dream	X	O	O
		Getcha Getcha	X	O	O
		Another One	O	X	O
2005 Compact Discs					
50 Cent	The Massacre (N=21)	Outta Control	O	X	O
		Ski Mask Way	O	X	O
		My Toy Soldier	X	X	O
		Hate It or Love It	O	O	X
The Game	Documentary (N=17)	Runnin'	O	O	X
		The Documentary	O	O	X
		Start from Scratch	O	O	X
		Church of Thugs	O	X	X
		Hate It or Love It	O	O	X
		Don't Need Your Love	X	O	X

Table 8.3 continued

ARTIST	ALBUM TITLE	SONG	THEMES		
			FRIENDS ARE FAMILY	SUCCESS BY ASSOCIATION	LOSS OF FRIEND
Lil Jon	Crunk Juice (N=13)	Grand Finale	X	O	O
		Stick That Thang Out	O	X	O
		What You Gon' Do	O	X	O
Ludacris	The Red Light District (N=15)	Get Back	O	X	O
		Spur of the Moment	O	X	O
		Large Amounts	O	X	O
		Two Miles an Hour	O	X	O
Kanye West	Late Registration (N=17)	Drive Slow	X	O	O
		Diamonds from Sierra Leone (Remix)	X	X	O
		Gone	X	O	X
2006 Compact Discs					
T.I.	King (N=16)	I'm Talkin' to You	X	O	O
		Live In the Sky	O	O	X
		Top Back	O	X	O
		Under Taker	O	O	X
		Good Life	O	O	X
		Told You So	O	X	O
Lil Wayne	Carter II (N=19)	Fly In	O	X	O
		Money On My Mind	X	O	O
		Lock and Load	X	O	O
		Hustle Music	O	X	O
		Shooter	O	X	O
		Get Over	O	O	X
		Feel Me	X	O	O

Table 8.3 continued

ARTIST	ALBUM TITLE	SONG	THEMES		
			FRIENDS ARE FAMILY	SUCCESS BY ASSOCIATION	LOSS OF FRIEND
B.I.G.	Duets (N=19)	It Has Been Said	0	X	X
		Spit Your Game	0	X	X
		Get Your Grind On	0	X	0
		Whateva	0	0	X
		Beef	0	0	X
		Hustler's Story	0	0	X
		Breakin' Old Habits	0	X	X
		Mi Casa	0	X	0
		Want That Old Thing Back	0	X	0
Chamillion-aire	Sound of Re-venge (N=18)	Intro	X	0	X
		Picture Perfect	0	X	0
		Void My Life	0	0	X
		Rider	0	X	0
Yung Joc	Young Joc City (N=13)	Hear Me Coming	0	X	X
		Picture Perfect	0	0	X
2007 Compact Discs					
Jay-Z	Kingdom Come (N=14)	Prelude	X	X	0
		Lost One	X	X	0
		Do You Wanna Ride	X	X	X
		30 Something	0	X	0
		Minority Report	0	0	X
Kanye West	Graduation (N=15)	Good Morning	0	X	0
		Champion	0	X	X
		Big Brother	X	X	0
		Glory	0	X	0

Table 8.3 continued

ARTIST	ALBUM TITLE	SONG	THEMES		
			FRIENDS ARE FAMILY	SUCCESS BY ASSOCIATION	LOSS OF FRIEND
Young Jeezy	Inspiration (N=16)	You Know What It Is	O	X	X
		I Luv It	O	X	O
		Go Getta	O	X	X
		Buy Me a G	O	X	O
		Dreamin	X	X	O
		Keep It Gangsta	X	X	O
T.I.	T.I. VS. T.I.P. (N=19)	Act 1: T.I.P.	O	O	X
		Big Shot Poppin	O	X	X
		Hurt	O	O	X
		Row	O	X	O
		We Do This	O	X	O
		Shot It To Me	O	X	O
		Hustlin'	O	X	O
		Touchdown	O	X	O
50 Cent	Curtis (N=17)	I'll Still Kill	O	X	O
		Come and Go	O	X	O
		Move On Up	O	X	O
		Straight to the Bank	O	X	O
		All of Me	O	X	O
2008 Compact Discs					
Lil Wayne	Tha Carter III (N=22)	You Ain't Got	X		
		Nuthin On Me	X		
		I'm Me	O	X	O
		Kush	O	X	O
		Love Me or Hate Me	O	X	O

Table 8.3 continued

ARTIST	ALBUM TITLE	SONG	THEMES		
			FRIENDS ARE FAMILY	SUCCESS BY ASSOCIATION	LOSS OF FRIEND
T.I.	Paper Trail (N=16)	56 Bars	X	O	O
		Ready for Whatever	O	O	X
		On Top of the World	O	X	X
		No Matter What	O	O	X
		Swing Ya' Rag	O	X	O
		What's Up, What's Happening'	O	X	O
		Every Chance I Get	O	X	O
		Swagger Like Us	O	X	O
		You Ain't Missing Nothing	O	O	X
		Dead and Gone	O	O	X
Rick Ross	Trilla (N=13)	Speedin'	O	X	O
		This Is Life	O	O	X
		This Me	O	X	O
		I'm Only Human	X	O	O
		Trilla	O	X	O
		We Shinin'	O	X	O
		Billionaire	O	X	O
		The Boss	O	X	O
Jay-Z	American Gangsta (N=14)	American Dreamin'	O	X	O
		No Hook	O	X	O
		Roc Boyz	O	X	O
		Sweet	O	X	O
		Say Hello	X	X	X
		Blue Magic	O	O	X
		American Gangster	O	O	X

Table 8.3 continued

ARTIST	ALBUM TITLE	SONG	THEMES		
			FRIENDS ARE FAMILY	SUCCESS BY ASSOCIATION	LOSS OF FRIEND
Young Jeezy	The Recession (N=16)	Crazy World	X	O	O
		What They Want	O	X	O
		Hustlaz Ambition	O	X	O
		Vacation	O	X	O
		Put On	X	O	O
		Get a Lot	O	O	X
		My President	O	X	X
Note: X means the theme is present in the song; O means the theme is not present in the song. N is the total number of songs on a compact disc					

STEP 2: Identify the text(s) to be analyzed. You must identify the communication medium or text best suited to yield an answer to your research question.

STEP 3: Identify your unit of analysis. Remember, your unit of analysis is the *what* of your study. A unit could be a book, article, commercial, or TV episode. But it must be identified early on in your research.

STEP 4: Draw a sample. In content analysis, there is usually a large body of items to be coded, and researchers can only code a limited amount of material. Therefore, random sampling is a good method to incorporate into content analysis when possible. Researchers must identify their population, create a sampling frame, and use random selection to draw a sample if random selection is best suited. Otherwise, the classic sampling methods are also suitable.

STEP 5: Create a coding system. Once researchers have identified their variable, this needs to be operationalized. Operationalization in content analysis happens when researchers create a coding system. For each variable, researchers have to determine what kind of coding they are most interested in using: actors, frequency, images, subjects, disposition, space, or prominence.

STEP 6: Construct and refine coding categories. This means that the researcher must create a clear and precise system of categories. The researcher has to draw distinctions between each aspect of each variable. If a researcher is studying violence, he or she has to decide whether to assess it as high, moderate, low, or additional levels of intensity (Neuman, 2009).

STEP 7: Code the data onto the recording sheets. Once you create your coding schedule and sheets or forms on which you record data, it is time to collect the data. Usually the researcher creates a form for data collection for each case. If you are studying newspaper articles and there are 50 newspaper articles, there should be 50 recording sheets.

STEP 8: Data analysis. The last step is to analyze the data recorded on each form. Collected data can be analyzed manually or with a software program. Text, audio, video, and photographs can be stored digitally. There are several qualitative data analysis software programs available, such as Nvivo, Atlas.ti, and Ethnograph. There are also some free software programs such as AnSWR and EZ-Text, ELAN and Ethno 2. These software programs allow researchers to do several things that would be difficult by hand (Remler & Van Ryzin, 2011):

- store data in electronic form (text, images, and audio);
- search interview transcripts or field-notes for key words or phrases;
- create coding categories and adjust those categories during the research process;
- accommodate multiple coders and provide data on inter-coder reliability;
- group and combine data together into themes;
- track the co-occurrence of themes; and
- visualize qualitative data in the form of graphs and models.

Validity and Reliability in Content Analysis

In content analysis, validity refers to how truthful the categories are and how meaningful they are as indicators of what the researcher is trying to measure. Researchers have to take steps to ensure that they have created valid indicators. The methods of assessing validity earlier in this text are also relevant in assessing validity in content analysis. Content validity is the most often used method of assessing validity in content analysis. Reliability in content analysis refers to the ability of a measurement to yield consistent results, which is also a reflection on the ability of researchers to apply their coding schemes consistently. It means that to ensure the reliability of their measures, researchers must be careful to precisely define categories and ensure that coding schemes are applied properly and consistently throughout the research process. Ensuring this requires coders to be trained on how to apply them.

In cases where there are a large number of documents to code (many books, articles, or hours of media), researchers recruit people to help them code. When multiple coders are used, they need to be trained to properly apply coding schemes. A researcher will typically assess inter-coder reliability by having them code the same material. One method of doing this is by calculating the percentage of assessments and categorizations that coders agree on:

$$\text{Percentage of Agreement} = \frac{2 \times \text{Number of Agreements}}{\text{Total Number of Observations Made by Both Observers}}$$

One thing to keep in mind when assessing inter-coder reliability is that coders may also be agreeing with one another by chance alone. Nevertheless, the accepted level of agreement in inter-coder reliability is 75% or higher. This percentage should always be reported along with the results of a study.

Limitations of Content Analysis

The limitations of content analysis are tied to its strengths. It is a technique that can only describe what is in a text, thereby revealing patterns (Neuman, 2009). For example, you can identify patterns in the roles that African American characters play in certain types of television shows, but you cannot state with any certainty how seeing those characters influences viewers. This is beyond the function of content analysis. Making those kinds of claims would require a researcher to use a different method, such as experimental design, which is best suited to measure cause and effect. This is why, as stated in the beginning of this section, content analysis works well when combined with other methods of data collection such as experimental designs, questionnaires, semi-structured interviews, and others. This way an investigation could provide a detailed description of messages or images and also assess their impact on viewers.

Content analysis is also only as good as the documents the researcher analyzes. For this reason it is important for researchers to ensure that the documents they analyze are authentic, credible, and representative. This means that the documents under study should be truly what they are believed to be. It should be verified that they have not been distorted, and they should be representative of other such documents. In content analysis, a considerable amount of interpretation is required for researchers to categorize material, especially in latent coding. Because of this, there is a risk of the researcher making invalid decisions. It is also important for researchers to understand that content analysis is not the best method of acquiring answers to questions about *why* phenomena occur. For example, one might be able to analyze the images of Black men in cigarette advertisements and find differences between the way Black men and White men are depicted in such advertisements. However, you won't be able to identify why such differences exist with content analysis. Researchers using content analysis can speculate about why, but it will remain speculation. Again, this dilemma presents an opportunity for content analysis to be combined with another method, such as interviews, to gather data on *why* differences exist.

Secondary Analysis

In most cases, researchers collect data themselves, a practice that enables them to gather information in a manner that will allow them to answer their research question. However, it is not always feasible to do so. Sometimes collecting certain kinds of data or collecting data under certain conditions or circumstances is too time consuming or expensive. In other cases it may not be necessary for a researcher to collect data when the data he or she needs to answer a research question already exists. This kind of data—that is, data that was collected through a previous administrative or research project—is called secondary data. When you engage in **secondary data analysis**, you are analyzing data collected by someone else. There are two types of secondary data: statistical data and documents. Some secondary data are statistical data on crime, health, births, and deaths, which are often collected by government agencies. Other forms of secondary data are documents or non-quantitative communication such as books, magazines, web pages, radio, television, and movies. Sometimes secondary data can be used in conjunction with other methods of data collection such as interviews, surveys, experiments, and so on.

Advantages of Secondary Analysis

Secondary data is advantageous to a research project for many reasons. It saves the researcher cost and time. It gives the researcher access to information for a small portion of the cost of collecting original data. Many of the secondary data sets that researchers have access to are of very high quality and cover large representative samples of populations. Many data sets, such as the General Social Survey (GSS), are conducted by highly experienced researchers who rigorously monitor the quality of the data they publish. Because many secondary data sets collect data from large samples, they can be especially advantageous for the study of underrepresented racial/ethnic populations. With secondary analysis, there is often the opportunity to study large samples of underrepresented racial/ethnic populations that often occupy small percentages of other research studies. When researchers engage in secondary analysis, they do not have to engage in data collection because the data are already available. This allows the researcher more time to engage in analysis.

Statistical Data

The U.S. Department of Health and Human Services (HHS) (2011) produced a report entitled *Combating the Silent Epidemic of Viral Hepatitis*. The report notes that between 3.5 and 5.3 million Americans are living with the virus, and between 65% and 75% are unaware of their infection status. Viral hepatitis is the leading cause of liver cancer. This news is especially critical for African Americans because this demographic is twice as likely as the general American population to be infected with the hepatitis C virus (HCV). Knowledge of this fact is important so that programs can respect the diversity of the population of infected people and target interventions for those who are most vulnerable to the virus. HHS is able to detect this and other such epidemics because it tracks hospital administrative data and surveys of the U.S. population. These data are used to guide HHS's approach to addressing epidemics and other public health emergencies. It does so largely through its analysis of secondary (available) data. Hospital administrators keep records on the number of people who enter the emergency room complaining of certain symptoms. Other quantitative data, such as patients' ages and income levels, are collected. Analysis of such already-existing quantitative data is secondary analysis of statistical data. Quantitative research involves the statistical analysis of quantitative or numerical data. Statistical data for secondary analysis can come from many different sources; some examples follow.

Administrative Data

Firms, organizations, and agencies collect quantitative data in the form of record keeping. They accumulate data on their own activities as well as on the groups and individuals they provide services for or have exchange relationships with. Administrative data are an important source of statistical information on programs and services. Remler and Van Ryzin (2011) identify several kinds of quantitative data found in administrative records:

- financial records of income and expenditures;
- employee records;
- records of the production and output of goods and services;
- records kept on patients, students, or clients; and
- performance indicators.

Often these data are kept in electronic form to facilitate the ease of entry and retrieval of information. However, most records are still kept in the form of paper documents. Paper documents are useful but problematic for researchers because they must be coded and entered into a statistical database. Administrative records are also kept on vital statistics such as births and deaths. The Uniform Crime Report (UCR) consists of administrative data that are reported by victims and logged by law enforcement agencies for their own administrative purposes (Remler & Van Ryzin, 2011). To assess the strengths of the economy, economists monitor administrative data collected by state agencies when people file for unemployment claims.

The use of administrative data does raise some ethical concerns. Much of the data gathered by organizations and agencies were not originally gathered for research purposes and may contain private information that wasn't collected with informed consent. The federal government sometimes regulates how such information is used. For example, the Health Insurance and Portability and Accountability Act (HIPAA) provides rules and guidelines for the use of health insurance and healthcare records to protect people's privacy. The key issue in the use of administrative data is privacy. Researchers making use of administrative data and agencies or organization that provide such data are obligated to make sure that the data is non-identifiable. Making the data non-identifiable means that the data should not contain information that would allow someone to discover the identity of any individual. Identifiable information should be removed before administrative data is ever provided to a researcher. Identifiable information includes names, social security numbers, addresses, and other information that would allow someone to identify an individual. Collecting administrative data properly is important for tracking and improving health conditions, educational achievement, and quality of healthcare services.

Official Statistics

Many statistical sources of secondary data come from federal agencies that serve as tools for shaping and making public policy decisions. Examples are the Federal Bureau of Investigation (FBI) and the National Center for Health Statistics (NCHS). Statistics from such organizations are often used in the news media to report increases in crime or unemployment.

Published Data Tables

Some agencies collect data and make them available in published tables or downloadable spreadsheets (Remler & Van Ryzin, 2011). For example, the U.S. Census Bureau publishes state-level data, thereby making them available to the public. The United Nations, the World Bank, the African Union, and the National

Survey of Black Americans all have published data tables available for public use. There are also data archives that store and document data from various surveys and studies. There are thousands of sources for statistics on different topics. The most valuable source is the *Statistical Abstract of the United States*, published by the U.S.

Table 8.4

SOURCE	TYPE OF DATA	LINK TO SOURCE
U.S. Census Data	Source for the most recent census data on the people and economy of the U.S. at the country, state, and county levels	http://quickfacts.census.gov/qfd/index.html
Bureau of Economic Analysis	A source of economic statistics that enable government and business decision makers, researchers, and the American public to follow and understand the performance of the nation's economy. To do this, BEA collects source data, conducts research and analysis, develops and implements estimation methodologies, and disseminates statistics to the public.	http://www.bea.gov/
Bureau of Justice Statistics	A source of data on crime, criminal offenders, victims of crime, and the operation of justice systems at all levels of government. These data are critical to federal, state, and local policymakers in combating crime and ensuring that justice is both efficient and evenhanded.	http://bjs.gov/
Bureau of Labor Statistics	A source of data on U.S. labor market activity, working conditions, and price changes in the economy	http://www.bls.gov/
Bureau of Transportation Statistics	Source of data on transportation statistical knowledge with public and private transportation communities and the nation.	http://www.rita.dot.gov/bts/
Economic Research Service	Source of data on economic information and research in the U.S. Department of Agriculture.	http://www.ers.usda.gov/
Energy Information Administration	Source of data on energy production, stocks, demand, imports, exports, and prices	http://www.eia.gov/
National Agricultural Statistics Service	Source of data on every aspect of U.S. agriculture, including production and supplies of food and fiber, prices paid and received by farmers, farm labor and wages, farm finances, chemical use, and changes in the demographics of U.S. producers.	http://www.nass.usda.gov/
National Center for Educational Statistics	Source of data on education in the United States and other nations.	http://nces.ed.gov/
National Center for Health Statistics	Source of data on topics related to public health importance, including diseases and conditions, injuries, life stages and populations, and health care and insurance.	http://www.cdc.gov/nchs/

Chamber of Commerce. Once you locate sources of data such *as Statistical Abstracts*, you can acquire them in book or CD-ROM format online. You can sometimes download them at a cost, although they are usually free. Table 8.4 includes a list of free web-based statistical data sources for different purposes.

You might also consider the University of Michigan's "Statistical Resources on the Web" website. For world statistics, you can look at the United Nation's *Demographic Yearbook* online; it contains vital statistics on births, deaths, and other global population data. You can also find graphic and mapping data online provided by sources such as the U.S. Census Bureau or the Social Explorer.

Limitations of Secondary Data

The Problem of Missing Data

Secondary data sets may include incomplete data on individuals or segments of populations. Researchers may not have collected data in a certain neighborhoods considered too dangerous for them to enter (Monette, Sullivan, & DeJong, 2005). Missing data in secondary data sets calls into question their representativeness. Such missing data can also result in misleading conclusions about populations. Whenever researchers use secondary data, it is important to consider the impact of such missing data on the results of their analysis.

Means of Data Collection and Misleading Conclusions

An example of the problem of missing data is seen in certain crime statistics, which can be misleading because in some cases they only include individuals who have been processed by agencies with the responsibility of compiling data on crime. According to Bryman (2008), an offense may be considered a crime if it meets two criteria: (1) a crime must be seen as a crime by a member of the public, and (2) the offense must be officially recognized as a crime before it's reported by the police. This means that a crime may not be reported by a member of the general public. A criminal act may go unnoticed, or it may simply not get reported to the police because it is not recognized as a criminal act. It may be noticed and recognized as criminal but not be reported to the police if a member of the public is not confident that the police will give it appropriate attention. (This often happens when the victim is afraid of reprisal for any number of reasons.) Moreover, Bryman (2008) adds that even if a crime is reported, police may not enter it into official statistics because they have considerable discretion about whether or not to proceed with a conviction or to let a person off with a warning. All of these factors influence the statistics that come to represent the "crime rate." The Uniform Crime Report (UCR) data from the Federal Bureau of Investigation (FBI) consist of annual crime statistics for the United States. However, UCR data is limited, since it only includes data from crimes that result in an arrest, while a substantial portion of crime is not reported to the police. Moreover, African Americans are less likely to report certain crimes to police than other races (Walker, Spohn, and Delone, 2012).

The Problem of Reliability in Secondary Analysis

Sometimes secondary analysis can be affected by the problem of reliability when the definitions of variables, attention to certain social phenomena, or policies about data collection change over time. If, for example, a local police station decides to crack down on drug trafficking in a particular area, they may be more likely to make arrests in response to such a policy decision, and in turn they may be less likely to let an offender off with a warning under such orders. Such decisions would affect fluctuations in statistics of drug trafficking crimes. In other cases, the United States has changed how it calculates statistics such as the unemployment rate. While at one time the unemployment rate was collected by dividing the number of unemployed people by the civilian workforce, it is now calculated by dividing the unemployed population by the civilian workforce plus the military.

The Implications of Data Availability

Sometimes there are more data available for some topics than others. But when this affects what studies get completed or not, researchers encounter data availability as a problem. Researchers may become *too data driven* when they only pursue questions that can be answered with available data. For minorities who have been notoriously underresearched or for whom available data are inadequate or biased, this is a tendency that does not bode well. Because of this tendency, some topics are more likely to be studied than others (Remler & Van Ryzin, 2011).

The Problem of Validity in Secondary Analysis

Validity refers to whether or not an instrument truly measures what it intends to measure. According to Monette and colleagues (2005), the issue of validity arises in three areas within secondary analysis. First, secondary data may or may not have directly measured the variable(s) that a researcher is interested in. This is not something that the researcher has control over; after all, the data were collected by someone else. In some cases researchers have to identify variables in secondary data sets that indirectly measure what they are interested in. As the researcher, you may be assessing the need to advocate for better working conditions by examining the rate of workforce injury at textile plants in a particular city. As Neuman (2009) asserts, you may define workforce injury in such a way that it includes minor cuts, bruises, and sprains sustained on the job. However, secondary data that are available may only include injuries that result in a documented visit to a physician or a hospital. The result would be that many of the injuries you would otherwise include are left out. The second issue arises when researchers adjust their operational definitions of variables so that they can measure the variables that are measured in secondary data sets. The third issue in which validity problems emerge is the change of data collected over extended periods of time. When definitions change, questions are added or eliminated, and it becomes difficult to compare data over time.

The Inductive and Deductive Challenge

When researchers are not engaging in secondary analysis and they collect data firsthand, they are often engaging in what is called the *deductive approach*. In the deductive approach, the researcher draws a hypothesis from a theory, variables are derived, and data are used to test the hypothesis. In this case, the theory and the research question determine the kind of data that are collected. When doing secondary analysis, the deductive approach is often impossible because the data needed to test an existing theory may not exist or may not have been collected. A theory about homecare providers might include a variable called *friendliness* to assess the relationship between the care provider and the person receiving the care. However, although friendliness may be a part of the theory, *friendliness* may not be a part of the data that are routinely collected by the hospital or care-providing agency. When this is the case, it is not possible to operationally define a variable in a way that fits a theory. Here it is important for the researcher to make a compromise and redefine his or her variables in such a way that they can be tested with the data available through secondary analysis. In the case of the homecare provider, we might have to measure friendliness based on other variables, such as a patient's overall satisfaction with the care provider and his or her rating of how courteous and respectful the care provider was. A researcher might use one, two, or a combination of all of the above alternative variables to examine *friendliness*. Ultimately, the researcher may have to adjust the scope of the study to fit the data that is available for secondary analysis.

Why Collect Original Data?

Sometimes it is necessary to collect original data. Large data archives do not always contain enough data on small local areas, cities, and neighborhoods. In other cases, as we now know, existing sources of data may not measure the particular variables that a researcher is interested in. Available data may be outdated and in need of updating, in which case it would behoove a researcher to collect new data.

Key Terms

Coding   Manifest Coding
Coding Manual   Physical Evidence
Coding Schedule   Secondary Data Analysis
Coding System   Semiotics
Content Analysis   Surface Coding
Latent Coding

Thinking about Science

Activity 1

- Find a public high school in or near your neighborhood. Go there approximately a half hour after school lets out and/or a half hour before school begins. Repeat this for 3 days. Observe the physical objects on the ground around the school. Categorize the different types of objects you observe. Create and explain the different themes you discovered among the objects you found on the ground. Explain each theme.

Activity 2

Find the website for the *Statistical Abstracts of the United States* and locate the following information:

- What is the last recorded number of foreign-born Black students enrolled in elementary school or higher grades in the United States?
- How many Black members of Congress are there currently? What percentage of the total number of congresspersons do they represent?
- What is the percentage of Black Americans who engage in regular physical activity that is moderate or vigorous?

CHAPTER NINE

Scales and Indexes

Some variables are more complex than others. The researcher has to adjust to the type of variable being measured and its level of complexity. To measure complex variables, the researcher needs to develop more complex measurements. This chapter explains the purposes, strengths, and limitations of scales and indexes. Scales and indexes provide measurements that allow the researcher to capture the full range and array of the dimensions of complex variables.

Indicators

In an earlier chapter we covered the complex topic of measurement. We learned that phenomena can be measured by asking a question or a series of questions that serve as indicators of the phenomena we are trying to measure. However, it is difficult to measure constructs with complex meanings using a single indicator. It is often useful to combine a set of indicators to create a single measure. When we do combine indicators (two or more) into a composite, we have created an index or a scale. An *index* or *scale* refers to a combination of variables used to measure an abstract concept. The terms *index* and *scale* are often used interchangeably. They both combine multiple indicators to measure a variable and rank order units of analysis on variables such as religiosity, prejudice, and socioeconomic status (Babbie, 2001). They are both effective at condensing information about variables and increasing measurement reliability and validity. This is done to better capture the full range of the concept being measured. However, there are some key differences. **Scales** are ordinal measures of the levels or intensity, direction, and potency of a variable established by arranging responses on a continuum (Neuman, 2009). Also, the items in scales usually need to be arranged in a particular order. It is important to have multiple indicators to measure the presence of complex variables, but scales are more appropriate in cases in which the researcher is interested in the degree to which a variable is present. An **index** is a composite measure that summarizes information from multiple indicators into a single score, or the sum of their values (Neuman, 2009). Different from scales, the items in indexes need not be arranged in any par-

Table 9.1

Instructions: In your day-to-day life, how often do any of the following things happen to you? Indicate your answer by placing an "X" on the line that best reflects how often you experience the following kinds of discrimination.						
	EVERY DAY	AT LEAST ONCE A WEEK	A FEW TIMES A MONTH	A FEW TIMES A YEAR	LESS THAN ONCE A YEAR	NEVER
1. You are treated with less courtesy than other people are.	____	____	____	____	____	____
2. You are treated with less respect than other people are.	____	____	____	____	____	____
3. You receive poorer service than other people at restaurants or stores.	____	____	____	____	____	____
4. People act as if they think you are not smart.	____	____	____	____	____	____
5. People act as if they are afraid of you.	____	____	____	____	____	____
6. People act as if they think you are dishonest.	____	____	____	____	____	____
7. People act as if they're better than you are.	____	____	____	____	____	____
8. You are treated with less politeness than other people are.	____	____	____	____	____	____
9. You are treated with less appreciation than other people are.	____	____	____	____	____	____

ticular order. Both scales and indexes are multi-indicator measures that assign individual scores for each item, which are then combined to create a composite score for a person. The key difference is that items in an index do not need to be in a particular order, and each item usually has the same weight or significance (Vogt, 1999). Nevertheless, in most cases scales and indexes are treated interchangeably.

Each variable in an index or scale is referred to as an item or indicator. For complex variables, multiple indicators are necessary to capture the multidimensionality of abstract concepts. Without having enough indicators to capture the multidimensionality of the abstract concepts being assessed, a measure will lack what we have previously defined as *content validity*. Some variables can be measured with a single indicator. For example, marital status can be measured with a single item, such as "What is your marital status? ○ married ○ single ○ separated ○ divorced ○ widowed ○ engaged ○ annulled ○ cohabitating." Similarly, you could measure sex with a single item such as "What is your sex? ○ male ○ female." However, more complex variables cannot be sufficiently measured with a single indicator, but instead require multiple indicators taken together. In this case a scale or index is more appropriate. For example, one cannot measure a complex construct such as *discrimination* using a single indicator. Instead, an abstract construct such as discrimination has to be measured using multiple items. Forman, Williams, and Jackson (1997) developed the Everyday Discrimination Scale (EDS) to study the relationship between experiences of discrimination and physical and mental health. The EDS consists of a nine-item scale in a modified format, displayed in Table 9.1.

The Importance of Indexes

Indexes can be extremely useful instruments of social change. However, single indicators are insufficient for individuals and institutions interested in improving service to citizens. For example, a single indicator would not be adequate for assessing *human development*. Since the 1980s there has been a move away from measuring human development based on economic growth alone. Human development is now defined by the United Nations Development Program (2012) as "a process of enlarging people's choices and enhancing human capabilities (the range of things people can be and do) and freedoms, enabling them to: live a long and healthy life, have access to knowledge and a decent standard of living, and participate in the life of their community and decisions affecting their lives." Therefore, to measure human development in a more comprehensive way, the United Nations Human Development Program adopted the Human Development Index (HDI) score. The HDI score is a composite score used to rank countries based on their degree of human development. The HDI score includes a country's life expectancy rates, literacy rates, educational levels, and standards of living.

Exhibit 9.1

How the Urban League Equality Index Works

For any given measure, the index represents the ratio of Blacks to Whites. To use median household income as an example, an index of 61%= $33,463\$54,671, whereas $33,463 is the median household income for Blacks and $54,671 is the median household income for Whites. Equality would be indicated by an index of 100%. Therefore, an Equality Index less than 100% suggests that Blacks are doing worse relative to Whites and an Equality Index greater than 100% suggests that Blacks are doing better than Whites (National Urban League, 2012).

There are many different ways to measure the health of a country's economy. The Consumer Price Index (CPI) score is used in many different countries to measure changes in the price level of a representative basket of goods and services. In order to create a valid measure, more than one good must be included to produce a valid measure.

The Index of African Governments (Table 9.2) is a composite score taking into consideration 57 indicators to measure governance across four categories of public goods: Safety and Rule of Law, Participation and Human Rights, Sustainable Economic Opportunity, and Human Development (Mo Ibrahim Foundation, 2012). In the United States, the National Urban League developed a similar Equality Index (Exhibit 9.1) to assess the relative status of Black and White people and, more recently, Latino/Latina Americans. The purpose of the Equality Index is to assess the progress toward achieving equal social, political, and economic opportunity in the United States. The Equality Index score is a calculation based on five areas: economics, health, education, social justice, and civic engagement.

Creating a Scale or Index

The first step in creating a scale or index is defining the concept to be measured. At this point, your review of the literature on your topic is critical. Draw upon your knowledge of the concept you are attempting to measure. You will come across definitions of the phenomena you are trying to measure. You should define the concept the way other experts have defined it unless there is good reason to warrant a change. There may be something others have left out. A new or different theoretical perspective may lead you to consider removing or adding some new aspects to the phenomena you intend to measure. In any case, it is the obligation of the

Table 9.2

CATEGORIES	SUBCATEGORIES	INDICATORS
SAFETY AND RULE OF LAW	RULE OF LAW	Judicial Process Judicial Independence Sanctions Transfers of Power Property Rights
	ACCOUNTABILITY	Accountability, Transparency, and Corruption in the Public Sector Accountability, Transparency, and Corruption in Rural Areas Corruption and Bureaucracy Accountability of Public Officials Corruption in Government and Public Officials Prosecution of Abuse of Office
	PERSONAL SAFETY	Domestic Political Persecution Social Unrest Safety of the Person Violent Crime Human Trafficking
	NATIONAL SECURITY	Cross-Border Tensions Government Involvement in Armed Conflict Domestic Armed Conflict Political Refugees Internally Displaced People
PARTICIPATION AND HUMAN RIGHTS	PARTICIPATION	Free and Fair Executive Elections Free and Fair Elections Political Participation Electoral Self-Determination Effective Power to Govern
	RIGHTS	Core International Human Rights Conventions Human Rights Political Rights Workers' Rights Freedom of Expression Freedom of Association and Assembly Civil Liberties
	GENDER	Gender Equality Gender Balance in Primary and Secondary Education Women's Participation in the Labor Force Equal Representation in Rural Areas Women in Parliament Women's Rights Legislation on Violence Against Women

continued on p 196

Table 9.2 continued

CATEGORIES	SUBCATEGORIES	INDICATORS
SUSTAINABLE ECONOMIC OPPORTUNITY	PUBLIC MANAGEMENT	Statistical Capacity Public Administration Inflation Diversification Reserves Budget Management Ratio of Total Revenue to Total Expenditure Ratio of Budget Deficit of Surplus to GDP Debt Management Ratio of External Debt Service to Exports Reliability of Financial Institutions
	BUSINESS ENVIRONMENT	Competitive Environment Investment Climate Investment Climate for Rural Businesses Rural Financial Services Development Bureaucracy and Red Tape
	INFRASTRUCTURE	Access to Electricity Road and Rail Networks Air Transport Facilities Telephone and IT Infrastructure Digital Connectivity
	RURAL SECTOR	Public Resources for Rural Development Land and Water for Low-Income Rural Populations Agricultural Research and Extension Services Agricultural Input and Produce Markets Policy and Legal Framework for Rural Organizations Dialogue Between Government and Rural Organizations
HUMAN DEVELOPMENT	WELFARE	Social Protection and Labor Social Exclusion Welfare Services (Health and Education) Equity of Public Resource Use Access to Water Access to Sanitation Environmental Policy Environmental Sustainability
	EDUCATION	Education Provision and Quality Ratio of Pupils to Teachers in Primary Schools Primary School Completion Progression to Secondary School Tertiary Enrollment
	HEALTH	Maternal Mortality Child Mortality Immunization (Measles and DPT) Antiretroviral Treatment Provision Disease (Cholera, Malaria, and TB)

Table 9.3

ENVIRONMENTAL FACTORS	Convenience Eating (eating in response to the presence of convenience foods in one's environment), Fruit and Vegetable Availability in one's home or neighborhood, and Social Acceptance or social norms and supports that influence food intake
BIOLOGICAL FACTORS	The Sensation of Hunger and Food Taste Preferences
PSYCHOLOGICAL FACTORS	Self-Efficacy, Emotional Eating, and Dietary Restraint

researcher to justify those differences. Cahill, Freeland-Graves, Shah, Lu, and Klohe-Lehman (2009) were interested in studying the eating stimuli of low-income, post-partum women who belong to underrepresented racial/ethnic groups because previous studies had not focused on this population at such a critical time in their lives. They drew upon the knowledge they acquired through a careful review of the literature to define *eating stimuli* as *motivations to eat* divided into three categories: environmental motivations, biological motivations, and psychological motivations. Based on this definition, Cahill and colleagues (2009) developed the Eating Stimulus Index (ESI) (Table 9.3).

The second step involves carefully selecting the items that will comprise your composite measure. A major source for the items that will make up your composite scale or index is the previous research that has been done on your topic of interest. However, once you have reviewed the previous literature and are familiar with what has been done and the strengths and weaknesses of the existing research on your topic, your own imagination as the researcher is also a valuable source of potential items (Monette, Sullivan, & DeJong, 2005). Another source is people who are especially knowledgeable about your topic. If you are creating a scale measuring learning styles, teachers would be key informants. You might also identify scholars who have done substantial research on the topic. Other potential sources of items are the people who are the focus of your study. In the case of learning styles, those people would be students themselves (Monette et al., 2005). Conducting preliminary interviews with people who are especially knowledgeable about the phenomena you are measuring can be a valuable source of items to include in your scale or index. As you engage in item selection, you must be concerned about several factors: face validity, unidimensionality, exhaustiveness, and mutual exclusivity.

Face validity

Face validity in the context of creating items means that there should be at least a reasonable relationship between the item and the concept to be measured. In a measure of eating motivations, each item should be logically related to motivations to eat. For example, a measure of eating motivations would reasonably include an item about the availability of fresh fruits in one's home.

Unidimensionality

Items should also be **unidimensional**, meaning that scales and indexes should measure one dimension. Being unidimensional means that all of the items in scales and indexes should fit together or measure a single concept that may consist of multiple dimensions. This is important because when all of the items are scored, their total should measure a single concept.

Exhaustiveness

Items should also be **exhaustive**, meaning they should assess all of the possible nuances and aspects of the concept being measured. For instance, Cahill and fellow researchers (2009) divided eating stimuli into three broad areas covering the full range of motivating factors contributing to eating behaviors. Thus, their Eating Stimuli Index included items that measure each subsection of eating stimuli, including environmental factors, biological factors, and psychological factors. If an index only measured biological factors, it would not include all of the nuances of eating stimuli. The following questions about frequency of aerobic exercise are not exhaustive. Try to determine why (Neuman, 2009).

> On average, how many times per week do you engage in an aerobic exercise for at least 20 continuous minutes? (circle the correct answer)
> 1. Never
> 2. Less than 1 time per week
> 3. 1–2 times per week

The problem here is that the item is not exhaustive because individuals who engage in an aerobic exercise for at least 20 continuous minutes three or more times per week have no answer choice. The item could be written this way:

> On average, how many times per week do you engage in an aerobic exercise for at least 20 continuous minutes? (circle the correct answer)
> 1. Never
> 2. 1 time per week
> 3. 1–2 times per week
> 4. 3 or more times per week

Mutual Exclusivity

Now the above item does satisfy the criterion of exhaustiveness. However, it does not satisfy the requirement of mutual exclusivity. **Mutual exclusivity** means that in any quality index or scale, the quality of your variables should be both mutually exclusive and exhaustive. In a mutually exclusive item, a respondent's answer cannot fall into more than one category. A unit should go into one and only one category of a variable. For example, my response to the item about exercising should fit into only one response category. But are the response options mutually exclusive? No. An individual who engages in an aerobic exercise for at-least 20 continuous minutes 1 time per week could answer by circling either response option 3 or response option 4. In a mutually exclusive scale or index, a respondent should need to circle only one option. To ensure that this item is both mutually exclusive and exhaustive, it would be appropriate to remove response option 3. Thus:

> On average, how many times per week do you engage in an aerobic exercise for at least 20 continuous minutes? (circle the correct answer)
> 1. Never
> 2. Less than 1 time per week
> 3. 1–2 times per week
> 4. 3 or more times per week

Now the item is both mutually exclusive and exhaustive. Every item in a good scale or index should possess these characteristics.

Variance

An index or scale is expected to produce some degree of variance. **Variance** refers to the spread or dispersion of scores. If an item is expected to measure religiosity, then you should be able to note which respondents are religious, or how more or less religious some respondents are compared to others. But if that item identified no one as religious or everyone as religious, then the item would not be very useful because it does not indicate any variance. Items that offer no variance should be eliminated. The only way to determine how much variance an item offers is to pretest your scale or instrument.

Empirical Relationships

There should be a relationship between the items in an index or scale. If the items in an index or scale are measuring the same thing, it is reasonable that the answer a respondent gives to one item should be related to, or help predict, how the respondent is likely to answer several other items. For example, in a scale that measures communalism, you might find an item such as "I think the health of my community is more important than my personal health." An individual who agrees or strongly agrees with this statement should agree or strongly agree with a statement such as "Being involved in my community is important to me." It is possible that someone could agree with one and disagree with the other, but because the instrument is measuring similar general phenomena, there should typically be a relationship between the answers to them. In other words, the answer to one should predict the answer to the other. The relationship between variables can be tested by pilot testing a scale or index and using statistical software such as the Statistical Package for the Social Sciences (SPSS) to calculate the numerical relationships between variables. Some items may not correlate with others; if this is the case, those items may not be measuring the same variables, or they may simply measure different aspects of the same variable and vary independently. Nevertheless, each item in a scale should correlate with several others. In a perfect scale, each item should correlate somewhat with the others, but not too highly. If we discover that two items correlate perfectly with one another, then only one of them is necessary in the scale. If two items correlate nearly perfectly, then they are redundant, and having both of them adds nothing substantial to the scale. However, keep in mind that sometimes highly correlated items phrased in different wording are used in a scale to assess whether a respondent is answering honestly or just randomly marking answers.

Scaling Formats

The Likert Scale

In contrast to indexes, scales are especially suited to capturing the intensity of a phenomenon. Usually they are good for measuring people's beliefs, feelings, and opinions at the ordinal level. Although less common, they are also used at the interval and ratio levels. One kind of scale is the **Likert-type scale**, which consists of a series of statements followed by four to six response options. This kind of scale was invented by Rensis Likert (1932), and it has become one of the most widely used approaches to scaling. The typical number of response formats in Likert scaling is five; however, sometimes more or fewer are used, depending on the objective of the researcher. The purpose of the Likert scale is to move beyond the dichotomous response format to a response format that captures the relative intensity of an attitude or opinion.

The Racial Identity Attitude Scale (RIAS) (Table 9.4) uses a five-response agreement scale ranging from strongly disagree to strongly agree. Racial identity has been found to be related to self-esteem and many other indicators of psychological well-

Table 9.4

The Racial Identity Attitude Scale (RIAS)					
Read each of the following statements and decide to what extent you would agree or disagree with that statement. Indicate your answer by circling (SD) if you strongly disagree, (D) if you disagree, (U) if you are uncertain, (A) if you agree, or (SA) if you strongly agree, as the response that best describes how you feel most of the time.					
	STRONGLY DISAGREE	DISAGREE	UNCERTAIN	AGREE	STRONGLY AGREE
1. I believe that being Black is a positive experience.	SD (1)	D (2)	U (3)	A (4)	SA (5)
2. I know through experience what being Black in America means.	SD (1)	D (2)	U (3)	A (4)	SA (5)
3. I feel unable to involve myself in White experiences and am increasing my involvement in Black experiences.	SD (1)	D (2)	U (3)	A (4)	SA (5)
4. I believe that large numbers of Blacks are untrustworthy.	SD (1)	D (2)	U (3)	A (4)	SA (5)
5. I feel an overwhelming attachment to Black people.	SD (1)	D (2)	U (3)	A (4)	SA (5)
6. I try to involve myself in causes that will help oppressed people.	SD (1)	D (2)	U (3)	A (4)	SA (5)
7. I feel comfortable wherever I am.	SD (1)	D (2)	U (3)	A (4)	SA (5)
8. I believe that White people look and express themselves better than Black people.	SD (1)	D (2)	U (3)	A (4)	SA (5)
9. I feel uncomfortable around Black people.	SD (1)	D (2)	U (3)	A (4)	SA (5)
10. I feel good about being Black, but I do not limit myself to Black activities.	SD (1)	D (2)	U (3)	A (4)	SA (5)

being for Black people. The true RIAS is a 50-item Likert-type scale; however, only 10 items are used in Table 9.4 for the purpose of illustration. You will notice that the response options for the items in the RIAS scale have numbers next to them ranging from 1 to 5. These represent the point values of the RIAS ranging from 1 point for strongly disagree to 5 points for strongly agree. These numbers would not be displayed in the actual scale as administered to research participants because it could bias or influence respondents' answers. The numbers are only included here for the purpose of illustrating the scoring system used for the RIAS and similar scales. This instrument is scored by adding up respondents' point values on each of the subscales of the RIAS and dividing them by the number of items to maintain the scale metric.

The Likert scale adds a new dimension to measurement, especially when applied to opinions, attitudes, or beliefs. Consider the first questions in the RIAS: "I believe that being Black is a positive experience." Imagine that the response options to this item were dichotomous, "Agree" or "Disagree." What the Likert scale does that the dichotomous response format does not do is capture the *intensity* of a respondent's agreement with this statement by offering five response formats. Twenty people might agree with this statement; however, they might agree with different levels of intensity. The Likert scale offers five response options: strongly disagree, disagree, uncertain, agree, and strongly agree. The differences in intensity are what the Likert scale captures well, and this is what makes it an ideal scale for the measurement of attitudes, beliefs, and opinions.

The Likert scale must also have a balanced set of response options. For example, imagine that the response scale for the first item in the RIAS was strongly agree, agree, uncertain, and disagree. What is the problem? The scale is unbalanced because it provides more opportunity for positive responses than negative ones. People should have the same options for expressing disagreement as they have for expressing agreement and vice versa.

There are many different kinds of Likert-type response formats (Table 9.5). The responsibility of the researcher is to make sure the item (question or statement) matches the response format. Consider item 10 from the RIAS: "I feel good about being Black but I do not limit myself to Black activities." What if the response format were:

Never   Rarely   Some of the time   Often   Always

What is the problem with this response format? It is a frequency scale, and it doesn't match the item (statement). The response scale should be an agreement scale instead

Table 9.5

DIFFERENT LIKERT-TYPE RESPONSE FORMATS				
General	Not at All	Very Little	A Moderate Amount	Very Much	Completely
Level of Agreement	Strongly Disagree	Disagree	Not Sure (or Undecided) (or No Opinion)	Agree	Strongly Agree
Level of Importance	Unimportant	Of Little Importance	Moderately Important	Important	Very Important
Frequency	Never	Rarely	Some of the Time (or About Half the Time)	Most of the Time (or Often)	Always
Likelihood	Almost Never True	Usually Not True	Occasionally True	Usually True	Almost Always True
Level of Belief	Strongly Disbelieve	Disbelieve	Undecided (or Don't Know)	Believe	Strongly Believe
Level of Certainty	Definitely Not	Probably Not	Unsure	Probably	Definitely

of a frequency scale. When you offer a response format that doesn't match the item, what happens? A respondent may skip the item and not provide any data. The respondent may also circle any answer, which provides you with data that is invalid and limits your ability to draw any valid conclusions based on the respondent's score.

The term *worldview* refers to the philosophical assumptions that guide the way people think and perceive and experience the world around them (Obasi, Flores, & James-Myers, 2009). The Worldview Analysis Scale (WAS) was developed to measure worldview on a continuum from an African-centered worldview (Collectivism, Spiritualism) to a European-centered worldview (Individualism, Materialism). The WAS consists of 55 items, although only 10 are presented in Table 9.6 for the purpose of illustration. The WAS scale is a Likert-type agreement response scale, but its response format is different from the RIAS response format. Instead

Table 9.6

Worldview Analysis Scale (WAS)						
Direction: Answer each question as honestly as you possibly can by circling the response that best reflects your agreement/disagreement with each item ["Strongly Disagree" (1), "Disagree" (2), "Slightly Disagree" (3), "Slightly Agree" (4), "Agree" (5), "Strongly Agree" (6)]. There is no right or wrong answer, so please respond honestly. Provide only one response to each item.						
	STRONGLY DISAGREE	DISAGREE	SLIGHTLY DISAGREE	SLIGHTLY AGREE	AGREE	STRONGLY AGREE
1. I enjoy participating in family reunions.	1	2	3	4	5	6
2. My cultural heritage is often misrepresented and/or ignored in U.S. educational systems.	1	2	3	4	5	6
3. I do not feel like a spiritual person.	1	2	3	4	5	6
4. Spiritually blessed objects can protect a person from harm.	1	2	3	4	5	6
5. I existed spiritually before I was born.	1	2	3	4	5	6
6. Knowledge is restricted to the limitations of our five senses.	1	2	3	4	5	6
7. Everything in the universe is joined together by spiritual forces.	1	2	3	4	5	6
8. Being involved in community is very important to me.	1	2	3	4	5	6
9. There are visible and invisible dimensions of this universe.	1	2	3	4	5	6
10. Spiritual phenomena are not really real.	1	2	3	4	5	6

of having an undecided option, it has two additional response options: "slightly disagree" and "slightly agree." Researchers are divided on the question of whether or not to include a neutral response option such as "undecided." Those who support the use of a neutral response option believe that it is better to provide a neutral option than to force people to guess or to select a response option that does not reflect their honest opinion.

One problem that must be avoided in Likert-type scales is the problem of *response set*. This often occurs in scales that use the same response options for a long set of items on the same issue. For example, a respondent may be responding to 20 items on racial identity, and the items are set up in such a way that answering "strongly agree" always indicates positive attitudes about one's racial identity, and answering "strongly disagree" always indicates negative attitudes about one's racial identity. If this is the case, the respondent may stop reading after a while and simply mark "strongly agree" for the remainder of the items or vice versa, creating a **response set**.

The solution to a response set is reverse wording options. For example, the WAS is designed in such a way that high scores indicate a more African-centered worldview. But if you look closely at the items on the WAS, you will notice that items 3, 6, and 10 are reverse worded such that strongly agreeing with them does not indicate an African-centered worldview at all. On the contrary, strongly agreeing with those items indicates a rejection of spirituality and collectivism. For the majority of the items, strongly agreeing would indicate an African-centered worldview. For example, for the first item, "I existed spiritually before I was born," strongly agreeing would be an indication of spiritualism. However, item 3, "I do not feel like a spiritual person" is reverse worded such that strongly agreeing would actually indicate a rejection of spiritualism. Because some of the items are reverse worded, a person who has a strongly African-centered worldview cannot simply go through and strongly agree with all of the items. Instead, they have to switch from agreeing to disagreeing and take each item on an individual basis. Because items are reverse worded, they must also be reverse scored (Table 9.7). For example, the WAS is scored by adding respondents' scores and dividing them by the number of items. Higher scores indicate a more

Table 9.7

Scoring and Reverse Scoring						
Scoring	1	2	3	4	5	6
	Strongly Disagree	Disagree	Slightly Disagree	Slightly Agree	Agree	Strongly Agree
Reverse Scoring	6	5	4	3	2	1

African-centered worldview, and lower scores indicate a more European-centered worldview. However, because some items are reverse worded, those items need to be reverse scored so that high and low scores are still meaningful.

In table 9.6 you will notice that items 3, 6, and 10 have a small ® next to each statement. This is to indicate that they are to be reverse scored. Those symbols should not appear on the actual scale presented to respondents, but are there only to help the researcher keep track of which items are to be reverse scored. For most of the items in the WAS, strongly agreeing counts for the highest number of points, and a cumulative high score will indicate a spiritually grounded, African-centered worldview. To maintain the meaning of a high and low score, strongly agreeing with items 3, 6, and 10 should earn one point instead of 6 points. Reverse scoring is illustrated in Table 9.7. The Likert scale is an ordinal-level measure ranging from strongly agree to strongly disagree, for example. And because the Likert scale's total score is often the sum of a respondent's answers to individual ordinal-level items, people assume that it is ordinal in nature (Monette et al., 2005). Technically, researchers are encouraged not to calculate means and standard deviations and other interval-level procedures from ordinal-level data. However, it is common for Likert scale data to calculate means and standard deviations, thus treating Likert scale data as if they were interval-level data.

Social Distance Scale

Des Courtis, Lauber, Costa, and Cattapan-Ludewig (2008) were interested in studying and comparing the attitudes of Brazilian and Swiss mental health professionals toward people with mental illnesses. One of the methods they used was to ask them the following series of questions after being presented with a description of a patient fitting the criteria for major depression. (Let's use the pseudonym "Jason" for the sake of the example.)

1. Would you be willing to work with a person like Jason?
2. Would you like to move next door to a person like Jason?
3. Would you be willing to make friends with a person like Jason?
4. Would you recommend a person like Jason for a job?
5. Would you rent a room to a person like Jason?
6. Would you like your child to marry a person like Jason?
7. Would you trust a person like Jason to take care of your child?

The questions purposefully increase contact, in terms of closeness or intimacy, with someone with a mental illness. Therefore, this questionnaire accomplishes its purpose of measuring the intensity of the variable "attitudes toward people with mental illnesses." The combination and arrangement of these kinds of items is what is called a Bogardus **social distance scale** (created by Emory Bogardus). The purpose of this kind of scale is to measure the amount of social distance separating groups or to determine the willingness of people to engage in varying degrees of intimacy in social relations with others. The items in the Bogardus scale are ordered based on their level of intensity, from the most socially distant to the most socially intimate. It is a scale that indicates the point at which people no longer feel comfortable. It is presumed that if a person were willing to accept one level of intensity of association, s/he would be willing to accept all of those associations preceding it on the list (those with lesser associations). For instance, if a person is willing to rent a room to a person who is mentally ill, it is likely that he or she would be willing to work with that person. Nonetheless, he or she may not trust a person who is mentally ill to take care of his or her child. The items with weaker levels of intensity of association are called "easy" items, and those with stronger levels of association are called "hard" items. Typically, people agree more with the easy items compared to the hard items, with some exceptions.

Guttman Scale

Researchers often attempt to make scales that are unidimensional or measure a single variable or a single aspect of a variable. **Guttman scaling** is used in the process of scale construction to ensure that a scale is unidimensional (Monette et al., 2005). The Guttman scale was invented by Louis Guttman and is based on the assumption that some items in a scale are more extreme indicators of a variable than others (Babbie, 2001). In contrast to other scales, the Guttman scale is used on data after they have already been collected. The scale tells a researcher whether or not a particular structure or sequence holds true among a set of items.

The patterns in a Guttman scale are hierarchically arranged from easier (basic or lower) to harder (advanced or difficult) items. In Guttman scaling, the researcher arranges the items from easier items to lower items and tests the extent to which the data you collect actually fit that pattern. Koslowsky, Pratt, and Wintrob (1976) investigated the nature of physicians' attitudes toward abortion based on individual patient circumstances. Interviewees in this study pretested the interview questions and arranged 11 questions from easiest to hardest. Each participant was asked his or her personal opinion about the decision to have an abortion based on 11 different circumstances arranged in a hierarchical order. The Guttman scale was used to measure the extent to which interviewees' acceptance or rejection of each circumstance fit the hierarchical sequence or pattern in which the researchers arranged the items or circumstances. The Guttman scale provides a coefficient of reliability score, which is the degree to which answers to questions fit a sequence

Table 9.8

Percentage of Acceptance and Rejection and Number of Errors for Each Circumstance in Guttman Scale				
	RESPONSE PERCENTAGE		ERROR	
CIRCUMSTANCE	REJECT	ACCEPT	REJECT	ACCEPT
1. Career of education would be disrupted.	60	40	0	3
2. Too young to have a child.	57	43	0	3
3. Financially unable to support the child.	55	45	2	1
4. Too old to have the child.	55	45	2	1
5. Does not want the child.	54	46	2	1
6. Being unmarried would be a problem.	48	52	2	2
7. Pregnancy or childbirth is a threat to mental health.	32	68	0	1
8. Pregnancy of childbirth is a threat to physical health.	28	72	1	2
9. Pregnancy is a result of rape or incest.	28	72	3	1
10. Risk of congenital abnormality.	25	75	2	1
11. Pregnancy or childbirth is a threat to life.	23	77	2	0

ranging from 0 to 1, with 0 indicating the pattern of response and 1 indicating that everyone's answers fit the hierarchical sequence of the items. A coefficient of reliability score of .90 is considered to be evidence of a reliable Guttman scale, and a unidimensional instrument. The results of Koslowsky and colleagues' (1976) 11 Guttman scale items are illustrated in Table 9.8. As shown, the physicians who participated in the study produced a gradient of responses. Using SPSS, Koslowsky and fellow researchers (1976) calculated a coefficient of reliability of .96, which is significant and indicates the unidimensionality of their items or circumstances that fit the Guttman scale pattern. Their research indicated that physicians had high rates of approval of abortion for medical reasons and lower rates of approval for sociocultural or non-medical reasons, with the exception of rape or incest as a reason for abortion.

Thurstone Scale

Thurstone scaling is a method of scale construction in which judges assign weights and degrees of intensity to scaled items (Vogt, 1999). In constructing a Thurstone scale, the researchers begin by identifying hundreds of items or statements that are indicators of the variable being measured. A group of 10–15 judges is selected by the researchers and given the task of assigning a score indicating the strength of each item on a scale of 1–11. If the variable were sexism, for example, judges would be given the task of assigning a score of 1 to the weakest indicators of sexism and 11 to the strongest indicators of prejudice, and also intermediate scores to those items that are felt to be somewhere in between (Babbie, 2001). After a group of judges assigns scores to each item, the researcher(s) must then analyze all of the items and identify the percentage of agreement among the scores assigned to each item.

The objective is to determine which items have the most agreement among the judges. Those items with the least amount of agreement are considered ambiguous and are discarded. Among the items with the most agreement, one or more of them will be assigned to represent each point on a scale from 1 to 11. The final items are arranged randomly and are presented to and completed by research participants. However, there must be an equal number of favorable and unfavorable items. Participants are typically asked to indicate which items they agree with, which makes the Thurstone scale easy for respondents to complete. Participants are also assigned a score based on their completed scales. Scores are calculated based on the mean of the scale values a respondent agrees with. Thurstone scales are easier and quicker to complete than Likert scales, but they are also more costly and difficult to construct.

Semantic Differential

Osgood, Suci, and Tannenbaum (1957) developed the semantic differential scaling format. The **semantic differential** is a scaling format in which "respondents are asked to locate their attitudes on a scale ranging between opposite positions on a particular issue" (Vogt, 1999, p. 261). The respondents usually indicate their attitudes by marking points on a scale from 1 to 7, with qualifiers between the two opposites. The semantic differential scale usually consists of seven points but can have more or fewer. To create the scale, you must first identify the dimension of the variable on which you want respondents to rate their attitudes. Then you must identify the relevant adjectives that represent polar opposites for each dimension. Semantic differential scores can be computed by calculating the sum of each individual adjective pair separately. The scores for semantic differentials can also be computed by summarizing the scores for all of the pairs in each dimension. Semantic differentials usually require 4–8 adjective pairs for each dimension of the variable being measured.

Durrheim, Dixon, Tredoux, Eaton, Quayle, and Clack (2011) studied racial attitudes in South Africa. They used a semantic differential to measure respondents' attitudes about Blacks and Whites using five polar opposite adjectives on a point

Table 9.9

Racial Attitudes about Black and White South Africans											
	1	2	3	4	5	6	7	8	9	10	
Negative	—	—	—	—	—	—	—	—	—	—	Positive
Cold	—	—	—	—	—	—	—	—	—	—	Warm
Hostile	—	—	—	—	—	—	—	—	—	—	Friendly
Suspicious	—	—	—	—	—	—	—	—	—	—	Trusting
Disrespect	—	—	—	—	—	—	—	—	—	—	Respect

scale from 1 to 10: negative/positive, cold/warm, hostile/friendly, suspicious/trusting, disrespect/respect. The adjective pairs used in their study are illustrated in Table 9.9. Their scale provides the respondent with the opportunity to rate each pair of adjectives on one of ten points between each value.

Researchers' decisions about which index or scaling procedures to use should be based on their research question. Different objectives call for different indexing and scaling techniques. Be familiar with all of them so that you are prepared to choose the most appropriate techniques.

Key Terms

Exhaustive   Scale
Guttman Scaling   Semantic Differential
Index   Social Distance Scale
Likert-Type Scale   Thurstone Scaling
Mutual Exclusivity   Unidimensional
Response Set   Variance

Thinking about Science

The CDF Freedom Schools program provides summer and after-school enrichment that helps children fall in love with reading, increases their self-esteem, and generates more positive attitudes toward learning. Children are taught using a model curriculum that supports children and families around five essential components: high-quality academic enrichment; parent and family involvement; civic engagement and so-

cial action; intergenerational leadership development; and nutrition, health and mental health.

—CHILDREN'S DEFENSE FUND, 2012

Activity 1

- Based on the Children's Defense Fund's description of its Freedom Schools program, if you were to create an index measuring the effectiveness of the Freedom School program's summer school enrichment, what *dimensions* of summer school effectiveness might you measure?

Activity 2

- Based on the stated goals of the Freedom School program in the United States, develop six Likert-type items to assess the effectiveness of Freedom Schools. Keep in mind that your items will be completed by students between the ages of 9 and 12 who are currently enrolled in the Freedom Schools program. Your items should measure their attitudes about their Freedom School experience based on the goals of the Freedom Schools program.

Activity 3

Imagine that the following questions and others were asked of Freedom Schools students to assess the effectiveness of the program. Explain whether or not each of the following questions has face validity and content validity.

- What did you enjoy most about the readings you had in the Freedom Schools program?
- Does participating in Freedom Schools make you enjoy reading more than you did before you were in Freedom Schools?
- Does participating in Freedom Schools make you feel better about America?

CHAPTER TEN

Survey Design: Asking Questions

Toddlers quickly learn that when there is information they would like to know, one of the easiest tools at their disposal is the "question." They ask lots of questions because, unlike adults, they are unburdened with presumptions about knowing the answers. They know they don't know; therefore they are insatiable askers of questions. A disciplined researcher can learn a lot from toddlers, especially their willingness to question things that most people take for granted. Too often we ignore or dismiss that voice inside that has a question. That voice is a researcher's antennae. If we can learn to listen to it, we will never be without a research question. This chapter is about questioning—specifically it is about survey design. The chapter covers the various types of surveys and questionnaires. It also explains the common pitfalls that present themselves during the survey process, how they can affect your research, and how to avoid them.

The Joint Center for Political and Economic Studies conducted an investigation of African Americans' attitudes about social security and retirement savings. The study found that African Americans and White Americans had some similar and different attitudes about social security and retirement policies. Leigh and Wheatley (2010) surveyed 850 African Americans and 850 members of the general public; 721 Whites were surveyed. African Americans were more likely than Whites to expect social security to be their major source of income after retirement (Leigh & Wheatley, 2010). African Americans were more likely than Whites to support the social security system as it is, believe that its benefits should be means-based, and think that the retirement age should not be raised. Such survey data would be important for any interest groups concerned with formulating and advocating a public policy agenda that would benefit African Americans.

But what are surveys? A **survey** is a tool for collecting data from individuals called respondents by having them respond to items (questions and statements). It is the most widely used data collection technique in the social sciences. You have likely been asked to participate in a survey at some point(s) in your life. It involves asking a relatively large sample of people questions regarding a variable over a short period of time and analyzing the results to describe a situation (Babbie, 2001). Surveys have the following characteristics:

- Surveys are best suited to large populations; thus, their strength is their generalizability or their ability to produce data that are representative of large populations that are difficult to study using other methods.
- Surveys involve presenting respondents with a series of questions related to a given topic or variable. Survey data represent peoples' answers to those questions.

Exhibit 10.1

Poll on Daily Twitter Usage

"The number of adults using Twitter every day has doubled since 2011, according to a new survey. Eight percent of adult Internet users said they log on to Twitter every day, up from the 4% who said the same last year, according to the Pew Research Center, which conducted the survey. That number was even higher for young adults. One in five Internet users ages 18 to 24 are using the website each day, and nearly one-third of all users that age are on Twitter. The reason for the increase in daily usage is likely because of the rise of smartphones, the survey suggests. "Those ages 18-24 are not just the fastest growing group when it comes to Twitter adoption over the last year," the survey reads. "They also experienced the largest increase in smartphone ownership of any demographic group over the same time period." The survey shows that 20% of smartphone users are also Twitters users while those who own basic phones are half as likely to use Twitter. The bad news for Twitter, however, is its overall adult usage did not pick up by much. Last year, 13% of adults on the Internet were using Twitter. That number went up to only 15% in the latest results. Another interesting fact from the survey is African Americans use Twitter twice as much as other ethnic groups. More than a quarter, 28%, of black Internet users are on Twitter as opposed to Hispanic, 12%, and white Internet users, 14%." (Rodrigez, 2012)

—From the *LA Times* website, May 31st, 2012

- Surveys are not well suited for research on topics that people are unaware of or unwilling to share information about (Neuman, 2009).
- Surveys are an effective tool for analyzing the attitudes and opinions of large populations that are not easily accessible.
- Surveys are best suited to descriptive, explanatory, and exploratory purposes.

Surveys are most effective when they are used to investigate topics that people are able and willing to report on. However, it is important to remember that surveys measure what people say about their thoughts, opinions, and behaviors. Surveys do not directly observe those thoughts, attitudes, and behaviors; rather, it is indirect. For example, a survey on people's dietary habits might indicate that a respondent consumes 2,000 calories per day, but we cannot conclude that this is exactly how much that person consumes. Surveys involve what people say they do, not what they do indeed (Monette, Sullivan, & DeJong, 2005). Instead, we can infer that this is how much they consume based on what they have said.

A poll is a certain kind of survey. If you follow the news (*The Washington Post*, CBS, CNN, Fox News, etc.) you will hear reports of many different poll results. Opinion polls are shorter than most surveys; they take place over a shorter period of time and cover current issues. Exhibit 10.1 explains the results of a Pew Research Center Poll on changes in Twitter usage.

The Survey Process

It is first important to determine whether or not the survey method is the most appropriate method to help you answer your research question. Neuman (2009) identifies several steps in the survey process.

The beginning of the survey process consists of identifying who the respondents will be for your study, since this will have an influence on the topic and vice versa. The researcher must also select the research population best suited to providing the information necessary to answer the research question. In step one, the researcher must also identify what he or she wants to know from the respondents or research participants. Knowing what you eventually want to be able to say is essential in the development of questions.

Once the researchers have identified the population and purpose of the study, they can begin to develop items (questions or statements) related to the topic. It is important to look for questionnaires developed by other researchers that may be helpful. The researcher should anticipate going through the process of writing and re-writing questions and statements until the items are as clear and precise as possible. It is essential to pilot the survey or to conduct a preliminary trial run of the survey questionnaire. To do this, the researcher administers the survey to a sample population similar to the target population. What the researcher wants to know from the pilot research participants is whether or not the items (questions or statements) were clear, whether or not their answer choices were sufficient, and whether or not they interpreted the questions and statements the way the researcher intended them to. As a result of the feedback a researcher gets from the pilot survey, she may want to rephrase or reformat the survey to improve it.

The next step is actually carrying out the survey, which involves contacting the population and explaining to them how the survey must be completed. The researcher has to record all of the respondents' responses and prepare the data to be analyzed statistically. The last steps in the survey process involve analyzing the data, reporting, and presenting the results.

Practical Function of Surveys

A bank may survey its employees to assess employee job satisfaction. Coordinators of an after-school reading program for youth may be interested in measuring its effectiveness. The coordinators might do this by surveying its youth members. A hospital office may distribute an outpatient survey to assess how well it has served patients. A health education intervention program may distribute a survey to assess any changes in its participants' dietary habits. Surveys can be crucial instruments in the formation and improvement of organizations interested in becoming agents of social change or delivering critical services to different populations.

Two Means of Collecting Survey Data

Survey data are collected using two major tools: questionnaires and interviews. **Questionnaires** consist of questions meant for research participants or subjects to respond to without being read by the interviewer. Questionnaires can be distributed to respondents in person or they can be mailed. Questionnaires can also be distributed to participants via the Internet—by email, for example. **Interviews** involve an interviewer reading questions to respondents and recording respondents' answers.

Constructing Survey Items

The term *questionnaire* can be misleading in some respects because actual questionnaires often contain more than questions; they contain statements as well. In fact, instead of using the term *question*, the term **item** is used to refer to both questions and statements. **Questions** are requests for information and end with a question mark. **Statements** are sentences or phrases designed to gather information about a respondent. They are used when researchers want to measure the extent to which a respondent holds a particular attitude or opinion. Instead of asking a question, the researcher can develop a statement that embodies a particular attitude or belief, present it to a respondent, and ask the respondent to indicate the extent to which he or she agrees or disagrees with it. For example, McGee (1996) developed the Violent Victimization Survey to assess the extent of violent victimization and psychological trauma among students at predominantly Black high schools. The instrument (survey) contains questions, but it also contains statements. Here are some of the statements in the Violent Victimization Survey using an agreement scale (SD = strongly disagree, D = disagree, A = agree, and SA = strongly agree):

My neighborhood is a safe place to live.	SD (1)	D (2)	A (3)	SA (4)
There is a lot of violence in this school.	SD (1)	D (2)	A (3)	SA (4)
When I am in school I am scared most of the time.	SD (1)	D (2)	A (3)	SA (4)

Of course these are not questions; they are statements. However, they can also be posed in the form of questions:

Is your neighborhood a safe place to live?	Yes	No
Is there a lot of violence in this school?	Yes	No
When you are in school are you scared?	Yes	No

Ultimately, using both questions and statements diversifies a survey and keeps respondents engaged. In survey research, researchers can pose open- or closed-ended items. **Open-ended items** are statements or questions that give respondents the opportunity to provide their own answers. An example of an open-ended question can be found in Exhibit 10.2.

Exhibit 10.2

In your opinion what is the most important challenge facing the Black community?

_____

_____

_____

_____

Exhibit 10.3

Advantages and Limitations of Open-Ended Items

Advantages

- All possible answers are permitted
- Make it possible for unanticipated findings to emerge
- Permit sufficient answers to complex issues
- Allow respondents to express themselves in their own words
- The respondents thought process is revealed
- They are useful for exploratory research

Disadvantages

- Time consuming for the researcher to administer and analyze the data
- Require more effort from the respondent
- Highly articulate and literate respondents have an advantage
- Respondents may give irrelevant or unclear answers
- Comparison is difficult

Open-ended items, however, do place additional burdens on the respondent, and the researcher should be aware of that. Open-ended items in a survey also require a greater level of verbal skill on the part of research participants, who must express their attitudes and opinions. See the advantages and limitations of closed ended items in exhibit 10.3. Open-ended items can also be very tedious for the researcher who must sometimes read hundreds of different open-ended answers and analyze them, which takes quite a bit of time. They are best when used on small populations (fewer than 200 people) and with a short number of items (fewer than 20). Open-ended questions are good for exploratory studies when the researcher is pursuing a topic that there is little research on and little theoretical development about. In these kinds of studies it is best to place few restrictions on respondents' answers.

Closed-ended items are statements or questions designed to provide respondents with a fixed set of response options, often multiple choices. See the advantages and limitations of closed-ended items in exhibit 10.4. Closed-ended items are often preferred because they are uniform, which makes them easy for the researcher to analyze. However, the researcher must be sure to use closed-ended items when all the possible response options can be anticipated in advance. For example, there are a known number of response options to a question such as "What is your marital status?" Therefore, it is suitable for a closed-ended response format such as:

Exhibit 10.4

Advantages and Limitations of Closed-Ended Items

Advantages
- Quicker and easier for respondents to answer
- Answers are easier to code, process and statistically analyze
- Respondents are more likely to respond to sensitive questions
- Respondents' answers are clear
- Suitable for less literate and less articulate respondents
- Answers are easier to compare
- Make it easier to replicate research

Disadvantages
- Loss of spontaneity in respondents answers
- Respondents with no opinion or knowledge may provide invalid answers
- They may suggest answers that respondents would not have thought of
- Respondents desired answers may not be available
- Respondents may be forced to give simplistic answers to complex issues
- Respondents may be forced to make choices they may not have to make in the real world

---

a. married
b. single
c. separated
d. divorced
e. widowed
f. engaged
g. annulled
h. cohabitating

The challenge of closed-ended responses is that researchers may not anticipate all of the possible responses that respondents may want to choose from. When this happens, respondents may be forced to choose an answer that is not the best reflection of their attitudes. For example, the researcher may ask the question, "In your opinion, what is the most important challenge facing the Black community?" using a closed-ended format. If this happens, the fixed response options may not include options such as "lack of educational resources" or "joblessness." In some cases it is appropriate to pose partially open-ended items. For example, the researcher might be interested in knowing a respondent's religious affiliation and include the following item in a survey:

What is your religious affiliation?
  a. Protestant Christian
  b. Roman Catholic
  c. Evangelical Christian
  d. Jewish
  e. Muslim
  f. Hindu
  g. Buddhist
  h. Other: _____

This item is *partially* open-ended because, although we may be able to anticipate the religions that have large numbers of people affiliated with them, there are likely to be individuals who affiliate with a less-known and less-popular religion. In this case the researcher can offer an open-ended "other" option that allows a respondent to write in a less-common response to the question. This accommodates persons with less-common views instead of leaving them without a response option. Monette, Sullivan, and DeJong (2005) suggest that educated respondents may become dismayed with completely closed-ended instruments because they are overly simplistic ways of addressing complex issues. However, open-ended questions are often seen by respondents as more satisfying and make respondents more likely to complete the instrument.

It is important for a researcher to think about the type of question that is being asked. What follows is a discussion of three additional types of questions.

Factual items are those questions or statements that have a definitive answer. These questions ask respondents for objective information. Factual questions are questions such as: "Are you a vegetarian?" or "Do you eat meat?" Factual questions are also those that ask respondents about their income levels, their educational levels, or their ages. Factual questions often require dichotomous "yes/no" response formats or other closed-ended response formats.

Opinion items are questions or statements that don't have definitive answers. Opinion-based questions often ask respondents for their attitudes or their beliefs, such as their political attitudes or their religious beliefs. Opinion-based questions often require Likert-type response formats and open-ended response formats.

Vignette Questions

The **vignette question** is a technique that is used to investigate people's normative standards. The vignette approach involves presenting respondents with one or more scenarios, then asking them how they would respond if they were confronted with the circumstances in that scenario (Bryman, 2008). Brown and fellow researchers (2011) designed a study to assess "differences in the perceptions of depression of Black African and White British women that may influence lower detection and to investigate whether there are ethnic group differences in reasons for not seeking formal help" (p. 362). Participants in this study were presented with the following vignette:

> You have been feeling unusually sad and miserable for the last few weeks. Even though you are tired all the time, you have trouble sleeping nearly every night. You don't feel like eating and have lost weight. You can't keep your mind on your work and put off making decisions. Even day-to-day tasks seem too much for you. This has come to the attention of your boss who is concerned about your lowered productivity. (Brown et al., 2011, p. 364)

Respondents were asked to imagine themselves as the character in the vignette, and then they were asked to answer several questions. The purpose of the study was to assess the participants' own illness perceptions. Participants were asked to respond to the situation of the vignette character. They were asked to answer questions such as: "How much do you think treatment can help these difficulties?" "How long do you think these difficulties will continue?" "How concerned are you about these difficulties?" "How well do you understand these difficulties?" Vignette questions are very helpful when researching sensitive issues because it creates a distance between the person and the question. This is because the questions are about other people (characters in the vignette) and not the respondents themselves.

Avoiding Problems in Asking Questions: The Rules of Item Construction

CLARITY: Items should have one and only one interpretation. A question such as "What is your income?" may seem simple and unambiguous. However, this question is not as clear as it could be. Respondents needs to know whether or not you are asking about their monthly, weekly, or annual income. Item ambiguity is a threat to the validity of a survey because you will get responses from respondents who have interpreted items in different ways. Consider the question "What do you think about the president's comments about Iran?" Such a question simply provokes another question: "Which comments and when?" Ambiguous wording also leads to lack of item clarity. A question such as "Do you eat fast food regularly?" is likely to be met with another question, "What is meant by 'regularly'?" If you mean "once a day" or "once a week," use those specific terms in the question instead.

DOUBLE-BARRELED QUESTIONS: Sometimes a researcher can pose an unfair question to respondents by requiring them to provide one answer to a question with two or more parts. Double-barreled questions occur when you ask more than one question and only allow for one answer. Consider the following item, "I cry over the slightest thing and my mood changes from day to day. ○Agree or ○Disagree." Some people would agree with this statement; others would disagree. However, how will people answer whose mood changes from day to day, but they don't cry over the slightest thing? These individuals might skip the question or provide a misleading answer. The solution to the double-barreled question is simply to ask one question at a time.

RESPONDENTS MUST BE COMPETENT TO ANSWER: Respondents should not be expected to provide answers to questions about which they don't have any knowledge. You might ask respondents to identify the age at which they were first punished for misbehaving. Outside of the issue about what counts as punishment, they are not likely to accurately remember when they were first punished. As such, it would not make sense to ask respondents about the functioning of iPads if they have never used one. If you were researching a sample population that is in elementary school grades 4–5, it would not be a good idea to ask them to self-report their grade point averages (GPAs) because they are not likely to be knowledgeable about them. Instead, with parental consent, you could get their GPAs from school administrators. If you ask young children for their GPAs, they are likely to leave the question blank or take a guess, which would invalidate your data.

ITEMS MUST BE RELEVANT TO RESPONDENTS: It is important for the researcher to avoid asking respondents to provide information on issues that they haven't thought about or don't care about (Babbie, 2001). When an item is not relevant to a respondent, it helps to offer response options such as "I don't know," "undecided" or "no opinion."

NEGATION: The problem with items that use the word "not" is that respondents can easily miss that word and answer in the opposite way from the way you intended. If the word "no" is used in an item, it is important to use bold, underline or italicize it, or use all caps in order to be sure that the word "no" is recognized. For example, when reading the statement "Congress should not approve more funds for health care and social assistance," some respondents are likely to miss the word "not." If they believe that Congress should approve the new stimulus package, they are likely to agree with this statement. If you use the word "not," be sure that the word appears in boldface, is underlined or italicized, or is printed in capital letters so that the word is recognized. For example, "Congress should **not** approve more funds for health care."

THREATENING/INSENSITIVE LANGUAGE: There is a reason why questionnaires ask people if they have been convicted of a crime instead of whether or not they are criminals, or what their income level is instead of whether they are rich or poor. It is important to avoid insensitive, threatening, and judgmental language. For example, the researcher should avoid outdated ethnic or racial terms as well as insensitive language to describe a particular sexual orientation. Such questions can lead respondents to provide misleading answers or to refuse to answer at all.

LENGTH OF ITEMS: If you are researching a complex phenomenon, it is tempting to create items that are very long. This should be avoided, and items should be short and concise. Respondents are often unwilling to do a lot of reading. Wordiness can discourage them from completing a survey. Respondents often want to answer questions quickly and may simply skim long items and answer them without a complete understanding. The researcher should be sure to provide short and clear items. Concise items are least likely to be misinterpreted.

JARGON: It is important for the researcher to avoid using sophisticated language or technical jargon. The researcher has the responsibility of keeping the language in a survey at the level of the respondents. Plumbers use puller kits, fitting brushes, and snakes; bankers speak of junk bonds, bearer bonds, and convertible bonds; psychologists speak of memetics. This kind of language should be avoided in the design of questions. You would not ask respondents, "Do you favor or oppose an increase in the *excise* of tobacco *consumption?*" Instead you would ask, "Do you favor or oppose an increase in taxes on cigarettes?" If you wanted to assess the degree of homework difficulty for a group of fifth-grade students, you would not ask them, "Do you feel *overwhelmed* with the homework you get?" "Overwhelmed" is too sophisticated a word. The researcher's objective is to be sure that participants understand the questions being asked. You wouldn't ask a student, "Do you feel alienated by the curriculum in your classes?" You would ask, "Do you feel that you can relate what you are learning to your personal life?" Simple language is always the best approach. The researcher should generally keep the wording at the eight-grade level.

BALANCE AND SYMMETRY: A researcher must maintain balance and symmetry between items and response options. Sometimes a researcher will design a survey with an imbalance of negatively or positively worded items. If a survey is attempting to assess the level of violence in people's neighborhoods, you might find that the majority of their items are negatively worded such that a respondent is asked:

- Have you witnessed someone being physically attacked in your neighborhood?
- Do you consider your neighborhood to be a "violent neighborhood"?
- Have you ever witnessed someone being robbed in your neighborhood?
- Are you afraid to be outdoors in your neighborhood?

These are primarily negatively worded items; they are not very balanced. The researcher should add more positively worded items to such questions. There should be questions such as, "Do you consider your neighborhood to be a safe neighborhood?" and "Do people in your neighborhood show concern for one another's safety?" Moreover, there should also be balance and symmetry among the response options for survey items. You should not write in a survey "Please indicate on a scale from 1 to 5 how violent you feel your neighborhood is, 1 being not violent and 5 being very violent." Instead, write "Please indicate on a scale from 1 to 5 how safe or violent you feel your neighborhood is." You should not have an item with the following response format:

1. I believe that being Black is a positive experience.
   Strongly Disagree   Disagree   Undecided   Agree

This response format is skewed or unsymmetrical because it presents the respondent with more opportunities to disagree with this statement than to agree. It suggests that the researchers are less interested in responses that indicate positive feelings about Blackness. Instead, it should offer the respondent a balanced set of response options such as:

1. I believe that being Black is a positive experience.
   Strongly Disagree   Disagree   Undecided   Agree   Strongly Agree

LEADING QUESTIONS: The researcher should always avoid leading questions. Some questions appear to be leading respondents to answer in a certain way. For example, "Would you agree with raising taxes on cigarettes even though doing so might result in a reduction in cigarette-industry donations to early childhood education?" The problem with such a question is that it appears to be leading the respondent toward disagreement. Consider the following question: "Did you vote for your fellow African American presidential candidate Barack Obama in the presidential election?" Although the researcher is interested in knowing how the respondent voted, the item is leading the respondent to respond by saying "yes." Dishonest researchers who want to manipulate the results of a survey use leading questions. The researcher's goal should be to construct a survey in which respondents don't know what answer the researcher would prefer and feel completely free to provide the answer that best represents how they think.

SOCIAL DESIRABILITY BIAS: This occurs when respondents attempt to give answers that present themselves in a positive light or conform to social norms. For example, if you ask people whether or not they are racist, they are likely to say "no" because being a racist is something that most people know is not socially desirable, even if they are racist. Therefore, it is important for the researcher to be sure to let the respondent know that there are no preferred answers. It is also helpful to phrase questions so that the atypical answer doesn't seem to be undesirable. According to Neuman (2009), "The National Election Survey asked about voting in the following way to reduce the social desirability bias: 'In talking to people about elections, we often find that a lot of people were not able to vote because they weren't registered, they were sick, or they just didn't have time. Which of the following best describes you?—One, I did not vote; Two, I thought about voting this time but didn't; Three, I usually vote but didn't this time; Four, I am sure I voted'" (p. 165).

Self-Administered Questionnaire Design

A questionnaire is a group of written questions to which a research subject or participant is expected to respond. Sometimes researchers hand questionnaires to respondents, in which case respondents have the opportunity to ask the researcher questions for clarification. In other instances, such as when questionnaires are distributed online through email, the respondent does not have the opportunity to ask questions for clarification. In any event, the researcher must take care to be sure that the questionnaire is self-explanatory and clear enough that the respondent doesn't need to ask for clarification. When there is no interviewer to ask questions of, the respondent needs to be able to read the questionnaire for him or herself and capture its intended meaning. Because of this, questionnaires tend to:

- have more closed-ended questions since they tend to be easier to answer;
- have easy-to-follow formats and designs to minimize confusion; and
- be shorter in length to reduce the likelihood that respondents will become exhausted.

Exhibit 10.5

Directions for African Self-Consciousness Scale

Instructions: *The following statements reflect some beliefs, opinions, and attitudes of Black people. Read each statement carefully and give your honest feeling about the beliefs and attitudes expressed. Indicate the extent to which you agree by using the following scale:*

1	2	3	4	5	6	7	8
Strongly Disagree		Disagree		Agree		Strongly Agree	

Circle the number closest to your own feelings. Note that the higher the number you choose for the statement, the more you agree with that statement; conversely, the lower the number you choose, the more you disagree with that statement. Also, there is no right or wrong answer, only the answer that best expresses your feelings about the statement. Please respond to all statements (do not omit any).

Instructions

One of the researcher's most basic responsibilities in questionnaire design is to provide clear instructions. Exhibit 10.5 illustrates a clear set of directions for the African Self-Consciousness Scale, which was designed to assess the Black personality (Baldwin & Bell, 1985). Instructions are not just for the respondent; good instructions improve the quality of data that the researcher gets back.

The directions to a questionnaire should be preceded by a sentence or two about the purpose of that instrument. For example, "The following statements reflect some beliefs, opinions, and attitudes of Black people." If respondents are expected to insert an "X," fill in a circle, or circle an answer, then they should be clearly instructed to do so. However, sometimes questionnaires require different response formats or ways of answering questions. Every time the response format changes, there needs to be a new set of instructions. If questions 1–3 require an individual to fill in the blank, and Question 4 requires the respondent to circle their answer, then there needs to be a new set of instructions after Question 3 (Exhibit 10.6).

Order of Questions

What comes when? Careful consideration needs to be given to the order of items in a questionnaire. A poorly ordered questionnaire can bias respondents' an-

Exhibit 10.6

New Directions Each Time There Is a Change in Response Format

Please fill in the correct answers.

1. What grade are you in?_____
2. What is your age?_____
3. What is your zip code?_____

Please circle the correct answer.

4. In my home, I have a space dedicated to study?   Yes   No

---

swers or reduce their response rates. Researchers should try not to ask questions early in a questionnaire that will bias subjects' responses to later items. For example, if a researcher designs a questionnaire with several factual questions about healthcare in the Black community early in a questionnaire and later asks respondents what they think is the most critical issue facing the Black community, the respondents are more likely to mention healthcare because they will want to answer in a way that they believe to be consistent. This problem can be avoided by placing opinion questions and open-ended questions early in a questionnaire and factual questions later. It is also helpful to ask intriguing or interesting questions first. Placing opinion questions first helps because people like to express their opinions. This way, once people have begun a questionnaire, they are more likely to finish it. Avoid placing demographic items first, such as questions about age, sex, and income. Such items often strike respondents as routine and mundane. If people see demographic items first, they are more likely to become bored with the instrument. It is also important to avoid beginning an instrument with sensitive questions about sexuality, drug abuse, and criminal history. Instead, sensitive items should be reserved for later in an instrument.

Questionnaire Format

Not surprisingly, a clear and attractive questionnaire layout increases response rates. However, some researchers use tactics that reduce response rates. To create a questionnaire that appears short to respondents, researchers sometimes place items one after the other, with little space in between, and reduce the page margins to get as many words as possible on a page. However, this actually makes the questionnaire look cramped and confusing and makes it difficult to distinguish one question from another. Items should be spread out instead. However, they shouldn't be too spread out because you don't want your questionnaire to be too long. The researcher must find a suitable middle ground between the two. The layout should be easy on the eyes. It is also important to be sure that questions and answers remain together. In some cases a question can be on one page and the response options can be on the next page. This creates confusion and should be avoided.

In some questionnaires you will notice that not every question is relevant to every respondent. Researchers should always be sure that respondents are answering questions that are relevant to them. You may run an alcohol rehabilitation center and design a questionnaire to identify how many people in an area could use your services. The questionnaire may ask a series of questions about alcohol consumption. You may want to know whether or not people drink alcohol and if they do so, how much they drink. However, you don't want people who don't drink alcohol answering a question about how much they drink. This presents an opportunity to use what are called filter questions. A **filter question** screens respondents by guiding them to questions that are relevant to them. A filter question leads to a contingency question. The answer to a filter question determines the question the respondent answers next. A **contingency question** is a question that is answered depending on a participant's response to a previous question (a filter question). Exhibit 10.7 presents an example of a filter question and a contingency question.

Sometimes a questionnaire will have a series of questions or statements with identical response options. These are called matrixes. This is typically the case when Likert-type response options are used. Indexes and scales with multiple items often use matrixes. Matrixes make questionnaire completion easier and quicker for the

Exhibit 10.7

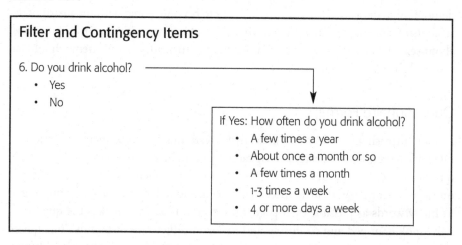

Filter and Contingency Items

6. Do you drink alcohol?
   - Yes
   - No

   If Yes: How often do you drink alcohol?
   - A few times a year
   - About once a month or so
   - A few times a month
   - 1-3 times a week
   - 4 or more days a week

respondent. The best way to identify errors and weaknesses in a questionnaire is to **pretest** it by administering it to a sample that is similar to your population of interest. It is easy for a researcher to miss something, and it always helps to ask people to go through your instrument and look for errors.

Conducting the Self-Administered Questionnaire

There are three main ways of administering survey questions to respondents: surveys administered by researchers in face-to-face settings, surveys conducted by telephone, and self-completed questionnaires in which respondents are expected to administer the questionnaire themselves (Babbie, 2001).

The most common self-administered questionnaires are mailed questionnaires. These are sent through the mail with a letter explaining the purpose of the research and a self-addressed, stamped envelope for the return of the completed questionnaire. There are many advantages to mailed questionnaires. They are popular because they are relatively easy and inexpensive. Mailed questionnaires allow the researcher to cover a large geographic area. They also provide anonymity to the respondent. The response rates (the percentage of questionnaires returned to the researcher) for mailed questionnaires tend to be high for highly educated target populations with interest in the topic. However, there are some disadvantages to mailed questionnaires. By far the biggest problem is low response rates. It could be that only people who are particularly interested in the topic in question respond. This means that when you get a low response rate, those who do respond may be systematically different from the rest of the population in some key ways. Another challenge is that the researcher cannot control the conditions under which the respondent completes the questionnaire. The respondent could be distracted and complete the questionnaire under less than ideal circumstances. When a respondent is completing a mailed questionnaire (as opposed to a survey), he or she cannot ask questions for clarification. As a consequence, researchers can receive some incomplete questionnaires.

What can researchers do to resolve this problem? It is important for researchers to monitor their returns. The researcher should record the dates and demographic characteristics of respondents' forms as they are returned. By collecting data from respondents, the researcher can keep track of sampling bias by noting the characteristics of those who have returned questionnaires. Returned questionnaires may be primarily from those who have high levels of education, those who are unemployed, or those who with high levels of income. Increasing response rates thus becomes a challenge to the researcher.

Follow-Up Questionnaires and Letters

Sending follow-up questionnaires to respondents also increases response rates. If respondents have not returned their questionnaires after 2 or 3 weeks, researchers should send a follow-up questionnaire. Sending three follow-up letters has been found to be most efficient (Babbie, 2001). With two follow-up letters, the researcher can expect to receive a 15–20% increase over the initial return rate.

The response rate of a research study using mailed questionnaires indicates quite a bit about the study. A high response rate decreases the likelihood of bias in the sample. However, low response rates indicate a greater likelihood of a biased sample. A response rate of 50% is acceptable; 60% is good; and 70% or above is very good (Babbie, 2001).

Cover Letter

Having a good cover letter increases the response rate. Mailed questionnaires should be accompanied by a cover letter that introduces and explains the questionnaire to the researcher. The cover letter should explain who the researcher is, what institution or organization is sponsoring the research, an explanation of the purpose of the research, and the address and contact information of the researcher. In addition, it is always important to remind research participants of the confidentiality of their responses.

Length and Appearance

In general, the longer the questionnaire, the lower the response rate will be. The questionnaire should be no longer than five pages and take no longer than 30 minutes to complete. However, there is no strict rule on these limits, and a researcher shouldn't try to force items to meet these limits. Therefore, the researcher should go through every item and be sure to remove all non-essential items. The questions should be as short as possible to encourage completion. Because people are discouraged by having to do a lot of writing, mailed questionnaires should also have as few open-ended items as possible.

Payment

Offering potential respondents payment or other incentives has a positive effect on cooperation or participation. This approach usually has a greater effect if the payment is accompanied by the questionnaire rather than being promised once the questionnaire is returned. However, it is a misconception that payment needs to be large. Payments between $2 and $20 are known to increase response rates by 10% (Monette, Sullivan, & DeJong, 2005).

Diaries

Sometimes a researcher is interested in a research topic that requires analyzing precise estimates of human behavior. This presents an opportunity to use the **diary method**. Using the diary method, the research participant observes his or her own behavior. For example, a researcher might be interested in studying the number of hours people spend watching television, how often and what kind of vegetables they eat, or how often they engage in exercise. These interests are suitable to the diary technique. In each case, the participant is instructed to systematically record a particular behavior of interest. If you use the survey approach and ask people how many hours of television they watch per day, their answers are more likely to be subject to forgetting or misremembering. However, the diary approach limits the interference of memory problems.

The diary approach is most appropriate when the researcher is interested in analyzing precise sequences of events or the frequency of behaviors. Diaries are also more appropriate than observations for personally sensitive topics. However, diaries can still be time consuming because of the researcher's responsibility to be sure that diaries are being kept properly. Diaries can also suffer a high attrition rate because people grow tired of recording their behavior over long periods of time. Moreover, people are not always diligent in recording their behavior and may forget to do so. When this happens, memory problems can affect the accuracy of the recordings.

Advantages of Questionnaires

Self-completion questionnaires are quicker and more inexpensive than interviews. A researcher is able to collect data from more participants in a shorter amount of time than it would take to interview the same number of people. Data can be collected from geographically dispersed populations in an inexpensive way compared to traveling to individual households. When topics are of a sensitive nature, respondents are more likely to answer self-completion questions because they do not have to worry about being judged by an interviewer. The self-completion questionnaire also reduces what we described earlier to be social desirability bias. Self-completion questionnaires also eliminate the problem of interviewer bias, that is, the effect that interviewers can have on respondents because of their body language, vocal tone, facial expressions, and overall demeanor in reaction to respondents' answers.

Disadvantages of Questionnaires

Because self-administered questionnaires do require a certain level of literacy, some respondents will be at a disadvantage. For this reason, mailed questionnaires are more likely to be completed by respondents with higher levels of education. With mailed questionnaires, researchers also don't have the opportunity to answer respondents' requests for clarity. This can result in respondents skipping questions they don't understand, which results in a greater risk of missing data. There is also no opportunity to ask respondents to provide more information or to rephrase their answers. When respondents complete a questionnaire on their own, they have to contend with the fact that there is no assurance that the person they intended to complete the questionnaire is the one who actually completes it. Finally, researchers must contend with non-response bias, or the threat that those who do not return questionnaires will differ in some systematic way from those who do respond.

Interviews

Interviews are a part of everyday social life. The interview is a form of data collection that typically involves orally asking people questions and recording their answers. Interviews can take place face to face, over the telephone, or through the Internet. Face-to-face interviews have the highest response rates. Properly done face-to-face interviews should have an 80–85% response rate. The presence of an interviewer provides the opportunity to probe interviewees for more explanation and clearer answers. This type of interview is best for the use of longer questionnaires and more complex topics. However, face-to-face interviews can be very expensive and time consuming for interviewees in terms of travel and personal costs, and the interviewer's tone of voice, appearance, and demeanor all increase the risk of interviewer effect.

Monette, Sullivan, and DeJong (2005) identify three levels of interviews: (1) structured, (2) semi-structured, and (3) unstructured interviews. These interview types differ primarily in their degree of rigidity. This section will deal specifically with structured interviews, while semi-structured and unstructured interviews will be covered in Chapter 13. The **structured interview**, the most rigid approach, involves asking a specific standardized set of questions in a fixed order. These questions have to be presented to each respondent in the exact same way because the objective is to make each interview comparable to all the others. Most of the questions are likely to be closed-ended, although some may be open-ended. Instead of having respondents read the questions themselves, in structured interviews only the interviewer asks the questions. All interviewees respond to the same questions read to them in the same order and in the same wording. These questions are delivered in exactly the same way to each interviewee so that different interviewees' responses will be comparable. Structured interviews are best when researchers are dealing with large populations. They are also useful in longitudinal studies in which the researcher is interested in collecting the same information at different points in order to measure change over time.

Conducting Interviews

KNOW THE INTERVIEW SCHEDULE

One of the first responsibilities of the interviewer is to be familiar with the interviewing schedule. An **interview schedule** contains specific instructions for conducting an interview, the specific questions to be asked, and the order in which interview questions should be asked. If the interviewer is not conversant with the questions, he or she can miss questions or ask the wrong questions during an interview. If there are multiple interviewers, each of them needs to be trained so that they are not asking questions in different ways.

INTRODUCING THE RESEARCH TO THE RESPONDENT

Respondents are more willing to participate in an interview when they have been presented with an adequate rationale for the study. Consider that your respondent is giving his or her valuable time to participate in your study. At a minimum, the researcher should explain why this study is directly or indirectly important to the respondent's community, the Black community, the country, or the world. The interviewer should explain to the interviewee his or her intentions and the conditions under which the research is being conducted (for university research, market research, professional research, etc.). The interviewer must explain to the interviewee the purpose of the research and why the interviewee has been selected. Interviewees must be reminded that their participation is voluntary and that their identification is confidential.

Rose, Kim, Dennison, and Hill (2000) conducted semi-structured interviews with 19 Black males living with high blood pressure. The study assessed their perceptions of health, health problems, and their concerns with daily living that influence their appointment keeping. However, before their interviews, the researchers began with the following statement:

> I am interested in what it is like for you in your daily life to manage health problems and concerns, including high blood pressure and the things that might make it easy or hard to get treated for those problems. (Rose, Kim, Dennison, & Hill, 2000, p. 589)

APPEARANCE OF THE INTERVIEWER

The interviewer should dress in a similar way as the population being interviewed. Generally, this means dressing in a way that is acceptable to a wide variety of people. An interviewer who is dressed in formal wear may have trouble getting interviewees who are dressed casually to open up. Conversely, an interviewer who is dressed casually may have the same trouble with interviewees who are dressed in a very formal way. The way you dress can be interpreted as a sign of your assumptions, attitudes, and beliefs. In general demeanor, the interview should seek to be pleasant. Interviewers should conduct themselves in ways that make the interviewee feel comfortable.

WORDING

In structured interviews, an interviewer must be sure to stick to the wording of questions. When questions are worded uniformly, interviews are comparable. However, if questions are differently worded to multiple respondents, there is a risk that the wording of the questions will influence the answers. On the other hand, when recording answers given by respondents, the researcher must be sure that answers are recorded exactly as the respondent gives them. If researchers paraphrase interviewees' words, they risk distorting their views and introducing error to the research. This means that interviewees' words should not be summarized, nor their grammar corrected.

PROBING

In some cases an interviewee may give an unclear or incomplete answer. In this case it is important for an interviewer to **probe**, or request that interviewees elaborate or provide more explanation. For example, if a researcher poses the question "What in your opinion is the most important problem facing the Black community?" and the respondent replies, "Schools," this answer is incomplete. The interviewee must then probe the respondent, possibly by saying "How are schools the most important problem?" or "In what ways are schools the most important problem?" Other useful probes are: "Could you say more about that?" "Why do you think that?" or "In what ways?" Other times, silence is a useful probe. Silence lets respondents know that you are expecting more explanation from them. However, the interviewers need to be sure that the probes they use do not influence the respondent's answer.

TRAINING INTERVIEWERS

In situations where a researcher hires interviewers to conduct large numbers of interviews, those interviewers must be trained. It cannot be assumed that they will all be on the same page. The risk of some interviewers asking different questions than other interviewers has to be minimized. Interviewers working on the same project have to be trained and supervised as they contact prospective interviewees. They also have to be instructed about how to read and ask questions properly, use probes, and record answers. Interviewers can be trained by having them conduct mock interviews, and their styles can be monitored by recording individual response rates. Also, contacted respondents can be called back and asked to report on their interviewer's conduct.

UNDERREPRESENTED GROUPS IN INTERVIEWING

Social desirability bias refers to respondents' tendency to want to present themselves in a way that they believe will appear socially desirable to their interviewer. This is especially true when questions deal with issues of race, ethnicity, gender, and sexuality. The general rule of thumb is that the smaller the social distance, the more honest respondents' answers will be. Blacks are more likely to honestly discuss issues of race when a Black person interviews them. Women are more likely to discuss issues of rape openly when interviewed by a female. However, there can also be intraracial- and intragender-based bias. It is up to the researcher to ensure that respondents are comfortable and give their most honest answers with as little bias as possible.

ENDING THE INTERVIEW

The interviewer should thank the respondent before leaving. The interviewer should then organize his or her interview notes (date, time, and place of interview). This should be done as soon as possible. The longer you wait, the more likely you are to misremember or leave important information out of your notes.

Telephone Interviews

Face-to-face interviews are a relatively expensive means of collecting data. **Telephone interviews**, however, are relatively inexpensive and require no travel. They are a common data collection technique used in marketing research in which the interviewer asks questions over the telephone instead of being face to face. In fact, you may have recently encountered some form of telephone-based marketing research. Lots of academic research is based on face-to-face interviews.

There are many advantages to conducting telephone interviews. Telephone interviews are cheaper to administer than face-to-face interviews. Like mailed questionnaires, telephone interviews make it easier for the researcher to access a geographically dispersed population. When using more than one interviewer, conducting interviews over the telephone makes monitoring or supervising interviews much easier. This helps to guard against interviewer falsification. Telephone interviews limit the effect of the interviewer on the respondents' answers, although the interviewer's voice may still have some effect on the interviewer. In telephone interviews the interviewers are far more remote (not physically present) than in face-to-face interviews and have a lesser likelihood of their characteristics affecting the respondent's answers. In fact, interviewees may be more likely to provide the interviewer with answers that are socially undesirable if they don't have to look the interviewer in the eye. Finally, it is difficult for mailed questionnaires to accommodate non-English-speaking populations unless the languages that potential respondents speak are already known. However, telephone interviews make it easier to accommodate languages because multilingual interviewers who are conversant in the respondent's language can be made available.

As with other methods, the telephone interview has its limitations. The most obvious limitation is that it is, by definition, limited to people who own telephones. Depending on what country you are conducting research in, disadvantaged populations may be underrepresented among those who own telephones, which introduces sampling bias. Those who elect to have their numbers unpublished are typically richer. Another form of bias that may affect telephone interviewing is the difficulty encountered by potential respondents who have hearing problems. Telephone interviews also tend to be shorter, typically not lasting beyond 20–25 minutes. This time limitation restricts the amount of information and depth of information that can be explored in telephone interviews. Telephone interviewing also eliminates the possibility of making observations of interviewees' nonverbal behavior in response to questions.

Computer-Assisted Interviewing

Computer technology is influencing telephone interviewing by way of **Computer-Assisted Telephone Interviewing** (CATI) techniques. CATI is an increasingly popular method of interviewing. Using CATI, the interviewer is able to sit at the computer and use the computer program to randomly dial telephone numbers and present the person who answers the phone with a series of questions that the researcher programs it to ask. The program may ask the interviewee, "How many people live in this residence?" and the interviewee is given a number (code) to enter for a closed-ended question, or will verbally respond to an open-ended question. In any event, the respondents' answers are displayed and recorded by the researcher, who sits at the computer and records respondents' coded responses and copies their verbatim open-ended responses. **Computer-Assisted Personal Interviews** (CAPI) are similar to CATI except that they are used in face-to-face interviews instead of over the telephone. **Computer-Assisted Self-Interviews** (CASI) occur when a researcher brings a laptop to the respondent, and the respondent reads and answers the questions him or herself.

Online Surveys

Online surveys are surveys that are often sent as email attachments or links to web-based questionnaires. Online surveys work best when the researcher has access to the online contact data for a population of interest. They are also well suited for surveying regular visitors to particular websites. Online surveys have many advantages. They are faster, inexpensive, and are able to reach people all over the globe. Internet surveys also make it easier to incorporate visual and auditory aids. Because online surveys are automated, they reduce error and make filter and contingency items easy to follow. Social desirability bias and interviewer effects are limited, given that there is no interviewer.

Online surveys also have disadvantages. Not everyone has access to the Internet. In fact, often it is those who are in most need of basic human services who lack access to the Internet. Because of this and the fact that not everyone chooses to respond to online surveys, some researchers believe that online surveys should be considered convenience samples instead of probability samples. Typically, online surveys are considered skewed toward those who are richer, have higher levels of education, and are young and male.

Key Terms

Closed-Ended Items

Computer-Assisted
Personal Interviews
(CAPI)

Computer-Assisted Self
Interviews (CASI)

Computer-Assisted
Telephone Interviews
(CATI)

Contingency Question

Diary Method

Factual Item

Filter Question

Interview

Interview Schedule

Item

Online Surveys

Open-Ended Items

Opinion Items

Probe

Question

Questionnaire

Social Desirability Bias

Statement

Structured Interview

Survey

Telephone Interviews

Vignette Question

Thinking about Science

Activity 1

Find a survey on the Internet and critique it according to the rules of survey item construction discussed in the chapter. Identify any violations of the rules of item construction in the survey and indicate what could be changed about the survey to remedy the violations.

Activity 2

Look at the following list of open-ended questions and turn them into closed-ended items.

- How often do you spend time with your child?
- What is your race?
- What is your age?
- How important is culture in your daily life?

Activity 3

Look at the following research variables and determine whether or not the survey approach is the best tool for collecting data on them. Explain why or why not. If not, what do you think is a more appropriate tool for collecting data?

- The voter turnout rate of Black youth in your country's last presidential election.
- Black people's attitudes about the relationship between physical health and spirituality.
- The average annual income of Black people.
- The effects of a new approach to teaching literature on the reading comprehension of a group of high school students.

Activity 4

You are conducting an interview about Internet access and you have asked a respondent why he or she thought access to the Internet was important. The reply was "access to jobs and healthcare." Identify three different things you might say to the respondent to probe for a better answer.

CHAPTER ELEVEN

Experimental Design

We have now stumbled upon another area in which infants have demonstrated their heightened instincts for research, *the experimental design*. We have to protect infants from their unbridled propensity for experimentation. They have an insatiable curiosity to discover "what would happen." To protect them, we have to cover electric outlets, make sure sharp objects are out of reach, and lock away hazardous substances. Have you ever asked yourself, "What would happen if...?" taken some action, and then observed the consequences? If you have, then you have conducted an **experiment**. An experiment involves manipulating a treatment condition or initiating a cause and systematically observing the consequences. Experimentation is natural. It involves the researcher taking an action and observing the consequences in a systematic way. This chapter explores the basic types of experimental designs and assesses their strengths and limitations. It also explores threats to the internal and external validity of experimentation and how to avoid them.

The basic purpose of an experiment is to identify and explain cause-and-effect relationships. Experiments are best for topics that have well-defined concepts and are the best-suited method for hypothesis testing and identifying causation. Do you remember the criteria for causation mentioned in Chapter 1? Experimental designs are the best-suited methods for establishing causation because they are the most likely to meet all three of the major criteria for establishing causation. The studies described at the beginning of this chapter identify story framing as the cause of judgments about newsworthiness and attitudes about colon cancer screening.

Exhibit 11.1

Newsworthiness and African American Public Health?

Nicholson, Kreuter, Lapka, Wellborn, Clark, Sanders-Thompson and Casey (2008) conducted an experiment to investigate how underrepresented racial\ethnic groups react to public information about racial disparities in the prevalence of colon cancer. First, participants were asked to complete surveys asking them whether or not they had been screened for colon cancer; the extent to which they were planning to be screened in the next 6 months; and the extent to which they agreed that colon cancer was an important health problem. Participants in this study included 300 African American male and female adults. Participants were randomly assigned to read one of four mock news stories based on the same information from the U.S. Surgeon General, but framed differently. The four mock news articles had four distinguishing features; 1.) Impact: one story emphasized the impact of cancer on African Americans, 2.) Disparity, another story emphasized that Blacks are doing worse relative to Whites as it relates to the effects of cancer, 3.) Disparity, another story emphasized that over time Blacks were improving but less than Whites, 4.) Progress, the last story emphasized that Blacks were improving over time. Participants were randomly assigned to read one of the four articles. Afterward they completed a survey measuring how positively or negatively they felt about the article they read and the extent to which they wanted to be screened for colon cancer. The results indicated that individuals in the positively-framed stories felt more positively about their story than those who read the disparity stories and the impact story. Individuals who read the disparity-framed stories felt significantly more negatively about their story than those who read the impact or progress-framed stories. Those who read the progress-framed story were more likely to want to be screened for colon cancer than those who read the disparity- and impact–framed stories. Those who read the impact-framed story were more likely to want to be screened than those who read the disparity-framed story.

Hinnant, Oh, Caburnay, and Kreuter (2011) conducted an experiment to investigate how health journalists make decisions about news stories. They selected a sample of 175 journalists to participate in the experiment. There were 51 males, and 124 females, 143 Whites, and 9 Blacks. Interviewees were presented with four different experimental links via the Internet. Some participants received a story about the results of the Nicholson study and how stories emphasizing disparities affect readers, others received a control story about a non-medical-related topic about bats avoiding flying near street lights. Then participants were presented with two types of news stories (stimuli): progress-framed stories and disparity-framed stories. The stories covered health issues facing African Americans, but were distinguished by their framing. Disparity-framed stories would have a headline such as "Black-White Gap in Colon Cancer Deaths Growing," a progress-framed story would have a headline such as, "Blacks Making Great Strides Against Colon Cancer." Lastly, the partici-

Cont. on p. 239

Exhibit 11.1 cont

pants were asked to evaluate the "newsworthiness" of the story they read. The results indicated that most journalists judged the disparity-framed news story as more newsworthy than the progress-framed news story. However, those who read the results of the Nicholson study were significantly less likely to evaluate the disparity-framed studies as newsworthy and more likely to evaluate the progress-framed stories as newsworthy. What we know from both of these stories is that Black readers feel more positively about positively framed public health stories with the same information and that they are more likely to want to be screened for colon cancer when they are exposed to a progress-framed story than when they are explored to disparity-framed stories. However, journalists judge disparity-framed stories more newsworthy than progress-framed stories.

Classic Experimental Designs

Let's first examine the features of the **classic experimental design**, also known as the **true experimental design**. The classic experimental design has *random assignment* and consists of an *experimental stimulus*, an *experimental group*, and a *control group*. The stimulus is otherwise known as the independent variable or the criterion variable. It is this experimental stimulus that researchers directly manipulate to measure its effect on thinking, behavior, or other outcomes. The research participant may be in a group that experiences the stimulus or does not experience the stimulus. There is also the *effector variable*, or the dependent variable, which is the variable that is expected to change as a result of being exposed to the stimulus. One way to think of it is that the stimulus is the cause and the dependent variable is the effect. In a classic experimental design, the dependent variable is measured on two occasions: in a pretest and a posttest. A *pretest* involves measuring the dependent variable before exposure to the stimulus or independent variable. A *posttest* involves measuring the dependent variable after exposure to the experimental stimulus or independent variable. Having a pretest and a posttest allows the researcher to com-

Exhibit 11.2

Classic Experimental Design		
Pretest	Experimental Treatment	Posttest
Pretest	Control Condition	Posttest

pare where individuals stand in relation to the dependent variable before they experience the stimulus and after they experience the stimulus. The *experimental group* is the group that is exposed to the experimental stimulus. In the classic experimental design, there is also a *control group* that is not exposed to the experimental stimulus. In true experimental designs, participants are randomly assigned to either the control group or the experimental group. Having the control group allows the researcher to compare what happens when the stimulus is present to what happens when it is not. In the 1920s and 1930s, Roethlisberger and Dickson (1939) were interested in investigating the effects of working conditions on employee productivity and satisfaction. They did so by investigating the working conditions at Western Electronic Works in Hawthorne, Illinois. They found that improving working conditions resulted in an increase in worker productivity and satisfaction. For example, when the workroom was brightened by better lighting in the building, work productivity increased. However, to substantiate these results, the researcher dimmed the lights and productivity increased again! Why? The workers were responding to the attention they were getting from the researchers and not the improved working conditions. This phenomenon has since been known to social scientists as the Hawthorne Effect, or the effect that experimentation itself has on outcomes. Research participants adjust their behaviors when they know they are being observed. Having a control group allows the researcher to identify the effects of the experiment itself. Had there been a control group in the Hawthorne study, this effect would have been detectable without dimming the lights.

The following are symbols that represent the logic of experimental designs.

O = Observation or measurement of the dependent variable
X = Exposure to the experimental stimulus or independent variable
R = Random assignment to conditions

Using these symbols, the following is an example of the classic experimental design:

R O X O
R O O

There are two different types of experiments: lab experiments and field experiments. Lab experiments are conducted in artificial settings to isolate variables from the natural environment so that their effects can be measured. Field experiments are conducted in natural environments as people go about their daily activities. Here is an example of a lab experiment. Let's assume that you are interested in enhancing cultural sensitivity by reducing intolerance of same-gender loving in communities. You may bring participants into a laboratory setting and randomly assign them to either the pretest or posttest group. You may pretest participants in both the experimental and control groups by administering an Intolerance Survey to measure their levels of prejudice against lesbians, gays, bisexuals, transgendered, and queer individuals. Next, you may expose the experimental group to a documentary about cultural sensitivity, tolerance, and the impact of prejudice on people's well-being. Last, the control group and the experimental group are given the Intolerance Survey to measure changes in their levels of prejudice from pretest to posttest. The pretest is the Intolerance Survey, the stimulus is the documentary, and the posttest is a second Intolerance Survey. In the analysis, the researcher would compare the pretest of the experimental group to the posttest of the experimental group. Any change that occurs from pretest to posttest can be attributed to the documentary or stimulus.

However, the use of the control group allows the researcher to identify the effect of experiencing the experiment itself. Let's say the experimental group got an average score of 75 percent out of 100 on the Intolerance Survey pretest, and the control group got an average score of 70 on the Intolerance Survey pretest. Let's also say that the experimental group got an average score of 50 on the Intolerance Survey posttest. This means that we can attribute a 25% decrease in their levels of prejudice to the effects of having watched the cultural sensitivity documentary. But wait. What if we discover that the control group got an average score of 45 on the Intolerance Survey posttest? This would mean that the 25-point decrease in the prejudice levels of the experimental group cannot be attributed to the stimulus (documentary) because the control group's levels of prejudice decreased without being exposed to the stimulus. However, if the control group's average score on the Intolerance Survey posttest was 60, then we can attribute the change in the experimental group's scores from pretest to posttest to the stimulus (the documentary).

Let's think of an example of a field experiment. Imagine the following scenario. Karina and Chanel worked for Girl Power, a 6-week science and engineering summer camp for girls ages 12–14 for 7 years. The camp is designed to increase girls' knowledge of science and engineering, as well as their self-esteem and sense of social responsibility. However, Karina and Chanel learn that young Black girls who participate in the program often feel isolated from their peers and grow disillusioned with the program. Karina and Chanel decide that they want to develop a similar program for young Black girls from urban areas called Kujichagulia summer camp (Kujichagulia is a Swahili word meaning self-determination). Their objective is to develop a more culturally relevant camp that will have a greater effect on Black girls. To measure the effect of cultural relevance, they agree to develop the program, but they want to be sure that it meets its desired outcomes: increased knowledge, self-esteem, and social responsibility. They decide to develop an experimental design to test the effect that their 6-week program for Black girls has on the girls' knowledge, self-esteem, and sense of social responsibility.

On the first day of camp, Chanel and Karina give the girls a Science and Service pretest consisting of questions assessing their knowledge of science and engineering concepts, their self-esteem, and their sense of social responsibility. Chanel and Karina also want to have a control group that doesn't experience the Kujichagulia camp, so they also administer the Science and Service pretest to girls at Girl Power. Then the girls experience 6 weeks of the Kujichagulia summer camp curriculum, which integrates hands-on learning about science and engineering with history lessons about African American contributions to science and engineering, the Black community's need for infrastructural services that require science and engineering skills, and an extensive rite-of-passage ceremony symbolizing their transition through the program. When the summer camp is over, Karina and Chanel administer a Science and Service posttest to the girls to measure how effective the summer program has been at increasing the girls' knowledge of science and engineering, their self-esteem, and sense of social responsibility. The results indicate that the girls who participated in the Kujichagulia summer camp scored higher overall on the Science and Service posttest compared to the girls at the Girl Power summer camp. However, the study reveals that the girls in the Kujichagulia camp did no better on their science and engineering knowledge than the Girl Power group.

In this experiment the pretest is the Science and Service survey; the stimulus is the experience of the Kujichagulia camp curriculum; and the posttest is the Science and Service posttest. The experimental group is the Black girls who experience the Kujichagulia summer camp curriculum; and the control group is the girls who experience the Girl Power summer camp curriculum. A change in the experimental group's Science and Service survey scores from pretest to posttest can be attributed to the stimulus or the Kujichagulia camp curriculum. For example, if there was an increase in the Science and Service scores of the experimental group from pretest to posttest, the change can be attributed to the experience of the stimulus. For example, if the experimental group scored an average of 65 on their Science and Service pretest and an average of 90 on their Science and Service posttest, then the 25-point change can be attributed to the Kujichagulia camp curriculum. However, if the girls from the control group also received an average score of 65 on their Science and Service pretest and an average score of 90 on their Science and Service posttest, then the 25-point change cannot be said to have a greater effect on Black girls' increased knowledge, self-esteem, and sense of social responsibility compared to the Girl Power summer camp.

There is another way to use a true experimental design and still resolve the problem presented by the effect that being pretested might have on research participants. The Solomon Four Design uses four comparison groups to detect the effects of the stimulus, pretesting, and the interaction between pretesting and the stimulus. Let's apply the Solomon Four Design to the intolerance experiment measuring the effect of watching a cultural sensitivity documentary. The Solomon Four Design is a more

Table 11.1

Solomon Four Design			
	PRETEST	STIMULUS	POSTTEST
EXPERIMENTAL GROUP 1	O	X	O
CONTROL GROUP 1	O		O
EXPERIMENTAL GROUP 2		X	O
CONTROL GROUP 2			O

complex assessment of what causes changes in the independent variable. If we used a Solomon Four with a sample of 80 people, we would randomly assign 20 participants each to experimental group 1, control group 1, experimental group 2, and control group 2. Experimental group 1 receives the pretest (Intolerance Survey), stimulus (cultural sensitivity documentary), and posttest (Intolerance Survey). Control group 1 experiences the pretest (Intolerance Survey) and posttest (Intolerance Survey). Experimental group 2 experiences the stimulus (cultural sensitivity documentary) and the posttest (Intolerance Survey). Control group 2 experiences the posttest (Intolerance Survey). If our hypothesis is that exposure to the stimulus (cultural sensitivity documentary) will result in a decrease in intolerance, then

- Experimental group 1's posttest intolerance scores should be lower than their pretest intolerance scores.
- There should be less intolerance in the experimental group 1 posttest than in the control group 1 posttest.
- The experimental group 2 posttest should show less intolerance than the control group 1 posttest.
- The experimental group 2 posttest should show less intolerance than the control group 2 posttest.

The limitation of the Solomon Four Design is that it requires more people, time, and resources to conduct. The true experimental designs covered above are widely used because they are especially good for controlling internal validity.

Threats to Internal Validity

By using true experimental designs we increase our ability to attribute changes in research participants' attitudes and behaviors to the effects of our stimuli. However, our ability to attribute change in our research participants to the stimulus depends on the research design. Sometimes we cannot attribute change in research participants' behavior and attitudes to our stimulus because of threats to internal validity. Threats to internal validity are factors other than the stimulus that affect the dependent variable. Suppose we are interested in increasing the parenting skills and competencies (dependent variable) of Black teenage fathers by exposing them to an intensive, 6-week parenting workshop (stimulus).

O At pretest, the young fathers in the experimental group are given a Parenting Skills and Competencies Survey.

O At pretest, the young fathers in the control group are given a Parenting Skills and Competencies Survey.

X The stimulus, Parenting Skills Workshop, is experienced by the experimental group. The workshop is meant to increase the young fathers' skills and competencies.

O At posttest, the fathers in the experimental group are given another Parenting Skills and Competencies Survey.

O At posttest, the fathers in the control group are given another Parenting Skills and Competencies Survey.

Suppose we find that there is a significant increase in the parenting skills of the fathers in the experimental group from pretest to posttest. The change could be due to exposure to the workshop. However, or it could be due to any of the following threats to **internal validity**. Internal validity is the extent to which the results of experimentation are a result of what happened in the experiment. Things other than the experiment itself that have an effect on the result are threats to internal validity. The following are threats to internal validity:

1. History: History refers to environmental influences on research subjects between pretest and posttest. Events between pretest and posttest can confound the results of an experiment. A significant speech by a Black president on Black fatherhood and parenting skills during the course of the experiment is an example of an event that might influence the parenting survey results of participants in the parenting workshop. Or, perhaps some of the participants read a book on Black fatherhood after the pretest and before the posttest. The more time an experiment takes, the more likely it is that history may become a threat.

2. Maturation: People grow and change whether they are in an experiment or not. Maturation refers to the physical, emotional, and psychological growth of research participants that may be the cause of change in the

dependent variable. Participants can grow older, more tired, or wiser. The growth of participants may change their thinking or behavior during an experiment. Participants may change their attitudes about fatherhood over a period of time, regardless of the stimulus. Like history, maturation is more likely to have an effect on an experiment the longer the experiment lasts.

3. Testing: Testing is the threat that being exposed to multiple measurement devices can have on the dependent variable. People who take the Scholastic Aptitude Test (SAT) twice usually score higher the second time. Even when researchers use alternative forms of a test, subjects may score higher on it the second time. Simply taking the Parenting Skills and Competencies Survey at pretest may cause the participants to think about the meaning of the questions being asked, thus influencing their answers to similar questions on a pretest. The use of control groups helps the researcher to detect this influence.

4. Instrumentation: Sometimes the tests used at pretest and posttest can be significantly different. If this happens, how can the researcher be sure that the two tests are comparable? If the Parenting Skills and Competencies Survey pretest is more difficult than the posttest, then the increase from pretest to posttest could simply be a consequence of the change in degree of difficulty from pretest to posttest. The pretest and posttest should not be identical, but they should be comparable in order to guard against the effect of instrumentation.

5. Statistical Regression: Statistical regression refers to the tendency of scores to gravitate toward the mean. This typically occurs when researchers deal with extreme scores. If a researcher is experimenting with approaches to increasing math skills starting with students who have the lowest scores in their schools, it is likely that their scores will increase over time whether they experience the stimulus or not. If subjects are placed in groups based on extreme scores as they relate to the dependent variable, they can be expected to improve the next time they are tested based on this principle of statistical regression toward the mean. This is usually due to the fact that extreme scores are often the result of an unlikely combination of factors that led to their scores that are unlikely to repeat themselves. This would be expected to happen if young fathers who have the least knowledge of parenting skills and competencies were selected to participate in the experiment described above.

6. Experimental Attrition: Experimental attrition occurs when participants drop out of a study before the experiment is done. It is a threat to validity when there is a differential dropout of participants in the experimen-

tal group and control group. When experiments extend over long periods of time, this threat is more likely to occur. If attrition has a greater effect on the control group than the experimental group, then the two groups may not be comparable at the posttest. For example, if half of the control group of fathers drop out, they may no longer be comparable to the experimental group. In any case, it is incumbent upon the researcher to find out why participants are dropping out. It could be that they are dropping out for some common reason that needs to be explained in the research.

7. Diffusion of Treatment: Diffusion can be a threat to internal validity when participants in the experimental and control groups communicate with one another and share knowledge of the experimental stimulus. For example, members of the experimental group may share information about what they are learning in the parenting workshop with members of the control group. This would undoubtedly affect the control group's answers on the posttest. In this case, the control group is no longer a control group.

8. Causal Time Order: When the causal time order is unclear, there can be doubt about the effect of the stimulus on the dependent variable. Members of the experimental group must experience the stimulus before they complete the posttest. If not, the stimulus cannot be responsible for the posttest scores.

9. Compensation: Compensation becomes a threat when the control group is exposed to influences similar to the stimulus by the researcher or confederates to compensate them for the stimulus they have been deprived of.

10. Compensatory Rivalry: This occurs when members of the control group attempt to compensate for not having received the stimulus by working or trying harder on the pre- and posttests.

11. Experimenter Expectancy: The behavior of the experimenter can bias the outcomes of an experiment. Experimenters can unintentionally communicate expectations to research participants. Imagine that we decide to conduct an experiment by testing the effects of a culturally relevant method of teaching Afro British high school literature, as compared to the typical method of teaching high school literature in the UK. We may randomly select a control group and an experimental group. However, our teachers may try harder when teaching the culturally relevant approach. They may inadvertently be more enthusiastic, provide more examples, and give more encouragement. In this case, experimenter expectations can threaten the internal validity of the study.

12. Demoralization: This occurs when members of the control group feel deprived as a consequence of not experiencing the stimulus. They may give up or become demoralized.

13. Selection: Selection can become a threat to internal validity when groups are not selected at random. Therefore, participants in one group are significantly different from participants in another group. For example, it could be that the control group participants of young fathers were formerly incarcerated and the experimental group participants were college students who had never been incarcerated. If this is the case, then the fact that the experimental group scores higher than the control group on the Parenting Skills and Competencies Survey could be due to selection, or the fact that the two groups were not comparable from the beginning. Random selection and matching limit the likelihood of this threat to internal validity.

Matching and Random Selection

If you use a control group in a study, it is important to be sure that the members of the control group and those of the experimental group are similar if you want to make meaningful comparisons. Imagine that you are inspired by Bailey and Boykin's (2001) research, which demonstrated African American youth's tendency to have increased academic achievement in classrooms characterized by high energy and variation of learning tasks. You happen to teach two math classes—one in the afternoon and another in the morning. You decide to test out your High Energy, Socially Oriented Math (HESOM) teaching approach on the morning class (experimental group) and your typical approach on the afternoon class (control group). At the end of the quarter you may discover that the students in the morning class did significantly better on their tests than the students in the afternoon class. Can you assume that the difference was due to the new teaching technique? You can't be certain because the students in the morning class may have been better at math from the beginning. Two ways to avoid this problem are matching and random selection.

Matching refers to matching individuals in the experimental group with similar individuals in the control group. This technique matches individuals based on variables that could have an effect on the dependent variable. Matching makes experimental and control groups equivalent on key variables. In our teaching example, you as the teacher and researcher could match students with high GPAs in the experimental group with students who have high GPAs in the control group. Then use the same approach to place students who have moderate and low GPAs in the experimental and control groups. Having the same amount of high, moderate, and low GPA students in each group would make the experimental and control groups more comparable. Ultimately, you should end up with an even amount of high, moderate, and low GPA students in the experimental and control groups. One problem with matching is that the researcher has to be aware of variables that might affect the dependent variable in advance.

Random sampling is another way to ensure that there is little variation between individuals in the experimental and control groups. For example, every student could be assigned a number, and a computer randomization program can be used to randomly assign each student to either the experimental or control group. The problem is that randomization is based on chance, and there still exists a possibility that the groups may turn out to be non-equivalent. Sometimes matching can be a better technique than randomization, especially when dealing with small sample sizes.

Pre-Experimental Designs

Designs that lack random assignment and other qualifications of true experiments are considered **pre-experimental designs**. Because of their limitations they are far more susceptible to the threats to internal validity discussed above. Sometimes these kinds of designs are used in less-than-professional research, preliminary research, time-sensitive research, and field research in which random assignment and control groups are unrealistic. One such design is the *One Shot Case Study* (Table 11.2). As you can see, the One Shot Case Study includes an experimental group that receives a stimulus followed by a posttest, but no pretest. Let's think back to our experiment testing the High Energy, Socially Oriented Math (HESOM) approach to teaching algebra. If we conducted this experiment using the One Shot Case Study Design, our research participants would simply be exposed to the HESOM approach and then have their algebra tested afterward.

For simply teaching math, this is fine. In fact, if you are a student it happens all the time. However, if the researcher is interested in whether the HESOM approach led to students' algebra knowledge demonstrated on the posttest, this experiment is useless because there is no comparative randomly selected control group and no pretest to compare to their algebra knowledge in the posttest. For all we know, the knowledge students demonstrated on the posttest is at the same level it was before they were exposed to the HESOM approach.

Table 11.2

One Shot Case Study			
	PRETEST	STIMULUS	POSTTEST
EXPERIMENTAL GROUP 1		X	O

Table 11.3

Static Group Comparison Design			
	PRETEST	STIMULUS	POSTTEST
EXPERIMENTAL GROUP		X	O
CONTROL GROUP			O

To address the issues of comparison, some research is based on the *Static Group Comparison Design* (Table 11.3). This design includes experimental and control groups but has no pretests and lacks random assignment. For example, the experimental group may be exposed to the HESOM approach, but not the control group. (They would instead receive the typical approach to teaching algebra). However, all would experience a posttest, and their posttest scores would be compared to measure changes in the algebra knowledge of both groups.

If the experimental group had better algebra scores, we might be tempted to assume that the HESOM approach was responsible. But we do not know how much algebra they knew in the beginning because there was no pretest. It could be that the experimental group knew algebra better than the control group before they experienced the HESOM approach.

The *One-Group Pretest Posttest Design* is an approach that includes one group, a pretest, a stimulus, and a posttest (Table 11.4). However, it lacks random assignment and a control group. It has a pretest and posttest, but its lacks a comparison group (control group) that allows a researcher to measure change over time. Because of this deficiency, it is not possible to be certain that changes in the dependent variable from pretest to posttest are due to the independent variable (stimulus). In this case, we administer a pretest to our research participants, expose them to the HESOM approach, then administer a posttest to measure change in students' ability to do algebra. We may attribute change in the experimental group's algebra knowledge from pretest to posttest to their exposure to the HESOM approach.

Table 11.4

One-Group Pretest Posttest Design			
	PRETEST	STIMULUS	POSTTEST
EXPERIMENTAL GROUP	O	X	O

Table 11.5

Two-Group Posttest-Only Design			
	PRETEST	STIMULUS	POSTTEST
EXPERIMENTAL GROUP		X	O
CONTROL GROUP			O

However, because of the lack of a control group in the One-Group Pretest Posttest Design, we do not know whether something other than the stimulus was responsible for change in the experimental group's algebra ability. Without the control group, we cannot be certain that the change from pretest to posttest was due to exposure to the HESOM approach.

Quasi-Experimental Designs

Pre-experimental designs do a poor job at testing causal relationships. True experimental designs do the best job at testing causal relationships, while quasi-experimental designs do a moderate or intermediate-level job at assessing causal relationships. **Quasi-experimental designs** are designs that allow you to effectively test causal relationships in situations in which conducting a true experimental design is impossible or inappropriate.

The *Two-Group Posttest-Only Design* is a quasi-experimental design (Table 11.5). This design has every element of the classic experimental design except the pretest. Pretesting is not always the best idea. Sometimes, exposing research participants to a pretest can sensitize them to the independent variable under study. The Two-Group Posttest-Only Design is like a true experiment because it has random assignment. However, the problem with the Two-Group Posttest-Only Design is that the only assurance that the experimental group and the control group are equivalent is random assignment. A Two-Group Posttest-Only Design would involve exposing an experimental group to the HESOM approach and the traditional approach to teaching algebra to the control group. Then both the experimental and control groups would receive the posttest of participants' knowledge of algebra. If the experimental group had significantly higher scores on the posttest compared to the control group, we could attribute the difference to the HESOM approach.

However, because there is no pretest, the experimenter cannot be completely sure that the two groups (experimental group and control group) were equal in their ability to do algebra before the study began. The *Non-Equivalent Control Group Design*

Table 11.6

Non-Equivalent Control Group Design			
	PRETEST	STIMULUS	POSTTEST
EXPERIMENTAL GROUP	O	X	O
CONTROL GROUP	O		O

is also a quasi-experimental design (Table 11.6). It includes every feature of the classical experimental design except random assignment. It includes an experimental group, a control group, a pretest, and a posttest. This design is especially useful in cases when random assignment is impossible or unethical. If we are interested in testing the HESOM approach at a school, it may be impossible or unethical to reassign students to a class that does not receive the HESOM approach and another that does receive the HESOM approach, especially if they have already registered for their classes. In this kind of case it may be more appropriate to use the non-equivalent control group design. The challenge presented by such a design is that the researcher may have to use matching to ensure that equivalent comparisons are being made, because lack of random assignment means that the two classes being compared may not be equivalent in their math ability from the beginning of the study.

The *Interrupted Time Series Design* is a quasi-experimental design that includes only one group. It also involves multiple measures of the dependent variables both before and after the stimulus is administered. In this case we may expose our experimental classroom of student participants to a 12-week math class. They would be administered a pretest, then for the first 6 weeks we would expose them to the traditional approach to teaching algebra. However, for the last 6 weeks we would instruct them using the HESOM approach to teaching algebra. After every 2 weeks of class we would test their algebra knowledge. They would receive three tests while they were experiencing the traditional approach to teaching algebra and three tests while they were receiving the HESOM approach.

The *Equivalent Time Series Design* is another quasi-experimental design that involves only one group. It is like the Interrupted Time Series Design, only instead of having just one stimulus it includes a pretest followed by a stimulus, then a posttest, followed by another stimulus and posttest, and so on, with alternating stimuli or treatments. For example, in this case we could expose our youth participants to a 12-week math class. They would be pretested then exposed to the 2 weeks of the traditional approach to teaching algebra followed by a posttest, then exposed to 2 weeks of the HESOM approach followed by a posttest, then exposed to another 2 weeks of the traditional approach followed by a posttest, and so on, until the

Table 11.7

DESIGN	RANDOM ASSIGNMENT	PRETEST	POSTTEST	CONTROL GROUP	EXPERIMENTAL GROUP
Pre-Experimental					
ONE SHOT CASE STUDY	No	No	Yes	No	Yes
ONE-GROUP PRETEST POSTTEST	No	Yes	Yes	No	Yes
STATIC GROUP COMPARISON	No	No	Yes	Yes	Yes
True Experimental					
CLASSICAL	Yes	Yes	Yes	Yes	Yes
SOLOMON FOUR GROUP	Yes	Yes	Yes	Yes	Yes
Quasi-Experimental Design					
TWO-GROUP POSTTEST-ONLY	Yes	No	Yes	Yes	Yes
INTERRUPTED TIME SERIES DESIGN	No	Yes	Yes	Yes	Yes
TIME SERIES DESIGNS	No	Yes	Yes	No	Yes

6 weeks were over and the last posttest was completed. The advantage to the Time Series Designs are that they involve a single group of participants, which means that we don't have to worry about there being an identical comparison group. Table 11.7 borrows from Remler and Van Ryzin's (2011) summary of experimental design qualities. The disadvantage of the Equivalent Time Series Design is that the participants will experience an interference effect, that is, when they experience the second stimulus they will have already been exposed to and possibly changed by the first stimulus.

Threats to External Validity

External validity refers to the generalizability of research findings to the larger context of society at large or the "real world." If a study's findings do not hold true in the real world outside of the experimental condition, then we say that the study lacks external validity. This is because experimental designs often involve researchers making things happen that would otherwise not happen and observing their effects. Because of their effects, threats to external validity must always be kept at bay. But what are they? The following list contains the major threats to external validity:

1. Unrepresentative Samples: The researcher must ask the question, "To what extent can a study be generalized to a larger, diverse population?" However, this depends on the purpose of the researcher. If the researcher intends to take the findings of a research study and make generalizations to Black people in the United Kingdom (UK), then the sample should reflect the general characteristics of Black people in the UK. However, if the researcher's sample includes only Black people in the UK who are of low socioeconomic status, then that sample may be said to be unrepresentative. And that unrepresentativeness can cause the experiment to lack external validity because the findings of the study may not reflect the behaviors of Black people in the UK who are of middle and high socioeconomic status. Representativeness is extremely important for people of African descent. In the United States, for example, African Americans are underrepresented in many experimental designs, and this limits how representative such research findings are to African Americans. Individuals who participate in experiments usually volunteer and often have higher incomes, higher levels of education, and achievement motivations. Even in an all-Black country or community, the researcher must be sure that if he intends to have a representative sample of a particular people, a representative sample is taken. Nevertheless, having a representative sample is always difficult in experimental designs because they are usually volunteer based and involve small samples.

2. Artificial Setting: Researchers often bring research subjects or participants into artificial settings such as research laboratories on college campuses in order to conduct their experiments. This approach prevents threats to internal validity that were discussed earlier. However, such settings can be a threat to external validity. For example, results found in laboratory settings might not occur in natural settings such as schools, playgrounds, street corners, and households.

3. Pretesting: Being pretested may sensitize research subjects to the stimulus before they are ever exposed to it. For example, consider our earlier experiment testing the effects of a documentary about cultural sensitivity on research participants' tolerance levels. When individuals are pretested by completing an Intolerance Survey, they may be sensitized to the independent variable or stimulus. This may affect the way they respond to the stimulus—in this case the cultural sensitivity documentary. As a result, they may not be comparable to individuals in the "real world" because most people are not pretested on such issues. Researchers should consider whether or not pretesting will cause a reactive effect among

their participants, and if the effect may be too great, they should choose a design without a pretest.

4. Reactivity: Reactivity refers to the idea that when research participants take part in research, they know they are being observed and they behave differently than they would in real life. This is similar to the idea explained earlier as the Hawthorne Effect. People in experiments tend to be more cooperative, accommodating, and responsive than they would be in natural settings. The fact that participants respond differently when they know they are being observed in an experiment means that the external validity of the measure is affected.

Strengths and Weaknesses of Experimental Designs

The strength of the experimental design is that it is the best-suited method for establishing causation or causal relationships between variables. This is mostly because experimental designs have the most control over the research environment and the research variables. This provides assurance that the independent variable is having an effect on the dependent variables. Experimental designs are also usually smaller in sample size, which makes the research process less expensive.

There are also several disadvantages to experimental designs. Experimental designs are less suitable for exploratory research or the beginning phases of research. This is because experimental designs require that the independent variable(s) be well defined at the outset of the research. Because the independent variable has to be applied consistently and uniformly to participants, it must be clearly defined and not subject to change, as is the case in some exploratory research. True experimental designs are often ruled out in human services because the control group is often deprived of a potentially important stimulus. This raises an ethical concern for administrators, who are often unwilling to have one group receive nothing or not receive a more effective treatment.

Experimental designs also face the challenge of artificiality. Experiments are often done in laboratory settings that filter out the elements of the natural environment. This makes it difficult to determine whether or not people will behave the same way in their natural environments as they do in experimental settings. The amount of control that experimental designs demand often requires researchers to recruit small samples, as noted earlier. These smaller samples are easier to control; however, they limit the generalizability of findings from experiments. There is also concern that experiments, while they offer strong causal evidence, are less suitable for conducting research over the short term or when quick results are needed.

Key Terms

Classic Experimental
Design
Experiment
External Validity
Internal Validity

Matching
Pre-Experimental Designs
Quasi-Experimental
Designs
Random Sampling

Thinking about Science

Activity 1

Some research shows that there is a relationship between level of education and overall physical health such that the higher a person's level of education, the better they rate their overall physical health. Does this relationship suggest causation? What are some alternative explanations?

Activity 2

Pick two threats to internal validity and two threats to external validity discussed in the chapter. Create examples that demonstrate each one. (Do not use examples already explained in the chapter).

Activity 3

Go to your library search engine and find a research study that makes use of one of the many different types of experimental designs discussed in the chapter. Make sure that the study involves African/Black people. Identify that study's title, its author(s), independent variable(s), dependent variable(s), and stimulus. If the author(s) note any threats to internal or external validity that the study had to contend with, identify them.

CHAPTER TWELVE

Qualitative Field Research and Data Analysis

Qualitative Methods

Observation is a widely used term in research methods. Observational techniques refer to the "collection of data through direct visual or auditory experience of behavior" (Monette, Sullivan, & DeJong, 2005, p. 218). Researchers may choose to use qualitative or quantitative observational techniques depending on the nature of what they are investigating. This chapter explores different types of qualitative methods and the circumstances under which each method is most useful. The strengths and weaknesses of each method will also be explained. Finally, we will explore the basic techniques for qualitative data analysis.

Qualitative research data comes in the form of words, narratives, pictures, and descriptions. These kinds of data produced in qualitative research are not as easily reduced to numbers as data that comes from more quantitative methods such as surveys. Therefore, they require unique techniques of data reduction. Neuman (2009) identifies three key features of qualitative methods:

1. Inductive: Qualitative methods usually take an approach to the development of theory from data collection as opposed to more quantitative approaches that begin with theories and test them through data collection.
2. Interpretivist: They take an epistemological approach that is interpretivist, meaning that this approach to research emphasizes the interpretation or

understanding of the social world through the analysis or perspective of cultural insiders or participants in those cultures.;

3. A constructionist ontological position: This position, adopted in qualitative methods, is grounded in the assumption that social properties are the consequence of interaction between individuals and not phenomena separate from those involved in the construction.

Qualitative approaches are meant to offer more descriptive data on peoples' lives, behaviors, and subjective experiences compared to quantitative methods. Qualitative approaches are said to be non-positivist. Positivism asserts that ideas, emotions, morality and other human qualities could be studied quantitatively (Vogt, 1999). While positivism asserts a world independent of people's subjectivities, qualitative approaches are non-positivist in that their interpretivist or *versterhen* approach privileges understanding human subjectivities and how they perceive their own realities. According to Monette, Sullivan, and DeJong (2005), researchers cannot capture the meaning people attach to their lives adequately through quantitative methods; instead they need a subjective—or what Max Weber called a *versterhen*, understanding (Weber, 1957).

Field Research

Field research is a qualitative approach to collecting data on people or research elements in natural settings. W.E.B. Dubois, one of the premier Black intellectuals of the 20th century, pioneered *urban ethnography* in the social sciences using field research. Dubois introduced this approach to social sciences in his landmark study of the Black Population in Philadelphia's 7th ward. Field research involves observations made of people in naturalistic settings. Data produced in field research is not collected in laboratory or contrived settings but in real-life or natural settings where people act or behave as if they were not subjects of research observations. Survey researchers indirectly observe the phenomena they study, while field researchers use techniques that allow them to see and hear what they are studying in the field or natural setting. Field work is meant to be a method that reveals human attitudes and behaviors that might be missed by researchers using other methods. Lofland and Lofland (1995) and Babbie (2001) discuss several key elements of the field research method:

- Practices: Various kinds of behavior such as talking or reading a book;
- Episodes: A variety of events such as divorce, crime, and illness;

- Encounters: Two or more people meeting or interacting;
- Roles: The analysis of the positions people occupy and the behavior associated with them. For example, occupations, family roles, and ethnic groups;
- Relationships: Behavior appropriate to pairs or sets of roles. For example, mother-son relationships, friendships, and the like;
- Groups: Small groups such as friendships, athletic teams and workgroups;
- Organizations: Formal organizations such as hospitals or schools;
- Settlements: Small scale "societies" such as villages or ghettoes, and neighborhoods, as opposed to large societies such as nations, which are difficult to study;
- Social Worlds: Ambiguous entities with vague boundaries and populations, such as "the sports world" and "Wall Street";
- Lifestyles or subcultures: How large numbers of people adjust to life in groups such as a "ruling class" or "urban underclass."

For example, Saayman, and Crafford (2012) investigated how workers at a South African manufacturing company negotiated and constructed their work identities. The authors were interested in how the workers understand their identity in the context of their jobs and the work they do. The researchers were also interested in the competing demands and tensions that impact the workers' processes of understanding their identities. The authors chose field research because they were primarily interested in how people create and share meaning in natural settings. Quantitative approaches are less suited to this kind of research objective. Some of the main conceptual frameworks used in field work are naturalism, ethnomethodology, and grounded theory.

Naturalism is about investigating social reality on its own terms or *as it is* by making thick, detailed descriptions of people and their interaction in natural settings. Naturalism is one of the oldest perspectives in qualitative research based on the positivist assumption that social reality is most objectively described and reported by a scientific researcher. **Ethnomethodology** is a perspective that is based on the presumption that social reality is socially constructed through communication and interaction. The ethnomethodologist rejects the idea that social reality is simply there for the researcher to observe. Instead of decrying social reality as it objectively is, the ethnomethodologist privileges and validates people's descriptions of social reality as their subjective ways of making sense of it. **Grounded theory** is not a theory as it may seem simply based on its name. Grounded theory is instead a method of developing theory (grounded in data) by recognizing patters or codes in data collected through qualitative methods. In the positivist methodology, first, data is to be collected; second, it is analyzed and; lastly, theory is developed. In the grounded theory methodology, each of these steps can occur simultaneously. A researcher may start by making observations and, depending upon these, may develop new concepts and seek explanation for them. Instead of starting with preexisting theories that may restrict the researcher's thinking, using grounded theory observations are made and concepts and theoretical explanations are developed during the processes of data collection and analysis. **Action research** is another approach which is designed to find the most effective way to bring about some desired social change. Central to action research is the integration of theory *and* practice. In action research, of which there are many different types, the collection of data is more tightly associated with the development of solutions. For instance, in **participatory action research**, the researcher and the members of a social setting collaborate in the process of studying a problem and developing a solution for it. Participatory research shares several things with action research, such as placing value on practical or useful knowledge and making change. However, participatory action research combines the added element of collaboration with members of a social setting in the data collection and change-making process.

Akom (2011) developed the framework, **Black Emancipatory Action Research** (BEAR), as an orientation meant to enhance qualitative methods in research involving people of African descent. BEAR is a framework for guiding research that seeks to liberate African Diasporic peoples from various forms of oppression. The core principals of BEAR are: 1) structural racialization; 2) Intersectionality and social construction of knowledge; 3) the development of critical consciousness and; 4) love, healing, and a commitment to social justice (Akom, 2011). The theory of structural racism is at the core of BEAR. The theory of structural racism rejects conceptualizations of racism that focus on individual acts of racial discrimination. BEAR incorporates this model to examine how individuals and institutions interact to produce enduring, radicalized, and unequal distributions of power and privilege. BEAR locates structural racialization at the intersection of multiple forms of oppression such as class, gender, religion, nationality, sexual orientation, immigrant status, surname, phenotype, accent, and special needs by explaining how they interact as a system of oppression. BEAR encourages everyday people to deconstruct the systems that oppress them through critical consciousness. BEAR locates healing as another central aspect of Black community development given the historical trauma that White Supremacy has had and continues to have on Black life. Lastly, BEAR seeks to develop love and self-determination in people of African descent through the research process by empowering them to conceptualize, study, and meet their challenges in a collective manner.

There are several main steps in conducting field research in general.

- Identify the topic: Explore the topic you are interested in. Review the existing literature and decide whether or not it is a topic that warrants the use of field research. Learn as much as you can about the population and social phenomena you are interested in. Finally, make a decision about how appropriate field research is in investigating it.

- *The formulation of a research question*: In field research the research question is more general than the research question in quantitative research. According to Nielson (2011), the African American shopper makes more trips to the grocery store and spends less money per trip than the average American shopper. Quantitative and qualitative questions on this topic might be as follows:
  - Quantitative: According to the Shoppers Choice Survey (SCS) how does race and ethnicity impact grocery shopping frequency and choice of goods among African American shoppers in Oakland, California?
  - Qualitative: How do African American shoppers negotiate where to shop and what groceries to buy?

- Selecting the Field Site: The field researcher has to decide which group of people are most appropriate to study to answer the research question or address the research problem at hand. Keep in mind that the setting doesn't have to be a single physical setting because a group of people can interact in many settings in a fluid way. Neuman (2009) identifies four factors that affect a field researcher's choice of a site:
  1. Containment: Bounded areas where small groups of people interact are easier to study while large open areas where many people pass through are more difficult;
  2. Richness: According to Neuman (2009) "More interesting data come from sites that have overlapping webs of social relations among people with a constant flow of activities and diverse events" (p.269);
  3. Unfamiliarity: A researcher can more easily be open-minded and attentive to detail in an environment that is new and unfamiliar to them;
  4. Suitability: The researcher's time, accessibility, safety, and skill should be taken into consideration when choosing a setting.

- Gaining Access: There are open public spaces (parks, airports, etc.) and closed spaces (schools, private homes, etc.). Closed spaces require permission from someone who controls access.

- Data Collection: In field research the researcher is the instrument of data collection. The researcher collects data on the physical setting, people's behaviors, interactions, and words.

- Interpretation of Data: Collected data must be analyzed for themes and patterns.

- Development of New Concepts and Theories: Often new concepts and theories emerge from the coding process.

There are several different kinds of qualitative research methods. The following sections will specifically cover qualitative interviewing, focus groups, observations, case studies, and discourse analysis. Three qualitative methods are interviewing, observation, and document analysis. **Ethnography** is the careful study of a culture through qualitative (unstructured or semi-structured) interviews, observations (complete observer, participant as observer, observer as participant, complete participant), and analysis of cultural documents. "Ethno" means "people," and "graphy" means "to describe something" (Neuman, 2009). Ethnography is based on the idea that people live in cultures and in order to understand them it is necessary to study them in their cultures. Those cultures can be micro cultures such as families, or macro cultures such as nations. The job of the ethnographer is to immerse him- or herself in the culture under study to see through the eyes of the people being studied and to make sense of it from a scientific perspective. What is most important to the ethnographer is how the members of a culture define their own reality. According to Bryman (2008), ethnography is a method in which the researcher:

- Is immersed in a social setting for an extended period of time;
- Makes regular observations of behavior of the members of that setting;
- Listens to and engages in conversations;
- Interviews informants on issues;
- Collects documents about the group;
- Develops an understanding of the group's and people's behavior in the context of that group;
- Writes a detailed account of that setting.

When the researcher has collected data about a culture through interviews, observations, and/or analysis of cultural documents from that culture, the next objective is pattern recognition. The researcher must find commonalities and logical patterns in the data that represent aspects of their existence. One of the major tools of the ethnographer is analysis of cultural documents, which has already been covered. Let's discuss the remaining two tools of ethnography: interviews and observations.

Observation/Participant Observation

Observation is a technique in which the researcher observes people in their natural environment. **Participant observation** involves observing and participating in the activities of people in their natural environment. In participant observation, researchers learn about the social world that they are studying by participating within and engaging with it. It is a way of generating researcher understanding through empathy (Monette, Sullivan, and DeJong, 2005). Observation in this context refers to taking note of and recording how people act and interact in their natural environment or social setting. For example, Richardson (2012) conducted participant research on the role of the African American coach as a source of social capital for at-risk African American male junior high school students. Richardson (2012) participated as a coach himself and observed students in multiple settings including their schools, their local communities, and their home environments. Richardson (2012) was able to find that African American coaches served as mentors, social fathers, supervisors, guidance counselors, motivators, and encouragers. Gold (1958) identifies four different participant observer roles: 1) the complete participant; 2) the participant as observer; 3) the observer as participant and; 4) the complete observer. The *complete participant* uses a covert approach to observation in which the researcher does not make those who are being studied aware that they are being observed. You, as the researcher, enter the field under the guise that you are a participant like the others. The researchers' goal is to be seen as natural members of the social setting without making known their identities as researchers. The role of the *participant as observer* is similar to the role of the complete observer with the exception that those who are being researched are aware that the researcher is observing them. In this role the researcher engages and interacts with individuals and they go about activities in their everyday lives. The participant as observer participates in the routines of people's everyday lives, but is overt about doing so for the purpose of research. This is the role that Richardson (2012) played in his research on coaches as social capital. The role of the *observer as participant* is similar to the role of the participant as observer in that they both make their status as a researcher known to members of the social setting being observed; however, they differ in the extent to which the researcher engages in the social setting and the amount of time the researcher spends in that setting. In this role, the researcher is more of an interviewer who engages in observation, but with little participation. The role of the *complete observer* is unobtrusive because the researcher observes but does not interact with the people being studied. This role is not considered participant observation because there is no participation alongside individuals in the social setting.

Taking Field Notes

The human memory is imperfect, and because of this, researchers have to take careful notes of their observations. These notes are called **field notes** or detailed descriptions of events and behaviors and the researcher's reflections on them. They are necessary even in the presence of audio or video recording devices which cannot capture the subtleties of social settings that a human being can. When in the field or social setting, it is the researcher's duty to take notes and record that which could not have been written down immediately after exiting the field. Field notes should be written down as quickly as possible when the researcher sees and hears relevant things in the field. Field notes that cannot be written down immediately should at the least be written down at the end of the day on which they were observed. The following are two different types of field notes:

1. Jotted Notes: These running descriptions are brief notes written down, such as in a notebook, to jog one's memory about events and action to be written up in more detail later. They usually need to be written down quickly and inconspicuously since detailed note-taking in front of people could make participants self-conscious. (Bryman, 2008; Monette, Sullivan, and DeJong, 2005).
2. Full Field Notes: These detailed notes should be written up as soon as possible because they serve as the researcher's main data source and should be completed at the end of the day at the latest.

What to Write About

You might be thinking, "I can't write up everything!" No, and you should not be expected to. However, you should record the most *relevant* or pertinent events and actions that occur in the social setting that you are observing. The researcher should primarily be observing the setting and the people in it. Observers should describe the physical and social aspects of the environment. It could be a home, a gymnasium, or a restaurant. Field notes should include a description of the conditions, the weather, and other physical aspects that might shape or have been shaped by the people in the social setting being observed.

The physical and social setting is important because it plays a role in the atmosphere in which people think and act. What is written on the walls, the floor, or the ceiling? These are relevant questions when making observations. The people should also be observed because they are often the key players. What do they look like, how are they dressed, how many of them are there, and how are they interacting?

Take note of their age and gender. Why? Because people often interact or behave differently based on these characteristics. People's actions should also be observed. Who interacts with whom and how do they do it? Do you notice any patterns in their behaviors and interactions with one another? The researcher should also take note of group behavior and interaction. On what basis do groups form, and how do groups interact with one another? Researchers should also pay attention to meaning. This refers to the meaning that people create for themselves, the perspectives they exhibit, and evidence of them. If the researcher is taking a quantitative approach to field notes, s/he enters the field with a set of predetermined categories or actions and behaviors that s/he is interested in observing. These things are noted on one's coding sheet. If the researcher is taking more of a qualitative approach, he or she must code field notes or analyze them for patterns.

Qualitative Interviews

Structured interviews are too rigid for qualitative research. Field research calls for less structured interviews. Qualitative interviewing makes use of two particular types of interviews: semi-structured interviews and unstructured interviews. Cashmore (2002) conducted **unstructured interviews** with 100 Black and Asian police officers in Britain about the importance of recruiting police officers who belong to underrepresented racial/ethnic groups. Using the unstructured approach, the interviewer develops interview questions as the interview progresses. This approach is called unstructured because the interviewer obtains different information from each respondent. In unstructured interviews the researcher is tasked with keeping the interview going while keeping the interviewee on topic. This approach is best for exploratory research, as the interviewer is essentially exploring the research topic with the interviewee. The researcher often begins the unstructured interview with a general question allowing the respondents to take the interview where they will. Using the unstructured approach, the interviewees are free to discuss the topic as they see fit and can touch on any particular issues they choose while relating them to their personal experiences. In an unstructured interview the role of the researcher is to record and ask the respondents for clarification and further explanation. The unstructured approach works best when the researcher does not need to make comparisons between respondents because each respondent is not being asked the exact same set of questions.

The **semi-structured interview** method is used with more specific topics. In the semi-structured interview each respondent is asked to answer a specific set of questions. However, the semi-structured interview maintains a conversational style in which the interviewer probes the respondent and is free to ask questions in a different order for all respondents. Although a semi-structured interview involves a standard set of questions, it also allows for interviewers to ask sub-questions and develop new questions based on interviewees' responses. Semi-structured interviewing does presuppose prior knowledge on the research topic. Qualitative interviews are more like conversations than structured interviews and should be understood as appropriate or less appropriate according to the nature of the research question.

Discourse Analysis

We have already covered content analysis. **Discourse analysis** is a research technique that allows you to systematically analyze the hidden and visible content in communication messages. Documents are among the sources analyzed in the process of conducting content analysis. However, this section will focus on the analysis of documents in qualitative research. In this case, documents refer to the texts, writings, manuscripts, and materials produced by members of the culture being studied.

Historians often use personal documents, but they may also be used in social science research. Personal documents are documents such as diaries, letters, and autobiographies produced by individuals being studied. In addition to letters and diaries, emails and text messages are also personal documents that could be analyzed in qualitative research. How such documents should be assessed is another matter. Scott (1990) identifies four criteria to help assess the quality of such documents studied in discourse analysis:

1. *Authenticity.* The researcher must know how genuine the document is. The researcher must make sure that the supposed author of the document is indeed the true author. This is an issue that arises in relation to autobiographies written by "ghost writers." However, it is also a concern related to other documents.

2. *Credibility.* The researcher must know that the document under study is free of error, misrepresentation, and falsehood. The researcher must assess the accuracy of information in the document. The researcher must also assess to what extent the document reflects the true attitudes and beliefs of the author. If individuals are aware that others will be reading their personal documents (for instance, those written by celebrities), they may present an image of themselves that they think will be appealing to others—not necessarily one that is representative of their true feelings.

3. *Representativeness.* The researcher must know to what degree the document under study is or is not representative of similar kinds of documents of its

kind and how representative it is of the population under study. For example, if an underrepresented racial/ethnic population produces less of a certain kind of document due to lack of access, capacity, or status, then the documents being studied may be less representative of that population.

4. *Meaning.* Is the evidence or document under study clear and understandable? When documents are difficult to read, undecipherable, or damaged, their meaning may be unreachable or unclear.

Visual objects such as photographs may also be used in qualitative research. They can be analyzed for what they reveal about those being studied, and they can also be used to evoke thought and dialogue from research participants. Official documents were discussed earlier as secondary sources of information. Official documents such as the minutes of meetings or transcripts of senatorial or congressional hearings can be subjects of analysis, as can mass media, such as movies, news programs, and episodes of television series. Virtual documents such as websites and Internet postings can also be subjects of research, as they reveal data about their creators or authors. Documents have to be interpreted and analyzed within the context that they were produced. Ultimately, they should be analyzed using techniques such as content analysis and other relevant qualitative data analysis techniques to be covered in the next chapter. There are some approaches to analysis of qualitative data that are concerned with contextualizing analysis, as opposed to attempting generalizations to larger populations. Five such approaches are conversation analysis, profiling, narrative analysis, case studies, and focus groups.

Conversation Analysis

Like discourse analysis, **conversation analysis** treats language as a topic rather than a resource. However, conversation analysis is focused on "talk," while discourse analysis is more flexible in that it can include things like texts such as newspapers and letters. Conversation analysis is the detailed analysis of naturally occurring spoken words. The purpose of conversation analysis is to discover the underlying structures of talk in interaction. The premise behind conversation analysis is that social order is constructed through social interaction, with a particular focus on conversational interaction. Given this premise, conversation analysis seeks to discover the assumptions in social life by analyzing the way people converse with one another. Heritage (1984) proposes three basic assumptions of conversation analysis:

1. *Talk is structured.* Talking is composed of structured patterns. Conversation analysis rejects the researcher's attempts to infer speakers' motiva-

tions from what they say; instead, the conversation analyst is interested in identifying the underlying structures revealed in talk.

2. *Talk is forged contextually.* Talk reveals action, and talk must be analyzed in context.

3. *Analysis is grounded in data.* Conversation analysts reject preexisting theories and argue that the sequences of talk must instead be induced from the conversational data itself.

Pallitt (2009) conducted a conversation analysis of South African primary school children's conversational interactions around email activities and how they communicate about resources in their environment. In conversation analysis, Pallitt's (2009) research demonstrated how students use the privacy of email technology, among other things, to gain or avoid individual attention from the teacher. Bertrand and Priego-Valverde (2011) used conversation analysis to investigate how conversational humor is produced and co-constructed in talk interaction. Their analysis of the patterns and sequences of conversational humor revealed how repetition, confirmation, and requests between conversationalists are key aspects of humor construction in conversation. Conversation analysis could also be used to study the structures and sequences in the use of Ebonics, or the Black vernacular among African Americans.

Profiling

Profiling in qualitative research refers to the use of excerpts about a person's experiences taken from qualitative interviews. Profiles are pieced together in a way that tells a story. Using profiling, the researcher transcribes an interview and then selects portions of the interview that are important in telling that person's story. The researcher goes through the passages to be sure that they flow together, that they have proper transitions, and that redundancies are eliminated. Although the researcher may include some commentary, the majority of the profile is in the person's own words. The researcher only adds commentary to clarify things or to make a transition from one topic to the next.

Narrative Analysis

Narrative analysis is similar to profiling. The objective of **narrative analysis** is to piece together narratives of people's lives and the world around them, using a number of sources. Narrative analysis focuses on people's stories and descriptive accounts of lives and events. Like profiling, it relies heavily on people's own words. However, unlike profiling, instead of relying solely on in-depth interviews, narrative analysis makes use of letters, autobiographies, interviews, and other sources. Koro-Ljung-berg, Bussing, Williamson, Wilder, and Mills (2008) used a narrative analysis to investigate how African American teenagers described and constructed stories about their personal lives and experiences with Attention Deficit/Hyperactivity Disorder (ADHD). The researchers' intention was to describe the experience of ADHD in a way that would be more culturally situated and useful for health professionals to understand the personal realities of African American teens with ADHD.

Case Studies

A **case study** is a detailed, intensive, and descriptive account of a single individual, group, or organization. Although it is often an individual or an organization, a case can also be a time period. Case studies are most commonly associated with, but not limited to, qualitative research. Focus in case studies is on the detailed description of the entity under study and the context that it is in. In case studies, people's lives are explained in great detail, but unlike profiles and narratives, they don't need to be primarily in the words of those being studied. Instead, case studies can make use of document analysis, interviews, official documents, observation, or a combination of these methods. The basic goal of the case study is to produce a detailed description of the particularities and complexities of the entity under study. Kinney (2012) conducted a case study of a young African American male participating in a song-writing exercise at the Music Resource Center (MRC) in Cincinnati, Ohio. The MRC has a literacy exercise that makes use of songwriting. By way of a case study, Kinney (2012) investigated how African American youth such as the one he investigated use songwriting as a form of self-expression and as a way of dealing with emotional trauma. For this case study, Kinney (2012) made use of semi-structured interviews, field notes from observations, compact discs (cds), and transcriptions of song lyrics.

Focus Groups

An interview is typically thought of as an act that takes place between one interviewer and one interviewee, but sometimes it is a good idea to bring research participants into the same room for interviewing. This is called a **focus group**—qualitative interviews of a group of research participants in an interactive group setting. Focus groups are appropriate for research questions that are concerned with collective or joint meaning making and the co-construction of ideas. Focus groups usually involve 4–15 people who are brought into the same room to discuss a topic, typically for up to three hours. The size of a focus group is kept small to allow the researcher to get a greater depth of information. Studies using focus groups are typically composed of 10–15 different groups, and only rarely just one group. Focus groups are best used for exploratory purposes rather than explanatory or descriptive purposes.

Focus groups are conducted using the unstructured or semi-structured interviewing styles. The facilitator or the moderator is the person who conducts the interview. If you are the interviewer, you should intend to be unintrusive. Your major responsibility is facilitating the focus group by using a set of broad and open-ended questions. To do so, it is important to have an understanding of the topic before formulating the questions and facilitating the focus group.

The careful selection of research participants is a critical feature of focus group research. If, for example, the researcher were interested in studying West African immigrants' perceptions of child and protective services in the United States, it would be important for the researcher to select for participation those who are in the best position to provide information about the topic. Participants who know each other should not be placed in groups together because they are likely to modify their answers in the presence of friends or acquaintances. In the case of perception of child protective services, the participants would be West African immigrants with children who have had relationships with child protective services. In general, participants should be selected to participate based on their level of involvement with the topic at hand.

There are several advantages to conducting focus groups. One of the strengths of focus groups is that they give participants the opportunity to discuss issues and question and build upon one another's answers. The key here is the collective construction of knowledge, which is the jewel of the focus group method. This gives the researcher the opportunity to record the participants' dialogue, agreements, and differences of opinion. The fact that participants can build upon and feed off one another can provide interviewers with deeper insights than they may have gleaned from interviewing individual participants separately. The focus group approach also allows the researcher to collect data from large groups of people in short periods of time. Given that African American males in the United States represent 47% of cases of police use of excessive force, it would be plausible to interview Black males about their perceptions of police officers. However, focus groups would allow one to analyze how Black males construe their perceptions of the police in conjunction with other Black males.

The group atmosphere of the focus group allows participants to probe and challenge one another in ways the interviewer might not be able to or may not have thought of. Participants can also bring up issues interviewers may not have asked about. In some cases this kind of atmosphere encourages participants to rethink and revise their attitudes. This evolution of thought in the group setting is important for the researcher to record. The focus group replicates the meaning-making process that takes place in everyday life. Moreover, for conducting action research dealing with resolving social problems, focus groups can also serve the purposes of problem solving and conflict resolution.

The moderator of the focus group begins by stimulating the conversation with one or two general questions. Ultimately, focus groups use fewer than 12 questions. However, the number of questions asked varies, and it is based on the complexity of the topic and the diversity of the participants. More complex topics and diverse groups use fewer or more specific questions. Groups that are less diverse in thought and share a similar outlook are likely to move through topics and questions more quickly than groups that are less homogeneous. As the focus group goes on, questions may become more specific. Such general questions are meant to allow the participants to discuss the issues of interest to them as long as they stay on topic.

As mentioned earlier, the role of the moderator in focus groups is not to be intrusive, but to skillfully allow the participants to articulate their perspectives by asking a small number of general, open-ended questions. The respondents should be allowed to discuss issues, probe, and respond to one another. However, the moderator needs to keep the participants on topic and prevent them from going off on unrelated tangents. The moderator should also probe participants in cases where a particularly interesting point is left unexplored or unexplained.

There are several limitations to the focus group approach. The researcher has less control of the research process in focus groups compared to structured interviews. However, this is not a true limitation because, for the focus group interviewer, it is advantageous to render control to the interviewees because doing so allows the participants to discuss issues on their own terms. Focus group recordings and transcripts produce lots of data, which are time consuming to analyze. They are also difficult to transcribe in some cases because participants often speak inaudibly or talk at the same time. Focus groups can be difficult to organize because of the high likelihood of people not showing up at an agreed-upon time or leaving early. Because of this, researchers often over-recruit participants to ensure that there are enough, or offer incentives for respondents ranging from money to gift certificates. There are also group effects on participants' responses in focus groups. Individuals in focus groups can be more likely to express attitudes they perceive to be socially desirable to the group, especially when sensitive topics are being discussed. When sensitive issues are being discussed, individual interviews are preferable.

Tips for Being Successful in the Field

Neuman (2009) described several basic strategies for success in field research:

- *Building relationships.* The researcher should build relationships with members of the social setting they are researching, but always keep a balance between social sensitivity and research goals. The researcher should be aware of how he or she appears to members of the social setting.
- *Perform small favors.* The researcher should be willing to engage in small acts of *kindness without expecting anything in return.*
- *Appearing interested and exercising selective inattention.* It is disrespectful to appear bored or disinterested in a social setting. The researcher should monitor his or her words and actions, including nonverbal cues that may signify disinterest.
- *Being an earnest novice.* The researcher should make an effort to try not to appear to be a *know-it-all* or *expert.* Instead, the primary mission of the researcher is to be a learner and to listen and ask questions.
- *Avoiding conflict.* It goes without saying that if the researcher is trying to collect data on an important issue that affects people's quality of life, being involved in a conflict within that group can only limit the researcher's ability to be of service.

Sampling in Qualitative Research

Probability sampling is rarely used in qualitative field research because of the difficulty of establishing a sampling frame. Field research usually makes use of non-probability sampling techniques such as purposive sampling and snowball sampling. Purposive sampling, as described in previous chapters, allows the researcher to select a sample directly related to the research question. Probability sampling is sometimes used in qualitative research; usually it is used in qualitative interviewing. If the researcher is interested in generalizing findings to a large population, it would be smart to use probability sampling.

Validity and Reliability

Internal validity in qualitative research refers to how good a match there is between the observations the researcher makes during the research process, the conclusions researchers draw, and the theories they develop. Internal validity is particularly strong in qualitative research because researchers often spend lots of time in the social setting they are studying, compared to relatively brief interactions between the researcher and the participants in quantitative research. External validity refers to how well conclusions can be applied to larger social settings. External validity can present a problem for qualitative research because qualitative research so often makes use of case studies of small sample sizes. In qualitative research there are several techniques that can be used by the researcher to enhance the validity of observations.

External reliability refers to the degree to which a study can be replicated. However, this is difficult in qualitative research because social settings are different. Internal reliability refers to the degree to which observers agree about what they observe in situations in which there is more than one observer. Methods of increasing reliability will be discussed below.

Some scholars argue that since the goals of qualitative research and quantitative research are different, they should be evaluated differently. Lincoln and Guba (1985) discuss two main criteria for evaluating a qualitative study: trustworthiness and authenticity.

Trustworthiness is made up of four different criteria: credibility, transferability, dependability, and conformability.

> *Credibility* is a concern in qualitative research because different researchers can create different accounts of the same phenomena that are observed. However, what is important about those observations is their credibility, or how correctly the researchers understood what they observed. This can be enhanced by ensuring that the researcher used ethical and best practices. Additionally, the researcher can confirm his/her observations with members of the social setting they observe to ensure that people's attitudes and behaviors were observed properly. *Triangulation* is another name for the researcher's practice of providing research participants with an account of their research and findings to seek confirmation or validation of the findings they arrived at.

> *Transferability* refers to the degree to which qualitative findings can be transferred to or applied to different social settings. According to Lincoln and Guba (1985), qualitative research is concerned with providing detailed descriptions of the uniqueness of social settings. They add that the thick description or rich detail of qualitative research provides the information necessary to determine how transferable findings are to other social settings.

> *Dependability* should also be assessed through an auditing process. Research must be monitored to ensure that complete records are kept, including all phases of the research process from problem formulation, sample selection, and field notes to the making of interview transcripts, data analysis, and the drawing of conclusions.

Conformability refers to the degree to which the researcher has acted in good faith by not letting his or her personal opinions or theoretical inclinations obstruct the conduct of research and interpretation of findings.

Authenticity consists of five components: fairness, ontological authenticity, educative authenticity, catalytic authenticity, and tactical authenticity.

Fairness is concerned with how justly or honestly the researcher represents the viewpoints of all members of the social setting under observation.

Ontological authenticity refers to how well the research allows members of the setting to gain a better understanding of their social conditions.

Educative authenticity refers to how well the research helps members of the social setting better appreciate the different perspective of other members of their social setting.

Catalytic authenticity refers to whether or not the research inspires members of the social setting to engage in social change to improve their condition.

Tactical authenticity refers to whether or not the research has empowered members of the social setting with the steps necessary to engage in social action (Bryman, 2008).

These criteria are very much relevant to action research and Black emancipatory action research. Monette, Sullivan, and DeJong (2005) suggest several procedures that can be employed in field research to enhance the validity of research:

- *Be as thorough as possible in describing and interpreting situations.* Thorough observations increase the likelihood that the most important aspects of the social setting are captured. It is better to have too much data and too much detail than too little.
- *Carefully assess your own values, prejudices, and dispositions to see how they might bias your research.* Researchers' expectations shape their perceptions. These expectations lead to what we have discussed earlier in this text as selective observation. To guard against this we should consciously look for cases or situations that contradict our expectations.

- *Have other researchers or confederates observe the same social setting to see if they have similar interpretations.* This can confirm the researcher's observation or alert him or her of bias.
- *Confirm the conclusions reached through field observations with those researched through other methods.* If other methods such as experimental designs and survey data confirm qualitative research, then the findings can be received with more confidence.
- *Consider how the conditions of the observer might influence the research.* The researcher's mental state (stress, anxiety, and other extreme emotions) might influence observations. The researcher should be aware of this and minimize these emotions' effect on how participants are described.
- *Look for illegal, risky, or embarrassing behavior.* If people engage in this kind of behavior when they know they are being observed, then it is more likely that they are acting naturally and not reacting to the observer.
- *If possible, make an audio or video recording of the social setting.* Recordings can pick up things that the researcher misses through human error. This is a good way of checking or validating researcher observations.

Because qualitative researchers are interested in observing the specifics of very particular social settings or cultures, reliability is not as easy to assess. However, if observations are done in a more structured way, they may be assessed by way of monitoring coding manuals and coding schedules mentioned earlier in the text. Researchers also assess reliability using inter-coder reliability or having more than one observer code the same data into categories to check for consistency.

Strengths and Limitations

Because field research is not limited to words and verbal statements, it is well positioned to observe the consistency between people's words and behaviors, or what they say during interviews and what they actually do in the real world. Because qualitative research often takes place over long periods of time, it is well suited to describe change as it takes place over time. Field research also provides a depth of information that is not often found in survey research or experimental design. Finally, field research can also be used to observe groups that might otherwise be inaccessible in other methods of research. Some groups may not be open to participating in experiments or survey designs.

However, there are some disadvantages to field research. Because the researcher is the primary tool of observation in field research, the possibility of observer bias is greater than in quantitative research. Because researchers and social settings are so different and qualitative studies are less structured, it is also more difficult to establish reliability in qualitative research. Because field research involves so much dense description and detailed observation, the data are much more difficult and time consuming to quantify. Field research is also less generalizable in most cases because it involves small sample sizes.

Qualitative Data Analysis

Qualitative analysis involves the analysis of data without converting them to numerical form (Babbie, 2001). However, there is not a clear delineation between quantitative and qualitative data analysis. Qualitative data analysis still relies on some level of numerical analysis, although far less in comparison to quantitative data analysis, which will be covered in the next chapter. As we know, qualitative methods produce lots of data in the form of words and narratives from field notes and in-depth interviews. That data has to be analyzed. In most cases, it must be coded.

Coding, or thematic analysis, involves translating or reducing data into categories based on patterns or themes. Researchers do *coding* by looking for patterns in data that provide understanding and meaning of phenomena being studied. The codes produced as a result are essential in the process of conceptualization and the development of theories such as in the *grounded theory* approach. Thomas, Manusov, Wang, and Livingston (2011) conducted semi-structured interviews with Black males to determine what characteristics and experiences contributed to their success in being admitted to and graduating from medical school. The semi-structured interviews produced lots of qualitative interview data, but they had to be coded. The researchers had to identify patterns or themes in the data; this process simplifies the mass of unstructured data derived from qualitative methods of data collection. Those themes would represent the characteristics and experiences that contributed to the men's success.

Consider the following two approaches to coding. One approach is to enter the process of coding with no pre-established coding scheme. This is characteristic of the grounded theory approach. Using this approach, coding is done during the research process. Themes in the data are identified as the researcher reads though transcripts. Thomas, Manusov, Wang, and Livingston (2011) identified six categories of factors from their analysis of interview data: social support, education, exposure to the field of medicine, group identity, faith, and social responsibility. Another approach involves going into field research with a pre-established coding scheme. This coding scheme would come from the researcher's review of relevant literature and theoretical knowledge. For example, a researcher conducting research on Black male success in medical school after Thomas and colleagues' study (2011) might decide to use the themes identified by them as a coding scheme. In this case they would conduct interviews or observations on a different set of Black males, looking specifically for semi-structured interview data that falls within the categories of social support, education, exposure to the field of medicine, group identity, faith, and social responsibility. This approach would test the preexisting coding scheme and possibly generate new categories.

According to Bryman (2008), there are several basic steps in the coding process. The researcher must code as soon as possible. Coding during the research process prevents the researcher from having to deal with a backlog of data to code when all data collection is completed. The researcher should first read through the data, taking note of significant or interesting aspects of the data. Data should be read through again and key words and themes identified. These will become your categories. The researcher should go over the codes s/he has generated to see if some categories are the same or if they should be separated into distinct categories. The researcher should, again, analyze the codes or categories created to determine if there is enough support for each of them. This means that there should be observational data to support each of them. For example, multiple interviewees in the study by Thomas and fellow researchers (2011) mentioned social support, education, exposure to the field of medicine, group identity, faith, and social responsibility. Some people may have mentioned other factors that contributed to their success, but these themes represent the most commonly recurring factors. Themes that do not have enough support should be eliminated.

Ryan and Bernard (2003) identify several things for researchers to look for when they are searching for themes: repetition, indigenous typologies, metaphors and analogies, similarities and differences, linguistic connectors, missing data, and theoretical material. *Repetition* is one thing to look for in the coding process. In particular, the researcher should be looking for the repetition of topics and subject matter. *Indigenous typologies* are also important to look for; they are expressions that are unfamiliar or used in an unfamiliar way. Researchers should pay attention to the *metaphors and analogies* that respondents use to represent their thoughts. Because *similarities and differences* reveal how respondents express the same or different ideas in unique ways, it is essential to take note of them. Paying attention to *linguistic connectors* such as the words "because" or "since" is important, because they often indicate respondents' perceptions of causal relationships. *Missing data* are equally important because what is not said is just as important as what is said, and this can present an opportunity for the researcher to ask about the kind of information that respondents omit. Finally, *theoretical material* refers to theoretical concepts in the social science literature that may be represented among the data being analyzed.

CAQDAS

Computer-assisted qualitative data analysis software (CAQDAS) refers to techniques that allow researchers to code qualitative text while on the computer. CAQDAS allows the computer to complete some of the previously mentioned tasks associated with qualitative data analysis such as marking patterns of text and organizing them in a sequential way. However, CAQDAS cannot perform other tasks associated with qualitative data analysis such as interpreting data. There are several software packages designed for CAQDAS such as NVivo, ATLAS/ti, and Ethnograph that can be downloaded from the following sites:

www.qsrinternational.com
www.atlasti.com
www.qualisresearch.com

Key Terms

Action Research
Black Emancipatory
  Action Research
  (BEAR)
Case Study
Coding
Computer-assisted qualitative data analysis software (CAQDAS)
Conversation Analysis
Discourse Analysis
Ethnography
Ethnomethodology
Field Notes
Field Research
Focus Group
Grounded Theory
Narrative Analysis
Naturalism
Observation
Participatory Action
  Research
Participant Observation
Profiling
Semi-structured Interviews
Unstructured Interviews

Thinking about Science

1. "Actions speak louder than words."
2. "If you make your bed you have to lie in it."
3. "I won't let the same bee sting me twice."
4. "A bird in the hand is worth two in the bush."
5. "The blind leading the blind."
6. "Don't bite off more than you can chew."

7. "Never burn your bridges behind you."
8. "You can't have your cake and eat it too."
9. "The blacker the berry, the sweeter the juice."
10. "What goes around comes around."
11. "One monkey don't stop the show."
12. "Don't be an education fool."
13. "You've got to work twice as hard to get half as much."
14. "Don't miss the forest for the trees."
15. "Don't be the pot calling the kettle black."
16. "Keep what you got and share what you have."
17. "Blood is thicker than water."
18. "It takes a village to raise a child."
19. "A closed mouth don't get fed."
20. "Until you know where you've been you can't know where you are going."

Activity 1

Read these 20 quotes and code them by grouping the quotes into categories based on common themes. Identify two or more common themes among the quotes. Create a name for each theme. Place the quotes into categories based on the themes they share. You may not be able to find a category for every quote. In this case, place the uncategorized quotes into the category called "miscellaneous."

Activity 2

Go to your library website and print out three field studies involving African/Black people.

Activity 3

Catch a local bus. Ride the bus from the beginning to the end of the line. Take field notes on the environment inside and outside of the bus as you ride. Take note of changes in the environment and interactions from the beginning to the end of the line.

CHAPTER THIRTEEN

Quantitative Data Analysis

People in Ancient Africa used notational marks on things like stones and bones in groups of fives and tens to indicate number systems. Ancient Kemetic (Egyptian) science moved beyond diagonal strokes grouped together; instead, single hieroglyphic symbols (Medu Neter) were used to represent numbers. Small symbols allowed the ancient Egyptians to understand more of the universe. These symbols allowed them to use numbers to survey land, prepare for floods, grow crops, build pyramids, and map the solar system. We know similar symbols today such as 1, 2, 3, 4, and 5. **Quantitative data analysis** refers to deriving meaning from numerical data collected during research. It involves numbers representing values that measure characteristics of research subjects or participants. These numbers help us understand the *social* universe. In this chapter we will explore different levels and approaches to quantitative data analysis. We will explore the data analysis techniques appropriate for data analysis based on how many variables are involved. Ultimately, we will explore how you go about making meaning of data through statistical analysis.

Statistics are the mathematical procedures that researchers use to produce numerical values for the purpose of summarizing and interpreting information. For instance, the National Urban League developed the Save Our Sons Diabetes Prevention Project (National Urban League, 2012). The program was designed to teach participating African American men how to recognize diabetes through workshops and other activities. The program also involved the men in a variety of physical fitness activities, including tennis, walking, bicycling, and swimming. The men also met regularly with "a personal trainer, dietician, and naturopathic doctor who discussed exercise routines, diets, and how to implement changes in health behaviors" (National Urban League, 2012, p. 178). Through statistical analysis of numerical data collected during the program, the Urban League was able to demonstrate that the men's health and knowledge of risk factors had significantly improved. Many of the men decreased their weight by 50 pounds and their cholesterol levels by 60 points, and saw improvements in their body mass index, glucose levels, and blood pressure. This brief example illustrates how statistics can be used to demonstrate the level of effectiveness of social interventions and other service-providing activities. Today, statistics can help us decipher and critique research about the social universe.

There are two basic purposes of statistics (Gravetter & Wallnau, 2004):

1. to help the researcher organize and summarize information, clarify what happened in the research, and communicate the results.
2. to help the researcher answer the research question(s) and determine what conclusions are justifiable based on the results.

Scales of Measurement for Different Types of Variables

The types of variables on which data are collected influence what statistical analysis can be undertaken. It is important for researchers to anticipate the types of variables on which they will be collecting data so that they know what kinds of analysis they will need to use. There are four levels of measurement ranging from the most simple to the most sophisticated.

Nominal scales are used to categorize data collected from observations. Measures using this scale involve labeling or naming things. Variables such as gender, job occupation, race, or religious affiliation are measured at the nominal level. Data can be differentiated based on what category they are assigned to at the nominal level, but you cannot say that one is more or less than the other. For example, if two people answer a question asking them what religion they are, and one checks Christian and the other checks Muslim, you cannot say that one has more religiosity than the other. Nominal scales simply categorize; they only identify qualitative differences, not quantitative differences.

Ordinal scales measure data on variables that can be rank-ordered. Ranks such as small, medium, or large or achievement levels ranked as low, medium, or high are measured at the ordinal level. However, ordinal measurement does not tell you how far apart individuals are. For example, if Rashid is at the high math proficiency level and Tamara is at the medium math proficiency level, you know that Rashid is a better mathematician, but you do not know how much better.

Ratio and interval scales measure data where the distance between categories is the same. For example, if you collected data on how many minutes people spend per day exercising, the difference between someone who spends 25 minutes and another person who spends 30 minutes would be the same as the difference between someone who spends 35 minutes and a person who spends 40 minutes. These scales are important to keep in mind when deciding how to analyze data.

Coding Quantitative Data

Once researchers collect raw data, those data have to be converted into a computer-readable format. This process is called **data coding**. Computers organize numerical data as **data records**. Data records are usually kept on a file card or computerized document. A single data record contains all information on each variable for one person. If you distribute and collect questionnaires from 200 people, then you have 200 data records. The researcher must assign numerical values to each attribute or category of each variable. (Numbers are necessary because the information must go into a computer program for analysis). For example, you may want to collect data on sex, grade point average (GPA), and college major. For sex, there are often two attributes: male and female. However, the researcher would be prudent to either provide an open-ended "other" option or to provide specific options for other categories of sex. Sex is a nominal-level variable, so male and female would have to be assigned numerical values so that they are computer readable. You might code male as 2 and female as 1. GPA is already a numerical value and can be entered directly into a computer data analysis program. If a Likert-type scale were used to measure an attitude such as self-esteem, you would need to assign numbers to each attribute of the scale so that they can be tabulated and measured. For example:

1. Strongly disagree
2. Disagree
3. Not sure
4. Agree
5. Strongly agree

Table 13.1

Sample Variable Code Book			
VARIABLE ID	VARIABLE NAME	DATA RANGE	MEASUREMENT SCALE
Variable 1	Sex	1 = F; 2 = M	Nominal
Variable 2	G.P.A.	0–4.0	Interval
Variable 3	Starting Salary	0–100	Ratio
Variable 4	Ending Salary	0–100	Ratio
Variable 5	SES	0–100	Ordinal
Variable 6	College Major	1 = Fine Arts 2 = Social Sciences 3 = Education 4 = Business Management	Nominal
Variable 7	Residence	1 = City 2= Suburb; 3 = Rural area	Nominal
Variable 8	Job Satisfaction	0–100	Interval

All of the data items in a study must be converted to numerical codes representing the attributes of each variable (See Table 13.1). A **variable codebook** is a document or chart that describes the names of each variable, the codes of its attributes, and the level at which they are measured. The variable codebook is a guide that tells you how to interpret and analyze each variable as it is entered into the computer.

Because of human error, data are not always entered properly. **Data cleaning** is the process of identifying and correcting errors in coding. Having errors in your data can invalidate your study. One method of cleaning your data is to go through your numerical values for impossible codes. For example, if sex consists of 1s and 2s and you find a code of 3 under the category "sex," then there has been a coding error. You must find the correct value and enter it.

Descriptive Statistics

There are two branches of statistics: descriptive and inferential. **Descriptive statistics** refers to a branch of statistics that is used to organize, summarize, and interpret data. **Inferential statistics** are used to make generalizations from sample data to the population they were sampled from.

Descriptive statistics are used to transfer and summarize raw data into a more simplified form. Descriptive statistics can be organized based on the number of variables that are considered at a given time: one, two, three, or more. In other words, there are *univariate* statistics (one variable), *bivariate* statistics (two variables), and *multivariate* statistics (three or more variables). Descriptive techniques are called **univariate analysis** when only one variable and its attributes are involved. An example of a univariate analysis would be an investigation of the average annual income for African American teachers. The only variable in that example is annual income; African Americans are a constant. This same investigation could be turned into a bivariate analysis by introducing a second variable such as: "How does gender affect the average income paid to African American school teachers?" Now the investigation has two variables: gender and level of income. A multivariate analysis could be done by adding additional variables such as age.

Univariate Analysis

Illustrations or charts, graphs, and images are all ways of simplifying the organization and presentation of data. There are many ways to illustrate univariate data, and several will be covered in this section. One of the easiest ways to illustrate numerical data about one variable is a **frequency distribution** (See Table 13.2). A frequency distribution is a description of the number of people (or animals or objects) that are classified in the same category of variable attributes. The frequency distribution simply shows you how many cases fall into each variable category. It also illustrates the variable categories that make up the measurement scale, and the frequency or number of individuals in each variable category (Gravetter & Wallnau, 2004). For example, you may have a frequency distribution of the ages of 83 high school students.

Table 13.2

Age Frequency Distribution			
		FREQUENCY	PERCENT
Valid	14.00	6	7.2
	15.00	11	13.3
	16.00	21	25.3
	17.00	27	32.5
	18.00	16	19.3
	19.00	2	2.4
	Total	83	100.0

Figure 13.1

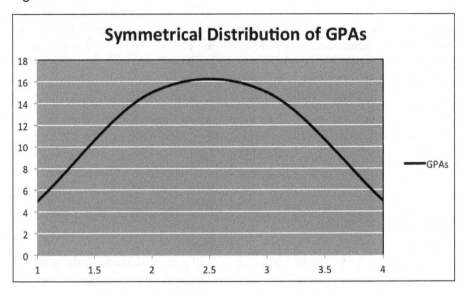

The frequency distribution would illustrate how many students fall into each category (14, 15, 16, 17, 18, or 19) of the variable "age" (see Table 13.2).

Types of Distributions

Frequency distributions present the range of values in a data set. This allows the researcher to evaluate the shape of the frequency distribution. The shape of the frequency distribution comes from the pattern created by the values in the data set. There are several labels that describe different kinds of distributions.

There are symmetrical and asymmetrical distributions. A **symmetrical distribution** is balanced, with one half of the distribution being exactly the same as the other half. However, in practice, data distributions only approach perfect symmetry (Figure 13.1). Asymmetrical or skewed distributions are noticeable because in them, most cases are gathered or clustered toward one end of the frequency distribution, with fewer cases trailing off in the other direction. A **positively skewed distribution** is one in which the long tail is extended toward the direction of the higher value (Figure 13.2), and the **negatively skewed distribution** is one in which the long tail is extended toward the direction of the lower values (Figure 13.3).

Frequency data can also be presented in the form or a pie chart, a bar chart, or a histogram. A **pie chart** is a good way to show how a whole group is divided into subgroups. The whole group is represented as a circle, and each subgroup is represented as a sector of that circle. The size of each slice in a pie chart shows the size

Figure 13.2

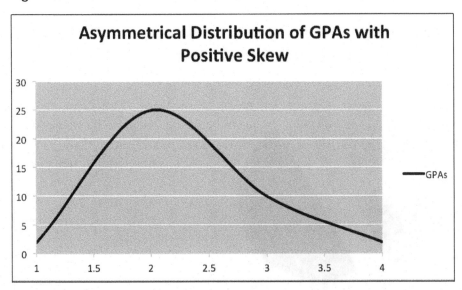

of that subgroup relative to the other subgroups. Figure 13.4 provides an example of a pie chart. Green jobs are defined as jobs that are necessary for producing products and services that increase energy efficiency, expand the use of renewable en-

Figure 13.3

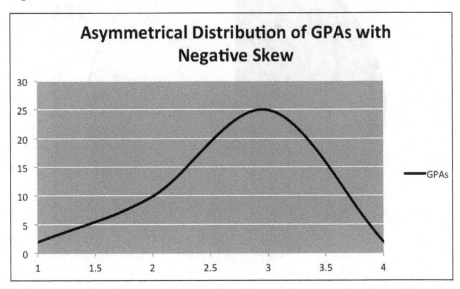

Figure 13.4

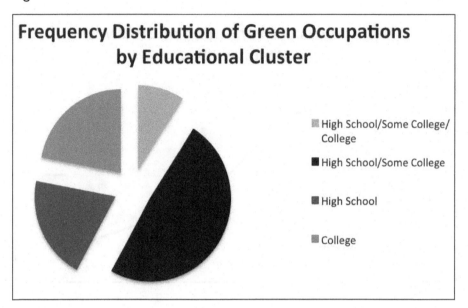

Figure 13.5

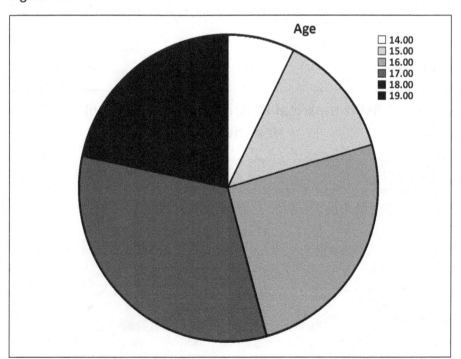

Figure 13.6

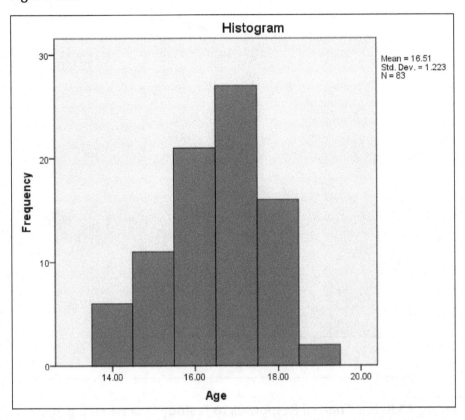

ergy, and support environmental sustainability. The Bureau of Labor Statistics provides data on the frequency of jobs by educational cluster. According to the statistics, 20% of green jobs are accessible to individuals with only a high school diploma, 49% to individuals with a high school diploma or some college, and 22% for individuals with a college degree (National Urban League, 2010) (Figure 13.4).

Another example of a pie chart is provided in Figure 13.5, an age pie chart.

A **histogram** refers to the use of vertical columns or lines to indicate how many times a particular score appears in a data set (Figure 13.6). Histograms are a good way of displaying interval or ratio data. In a histogram the baseline or horizontal axis corresponds to the observed scores on the dependent variable. The vertical axis is labeled with frequencies. The top of the bar represents the frequencies of each category. The differences between histograms and bar charts is that the columns or bars in a histogram represent ratio- or interval-level data, so they are not separated. However, the bars in bar chart data are separate. Because they are ratio- and interval-level variables, age and GPA are good for the histogram illustrations.

Figure 13.7

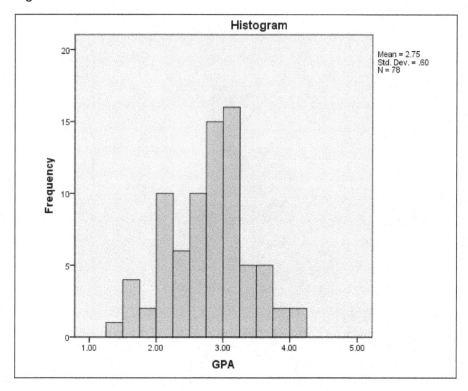

Figure 13.8: Bar Chart of Responses to "I study Best when it is quiet."

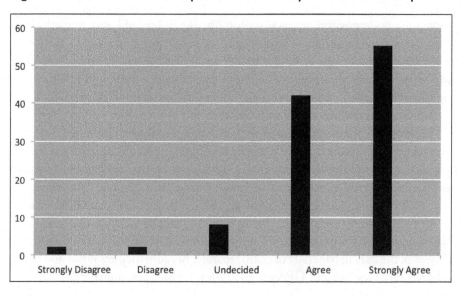

Figure 13.9: Frequency Distribution of Research Participants by Zip Codes

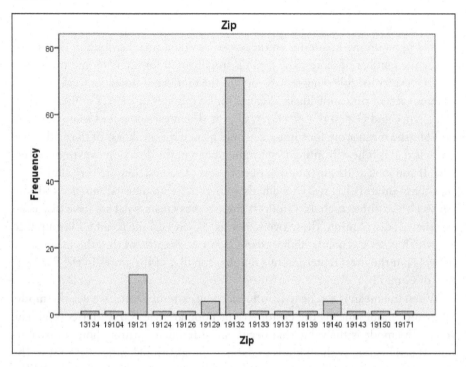

Bar charts are used to represent nominal- and ordinal-level data. The categories of measurement in a bar chart are listed along the baseline, or x-axis. The bar chart is the same as the histogram, except that there are spaces between the bars. This is because nominal and ordinal data do not have equal spaces between points, and you cannot be certain that ordinal categories are the same size. Figure 13.8 illustrates student responses to the item "I study best when it is quiet" using a Likert-type agreement scale. The results indicate that 2 people strongly disagree, 2 people disagree, 8 people are undecided, 42 people agree, and 55 people strongly agree. The bar chart illustrates that most students study best when it is quiet. Figure 13.9 illustrates the presence of research participants by zip code (a nominal variable) using a bar chart. Obviously, the great majority of the research participants (71 out of 101) lived in zip code 19132 in Philadelphia.

Measures of Central Tendency

The purpose of **measures of central tendency** is to identify a single score that is the most representative of the entire distribution. Measures of central tendency are meant to select the value that is most typical of a distribution of values. Using descriptive statistics, you can calculate three main measures of central tendency: the mean, median, and mode.

The **mean** is the arithmetic average of a distribution of values. The mean is calculated by summing or adding up the scores or values in a distribution and dividing by the number of scores. The mean is usually used for interval- and ratio-level data. Consider the following set of scores as the number of times per week that two different sets of nine individuals exercise for 20 minutes or more, Group A: 2, 2, 2, 3, 3, 5, 7, 9, 9 and Group B: 1, 1, 1, 1, 3, 5, 5, 22, 22. The mean score for Group A would be 4.66. The mean score for Group B would be 6.7. The weakness of the arithmetic mean is that is it heavily influenced by and drawn in the direction of extreme numbers. If you look at the distribution of both sets of values, they are very similar except that Group B has two individuals who exercise an unusual number of times per week—22 times each. In Group B these scores create what we have discussed as a skewed distribution. Those two scores have increased the mean for Group B to 6.7, which is several points higher than Group A. Because of this, the mean score of 6.7 is not the most representative number for all 9 of the scores in the distribution of Group B.

When the mean is too heavily influenced by extreme scores, we use the **mode**. The word "mode" means the customary or popular style (Gravetter & Wallnau, 2004). The mode is the value that occurs most frequently throughout a distribution. It can be used with all kinds of data: nominal, ordinal, interval, or ratio. The mode in Group A is clearly 2; there are no scores that occur more frequently. The mode for Group B is clearly 1. However, sometimes there is no mode. The mode is not used very often in formal studies, but it is sometimes used in informal studies.

The **median** is the middle score, or the midpoint of a distribution. It is the score in the distribution that divides the distribution exactly in half. To identify the median, you place the scores in the distribution in ascending order. Group A has an odd number of values, so the middle number is easy to identify: 3. Group B, however, has an even number of scores; therefore, to calculate the median, we must identify the two middle values of a distribution and calculate their average, which is 4. Whereas the mean is vulnerable to extreme scores in the distribution, the median is unaffected by them. For this reason, the median is best suited for calculating the central tendency of a skewed distribution. Because the mean will be influenced by extreme scores, the median is often used in official statistics that intend to identify the most representative number. For example, the U.S. Census Bureau reports the median family income because the average family income will be influenced by the few extremely wealthy individuals. The median can be used in calculating central tendency for interval-, ratio-, and ordinal-level data.

Measures of Dispersion

Dispersion refers to how values are distributed around a central value. **Measures of dispersion** are meant to identify how dispersed or spread out the values in a distribution are. Two distributions of scores may have the same average, but they could be dispersed very differently. For example, the means for distributions 2 and 3 below are the same, but their dispersion is quite different. The most obvious way of measuring dispersion is by identifying the range in a distribution of scores. The **range** is the difference between the maximum and the minimum scores in a distribution. Consider the following two distributions of scores on a 20-point math quiz:

Distribution 1: 2, 8, 10, 10, 11
Distribution 2: 1, 3, 5, 7, 8, 10
Distribution 3: 1, 4, 4, 5, 5, 15

The range for distribution 1 is 9 and the range for distribution 2 is also 9, but the range for distribution 3 is 14. Thus the range for distribution 3 is greater than the range of the other distributions. But the range does not take into consideration all of the values in a distribution; like the arithmetic mean, the range can be heavily influenced by outliers or extreme scores in a distribution. Because of this, the range is not the best indicator of dispersion in a distribution.

A more accurate measure of dispersion is the standard deviation, SD. The **standard deviation (SD)** is a statistic that describes the amount of variability in a distribution. Variability is the amount by which values in a distribution differ. As the standard deviation represents the average spread of the scores, the higher the SD, the more dispersed the scores in a distribution are from the mean. The smaller the SD, the less dispersed the scores are from the mean. The standard deviation takes into consideration the distance between each individual score and the mean. You might be worried that the SD could also be influenced by extreme scores in a distribution. The answer is yes, but those scores' impact is offset by dividing by the number of scores in the distribution. Considering the following scores on a different test from group 1, 2, and 3:

Group 1: 5, 10, 15, 20, 25, 30, 35
M = 20, SD = 10.8

Group 2: 19, 19, 19, 20, 21, 21, 21
M = 20, SD = 1

Group 3: 20, 20, 20, 20, 20, 20, 20
M = 20, SD = 0

Table 13.3

Descriptive Statistics						
	N	RANGE	MINIMUM	MAXIMUM	MEAN	STD. DEVIATION
Group 1	7	30.00	5.00	35.00	20.0000	10.80123
Group 2	7	2.00	19.00	21.00	20.0000	1.00000
Group 3	7	.00	20.00	20.00	20.0000	.00000
Valid N (listwise)	7					

The scores in these three distributions all have the same average, but they also have very different levels of variability. The scores in group 1 are different by 5 points, and therefore they have a higher SD (10.8) than the scores in group 2 (1). However, all the scores in group 3 are exactly the same; therefore the SD is 0.

The Normal Distribution

When a randomly selected sample approaches 100 or more, the shape of the distribution typically takes on a bell curve, formally called a normal curve or normal distribution. In a **normal distribution,** 68% of the scores or values in a distribution lie within one standard deviation of the mean, one standard deviation (34%) below the mean, and one standard deviation (34%) above the mean. Ninety-five percent lie within two standard deviations of the mean. For example, if a study re-

Figure 13.10

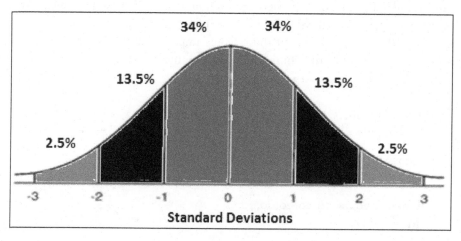

veals that the mean, $M = 75$ and $SD = 10$ in a normal distribution of math test scores then we know that 68% of the test takers scored between 65 (75 minus 10) and 85 (75 plus 10). A standard deviation takes into account how many points away from the mean it takes to capture 68% of the distribution. These statistics, such as 68%, cannot be expected in a distribution that is not normal (Figure 13.10).

Percentiles and Percentile Ranks

It is helpful for the researcher to be able to identify where specific scores in a distribution lie. When you take a test you may want to know in what percentile you scored. If you are a school principal or president, you may be interested in knowing in what percentile your students' scores rank in a distribution of state test scores. One way to identify this statistic is by calculating the percentile rank. **Percentile rank** is the number of scores in a distribution that are at or below a particular value. For example, imagine that you took a vocabulary test and earned 86 points, and you also know that 70 percent of your class scored at or below 86 points. Then your score has a percentile rank of 70%, and you scored in the 70th percentile. That score describes your position in a distribution. As we already know, the median of a distribution represents its 50th percentile. The 25th percentile represents the score at which 25% of the distribution are at or below that score. If you scored at the 90th percentile, then you scored better than 90% of the distribution and only 10% scored better than you. Knowing the percentile rank can tell you a lot about where a score lies with respect to other scores.

Z-Scores

Many of the previous measures that have been discussed in this section describe entire distributions. However, when describing a single score in a distribution, the researcher creates a standard score, or **z-score**. The z-score uses the mean and standard deviation of a distribution to calculate a z-score. The z-score expresses scores in terms of how many standard deviations they are above or below the mean. Z-scores also transform raw scores into standardized scores that allow you to compare across different distributions. Z-scores adjust for different distributions. This is useful when you want to compare the same variable in two populations.

Bivariate Analysis

In the previous sections of this chapter we looked at statistical procedures involving single-variable data sets. We looked at some examples wherein more than one

Table 13.4

Contingency Table of Student GPA and Hours per Day Spent Reading			
GPA LEVEL	LESS THAN 1HOUR	1-2 HOURS	3 OR MORE HOURS
2.5 and Above	8 (28%)	10 (50%)	20 (90%)
2.49 and Below	21(72%)	10 (50%)	2 (10%)
Total	29	20	22

variable were described, but they were described one at a time. However, most investigations involve statistical procedures that analyze the relationships between more than one variable. Here we will look at statistical techniques that help describe the relationship between two variables. Such statistical procedures are called bivariate. **Bivariate analysis** involves the analysis of two variables to determine whether or not there is a relationship between them.

Relationships between variables can be displayed in *contingency tables* and charts. A contingency table is a table that presents data on the relationship between variables as a distribution of percentages. Contingency tables are similar to frequency tables, but they are best suited to examine the relationship between two or more variables simultaneously. In most contingency tables, the independent variable is listed in the columns, and the dependent variables in the rows. The heading of a table should always describe exactly what data are being displayed. The variables and attributes of those variables should also be clearly described and explained. Table 13.4 illustrates data on two variables: high school students' grade point averages (GPA) and the number of hours per day they spend reading. The question these data can help to answer is whether or not there is a relationship between the number of hours per day high school students spend reading and their GPAs.

The contingency table reveals a positive relationship between GPA and hours spent reading. Bivariate relationships can also be displayed in a scattergram. A **scattergram** is a chart that allows you to see the relationships between two variables. In most cases, the independent variable is presented on the horizontal axis and the dependent variable on the vertical axis. Scattergrams are best used for interval- and ratio-level data. They do not work well for studies with only a few cases; they work best with large sample sizes. Scattergrams also reveal different kinds of relationships between variables. They can reveal independence between variables, which means that there is no relationship between variables. They can also reveal linear relationships between variables (Figure 13.11). The linear relationship, indicated by a straight line running from one corner of a table to the other, can be either positive or negative. *Positive* and *negative* indicate the directionality of a relationship be-

Figure 13.11

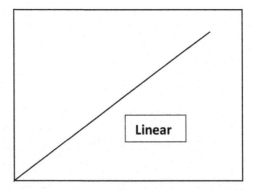

Figure 13.12

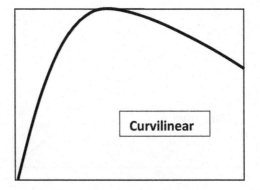

tween variables. There is also the curvilinear relationship, or non-linear relationship, which is indicated by a "U" shape or the shape of an upside down "U" (Figure 13.12). A positive relationship is illustrated by a line that starts at the lower left of a table and stretches to the upper right (Figure 13.13). A negative relationship is indicated by a line that begins at the upper left of a table and stretches to the lower right (Figure 13.14). The relationship between GPA and hours spent reading is a positive relationship.

Bivariate relationships have varying degrees of precision. The examples below indicate that a precise relationship describes a situation where all of the cases fit along the line that represents their direction and relationship (Figure 13.16). However, an imprecise relationship describes a situation where cases are more scattered near and far from the line representing their direction and relationship (Figure 13.15).

Figure 13.13

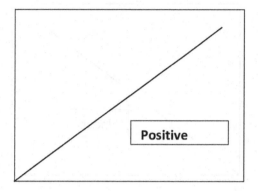

Figure 13.14

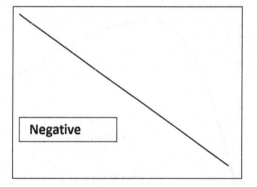

Figure 13.15

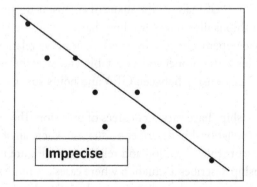

Figure 13.16

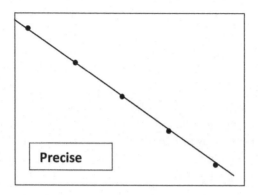

Strength of Association

Measures of association reduce the strength and direction of association between two variables to a single number. The most commonly used measure of the strength of association between two variables is the **Pearson Product Moment Correlation Coefficient**. The symbol for the Pearson correlation coefficient symbol is r. However, there are many other measures of association, such as Cramer's V, Lambda, Gamma, Tau, Rho, and Chi-Square. If the result of a measure of association is zero, this indicates statistical independence, meaning that there is absolutely no relationship between the two variables being measured. If the relationship is not zero, then there is a relationship between the variables. Pearson's r ranges from −1 to +1; negative numbers indicate an inverse or negative relationship, and positive numbers indicate a positive relationship (Figure 13.17). Let's consider our examples of the relationship between GPA and number of hours spent reading per day. If there were a correlation coefficient of 1 (r = 1), that would mean that there is a perfect positive correlation without error between GPA and number of hours spent reading per day such that every increase in hours spent reading per day corresponds with an equal increase in GPA. If there were a correlation coefficient of −1 (r = -1), that would

Figure 13.17

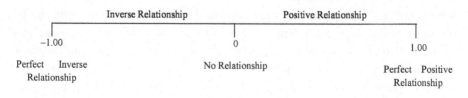

mean that there is a perfect inverse correlation without error between GPA and number of hours spent reading per day such that every increase in hours spent reading per day corresponds with an equal decrease in GPA. The closer a correlation coefficient is to 1 or −1, the stronger the relationship is (Figure 13.17). Pearson correlations can be thought of in terms of percentages. However, to do so the correlation coefficient must be converted into what is called a coefficient of determination symbolized as r^2. To compute this number, you square r. Therefore, if the relationship between the number of hours spent watching television per day and number of hours spent reading per day were −.85, there would be an r of −.85, r^2 = .72. If you multiply .72 by 100, the result is 72%. This means that 72% of the variance in hours spent watching television per day can be accounted for by the number of hours spent reading per day.

Multivariate Analysis

Multivariate analyses involve the simultaneous analysis of the relationship between three or more variables. Multivariate analyses are useful for many reasons. What we already know from earlier chapters is that just because there is a relationship between two variables, this doesn't mean that one is the cause of the other. Sometimes there is a third variable or spurious variable responsible for changes in both variables. To determine the impact of other variables on a relationship, researchers often include alternative variables. Outside of the impact of spurious variables, there may simply be other variables that impact the relationship between variables. For example, we may be interested in how much students' parents' levels of education are related to the number of hours per day students spend watching television or reading. Including other variables or control variables helps a researcher to provide a better explanation of the relationship between variables.

One method of analysis that is used for interval- and ratio-level data is the **multiple regression analysis**. There are many statistical computer packages that run multiple regression analyses. A multiple regression analysis allows the researcher to predict a dependent variable based on information about multiple independent variables. A multiple regression analysis produces a number referred to as R-squared, or R^2. An R^2 tells the researcher what percentage of accuracy in predicting the dependent variable can be accounted for by multiple independent variables. An R^2 of 35% means that the accuracy in predicting the dependent variable is improved by 35% by knowing the independent variables. This means that you would make 35% more errors in predicting the dependent variable without knowing the independent variables. Multiple regression analysis also tells you how much of an impact each independent variable has on the dependent variable in question. This is especially useful when the researcher is interested in knowing how much impact multiple independent variables have on a dependent variable, or which independent variable has the greatest impact on a dependent variable. For example, a multiple regression would be useful if we were interested in how much impact hours spent reading per day, hours spent watching television per day, and parents' levels of education, all taken together, have on students' GPAs, or which of them has the greatest impact.

Inferential Statistics

Inferential statistics moves from simply describing data to testing hypotheses and relating results from sample data to the populations they were drawn from. **Inferential statistics** allows the researcher to use probability theory to test hypotheses and evaluate the strength of relationships between variables. It is assumed that if the researcher uses inferential statistics, a random sampling technique has been used. One aspect of inferential statistics is the concept of statistical significance: the probability that a researcher's observations represent a genuine pattern and not just mere chance. There are many tests of statistical significance, such as the **t-test** and the **analysis of variance (ANOVA)**. Researchers use these tests of statistical significance to provide the data necessary to decide whether or not to accept or reject their hypotheses.

The reason that statistical significance is important is because researchers must always be concerned with the threat that the findings they arrive at from their sample will not be representative of the larger population they were selected from. As we already know, **sampling error** is the difference between the sample that a researcher selects and the population from which the sample was selected. Even when the researcher has used a probability sample, sampling error is still an ever-present threat. Moreover, researchers can never be certain that their findings apply to the population they were drawn from. All researchers can do is determine how confident they can be in their findings, and tests of statistical significance help the researcher make such determinations. These tests tell the researcher how much risk they are taking in making inferences about the larger population based on sample results.

Imagine that we selected a random sample of 1,000 African Americans adults from Baton Rouge, Louisiana. We may discover from our analysis of the 1,000 African American adults that there is a strong inverse or negative relationship between their strength of spiritual belief and their level of alcohol consumption, such that the stronger individuals' spiritual beliefs are, the less alcohol they consume. Tests of statistical significance tell us how confident we can be that this finding is true for other African American adult residents of Baton Rouge, and how much risk we are taking in applying this finding to the larger population. Technically, **statistical significance** tells you how likely the results from a sample could be due to random error (simply put, it's the probability of finding a relationship among sample data when there is none in the larger population).

Hypothesis Testing

Statistical significance often involves the testing of hypotheses. A **hypothesis** is a statement about the relationship between variables in a study. The researcher goes on to test that relationship. The researcher develops two contradictory or completely opposite hypotheses. The test of statistical significance tells the researcher which one of the hypotheses is most likely correct. The first hypothesis is called the **null hypothesis,** which states that two or more variables are not related in the population. For example, the null hypothesis in our spirituality and alcohol study would state that there is no relationship between strength of spiritual beliefs and level of alcohol consumption. Simply put, the null hypothesis guesses that there is no relationship between variable A and variable B in a population. The second hypothesis is called the **alternative hypothesis,** or the research hypothesis. The alternative hypothesis would be that there *is* a relationship between strength of spiritual beliefs and level of alcohol consumption. That is, the alternative hypothesis states that there is a relationship between variable A and variable B in a population. Statistical tests tell us which hypothesis is probable or improbable. These hypotheses exist because there is no way to prove the research hypothesis directly, but what a researcher *can* do is determine how likely the null and alternative hypotheses are to be false or true.

Tests of statistical significance provide the researcher with a **level of significance**. The level of significance provides researchers with a precise measure of how likely it is that their findings are due to chance alone, so that a researcher may use it to decide whether or not to accept or reject the null hypothesis. If the finding is not likely to be due to chance, then the relationship between variables in the sample is likely to be true for the larger population as well. In this case, the researcher would reject the null hypothesis and accept the alternative hypothesis. If the findings of a study indicate that the relationship between variables in a study have 5% or greater chance of being due to random chance, then the scientific community agrees that it is not statistically significant. In this case we would accept the null hypothesis and reject the alternative hypothesis. However, if the finding has less than a 5% chance of being due to the random process, then the finding is considered by the scientific community to be statistically significant. The level .05 is also referred to as the **alpha level,** or the level at which the null hypothesis will be rejected. Again, the level of significance tells the researcher the likelihood that results are due to random chance. Statistically significant results occur at three different probability levels:

- .05 Level
- .01 Level
- .001 Level

According to probability theory, if results are significant at the .05 level, you are likely to find these results as a consequence of random chance only 5 in 100 times. It also means that there is a 95% probability that the results are not due to random chance but are truly reflective of the larger population. It means you can be 95% *confident* that your sample findings are true for the larger population, too. Because we cannot say for certain that the findings we draw from a sample are true for the population the sample was drawn from, probability theory allows us to determine how likely it is that our results are the consequence of random error. Moreover, the scientific community has agreed that .05, or 5% chance of error or less, is small enough to take seriously.

There are two types of errors that a researcher can make in the process of drawing inferences based on statistical analyses: Type I errors and Type II errors. A **Type I error** occurs when the researcher rejects the null hypothesis when s/he should have accepted or confirmed it. When this happens, it means that the researcher claims to have found a relationship among the population when it was not a true relationship but was instead due to chance. If we draw our conclusions using a .05 level of significance, we are more likely to make a Type I error than when we are using a .01 level of significance. However, if you use a .01 level of significance—meaning you do not reject the null hypothesis unless there is less than a .01 chance of error—you are more likely to make a Type II error. A **Type II error** occurs when the researcher accepts the null hypothesis when s/he should have rejected it, meaning that the researcher has claimed to have found no relationship among the population when there was a true relationship that was not attributable to random chance.

Additional Statistical Procedures

In addition to previously mentioned statistical procedures such as the Pearson correlation and multiple regression, there are several other statistical procedures used to measure statistical significance levels. One test used to decide whether two sample means are significantly different from one another is the **t-test**. The t-test assumes that random sampling procedures have been used. If you are using a t-test of any inferential statistical procedure, the larger the sample, the smaller the likelihood that observed differences will be due to sampling errors. The t-test is well suited for dichotomous independent variables such as sex.

Imagine that we have a new, engaging method of teaching math. We might be interested in determining whether or not this new engaging method of teaching math

302 | RESEARCH METHODS IN AFRICANA STUDIES

is better for girls or boys. We might conduct a study in which we expose a randomly selected group of 100 students (50 boys and 50 girls) to this new and engaging method of teaching math. We might use a t-test to analyze the grades achieved by girls and boys at the end of the semester, and we might discover that the mean score of the boys was 85, and the girls' mean score was 93. However, we don't just want to know whether there was a statistical difference between the boys' and girls' scores; we want to know whether or not that score was statistically significant. Thus, we discover that the difference in their mean scores is statistically significant and that the probability level is .0345. Is this statistically significant? Yes! It is statistically significant because it is smaller than .05. This means that we can reject the null hypothesis and accept the alternative hypothesis because it is only less than 5 times out of 100 that the difference we found between boys and girls will be due to random chance.

The t-test was designed to compare the means of two groups and keep the experiment wise error rate at alpha .05. However, what happens when you need to compare the means of three or more groups—for example, freshmen, sophomores, juniors, and seniors? You could conceivably conduct a t-test on each group (i.e., you could compare freshmen with sophomores, then freshmen with juniors, then freshmen with seniors, and so on), but the error rate or alpha would be greater than .05, which means you have inflated your chance of making a type I error or claiming to have a significant finding when you do not. Multiple t–tests increase your chances of drawing an incorrect conclusion.

Analysis of variance (ANOVA) can be used to compare the means of three or more groups of subjects based on a single independent variable (or any number of means). ANOVA is designed to compare three or more means simultaneously, keeping the experiment wise error rate at alpha .05. ANOVA could be used to test whether or not there is a statistical difference between the scores of freshmen, sophomores, juniors, and seniors who are taught math using our new engaging methods of teaching mathematics. There are many more statistical procedures that are beyond the scope of this text. To go further into these and other procedures, readers are encouraged to pursue additional reading in statistical textbooks. All of the previously mentioned procedures vary in their usefulness, depending on the nature of the research being conducted. Be aware of the functions of each technique, and you will know when to use any particular technique.

Key Terms

Alpha Level

Analysis of Variance
(ANOVA)

Alternative Hypothesis

Bar Chart

Bivariate Analysis

Data Cleaning
Data Coding
Data Records
Descriptive Statistics
Frequency Distribution
Histogram
Hypothesis
Inferential Statistics
Interval Scales
Level of Significance
Mean
Measures of Central Tendency
Measures of Dispersion
Median
Mode
Multiple Regression Analysis
Multivariate Analysis
Negatively Skewed Distribution
Nominal Scales
Normal Distribution

Null Hypothesis
Ordinal Scales
Pearson Product Moment Correlation Coefficient
Percentile Rank
Pie Chart
Positively Skewed Distribution
Quantitative Data Analysis
Range
Ratio Scales
Sampling Error
Scattergram
Standard Deviation (SD)
Statistical Significance
Statistics
Symmetrical Distribution
T-Test
Type I Error
Type II Error
Univariate Analysis
Variable Codebook
Z-Score

Thinking about Science

Jamison (2006) examined the relationships between African Self-Consciousness, Cultural Misorientation, Hypermasculinity, and Rap Music Preference. African Self-Consciousness was measured using a 42-item African Self-Consciousness Scale. The scale assesses (1) individuals' recognition of themselves as having African identity and heritage, (2) the level of priority they place on the well-being of African/Black people, (3) the specific activity priorities they place on self-knowledge and the collective survival of African/Black people, and (4) their resistance to forces that threaten the well-being of African/Black people. The scale produces a score representing a person's level of African Self-Consciousness. Cultural Misorientation was measured using the 56-item Cultural Misorientation Scale, which assesses cultural misorientation across six dimensions: (1) materialism, (2) individualism, (3) alien self-orientation, (4) anti-self-orientation, (5) self-destructive orientation, and (6) integration orientation. Hypermasculinity was measured using the 30-item Hypermasculinity Inventory, which measures three dimensions of hypermasculinity, including (1) danger as exciting, (2) calloused sexual attitudes toward women, and (3) violence as manly. Rap music preference was categorized into three different subgroups: (1) reality rap (politically conscious), (2) conscious rap, (3) recreational rap, and (4) non-rap listeners.

Activity 1

Identify the level of measurement for the variables Rap Music Preference, African Self-Consciousness, and Cultural Misorientation.

Activity 2

African Self-Consciousness was divided into two categories: High African Self-Consciousness and Low African Self-Consciousness. There were a total of 72 participants in the study. Among those in the Low African Self-Consciousness group, 23 preferred reality rap, 3 preferred conscious rap, 9 preferred recreational rap, and 1 was a rap non-listener. Among those in the High African Self-Consciousness group, 12 preferred reality rap, 17 preferred conscious rap, 3 preferred recreational rap, and there were 4 rap non-listeners. Create a contingency table representing the information explained in Activity 2.

Activity 3

Jamison (2006) conducted an independent samples t-test to find out whether or not there was a significant difference between the Hypermasculinity scores of those who were low in Cultural Misorientation and those who were high in Cultural Misorientation. The test indicated that the group that had high Cultural Misorientation scores had significantly higher Hypermasculinity scores than those who had low Cultural Misorientation scores. The probability value was less than .05. What were the null and alternative hypotheses? Based on the information in Activity 3, would Jamison (2006) accept or reject the null hypothesis?

Glossary

ACTION RESEARCH: An approach to research that is designed to find the most effective way to bring about some desired social change.

AFRICANA STUDIES: The critical and systematic study of the thought and practice of African people in their current and historical unfolding.

ALPHA LEVEL: The level at which the null hypothesis will be rejected.

ANALYSIS OF VARIANCE (ANOVA): A test used to compare the means of three or more groups of subjects based on a single independent variable.

ALTERNATIVE HYPOTHESIS: A statement that there is a relationship between two or more variables in a population.

BAR CHARTS: Graphic displays of data used to represent nominal- and ordinal-level data. The categories of measurement in a bar chart are listed along the baseline, or x-axis. The bar chart is the same as the histogram except that there are spaces between the bars. This is because nominal and ordinal data do not have equal spaces between points, and you cannot be certain that ordinal categories are the same size.

BENEFICENCE: The researcher's responsibility to conduct research that contributes to the well-being of the population being studied.

BIVARIATE ANALYSIS: Analysis of two variables to determine whether or not there is a relationship between them.

BLACK EMANCIPATORY ACTION RESEARCH (BEAR): An orientation to research meant to enhance qualitative methods in research involving African diasporic peoples. BEAR is a framework for guiding research in the process of liberating African diasporic peoples from various forms of oppression.

CASE STUDY: A detailed, intensive, and descriptive account of a single individual, group, or organization. Although it is often an individual or an organization, a case can also be a time period. Case studies are most commonly associated with qualitative research, but they are not limited to qualitative research.

CLASSIC EXPERIMENTAL DESIGN: An experimental design that has random assignment and consists of an experimental stimulus, an experimental group, and a control group.

CLOSED-ENDED ITEMS: Statements or questions designed to provide respondents with a fixed set of response options, often multiple choices

CLUSTER SAMPLING: A procedure in which the final grouping of elements in a sample are drawn from larger units of elements called clusters.

CODING: A part of content analysis that involves synthesizing text into systematic categories of data (sometimes quantitative data).

CODING MANUAL: A statement of instructions for the coder. It includes all possible categories for each dimension being coded.

CODING SCHEDULE: A form onto which all data related to a particular item are recorded. The coding schedule is a form used to analyze each item (text or image).

CODING SYSTEM: A set of written rules that explains how a researcher is going to go about the process of categorizing and classifying observations.

COHORT STUDIES: Studies that involve the study of a specific subpopulation of people over time, but not necessarily the same individual members of that subpopulation each time.

COMPUTER-ASSISTED QUALITATIVE DATA ANALYSIS SOFTWARE (CAQDAS): Techniques that allow researchers to code qualitative text while on the computer.

COMPUTER-ASSISTED TELEPHONE INTERVIEWING: A data collection technique in which the interviewer is able to sit at the computer and use the computer program to randomly dial telephone numbers and present the person who answers with a series of questions that the researcher programs it to ask.

CONCEPTUAL DEFINITION: An abstract description of a variable that a researcher intends to measure.

CONFIDENCE INTERVAL: An estimation of the margin of error in a sample mean. The confidence interval indicates how precise a sample is.

CONSTRUCT VALIDITY: A type of validity that is derived from a theory that is relevant to the concept in question. Using construct validity, an instrument is validated by analyzing how it is correlated with the concepts and assumptions of a theoretical framework designed to explain the relevant variable.

CONTENT ANALYSIS: A research technique that allows you to systematically analyze the hidden and visible content in messages.

CONTENT VALIDITY: The extent to which a measure's items or indicators accurately represent the phenomena being assessed.

CONTINGENCY QUESTION: A question that is answered depending on a participant's response to a previous question (a filter question).

CONTINUOUS VARIABLES: Variables that have an infinite number of values such as temperature, age, and income.

CONVENIENCE SAMPLE: A sample based on population elements that are available to the researcher.

CONVERSATION ANALYSIS: The detailed analysis of naturally occurring talk or spoken words. The purpose of conversation analysis is to discover the underlying structures of talk in interaction.

COVERAGE BIAS: The problem presented by convenience samples in which subjects that are conveniently accessible to the researcher are not representative of the target population.

CRITERION VALIDITY: A concept by way of a standard or criterion. To establish the criterion validity of a measure, it is compared to another measure of the same concept or variable.

CROSS-SECTIONAL STUDY: A study that is conducted at a relatively single point in time by taking a cross section or snapshot of a sample of a population.

DATA CLEANING: The process of identifying and correcting errors in coding. Having errors in your data can invalidate your study.

DATA CODING: The process of converting raw data into computer-readable format.

DATA RECORDS: Collections of computer-readable numerical data.

DECEPTION: When researchers misrepresent their research to participants.

DEDUCTION: Research that moves from an expected pattern of behavior to observations that test whether that pattern actually exists. Deduction moves from established theories to testing the validity of those theories. It can be said that deduction moves from the general to the particular.

DEPENDENT VARIABLE: The variable that is affected by or dependent upon the independent variable.

DESCRIPTIVE RESEARCH: Research that describes phenomena as they exist, as opposed to experimental research, in which environments are controlled and manipulated.

DESCRIPTIVE STATISTICS: A branch of statistics that is used to organize, summarize, and interpret data.

DIARY METHOD: A data-collection technique in which the research participant observes his or her own behavior in a systematic way designed by the researcher.

DISCOURSE ANALYSIS: A research technique that allows you to systematically analyze the hidden and visible content in communication messages.

DISCRETE VARIABLES: Nominal- and ordinal-level variables. Continuous variables are interval- and ratio-level variables.

DISRUPTIVE CONCEPTUALIZATION: The development of concepts, paradigms, theories, or models that reject and debunk some of the fundamental premises of preexisting or prevailing frameworks.

DOMAIN OF INQUIRY: The specific aspects, subsets, or dimensions of reality on which a discipline focuses its thought.

ECOLOGICAL FALLACY: When you investigate an entire ecological unit but come to conclusions about the individuals who make up that group.

ETHICS: The philosophy of morality: what counts as good or bad, right or wrong.

ETHNOGRAPHY: The careful study of a culture through qualitative interviews, observations, and analysis of cultural documents.

ETHNOMETHODOLOGY: A perspective that is based on the presumption that social reality is socially constructed through communication and interaction. The ethnomethodologist rejects the idea that social reality is simply there for the researcher to observe. Instead of decrying social reality as it objectively is, ethnomethodology places value on people's descriptions of social reality as their valid subjective ways of making sense of it.

EUROCENTRISM: placing European culture and ideals at the center of all thought and behavior and imposing Western culture and ideology on other non-European-descended peoples.

EVALUATIVE RESEARCH: Research that is used to assess or monitor the implementation or effectiveness of a social intervention.

EXHAUSTIVE: Refers to items in a scale or index that assess all of the possible nuances and aspects of the concept being measured.

EXPERIMENT: Manipulating a treatment condition or initiating a cause and systematically observing the consequences.

EXPLANATORY RESEARCH: Research that seeks to understand phenomena by explaining the relationship between variables. Explanatory research is a continuation of descriptive research. Once you have descriptive information about a particular issue, you can go on to explain why or how it occurs or works the way it does.

EXPLORATORY RESEARCH: Research that looks for patterns, ideas, or hypotheses. Exploratory research is usually done on topics that have not been researched or have seldom been researched.

EXTERNAL VALIDITY: The extent to which a study's findings can be generalized to the population from which the sample was selected.

FACE VALIDITY: Refers to whether or not there is a reasonable relationship between a variable and a measure. Face validity is the minimum requirement that a measure must meet.

FACTUAL ITEMS: Questions or statements that have a definitive answer. These questions ask respondents for objective information. Factual questions are questions such as: "Are you a vegetarian?" or "Do you eat meat?"

FIELD NOTES: Detailed descriptions of events and behaviors and the researcher's reflections on them.

FIELD RESEARCH: The qualitative collection of data about people or research elements in naturalistic settings.

FILTER QUESTION: An item that screens respondents, guiding them to questions that are relevant to them. A filter question leads to a contingency question.

FOCUS GROUP: Qualitative interviews of a group of research participants in an interactive group setting.

FREQUENCY DISTRIBUTION: A description of the number of people (or animals or objects) that are classified in the same category of variable attributes.

GENERALIZING: Applying the results of a study of a sample to a larger population or a larger reality.

GROUNDED THEORY: A method of developing theory (grounded in data) by recognizing patterns or codes in data collected through qualitative methods.

GUTTMAN SCALING: A process used in the construction of scales that are unidimensional or measure a single variable or a single aspect of a variable.

HISTOGRAM: A graphic display of data using vertical columns or lines to indicate how many times a particular score appears in a data set.

HYPOTHESIS: A statement about the relationship between variables in a study. The researcher goes on to test that relationship.

INDEPENDENT VARIABLE: The predictor variable or causal variable that determines changes in the dependent variable.

INDEX: A composite measure that summarizes information from multiple indicators into a single score, or the sum of their values. Different from scales, the items in indexes need not be arranged in any particular order.

INDICATOR: An observation of evidence of the attributes or properties of a phenomenon.

INDUCTION: Research that moves from the particular to the general. You move from a specific set of observations to the discovery of patterns in those observations, hypotheses, and theories.

INFERENTIAL STATISTICS: Statistical procedures that allow the researcher to use probability theory to test hypotheses and evaluate the strength of relationships between variables.

INFORMED CONSENT: The research participants' right to know the purpose of a research project, how it may affect them, how it may benefit them, any possible risks in participation, and their right to decline to participate whenever they choose to.

INTERNAL RELIABILITY: The degree to which the indicators that make up an instrument are consistent and relate to one another.

INTERNAL VALIDITY: The extent to which the results of experimentation are attributable to what happened in the experiment.

INTER-OBSERVER RELIABILITY: An assessment of how similar or consistent observers or interviewers are when measuring the same research subject or object.

INTERSECTING INTERESTS THEORY: The IIT approach is designed to guide researchers in the process of producing research that is interesting and important to them and important to the community. Such an approach is meant to encourage and facilitate the production of scholarship that demonstrates creativity, quality, and relevance.

INTERVAL MEASURES: Measures that possess the same characteristics as both nominal and ordinal variables with the addition of the fact that there is a fixed distance between points in interval measures.

INTERVENING VARIABLE: The variable that helps to explain the relationship between the independent and dependent variable. It is affected by the independent variable and influences the dependent variable.

INTERVIEW: A form of data collection that typically involves asking people questions orally and recording their answers.

INTERVIEW SCHEDULE: Contains the specific instructions for conducting the interview, the specific questions to be asked, and the order in which interview questions should be asked.

INVERSE RELATIONSHIP: A relationship between variables in which an increase in one variable results in a decrease in another, or a decrease in one variable results in an increase in another.

ITEMS: The term item refers to the questions and statements that make up surveys and questionnaires.

LEVEL OF SIGNIFICANCE: The level of significance provides researchers with a precise measure of how likely it is that their findings are due to chance alone, so that a researcher may use it to decide whether or not to accept or reject the null hypothesis.

LEVELS OF MEASUREMENT: The rules that explain what mathematical procedures can be performed on data at different variables.

LIKERT-TYPE SCALE: A questionnaire format that consists of a series of statements followed by four to six response options.

LITERATURE REVIEW: A survey of scholarly articles, books, chapters of books, and dissertations relevant to a particular issue

MAAT: The ethical principle governing the laws of the universe, the standards by which human society should be shaped, and the principles by which human beings might best live.

MATCHING: Assigning individuals to the experimental group with similar individuals in the control group. Using this technique, individuals are matched based on variables that could have an effect on the dependent variable.

MEAN: The arithmetic average of a distribution of values.

MEASUREMENT: The process of describing abstract concepts in terms of specific indicators by assigning numbers or other symbols to these indicants in accordance with rules.

MEASURES OF CENTRAL TENDENCY: Measures used to identify a single score that is the most representative of the entire distribution.

MEDIAN: The middle score or the midpoint of a distribution.

METHODOLOGY: The Methodology is the aspect of research that contains the paradigms, theories, concepts, and methods that shape approaches to study and social intervention.

METHODS: Methods are tools of data collection, including experiments, questionnaires, interviews, observations, and other methods.

MIXED-METHODS RESEARCH: Research that incorporates multiple methods in the research process to employ a more holistic analysis of social phenomena.

MODE: The value that occurs most frequently throughout a distribution.

MULTIPLE REGRESSION ANALYSIS: A method of statistical analysis used on interval- and ratio-level data. It allows the researcher to predict a dependent variable based on information about multiple independent variables.

MULTIVARIATE ANALYSIS: The simultaneous analysis of the relationship between three or more variables.

MUTUAL EXCLUSIVITY: Refers to a quality possessed by items with response formats in which a respondent's answer cannot fall into more than one category.

NARRATIVE ANALYSIS: An approach to studying an individual that involves piecing together a narrative of the person's life and the world using a number of sources. Narrative analysis focuses on people's stories and descriptive accounts of lives and events. Like profiling, it relies heavily on the person's own words. However, unlike profiling, instead of relying solely on in-depth interviews, narrative analysis makes use of letters, autobiographies, interviews, and other sources.

NATURALISM: One of the oldest perspectives in qualitative research based on the positivist assumption that social reality is most objectively described and reported by a scientific researcher.

NEGATIVELY SKEWED DISTRIBUTION: A distribution in which the long tail is extended toward the direction of the lower values.

NOMINAL MEASURES: Measures that classify observations into mutually exclusive categories. Nominal data is only capable of indicating differences between categories.

NON-MALFEASANCE: The researcher's responsibility to do no harm to research participants in the research process. Research should never result in any serious or lasting harm to participants in the form of either physical or mental distress, including the experience of anxiety or loss of self-esteem.

NON-PROBABILITY SAMPLING: A sampling technique in which each population does not have a known probability of being included in a sample.

NON-RESPONSE: The degree to which members of a sample decline to participate in a study.

NORMAL DISTRIBUTION: A clustering of the sample means around the unknown population mean. The average of the sampling means, represented by $\bar{x}$, converges around the true population mean, μ. The mean μ is truly unknown, which is the reason that we study samples p, to attempt to estimate it with sample means, $\bar{x}$. If a distribution is a normal distribution, then there are certain claims we as researchers can make about the population the samples were drawn from.

NULL HYPOTHESIS: A statement that two or more variables are not related in the population.

OBSERVATION: A technique in which the researcher observes people in their natural environment.

ONLINE SAMPLING: The sampling of elements of a population by accessing them using the Internet.

ONLINE SURVEYS: Surveys that are often sent as email attachments or links to web-based questionnaires.

OPEN-ENDED ITEMS: Statements or questions that provide respondents the opportunity to provide their own answers.

OPERATIONAL DEFINITION: A definition stated in terms of the specific procedures and operations necessary to measure a variable.

OPINION ITEMS: Questions or statements that don't have definitive answers. Opinion-based questions often ask respondents about their political attitudes or their religious beliefs.

ORDINAL MEASURES: Measures that indicate order and rank among the categories of a variable. Ordinal measures represent a higher level of measurement than nominal measures because in addition to being made up of mutually exclusive categories, in ordinal-level measures categories can be rank-ordered.

OVERSAMPLING: A technique used in stratified sampling in which the researcher(s) select a disproportionately large number of elements from a particular stratum or group that might otherwise yield too few subjects.

PANEL STUDY: A long-term study in which data is collected from the same exact people each time. While a cohort study samples from the same population at different times, a panel study examines the exact same people at different times.

PARADIGM: A general way of understanding and approaching knowledge about the world. Paradigms guide a researcher through the experience of acquiring knowledge.

PARTICIPATORY ACTION RESEARCH: An approach to research in which the researcher and the members of a social setting collaborate in the process of studying a problem and developing a solution for it.

PEARSON PRODUCT MOMENT CORRELATION COEFFICIENT: The most commonly used measure of the strength of association between two variables.

PERCENTILE RANK: The number of scores in a distribution that are at or below a particular value.

PHYSICAL EVIDENCE: The analysis of physical evidence refers to the analysis of physical objects that are indicators of the variable(s) researchers are studying.

PIE CHART: A graphic way to show how a whole group is divided into subgroups. The whole group is represented as a circle, and each subgroup is represented as a sector of that circle.

POPULATION: The broad collection of elements (people or things) from which you select your sample. The population need not consist of people; instead, a researcher could be studying nations, cities, regions, photographs, teams, businesses, or houses.

POSITIVELY SKEWED DISTRIBUTION: A distribution in which the long tail is extended toward the direction of the higher value.

PREDICTIVE RESEARCH: Research that involves collecting and evaluating information for the purpose of envisaging or forecasting what may happen in the future.

PREDICTIVE VALIDITY: A kind of criterion validity in which a measure or instrument's validity is assessed based on its prediction of some future state of affairs.

PRE-EXPERIMENTAL DESIGNS: Designs that lack random assignment and other qualifications of true experiments.

PROBABILITY SAMPLING: Sampling techniques in which people or elements in a population have a known chance of being selected.

PROBE: A request that interviewees elaborate or provide more explanation.

PROBLEM: a circumstance where there is a difference between a desired state or condition and a present state or condition.

PROFILING: The use of excerpts about a person's experiences taken from qualitative interviews.

PURPOSIVE SAMPLING: A sampling process in which the researchers select individuals or elements that they think possess unique characteristics or perspectives that will provide insight into a particular topic.

QUALITATIVE RESEARCH: Research that involves the use of non-numeric observations of phenomena. Qualitative approaches to research are often carried out using research methods such as ethnography, interviews, questionnaires (with open-ended items), field observations, and analysis of cultural documents.

QUANTITATIVE DATA ANALYSIS: Deriving meaning from numerical data collected during social research. It involves numbers that represent values measuring characteristics of research subjects or participants.

QUANTITATIVE RESEARCH: Research that involves the use of methods such as experimentation and survey/questionnaire design. These methods are often selected to study phenomena by using numbers and counts.

QUASI-EXPERIMENTAL DESIGNS: Designs that allow you to effectively test causal relationships in situations in which conducting a true experiment is not possible or appropriate.

QUESTION: A request for information ending in a question mark.

QUESTIONNAIRE: A tool of data collection consisting of questions meant for research participants or subjects to respond to without being read by the interviewer.

QUOTA SAMPLING: A technique that involves dividing a population into categories and selecting a quota or certain number of them from each category.

RACIAL DIGITAL DIVIDE: This is the problem presented by the fact that the accessibility of information and communication technologies is unequal.

RANDOM DIGIT DIALING: A telephone sampling technique that involves replacing the last digits of listed telephone numbers with randomly selected digits. Once the random digits are selected, the numbers are called.

RANDOM SAMPLING: A selection process means that each element or person in a population has an equal chance of being selected.

RATIO MEASURES: Measures that possess all the characteristics of nominal, ordinal, and interval measures with one exception.

RELIABILITY: The consistency of a measure. A measurement is considered reliable when it yields consistent results.

RESEARCH: Logical systematic investigation of phenomena.

RESEARCH DESIGN: The critical components in the planning and strategy that guides the execution of research.

RESEARCH PROPOSAL: A detailed description of a research project that you intend to pursue.

RESEARCH QUESTION: A question representing the problem you intend to investigate in your study.

RESPONSE RATE: The percentage of a population that agrees to participate in a study.

RESPONSE SET: When a respondent stops reading an instrument and simply marks the same answer for the remainder of the instrument.

RIGHT TO PRIVACY: The researcher's responsibility to protect the identity of research participants.

SAMPLE: A selection of elements from a larger population. A sample is the specific segment of cases or elements that is selected from a population of interest for the purpose of investigation.

SAMPLING DISTRIBUTION: Represents the distribution of scores or percentages on a variable.

SAMPLING ERROR: The difference between the sample that a researcher selects and the population the sample was selected from.

SAMPLING INTERVAL: The elements selected in a systematic random sample. Represented as k, the sampling interval is determined by dividing the population count of the sampling frame) by the desired sample size.

SCALE: A combination of variables used to measure an abstract concept. Usually scales are ordinal measures of the levels or intensity, direction, and potency of a variable noted by arranging responses on a continuum.

SCATTERGRAM: A chart that allows you to see the relationships between two variables. In most cases the independent variable is presented on the horizontal axis and the dependent variable on the vertical axis.

SCIENTIFIC COLONIALISM: When the center of gravity for the acquisition of knowledge about a people is located outside of that people's lived reality.

SCIENTIFIC RESEARCH: Systematic investigation involving the discovery, explanation, and/or description of a subject or topic.

SECONDARY ANALYSIS: Analysis of data collected through a previous administrative or research project.

SEMANTIC DIFFERENTIAL: A scaling format in which respondents are asked to locate their attitudes on a scale ranging between opposite positions on a particular issue.

SEMIOTICS: The analysis of signs and symbols and the meanings they carry.

SEMI-STRUCTURED INTERVIEW: An approach to interviews in which each respondent is asked to answer a specific set of questions. However, the semi-structured interview maintains a conversational style in which the interviewer probes the respondent and is free to ask questions in a different order for all respondents.

SIMPLE RANDOM SAMPLING: The most basic kind of probability sample. Simple random samples ensure that every element in a target population has an equal opportunity to be selected to be included in a sample. Simple random samples are usually used in small-scale projects that deal with moderately sized populations in which it is easier to gather an accurate sampling frame.

SNOWBALL SAMPLING: A type of convenience sampling in which researchers make initial contact with a small number of research participants, then use them to gain contact with additional research participants.

SOCIAL DESIRABILITY BIAS: Social desirability refers to respondents' tendency to want to present themselves in such a way that they will appear socially desirable to their interviewer.

SOCIAL DISTANCE SCALE: A type of scale designed to measure the amount of social distance separating groups or to determine the willingness of people to engage in varying degrees of intimacy in social relations with others.

SPURIOUS VARIABLE: A variable that is the cause of both the independent and dependent variables.

STABILITY: The aspect that refers to how consistent a measure's results are over time.

STANDARD ERROR OF THE MEAN: Tells us how much a sample mean, $\bar{x}$, is likely to differ from a population mean, μ.

STATEMENT: A sentence or phrase designed to gather information about a respondent. Statements are used when researchers want to measure the extent to which a respondent holds a particular attitude or opinion.

STATEMENT OF THE PROBLEM: An explanation of the importance of the topic the research intends to pursue.

STATEMENT OF THE PURPOSE: An explanation of why you are conducting your research project.

STATISTICAL SIGNIFICANCE: The likelihood that results from a sample could be due to random error—that is, the probability of finding a relationship among sample data when there is none in the larger population. It represents the probability that a researcher's observations reveal a genuine pattern and not just mere chance.

STATISTICS: The mathematical procedures that use and produce numerical values for the purpose of summarizing and interpreting information.

STRATIFIED RANDOM SAMPLING: A sampling approach that divides the population into strategic strata or subgroups. After the population is divided, a sample is drawn separately and randomly from each stratum. When this is done, the strata must encompass or include the entire target population. Every element in the target population has to fit into a stratum. This sampling technique is used when a researcher wants to be sure that his or her sample reflects certain diversity in a target population.

STRUCTURED INTERVIEW: A technique of data collection that involves asking a specific standardized set of questions in a fixed order.

SURVEY: A tool for collecting data from individuals called respondents by having them respond to items (questions and statements).

SUSTAINABLE CONCEPTUAL DEVELOPMENT: The idea that it is up to theorists to recognize the limitations and inadequacies in existing theories and paradigms.

SYMMETRICAL DISTRIBUTION: A distribution that is balanced, with one half of the distribution being exactly the same as the other half. However, in practice, data distributions only approach perfect symmetry.

SYSTEMATIC RANDOM SAMPLING: Selecting every kth element in a sampling frame. When researchers use systematic sampling, they often use a table of random numbers to select a starting point in their sampling frame.

T-TEST: A statistical procedure used to decide whether two sample means are significantly different from one another.

TELEPHONE INTERVIEW: A common data collection technique used in marketing research in which the interviewer asks questions over the telephone instead of in person.

THEORY: A set of interrelated assumptions that seek to illuminate phenomena by explaining the relationship between variables.

THURSTONE SCALING: A method of scale construction in which judges assign weights and degrees of intensity to scaled items.

TYPE I ERROR: When a researcher rejects the null hypothesis when he or she should have accepted or confirmed it.

TYPE II ERROR: When a researcher accepts the null hypothesis when he or she should have rejected it, meaning that the researcher has claimed to have found no relationship among the population when there was a true relationship that was not due to random chance.

UNIDIMENSIONAL: Refers to items that measure one dimension of a variable or construct.

UNITS OF ANALYSIS: The elements (people or things) on which you measure variables and collect data.

UNIVARIATE ANALYSIS: Statistical analysis involving one variable and its attributes.

UNSTRUCTURED INTERVIEWS: An approach to interviews in which the interviewer develops interview questions as the interview progresses. This approach is called unstructured because the interviewer obtains different information from each respondent.

VALIDITY: The truthfulness, correctness, and accuracy of a measurement.

VARIABLE: A concept (trait or a characteristic) with two or more categories or attributes.

VARIABLE CODE BOOK: A document or chart that describes the names of each variable, the codes of its attributes, and the level at which they are measured.

VARIANCE: The spread or dispersion of scores.

VIGNETTE QUESTION: A technique that is used to investigate people's normative standards. The vignette approach involves presenting respondents with one or more scenarios, then asking them how they would respond if they were confronted with the circumstances in that scenario.

VOLUNTARY SAMPLING: Refers to instances when population elements are selected by putting out an explicit call for volunteers, such as an Internet post or posted paper advertisement for participants.

VOLUNTEER BIAS: The possibility that volunteers may differ from a more representative sample in ways that affect the outcomes of a study.

Z-SCORE: A standard score used to locate the position of a single score in a distribution of scores.

Works Cited

Adams, H. (2001). African observers of the universe: The Sirius question. In I. Van Sertima (Ed.), *Blacks in science* (pp. 27–46). New Brunswick, NJ: Transaction Publishers.

Akbar, N. (1981). Mental disorders among African Americans. *Black Books Bulletin, 7*(2), 18–25.

Akbar, N. (1994). *Light from ancient Africa*. Tallahassee, FL: Mind Productions and Associates, Inc.

Akom, A. (2011). Black emancipatory action research: Integrating a theory of structural racialisation into ethnographic and participatory action research methods. *Ethnography & Education, 6*(1), 113–131.

Aldridge, D.P. (2007). Black male-female relationships: The lens model. In C. Hudson-Wheems (Ed.), *Contemporary Africana: Theory, thought and action* (pp. 59–73). Trenton, NJ: Africa World Press, Inc.

Allen, A.J., Davey, M.P., & Davey, A. (2010). Being examples to the flock: The role of church leaders and African American families seeking mental health care services. *Journal of Contemporary Family Therapy, 32*, 117–134.

Allen, B.A. & Boykin, A.W. (1992). African American children and the educational process: Alleviating cultural discontinuity through prescriptive pedagogy. *School of Psychology Review, 21*(4), 586–596.

Asante, M.K. (1992). *Afrocentricity: The theory of social change*. Trenton, NJ: Africa World Press.

Asante, M.K. (1992). *The afrocentric idea*. Philadelphia, Pa: Temple University Press.

Asante, M.K. (2003a). *Afrocentricity: The theory of social change* (rev. ed.). Chicago: African American Images.

Asante, M.K. (2003b). Locating a text: Implications of Afrocentric theory. In A. Mazama (Ed.), *The Afrocentric paradigm*. Trenton, NJ: Africa World Press.

Azibo, D.A. (1989). African-centered theses on mental health and a nosology of Black/African personality disorder. *Journal of Black Psychology*, *15*(2), 173–214.

Babbie, E. (2001). *The practice of social research*. Australia: Wadsworth/Thomson Learning.

Babbie, E. (2007). *The basics of social research*. Australia: Wadsworth.

Bailey, C.T., & Boykin, A.W. (2001, Winter/Spring). The role of task variability and home contextual factors in the academic performance and task motivation of African American elementary school children. *The Journal of Negro Education*, *70*(1/2), 84–95.

Balani, M. (2011, August 5). Post office cuts would deliver a blow to the Black community. *The Griot*. Retrieved from http://www.thegrio.com/money/post-office-cuts-could-deliver-a-blow-to-the-black-community.php

Baldwin, J., & Bell, Y. (1985). The African Self-Consciousness Scale: An Africentric personality questionnaire. *The Western Journal of Black Studies*, *9*(2), 61–68.

Banks, J.A. (1993). Multicultural education: Historical development, dimensions, and practice. In L. Darling–Hammond (Ed.), *Review of research in education* (pp. 3–49). Washington, DC: American Educational Research Association.

Banks, J.A., & McGee-Banks, C.A. (Eds.). (2004). *Handbook of research on multicultural education*. San Francisco, CA: John Wiley and Sons.

Barna Group. (2005). African Americans. Retrieved March 27, 2005, from http://www.barna.org/

Baro, E.E., Onyenania, G.O., & Osaheni, O. (2010). Information seeking behavior of undergraduate students in the humanities in three universities in Nigeria. *Journal of Library & Information Science*, *76*(2), 109–117.

Beauchamp, T. L., Faden, R. R., Wallace, R. J., and Waiters, L. (1982). Introduction. In T. Beauchamp, R. Faden, R. Wallace, & L. Waiters (Eds.), *Ethical issues in social science research* (3-39). Baltimore: Johns Hopkins University Press.

Belgrave, F.Z., & Allison, K.W. (2006). *African American psychology*. Thousand Oaks, CA: Sage Publications.

Belgrave, F.Z., Cherry, V.R., Cunningham, D.M., Walwyn, S., Letlaka-Rennert, K., & Phillips, F.B. (1994). The influence of Africentric values, self-esteem, and Black identity on drug attitudes among African American fifth graders: A preliminary study. *Journal of Black Psychology*, *20*(2), 143–156.

Bell, D.A. (1992). *Faces at the bottom of the well: The permanence of racism*. New York: Basic Books.

Bertrand, R., & Priego-Valverde, B. (2011). Does prosody play a specific role in conversational humor? *Pragmatics & Cognition*, *19*(2), 333–356.

Billingsley, A. (1968). *Black families in White America*. New York: Touchstone Books.

Blackwell, A.G., Kwoh, S., & Pastor, M. (2010). *Uncommon common ground*. New York: W.W. Norton.

Bless, C., Higson-Smith, C., & Kagee, A. (2006). *Fundamentals of social research methods: An African perspective*. Cape Town, South Africa: Juta & Co. Ltd.

Bobo, L.D. (1999). Prejudice as group position: Microfoundations of a sociological approach to racism and race relations. *Journal of Social Issues*, *(55)*, 3, 445–472

Booth, W.C., Colomb, G.G., & Williams, J.M. (1995). *The craft of research*. Chicago: University of Chicago Press.

Boyd-Franklin, N. (2003). *Black families in therapy: Understanding the African American experience*. New York: Guilford Press.

Boyd-Franklin, N., & Bry, B.H. (2000). *Reaching out in family therapy: Home-based, school, and community interventions.* New York: Guilford Press.

Boykin, A.W. (2000). The talent development model of schooling: Placing students at promise for academic success. *Journal of Education for Students Placed at Risk, 5*(1/2), 3–25.

Boykin, A.W., & Cunningham, R.T. (2002). The effects of movement expressiveness in story content and learning context on the analogical reasoning performance of African-American children. *Journal of Negro Education, 70*(1/2), 70–83.

Brayboy, B.M. (2006). Toward a tribal critical race theory in education. *The Urban Review, 37*(5), 425–446.

Breitman, G. (1965). *Malcolm X speaks.* New York: Grove Weidenfeld.

Brown, J.L., Casey, S.J., Bishop, A.J., Prytys, M., Whittinger, N., & Weinman, J. (2011). How Black African and White British women perceive depression and help-seeking: A pilot vignette study. *International Journal of Social Psychiatry, 57*(4), 362–374.

Bryan, C.J., Rudd, M., & Wertenberger, E. (2013). Reasons for suicide attempts in a clinical sample of active duty soldiers. *Journal of Affective Disorders, 144*(1/2), 148–152.

Bryman, A. (2008). *Social research methods.* New York: Oxford University Press.

Cahill, J.M., Freeland-Graves, J.H., Shah, B.S., Lu, H., & Klohe-Lehman, D.M. (2009). Development and validation of the eating stimulus index in low-income, minority women in early postpartum. *Journal of the American Dietetic Association, 109*(9), 1593–1598.

Carmichael, C., & Hamilton, C.V. (1967). *Black power: The politics of liberation in America.* New York: Vintage Books.

Carr, Gregory E. 2007. "Towards an Intellectual History of African America Studies: Genealogy and Normative Theory." Pp. 338–352 in *The African American Studies Reader,* edited by Nathaniel Norment. Durham, NC: Carolina Academic Press.

Cashmore, E. (2002). Behind the window dressing: Ethnic minority police perspectives on cultural diversity. *Journal of Ethnic & Migration Studies, 28*(2), 327–341.

CBS News/*New York Times.* (2009). The state of race relations [Press Release]. Retrieved from http://www.cbsnews.com/htdocs/pdf/poll_042709_racerelations.pdf

Children's Defense Fund. (2012). CDF freedom schools program. December 2012 Retrieved online: http://www.childrensdefense.org/programs-campaigns/freedom- schools/

Chilisa, B. & Ntseane, G. (2010). Resisting dominant discourses: Implications of indigenous, African feminist theory and methods for gender and education research. *Gender and Education,* 22(6), 617–632.

Christensen, C.M. (1997). *The innovators dilemma: When new technologies cause great firms to fail.* Boston, MA: Harvard Business School Press.

Cohen, C.J. (2005). Punks, bulldaggers, and welfare queens: The radical potential of queer politics? In E.P. Johnson & M.G. Henderson (Eds.), *Black queer studies: A critical anthology.* Durham, NC: Duke University Press.

Collins, P.H. (2009). *Black feminist thought: Knowledge, consciousness, and the politics of empowerment.* New York: Routledge.

Communications in New Brunswick. (2004, March 25). Minister unveils literacy initiative as part of Quality Learning Agenda. Fredericton, New Brunswick. Canada: Author. Retrieved January 25, 2009, from www.gnb.ca/cnb/news/edu/2004e0357ed.htm

Crenshaw, K., Gotanda, N., Peller, G., & Thomas, K. (Eds.). (1995). *Critical race theory: The key writings that formed the movement.* New York: New Press.

Cross, W.E. (1971). The Negro-to-Black conversion experience: Towards a psychology of Black liberation. *Black World, 20,* 13–37.

Cross, W.E. (1978). The Cross and Thomas models of Nigrescence. *Journal of Black Psychology, 5,* 13–19.

Cunningham, G., & Regan, M. (2012). Political activism, racial identity and the commercial endorsement of athletes. *International Review for the Sociology of Sport, 47*(6), 657–669.

Darling-Hammond, L. (1998). Unequal opportunity: Race and education. *Brookings Review, 16*(2), 28–33.

Dean, C. (2007, October 25). James Watson retires after racist remarks. *The New York Times.* Retrieved from http://www.nytimes.com/2007/10/25/science/25cnd-watson.html?_r=0

Des Courtis, N., Lauber, C., Costa, C., & Cattapan-Ludewig, K. (2008). Beliefs about the mentally ill: A comparative study between healthcare professionals in Brazil and in Switzerland. *International Review of Psychiatry, 20*(6), 503–509.

DiClemente, R. Milhausen, R.R., Salazar, L.F., Spitalnick, J., McDermott Sales, J., Crosby, R.A., Younge, S.N. & Wingood G.M. (2010). Development of the sexual sensation-seeking scale for African American adolescent women. *International Journal of Sexual Health, 22,* 248–261.

Diop, C.A. (1989). *The cultural unity of Black Africa.* London: Karnak House.

Du Bois, W.E.B. (1898, January). The study of the Negro problem. *Annals of the American Academy of Political and Social Science, 11,* 1–23.

DuBois, W.E.B. (1944). My evolving program for Negro freedom. In R. Logan (Ed.)., *What the Negro wants* (31-70). Chapel Hill: University of North Carolina Press.

Du Bois, W.E.B. (1997). *The souls of Black folk: Essays and sketches.* Boston, MA: Bedford Books. (Original work published 1931)

Dubowitz, H., Lane, W., Greif, G.L., Jensen, T.K., & Lamb, M.E. (2006). Low-income African American fathers' involvement in children's lives: Implications for practitioners. *Journal of Family Social Work, 10*(1), 25-41.

Duenwald, M. (2002, November 12). Good health is linked to grocer. *The New York Times.* Retrieved from http://www.nytimes.com/2002/11/12/health/good-health-is-linked-to-grocer.html?sec=health&pagewanted=print

Dunning, E., Murphy, P., & Williams, J. (1988). *The roots of football hooliganism: A historical and sociological study.* London: Routledge.

Durodoye, B., & Hildreth, B. (1995). Learning styles and the African American student. *Education, 116*(2).

Durrheim, K., Dixon, J., Tredoux, C, Eaton, L., Quayle, M., & Clack, B. (2011). Predicting support for racial transformation policies: Intergroup threat, racial prejudice, sense of group entitlement and strength of identification. *European Journal of Social Psychology, 41,* 23–41.

Edin, K., & Kefalas, M. (2005). *Promises I can keep: Why poor women put motherhood before marriage.* Berkeley: University of California Press.

Eggen, P.D., & Kauchak, D.P. (2003). *Learning and teaching: Research-based methods.* Boston, MA: Pearson Education.

Envirocom. (2007). *Content analysis coding schedule.* Retrieved December 28, 2011, from http://envirocom.files.wordpress.com/2007/02/appendix-4-content-analysis-coding-schedule.pdf

Fairlie, R. (2005). Are we really a nation online? *Report for the Leadership Conference on Civil Rights Education.* University of California, Santa Cruz, and National Poverty Center, University of Michigan.

Fanon, F. (1952). *Black skin, White masks*. New York: Grove/Atlantic.

Ferguson, R.A. (2005) Race-ing homonormativity: Citizenship, sociology, and gay identity. In E.P. Johnson & M.G. Henderson (Eds.), *Black queer studies: A critical anthology*. Durham, NC: Duke University Press.

Fields, J. (2003). *Children's living arrangements and characteristics: March 2002*. U.S. Bureau of the Census, Current Population Reports, P20-547. Washington, DC: U.S. Government Printing Office.

Flournoy, R., & Treuhaft, S. (2002). *Regional development and physical activity: Issues and strategies for promoting health equity*. Oakland, CA: PolicyLink.

Floyd-Thomas, S., Floyd-Thomas, J., Duncan, C.B., Ray, S.G., & Westfield, N.L. (2007). *Black church studies: An introduction*. Nashville, TN: Abingdon Press.

Forman, T.A., Williams, D.R., & Jackson, J.S. (1997). Race, place, and discrimination. *Social Problems, 9*, 231–261.

Franklin, A.J. (2004). *From brotherhood to manhood: How Black men rescue their relationships and dreams from the invisibility syndrome*. Hoboken, NJ: John Wiley & Sons.

Franklin, A.J., & Boyd-Franklin, N. (2000). Invisibility syndrome: A clinical model of the effects of racism on African American males. *American Journal of Orthopsychiatry, 7*(1), 33–41.

Friedman, D., Corwin, S., Rose, I., & Dominick, G. (2009). Prostate cancer communication strategies recommended by older African-American men in South Carolina: A qualitative analysis. *Journal of Cancer Education, 24*(3), 204–209.

Friedman, D.B., Laditka, S.B., Laditka, J.N., & Price, A.E. (2011). A content analysis of cognitive health promotion in popular magazines. *International Journal of Aging & Human Development, 73*(3), 253–281.

Gagern, A., & van den Bergh, J. (2013). A critical review of fishing agreements with tropical developing countries. *Marine Policy, 38*, 375–386.

Galton, F. (1869). *Hereditary genius: Its laws and consequences*. London: Macmillan.

Galtung, J. (1967). After Camelot. In I. Horowitz (Ed.), *The rise and fall of Project Camelot*. Cambridge, MA: MIT Press.

Gardiner, P.S. (2004). The African Americanization of menthol cigarette use in the United States. *Nicotine & Tobacco Research, 6*(supp. 1), S55–S65.

Gardner, H. (1983). *Frames of Mind*. New York: Basic Book Inc.

Gentry, Q.M., Elifson, K., & Sterk, C. (2005). Aiming for more relevant HIV risk reduction: A Black feminist perspective for enhancing HIV intervention for low-income African American women. *AIDS Education and Prevention, 17*(3), 238–252.

Gold, R.L. (1958). Roles in sociological field observation. *Social Forces, 36*, 217–223.

Gordon, L.R. (2000). *Existentia Africana*. New York: Routledge.

Gordon, L.R. (2005). Black existentialism. In *The encyclopedia of Black studies*. Thousand Oaks, CA: Sage Publications.

Gordon, L.R., & Gordon, J.A. (Eds.) (2006). *Not only the master's tools*. Boulder, CO: Paradigm Publishers.

Gravetter, F.J., & Wallnau, L.B. (2004). *Statistics for the behavioral sciences*. Belmont, CA: Wadsworth/Thomson Learning.

Grigorenko, E.L., Geissler, P.W., Prince, R., Okatcha, F., Nokes, C., Kenny, D.A., Bundy, D.A., & Sternberg, R.J. (2001). The organization of Luo conceptions of intelligence: A study of implicit theories in a Kenyan village. *International Journal of Behavioral Development, 25*(4), 367–378.

Hall, G.S. (1905). The Negro in Africa and America. *Pedagogical Seminary, 12*, 350–368.

Hasnain, M.M., Levy, J.A., Mensah, E.K., & Sinacore, J.M. (2007). Association of educational attainment with HIV risk in African American active injection drug users. *AIDS Care, 19*(1), 87–91.

Helms, J.E., & Parham, T.A. (1996). The racial identity attitude scale. In R.L. Jones (Ed.), *Handbook of tests and measurements for Black populations* (pp. 167–174). Hampton, VA: Cobb & Henry.

Heritage, J. (1984). *Garfinkel and ethnomethodology*. Cambridge, MA: Polity.

Hill, R.B. (1998). Understanding Black family functioning: A holistic perspective. *Journal of Comparative Family Studies, 29*(1), 15–25.

Hilliard, A.G. (1998). *SBA: The reawakening of the African mind*. Gainesville, FL: Makare Publishing Company.

Hilliard, A.G., Williams, L., & Damali, N. (Eds.). (1987). *The teachings of Ptah Hotep: The oldest book in the world*. Grand Forks, ND: Blackwood Press.

Hinnant, A., Oh, H., Caburnay, C.A., & Kreuter, M.W. (2011). What makes African American health disparities newsworthy? An experiment among journalists about story framing. *Health Education Research, 26*(6), 937–947.

Hofstede, G., & Hofstede, G.J. (2005). *Cultures and organizations: Software of the mind*. New York: McGraw-Hill.

Hsin-hsin, H., & Coker, A.D. (2010). Examining issues affecting African American participation in research studies. *Journal of Black Studies, 40*(4), 619–636.

Hudson-Weems, C. (1994). *Africana womanism: Reclaiming ourselves*. Troy, MI: Bedford Publishers.

Humphreys, L. (1973). *Tearoom trade: Impersonal sex in public places*. Chicago: Aldine.

Jamison, D.F. (2006). The relationship between African self-consciousness, cultural misorientation, hypermansculinity, and rap music preference. *Journal of African American Studies, 9*(4), 45–60.

Jenson, A. (1969). How much can we boost IQ and scholastic achievement? *Harvard Educational Review, 39*, 1–23.

Johnson, E.P., & Henderson, M.G. (Eds.). (2005). *Black queer studies: A critical anthology*. Durham, NC: Duke University Press.

Johnson, K.A., Dolan, M.K., & Sonnett, J. (2011). Speaking of looting: An analysis of racial propaganda in national coverage of Hurricane Katrina. *Journal of Communications, 22*(3), 302–318.

Jones, J.M. (1972). *Prejudice and racism*. New York: McGraw-Hill.

Jones, J.M. (1991). Racism: A cultural analysis of the problem. In R.L. Jones (Ed.), *Black psychology* (3rd ed.). Hampton, VA: Cobb & Henry.

Jung, C.G. (1950). On the psychology of the Negro. Lecture to Zurich Psychoanalytic Society in 1912. In W. McGuire (Ed.), *Collected works of Carl G. Jung* (Vol. 18). Princeton, NJ: Princeton University Press.

Kambon, K.K. (1999a). *African/Black psychology in the American context: An African-centered approach*. Tallahassee, FL: Nubian Nation Publications.

Kambon, K.K. (1999b). *The worldviews paradigm; Foundation for African Black psychology*. Tallahassee, FL: Nubian Nation Publications.

Kambon, K.K., & Bowen-Reid, T. (2009). Africentric theories of African American personality. In H.A. Neville, B.M. Tynes, & S.O. Utsey (Eds.), *Handbook of African American psychology*. Los Angeles, CA: Sage Publications.

Karenga, M. (2002). *Introduction to Black studies* (3rd ed). Los Angeles, CA: University of Sankore Press.

Karenga, M. (2010). *Introduction to Black studies* (4th ed). Los Angeles, CA: University of Sankore Press.

Kershaw, T. (1992). Toward a Black studies paradigm. *Journal of Black Studies, 22*(4), 447–492.

Kershaw, T. (2003). The Black studies paradigm: The making of scholar activists. In J.L. Conyers (Ed.), *Afrocentricity and the academy: Essays on theory and practice.* Jefferson, NC: McFarland Publishers.

Khapoya, V.B. (1998). *The African experience.* Upper Saddle River, NJ: Prentice Hall.

King, G., Mallett, R.K., Kozlowski, L.T., & Bendel, R.B. (2003). African Americans' attitudes toward cigarette excise taxes. *American Journal of Public Health, 93*(5), 828–834.

King, K. (2010). *African American politics.* Malden, MA: Polity Press.

Kinney, A. (2012). Loops, lyrics, and literacy: Songwriting as a site of resilience for an urban adolescent. *Journal of Adolescent & Adult Literacy, 55*(5), 395–404.

Kitwana, B. (1994). *The rap on gangsta rap: Who run it? Gangster rap and visions of Black violence.* Chicago: Third World Press.

Klassen, P.E. (2004). The robes of womanhood: Dress and authenticity among African American Methodist women in the nineteenth century. *Religion & American Culture, 14*(1), 39–82.

Koro-Ljungberg, M., Bussing, R., Williamson, P., Wilder, J., & Mills, T. (2008). African-American teenagers' stories of attention deficit/hyperactivity disorder. *Journal of Child and Family Studies, 17*(4), 467–485.

Koslowsky, M., Pratt, G.L., & Wintrob, R.M. (1976). The application of Guttman Scale analysis to physicians' attitudes regarding abortion. *Journal of Applied Psychology, 61*(3), 301–304.

Kuhn, T.S. (1970). *The structure of scientific revolutions* (2nd ed.). Chicago: University of Chicago Press.

Ladson-Billings, G. (2009). Introduction. In L.C. Tillman (Ed.), *The Sage handbook of African American education.* Los Angeles, CA: Sage Publications.

Lao-Montes, A. (2007). Decolonial moves. *Cultural Studies, 21*(2/3), 309–338.

Leary, J.D. (2005). *Post traumatic slave syndrome.* Portland, OR: Joy Degruy Publications.

Leigh, W.A., & Wheatley, A.L. (2010). *African American perspectives on the Social Security system 1998 and 2009.* Joint Center for Political and Economic Studies. Retrieved, June 3, 2010, from http://www.jointcenter.org/sites/default/files/upload/research/files/African%20American%20Perspectives%20on%20the%20Social%20Security%20System.pdf

Levi, M. (2009). Abu Ghraib head: We were scapegoated. Retrieved April 22, 2009, from http://www.cbsnews.com/8301-503544_162-4961519-503544.html

Likert, R.A. (1932). Technique for the measurement of attitudes. *Archives of Psychology, 140*, 1–55.

Limb, J. (2005). Free speech row over racist academic. Retrieved from http://www.abc.net.au/pm/content/2005/s1422936.htm

Lincoln, Y.S., & Guba, E. (1985). *Naturalistic inquiry.* Beverly Hills, CA: Sage Publications.

Linnaeus, C.V. (1735). *Systema plutera.* Lugduni, Batavorum.

Lofland, J., & Lofland, L. (1995). *Analyzing social settings: A guide to qualitative observation and analysis* (3rd ed.). Belmont, CA: Wadsworth.

Loustalot, F., Wyatt, S., Sims, M., Ellison, C., Taylor, H., & Underwood, L. (2011). Psychometric testing of the daily spiritual experiences scale among African Americans in the Jackson Heart Study. *Journal of Religion and Health, 50*(3), 675–685.

Macionis, J.J. (1999). *Sociology*. Upper Saddle River, NJ: Prentice Hall.

Mandara, J., & Murray, C.B. (2002). Development of an empirical typology of African American family functioning. *Journal of Family Psychology, 16*(3), 318–337.

Marsh-Lockett, C. (1997). Womanism. In W.L. Andrews (Ed.), *The Oxford companion to African American literature*. New York: Oxford University Press.

Mastro, D.E. (2011). Characterizations of criminal athletes: A systematic examination of sports news depictions of race and crime. *Journal of Broadcasting & Electronic Media, 55*(4), 526–542.

Mazama, A. (2003). *The Afrocentric paradigm*. Trenton, NJ: Africa World Press.

McGee, Z.T. (1996). Violent victimization survey. In R.L. Jones (Ed.), *Handbook of tests and measurements for Black populations* (pp. 613–620). Hampton, VA: Cobb & Henry.

McLoyd, V. (1991). What is the study of African American children, the study of? In R. L. Jones (Ed.)., *Black Psychology* (419–440). Berkeley, CA: Cobb & Henry Publishers.

Mekgwe, P. (2003). Theorizing African feminisms: The colonial question. Paper presented at the *Department of English Seminar Series*, University of Botswana, in Gaborone.

Milgram, S. (1963). Behavioral study of obedience. *Journal of Abnormal and Social Psychology, 43*, 469–498.

Milgram, S. (1965). Some conditions of obedience and disobedience to authority. *Human Relations, 18*, 57–76.

Milgram, S. (1974). *Obedience to authority*. New York: Harper and Row.

Milliones, J. (1980). Construction of a Black consciousness measure: Psychotherapeutic implications. *Psychotherapy: Theory, Research and Practice, 17*, 175–182.

Mo Ibrahim Foundation. (2012). *The 2011 Ibrahim index of African governance*. Retrieved May 27, 2012, from http://www.moibrahimfoundation.org/en/media/get/20111003_ENG2011-IIAG-Structure.pdf

Modupe, D. (2003). The afrocentric phislosophical perspective. In: Mazama, A. (Ed.), *The Afrocentric paradigm*. Trenton, NJ: (pp. 55–72) Africa World Press.

Monette, D.R., Sullivan, T.J., & DeJong, C.R. (2005). *Applied social research*. Belmont, CA: The Thomas Corporation.

Moore, T. O. (1996). Revisited affect symbolic imagery. *Journal of Black Psychology, 22*(4), 443–452.

Moradi, B., Yoder, J.D., & Berendsen, L.L. (2004). An evaluation of the psychometric properties of the womanist identity scale. *Sex Roles, 50*(3/4), 253–266.

Morello-Frosch, R., Pastor, M., Sadd, J., & Shonkoff, S. (2009). *The climate gap*. Retrieved July 14, 2010, from http://college.usc.edu/pere/documents/mindingthegap.pdf

Munger, D. (2009). *Shooting unarmed suspects: A matter of race?* Retrieved July, 9 2010, from online: http://scienceblogs.com/cognitivedaily/2009/07/shooting_unarmed_suspects_a_ma_1.php

Murrell, P.C. (2009). Identity, agency, and culture. In L.C. Tillman (Ed.), *The Sage handbook of African American education* (pp. 89–101). Los Angeles, CA: Sage Publications.

Nápoles-Springer, A.M., Grumbach, K., Alexander, M., Moreno-John, G., Forte, D., Rangel-Lugo, M., et al. (2000). Clinical research with older African Americans and Latinos: Perspectives from the community. *Research on Aging, 22*, 668–691.

National Urban League. (2010). *The state of Black America: Jobs*. A National Urban League Publication.

National Urban League. (2012). *The state of Black America: Rebuild America*. A National Urban League Publication.

Neuman, W.L. (2009). *Understanding research*. Boston, MA: Pearson Education.

Neville, H.A., & Pieterse, A.L. (2009) Racism, White supremacy, and resistance. In H.A. Neville, B.M. Tynes, & S.O. Utsey (Eds.), *Handbook of African American psychology*. Los Angeles, CA: Sage Publications.

Nicholson, R.A., Kreuter, M.W., Lapka, C., Wellborn, R., Clark, E.M., Sanders-Thompson, V., & Casey, C. (2008). Unintended effects of emphasizing disparities in cancer communication to African-Americans. *Cancer Epidemiology, Biomarkers & Prevention, 17*(11), 2946–2953.

Nielson Company. (2011). *The state of the African American consumer*. San Francisco, CA: Nielson Media Research.

Nobles, W.W. (1991). Extended self: Rethinking the so-called Negro self-concept. In R.L. Jones (Ed.), *Black psychology*. Berkeley, CA: Cobb & Henry.

Nobles, W.W. (2006). *Seeking the sakhu*. Chicago: Third World Press.

Nobles, W.W., Goddard, L.L., & Cavil, W.E. (2012). *Theoretical and cultural foundations of the ABPsi African-centered behavioral change model*. Unpublished manuscript.

Nobles, W.W., Goddard, L.L., Cavil, W.E., & George, P.Y. (1987). *African American families: Issues, insights, and directions*. Oakland, CA: Black Family Institute Publications.

Nobles, W., Goddard, L.L., & Gilbert, D. (2009). Culturecology, women, and African-centered HIV prevention. *Journal of Black Psychology, 35*(2), 228–246.

Oakes, J. (1995). Two cities' tracking and within-school segregation. *Teachers College Record, 96*(4), 681–691.

Obasi, E.M., Flores, L.Y., & James-Myers, L. (2009). Construction and initial validation of the Worldview Analysis Scale (WAS). *Journal of Black Studies, 39*(6), 937–961.

Obenga, T. (2004). *African philosophy: The pharaonic period*. Paris: PER ANKH.

Obenga, T. (2007). *Ancient Egypt: Civilization & language*. Unpublished manuscript.

Ogunyemi, C. (1985). Womanism: The dynamics of the contemporary Black female novel in English. *Signs: Journal of Women in Culture and Society, 11*, 63–80.

Osgood, C.E., Suci, G.J., & Tannenbaum, P.H. (1957). *The measurement of meaning*. Urbana: University of Illinois Press.

Ossana, S.M., Helms, J.E., & Leonard, M.M. (1992). Do "womanist" identity attitudes influence college women's self-esteem and perceptions of environmental bias? *Journal of Counseling and Development, 70*, 402–408.

O'Sullivan, E., Rassel, G.R., & Berner, M. (2010). *Research methods for public administrators*. White Plains, NY: Pearson.

Oware, M. (2011). Decent daddy, imperfect daddy: Black male rap artists' views of fatherhood and the family. *Journal of African American Studies, 15*(3), 327–351.

Pallitt, N.M. (2009). Scarce resources: Conflict and sharing in discourse around primary school email use. *International Journal of Education & Development Using Information & Communication Technology, 5*(5), 22–32.

Parham, T.A., Ajamu, A., & White, J.L. (2011). *The psychology of Blacks: Centering our perspectives in the African consciousness*. Boston, MA: Prentice Hall.

Parrill, R., & Kennedy, B. (2011). Partnerships for health in the African American community: Moving toward community-based participatory research. *Journal of Cultural Diversity, 18*(4), 150–154.

Payne, Y.A., & Gibson, L.R. (2009). Hip hop music and culture: Site of resiliency for the streets of young Black America. In H.A. Neville, B.M. Tynes, & S.O. Utsey (Eds.), *Handbook of African American psychology*. Los Angeles, CA: Sage Publications.

Payne, Y.A., & Hamdi, H.A. (2008). "Street love": How street life oriented U.S. born African men frame giving back to one another and the local community. *Urban Review, 41*, 29–46.

Phillips, L. (Ed.). (2006). *The womanist reader.* New York: Routledge.

Pierre, M.R., & Mahalik, J.R. (2005). Examining African self-consciousness and Black racial identity as predictors of Black men's psychological well being. *Cultural Diversity and Ethnic Minority Psychology, 11*(1), 28–40.

Rabaka, R. (2002). Malcolm X and/as critical theory: Philosophy, radical politics, and the African American search for social justice. *Journal of Black Studies, 33*(2), 145–165.

Rabaka, R. (2006). Africana critical theory of contemporary society: The role of radical politics, social theory, and Africana philosophy. In M.K. Asante & M. Karenga (Eds.), *The handbook of Black studies.* Thousand Oaks, CA: Sage Publications.

Remler, D.K., & Van Ryzin, G.G. (2011). *Research methods in practice.* Los Angeles, CA: Sage Publications.

Renauer, B.C., & Covelli, E (2011). Examining the relationship between police experiences and perceptions of police bias. *Policing, 34*(3), 497–514.

Richardson, J. (2012). Beyond the playing field: Coaches as social capital for inner-city adolescent African-American males. *Journal of African American Studies, 16*(2), 171–194.

Rodriguez, S. (2012, May 31). Daily twitter usage among adults doubles in one year, survey finds. *Los Angeles Times.* Retrieved July 26, 2013, from http://articles.latimes.com/2012/may/31/business/la-fi-tn-twitter-adult-usage-doubles-20120531

Roethlisberger, F.J., & Dickson, W.J. (1939). *Management and the worker.* Cambridge, MA: Harvard University Press.

Roman, M.J., & Flores, J. (2010). *The Afro Latin@ reader: History and culture in the United States.* Durham, NC: Duke University Press.

Rose, L.E., Kim, M.T., Dennison, C.R., & Hill, M.N. (2000). The contexts of adherence for African Americans with high blood pressure. *Journal of Advanced Nursing, 32*(3), 587–594.

Ryan, G.W., & Bernard, H.R. (2003). Techniques to identify themes. *Field Methods, 15*, 85–109.

Saayman, T., & Crafford, A. (2012). Negotiating work identity. *SAJIP: South African Journal of Industrial Psychology* [online journal], *37*(1), 207–218.

Schrank, F.A., & Woodcock, R.W. (2002). Classroom behaviors observation form. In R.W. Woodcock, K.S. McGrew, & N. Mather (Eds.), *Report writer for the Woodcock-Johnson III Tests of Achievement.* Rolling Meadows, IL: Riverside Publishing.

Scott, J. (1990). *A matter of record.* Cambridge: Polity.

Shafer, E.F. (2010). The effect of marriage on weight gain and propensity to become obese in the African American community. *Journal of Family Issues, 31*(9), 1116–1182.

Shockley, K.G., & Frederick, R.M. (2010). Constructs and dimensions of Afrocentric education. *Journal of Black Studies, 40*(6), 1212–1233.

Shujaa, M.J. (2003). Education and schooling: You can have one without the other. In A. Mazama (Ed.), *The Afrocentric paradigm* (pp. 245–264). Trenton, NJ: Africa World Press.

Simmelink, J., Lightfoot, E., Dube, A., Blevins, J., & Lum, T. (2013). Understanding the health beliefs and practices of East African refugees. *American Journal of Health Behavior, 37*(2), 155–161.

Simmons, D. (2009, August 25). Hold out smokers: Who they are and why they can't quit. *Chicago Tribune.* Retrieved September 1, 2009, from www.chicagotribune.com/health/chi-who-still-smokes-21-aug25,0,4433587.story

Simpson, S.M., Krishnan, L.L., Kunik, M.E., & Ruiz, P. (2007). Racial disparities in diagnosis and treatment of depression: A literature review. *Psychiatry Quarterly, 78*, 3–14.

Skiba, R.J., Michael, R.S., & Carroll Nardo, A. (2000). The color of discipline. Indiana Education Policy Center, Policy Research Report #SRS1. Retrieved July 28, 2013, from http://www.indiana.edu/~safeschl/cod.pdf

Slavin, R. (1995). *Cooperative learning* (2nd ed.). Needham Heights, MA: Allyn & Bacon.

Smalls, C., & Cooper, S.M. (2012). Racial group regard, barrier socialization, and African American adolescents' engagement: Patterns and processes by gender. *Journal of Adolescence, 35*(4), 887–897.

Spencer, M.B. (1995). Old issues and new theorizing about African American youth: A phenomenological variant of ecological systems theory. In R.L. Taylor (Ed.), *Black youth: Perspectives on their status in the United States.* Westport, CT: Praeger.

Stanfield, J.H. (1989) Epistemological considerations. In J.H. Stanfield & R.M. Dennis (Eds.), *Race and ethnicity in research methods.* Newbury Park, CA: Sage Publications.

Staples, R. (1976). *Introduction to Black sociology.* New York: McGraw Hill.

Steady, F.C. (1992). Women of Africa and the African diaspora: Linkages and influences. In J.E. Harris, Global dimensions of the African diaspora. Washington, DC: Howard University Press, 167-187.

Stewart, A. (2007, September 6). Study finds new clues to breast cancer racial gap. *Star-Ledger* [Newark, NJ], p. 1.

Strauss, R.P., Sengupta, S., Kegeles, S., McLellan, E., Metzger, D., Eyre, S., et al. (2001). Willingness to volunteer in future preventive HIV vaccine trials: Issues and perspectives from three U.S. communities. *Journal of Acquired Immune Deficiency Syndromes, 26*, 63–71.

Sudarkasa, N. (1996). *The strength of our mothers.* Trenton, NJ: Africa World Press.

Swanson, D.P., Spencer, M.B., Dell'Angelo, T., Harpalani, T., & Spencer, T.R. (2002). Identity processes and the positive youth development of African Americans: An explanatory framework. In C.S. Lerner, C.S. Taylor, & A. von Eye (Eds.), *New directions for youth development.* San Francisco, CA: Jossey-Bass.

Szanton, S.L., Thorpe, R.J., & Whitfield, K. (2010). Life course financial strain and health in African Americans. *Social Science and Medicine, 72*(2), 259–265.

Tangwa, G.B. (2006). Some African reflections on biomedical and environmental ethics. In K. Wiredu (Ed.), *A companion to African philosophy.* Malden, MA: Blackwell Publishing.

Temple, C.N. (2005). *Literary Pan-Africanism.* Durham, NC: Carolina Academic Press.

Temple, C.N. (2006a). Rescuing the literary in Black studies. *Journal of Black Studies, 36*(5), 764–785.

Temple, C.N. (2006b). Strategies for cultural renewal in an American-based version of African globalism. *Journal of Black Studies, 36*(3), 301–317.

Terman, L. (1916). *The measurement of intelligence.* Cambridge, MA: Riverside Press.

Thomas, B., Manusov, E.G., Wang, A., & Livingston, H. (2011). Contributors of Black men's success in admission to and graduation from medical school. *Academic Medicine, 86*(7), 892–900.

Thompson-Brenner, H., Boisseau, C.L., & St. Paul, M.S. (2011). Representation of ideal figure size in *Ebony* magazine: A content analysis. *Body Image, 8*(4), 373–378.

Tillotson, M.T. (2011). *Invisible Jim Crow: Contemporary ideological threats to the internal security of African Americans.* Trenton, NJ: Africa World Press.

Trammel, M., Newhart, D., Willis, V., and Johnson, A. (2008). *African American male initiative.* Retrieved from http://kirwaninstitute.osu.edu/docs/publications/AAMaleInitiative_KelloggReport_April2008.pdf

Tsuruta, D.R. (2012). The womanish roots of womanism: A culturally-derived and African-centered ideal (concept). *The Western Journal of Black Studies, 36*(1), pp. 3–10.

United Church of Christ Commission for Racial Justice. (1987). *Toxic wastes and race in the United States.* New York: Commission for Racial Justice.

United Nations Development Program. (2012). Human development report 2012. Retrieved March 1, 2013 from http://hdr.undp.org/en/reports/

U.S. Census Bureau. (2010, December 4). *US population distribution and change: 2000–2010.* Retrieved January 25, 2007, from http://www.census.gov/prod/cen2010/briefs/c2010br-01.pdf

U.S. Department of Health and Human Services (HHS). (2011). *Combating the silent epidemic of viral hepatitis.* Retrieved December 21, 2011, from http://www.hhs.gov/ash/initiatives/hepatitis/actionplan_viralhepatitis2011.pdf

Vogt, W.P. (1999). *Dictionary of statistics and methodology.* Thousand Oaks, CA: Sage Publications.

Walker, A. (1983). *In search of our mothers' gardens: Womanist prose.* San Diego, CA: Harcourt Brace Jovanovich.

Walker, S., Spohn, C., & Delone, M. (2012). *The color of justice: Race, ethnicity, and crime in America* (5th ed.). Belmont, CA: Wadsworth.

Waller, M., & Plotnick, R. (2001). Effective child support policy for low-income families: Evidence from street level research. *Journal of Policy Analysis and Management, 20*(1): 89–110.

Walters, R.W. (1993). *Pan-Africanism in the African diaspora.* Detroit, MI: Wayne State University Press.

Washington, H.A. (2006). *Medical apartheid.* New York: Harlem Moon.

Weber, M. (1957). *The theory of social economic organization* (A.M. Henderson & T. Parsons, Trans.). New York: Free Press. (Original work published 1922)

Welsh-Asante, K. (2003). The aesthetic conceptualization of nzuri. In A. Mazama (Ed.), *The Afrocentric paradigm* (pp. 245–264). Trenton, NJ: Africa World Press.

Whitehead, N. (2004). The effects of increased access to books on student reading using the public library. *Reading Improvement, 41* (3), 165.

Wobogo, V. (1976). Diop's two cradle theory and the origins of White racism. *Black Books Bulletin, 4*(4), 20–29, 72.

Zeleza, P. (2011). Pan-Africanism in the age of Obama: Challenges and prospects. *Black Scholar, 41*(2), 34–44.

Index

ROCHELLE BROCK &
RICHARD GREGGORY JOHNSON III,
Executive Editors

Black Studies and Critical Thinking is an interdisciplinary series which examines the intellectual traditions of and cultural contributions made by people of African descent throughout the world. Whether it is in literature, art, music, science, or academics, these contributions are vast and far-reaching. As we work to stretch the boundaries of knowledge and understanding of issues critical to the Black experience, this series offers a unique opportunity to study the social, economic, and political forces that have shaped the historic experience of Black America, and that continue to determine our future. Black Studies and Critical Thinking is positioned at the forefront of research on the Black experience, and is the source for dynamic, innovative, and creative exploration of the most vital issues facing African Americans. The series invites contributions from all disciplines but is specially suited for cultural studies, anthropology, history, sociology, literature, art, and music.

Subjects of interest include (but are not limited to):

- EDUCATION
- SOCIOLOGY
- HISTORY
- MEDIA/COMMUNICATION
- RELIGION/THEOLOGY
- WOMEN'S STUDIES

- POLICY STUDIES
- ADVERTISING
- AFRICAN AMERICAN STUDIES
- POLITICAL SCIENCE
- LGBT STUDIES

For additional information about this series or for the submission of manuscripts, please contact Dr. Brock (Indiana University Northwest) at brock2@iun.edu or Dr. Johnson (University of San Francisco) at rgjohnsoniii@usfca.edu.

To order other books in this series, please contact our Customer Service Department:

(800) 770-LANG (within the U.S.)
(212) 647-7706 (outside the U.S.)
(212) 647-7707 FAX

Or browse online by series at www.peterlang.com.